Natural Law &
Human Dignity

Eberhard Schockenhoff

Natural Law &
Human Dignity

Universal Ethics in an
Historical World

translated by Brian McNeil

The Catholic University of America Press
Washington, D.C.

Originally published in the series *Welt der Theologie* as: *Naturrecht und Menschenwürde. Universale Ethik in einer geschichtlichen Welt,* Matthias-Grünewald-Verlag, Mainz, 1996.

The paper used in this publication meets the minimum requirements of American National Standards for Information Science—Permanence of Paper for Printed Library materials, ANSI Z39.48-1984.
∞

Library of Congress Cataloging-in-Publication Data
Schockenhoff, Eberhard, 1953–
[Naturrecht und Menschenwürde. English]
Natural law and human dignity : universal ethics in an historical world / Eberhard Schockenhoff ; translated by Brian McNeil.
p. cm.
Includes bibliographical references and index.
ISBN 0-8132-1339-8 (alk. paper) — ISBN 0-8132-1340-1 (pbk. : alk. paper)
1. Christian ethics—Catholic authors. 2. Natural law—Religious aspects—Catholic Church. I. Title.
BJ1249 .S36713   2003
241′.042—dc21
2002151508

Contents

Preface

It may at first sight seem surprising, after many years of silence among German-speaking moral theologians, that a monograph should take up anew the problems connected with the natural law. The appropriateness of such a study is suggested, first of all, by the contemporary debate within moral theology and social ethics. In the past, theologians' desire to identify the specifically Christian led many to dispute the possibility of providing rational justification for an "autonomous" ethics which would make substantial affirmations on individual points, thus confronting the human person with the claim reality makes; today, philosophical reasons lead many to reject this possibility altogether. Instead, moral theology is urged to abandon its ontological foundation and its epistemological claim to formulate judgments that conform precisely to reality, replacing these with the theological reception of procedural models such as those found in discourse ethics.

No one would wish to deny that the approaches discussed in today's philosophical ethics—whether transcendental-pragmatic, discourse-ethical, or orientated to behavior in a general sense—have great significance for Catholic moral theology, which can find helpful stimulus here in important questions, e.g., the confrontation with ethical relativism, the ultimate justification of ethical judgments, and the extent to which a transcendental-philosophical justification of human dignity is feasible. However, these proposals for the further development of a methodological approach in theological ethics entail more than the addition of new arguments or the reception of new questions: rather, their goal is the definitive elimination of an ethical model of thought that is conscious of being obligated to a basis antecedent to all procedural strategies that aim at a consensus. This basis provides the necessary orientation in the discussion about ethically correct behavior and the search for ethically justifiable resolutions to conflicts.

The present book, guided by the double concept of natural law and human dignity, argues against such positions that, thanks to the reality of the human person and of the existential ends sought in human life, there does exist such a basis antecedent to all strategies of consensus and procedures. This basis is capable of establishing a concrete ethics by means of substantial affirmations on individual points, without thereby lapsing into a circular justification or a naturalistic fallacy. This is why my proposal takes up the Thomistic theory of the practical reason and of the natural ends of human endeavor: here we already find an historical model of ethical thinking capable of meeting the classical objections to natural-law doctrines in the late scholastic and modern periods. An examination of the historical thinking of the twentieth century and an inquiry into the ultimate presuppositions of ethical self-determination will indicate how to arrive at a criterion of what is right on the basis of nature even under the conditions of today's philosophizing, and how such a criterion can be fruitful for ethics.

A second reason for taking up the theme of natural law anew today is the intellectual challenge faced by the church's moral proclamation in a world marked by the internal pluralism of democratic societies and the contemporaneous presence of totalitarian ideologies and forms of state in every region of the globe. For this reason, I shall analyze the growth of ethical relativism in European consciousness and inquire into the original intentions behind the discovery of historicity in the philosophy of the nineteenth and twentieth centuries, thereby investigating the historical transformation of our views about morality. The aim of these analyses is to demonstrate that the practical reason is in principle capable of grasping the truth and to determine the extent to which we can still maintain the universal validity of moral principles and norms in a world that has become aware of its inherent historicity and multicultural breadth. We shall see here that one must not understand the thesis of the universal validity of moral precepts as a statement with only one meaning; the meaning changes depending on whether moral norms and ethical directives prevent us from infringing the natural rights of others or remind us of those existential ends that allow our human life to succeed as a whole. This insight into the two stages of our practical reason allows us also to construct a systematic understanding of biblical ethics and of its universal claim, which is supported by the results of modern exegesis, especially research into the decalogue and the exposition of the Sermon on the Mount.

I am grateful to my colleagues in Freiburg, above all to Ernst-Wolfgang Böckenförde, Bernhard Casper, Alfons Deissler, Norbert Glatzel, and Lorenz Oberlinner, for suggestions on these topics, for criticism, and for conversations. Mrs. Gertrud Rothfuss and Mrs. Ingelore Schmidt worked on the manuscript, while Dr. Simone Rappel and Mr. Markus Ziegler have accompanied it from the very outset. I express my thanks to them all.

Freiburg im Breisgau, December 1995

Abbreviations

ARSP	*Archiv für Rechts- und Sozialpsychologie*
BK/AT	*Biblische Kommentare/Altes Testament*
CGG	*Christlicher Glaube in moderner Gesellschaft*
EKK	*Evangelischer-katholischer Komentar zum NT*
EvTh	*Evangelische Theologie*
GGB	*Geistliche Grundbegriffe*
GTA	*Göttinger theologische Arbeiten*
HWPh	*Historisches Wörterbuch der Philosophie*
JBTh	*Jahrbuch für biblische Theologie*
LS	*Lebendige Seelsorge*
LThK	*Lexikon für Theologie und Kirche*
NJW	*Neue Juristische Wochenschrift*
NTD	*Das Neue Testament deutsch*
PhJ	*Philosophisches Jahrbuch*
PhRv	*Philosophical Review*
Rech. de Sc. Rel.	*Recherches de science religieuse*
RGG	*Die Religion in Geschichte und Gegenwart*
SBS	*Stuttgarter Bibel Studien*
SdZ	*Stimmen der Zeit*
SVF	*Stoicorum Veterum Fragmenta*
ThPh	*Theologie und Philosophie*
ThQ	*Theological Quarterly*
ThZ	*Theologische Zeitschrift*
TRE	*Theologische Realenzyklopädie*
ZEE	*Zeitschrift für Evangelische Ethik*
ZkTh	*Zeitschrift für katholische Theologie*
ZThK	*Zeitschrift für Theologie und Kirche*
ZTK	*Zeitschrift für Theologie und Kirche*

Natural Law &
Human Dignity

🎚 1. *The unwished-for inheritance of natural law*

O F ALL THE CENTRAL concepts of Christian ethics, it is the concept of the natural law that most forcefully reminds theological ethical reflection of the debates and problems connected with the question of its own foundations. The term "natural law" has occurred seldom in the scholarly debates of the last few decades and has acquired an almost ominous character (except where it was employed in historical investigations of individual topics); nevertheless, even under other headings, natural law remained present in many ways as a substantial issue. In the debates about the justification of norms and the evaluation of goods, autonomous moral theology and teleological ethics, the historicity and immutability of morality, and the magisterium and the conscience, the answers given were always conditioned by problems that lie on a deeper level, and these problems were linked at an earlier period with the concept of natural law. The problems of justifying this concept may have been suppressed, but they simply re-emerged elsewhere, reminding both church and theology that one cannot neglect unresolved problems and go unpunished.

Whereas the dominant tendency in contemporary Catholic moral theology is to regard the term "natural law" as one of the historical burdens one would be glad to be rid of, there is an increasing willingness in Protestant ethics to confront the suppressed inheritance of one's own tradition. One symptom of this changed attitude is the title of a recently published professorial dissertation that investigates the continued influence of questions of the natural law on the Protestant ethics of the twentieth century: "The long shadow of the natural law."[1] In the wake of the Second Vatican Council, Catholic moral theology had good reasons to suspect the intellectual concept of "natural law" of bearing ideological freight; Tanner calls this a "perennial unresolved problem" of Protestant ethics and is emphati-

---

1. Cf. K. Tanner, *Der lange Schatten des Naturrechts. Eine fundamentalethische Untersuchung,* Stuttart 1993. On the disrupted relationship of Protestant ethics to its own natural-law inheritance, cf. also F. Wagner, "Naturrecht II," *TRE* 24, cols. 153–85, esp. 176–79.

cally open to the historical and fundamental potential of this concept, which he praises as a "hermeneutic sensitivity to fundamental problems of ethics."[2] Another Protestant theologian has recently designated the question of the status of natural law as the "sixty-four-thousand-dollar question" of every theological ethics—though a question more often passed over in embarrassed silence than openly discussed.[3]

On the other hand, the striking reserve of contemporary Catholic theology vis-à-vis the concept of natural law should not blind us to the fact that the classical concerns of this concept and some of its modes of argumentation are being developed in the context of different questions. Indeed, if one agrees with Max Weber's apposite definition of the natural law as the embodiment of those moral laws that have supra-positive validity (in the sense that they are not sanctioned by religious authorities) and can be justified rationally,[4] then one will see how appropriate it is, given the basic tendencies which are dominant in contemporary moral theology, to make this link to the substance of the "natural law." Critics are often over-hasty in synthesizing a generic concept, which they then call autonomous or teleological ethics; those who defend this approach justify it by appealing explicitly to the historical example of Thomas Aquinas' doctrine of the natural law. Sometimes, the lack of specific substance and of a reference to the present day in an ethics conceived in biblical and salvation-historical categories leads to the conclusion that one must argue on the lines of natural law.[5] In a broader sense, the term "natural law" in the context of moral theology also denotes a "cognitive" ethics, or one "guided by reason," which claims to be able to distinguish between good and evil, and correct and false, in such a way that it establishes substantial norms.

It is above all the autonomous moral theology of *Alfons Auer*—based on the supposition that reality is completely rational and can be known by human reason and justifying these philosophical implications in a wholly traditional manner—that is viewed by its interpreters as a "legitimate con-

2. Wagner, "Naturrecht II," cols. 19, 53.
3. P. Bubmann, "Naturrecht und christliche Ethik," *ZEE* 37 (1993), pp. 267–80, at 267.
4. Cf. M. Weber, *Wirtschaft und Gesellschaft. Grundriss der verstehenden Soziologie,* Tübingen fifth edn. 1972, p. 497.
5. Cf., e.g., J. M. Aubert, "Pour une herméneutique du droit naturel," *Rech. de Sc. Rel.* 59 (1971), pp. 449–92; B. Schüller, "Zur theologischen Diskussion über die lex naturalis," *ThPh* 4 (1966), pp. 481–503; Idem, "Die Bedeutung des natürlichen Sittengesetzes für den Christen," in: G. Teichtweiher and W. Dreier (eds.), *Herausforderung und Kritik der Moraltheologie,* Würzburg 1971, pp. 105–30; W. Korff, "Der Rückgriff auf die Natur. Eine Rekonstruktion der thomanischen Lehre vom natürlichen Gesetz," *PhJ* 94 (1987), pp. 285–96.

tinuation of the natural law in the circumstances created by the modern consciousness of freedom,"[6] or even as a "late representative of the classical Catholic natural-law ethics."[7] Depending on the position taken by the author in question, maintaining the objective foundations of the validity of moral theology's affirmations and the "ontological-ethical" basis that is claimed for these affirmations will be described emphatically as a justified decision or else lamented as a regrettable discontinuity within an otherwise consistent concept of autonomy.[8]

This clear disagreement in the evaluation indicates a critical boundary which lies beyond the alternative between an autonomous ethics of the reason and a theonomous ethics of faith—the alternative that compels every philosophical and theological ethics today to state its position unambiguously and to disclose its implicit attitude to its natural-law inheritance. This is because the simplified antitheses that often dominate discussion within the church (reason *or* tradition, autonomous insight *or* obedience to the law, responsible judgment of the conscience *or* authoritative decision by the magisterium) obscure the decisive point at issue. The *real* alternative that confronts those who reflect on the foundations of ethics in philosophy and theology today can be briefly outlined in the question of whether they acknowledge a criterion of their ethical judgment that is antecedent to the practical reason and belongs to the essential fundamental structures and absolutely unchallengeable presuppositions of human existence itself (although this criterion in its turn can be known only by means of the reason), or hold that such a criterion can be discerned only within the parameters of the reason, whether through consensus among the enlightened participants in a discourse about the resolution of a conflict or through the individual who posits his personal existential goals.

We can also translate this alternative into a form more akin to the traditional intellectual and linguistic form of moral theology: is the human person merely the formal instance of ethical judgments, in the sense that only whatever is in accord with the free self-disposition of the person can count

---

6. K.-W. Merks, "Naturrecht als Personrecht? Überlegungen zu einer Relektüre der Naturrechtslehre des Thomas von Aquin," in: M. Heimbach-Steins (ed.), *Naturrecht im ethischen Diskurs,* Münster 1990, pp. 28–46, at 43.

7. C. Kissling, *Gemeinwohl und Gerechtigkeit. Ein Vergleich von traditioneller Naturrechtsethik und kritischer Gesellschaftstheorie,* Freiburg 1993, p. 151.

8. On this controversial evaluation, cf. H.-G. Gruber, "Autonome Moral oder Moral der Autonomie," *SdZ* 118 (1993), pp. 691–99; H. Hirschi, *Moralbegründung und christlicher Sinnhorizont,* Freiburg 1992, pp. 169–72; 191–95.

as ethically justified? Or does the personal character of the human being, in the unity of bodily and intellectual existence, also denote an objective claim which can be elaborated in substantial terms, generating on the basis of an anthropological doctrine of goods a substantial criterion for what is justifiable vis-à-vis the person as a rational being? The answer to this question decides more than just whether the natural-law pattern of thought and its transposition to the level of personal thinking can provide viable ethical orientation in the great questions affecting the conduct of the individual's life. If the human person denotes merely the subjective origin of freedom and reason, but no objective claim or obligatory precept concerning life in common in state and society, there would no longer be any basis for the validity of the ethos of human rights in the European and American Enlightenment; and it is here, from the eighteenth century onwards, that natural-law thinking has had its greatest historical effect in the sociopolitical sphere.[9]

This indicates the basic thesis that will be elaborated in this book. We shall investigate the continued influence on contemporary ethical thinking of lines of argumentation involving the natural law, in order to employ these for a systematic justification of the ethos of human rights and of the underlying idea of the natural "dignity" of each human being. In this introductory chapter, our primary subject is the hermeneutical dilemmas and the difficulties of justifying the traditional doctrines of natural law; these must be borne in mind when one attempts to provide a theological-ethical justification of the concept of human dignity against the background of today's historical thinking. In the second and third chapters, we shall examine critically the implicit presuppositions of historicism and of ethical relativism. This will prepare us to investigate how one should understand the claim that ethical judgments have universal validity in an historical world. The last two chapters seek to offer a systematic answer to this fundamental problem of contemporary ethics by developing in two tiers the philosophical and theological implications of the idea of human dignity. One may then inquire into the meaning attributed in theological ethics to classical structures of natural-law argumentation such as the concept of intrinsically evil actions or the distinction between negative obligations to omission and positive obligations to act.

9. On this, cf. H. Welzel, *Naturrecht und materiale Gerechtigkeit. Problemgeschichtliche Untersuchungen als Prolegomena zu einer Rechtsphilosophie*, Göttingen 1960, pp. 160f.; K.-H. Ilting, "Naturrecht," *GGB*, IV, cols. 245–313.

1. What the loss costs us

A simple intellectual experiment can help us assess correctly the significance of the natural law for ethical thinking. Let us imagine the consequences for human society that would necessarily follow from a rejection,
not only of the word, but of the matter itself, and of its theoretical implications. The Jewish philosopher Leo Strauss, who was forced to emigrate to
America under the Nazi tyranny, describes soberly and without illusions the
consequences of such an intellectual experiment, which he saw as only hy-
pothetically possible. In Strauss' eyes, calling the natural law into question
leads to an unacceptable nihilism which is only seldom intended by the intellectual despisers of this venerable stream of tradition within political-
ethical thought. One who rejects the intentions of natural-law thinking
must logically accept in equal measure all personal lifestyles and modes of
behavior in the private sphere and all the forms of society which have developed in the course of history. It would then be no longer possible to discern
any morally significant differences between the totalitarian and the democratic forms of state that have come into being in the course of human history and that now compete with one another for control of the future in
Asia, Africa, and Latin America. From the perspective of cultural history,
we would have to place enlightened forms of life on the same level as a society of cannibals.

In the final analysis, it would be impossible for us to look at our own
societal system with any critical distance: we would thus be compelled to
justify all the attitudes toward values, needs, and modes of conduct found
in that society, without any distinctions. "If there is no standard higher
than the ideal of our society, we are utterly unable to take a critical distance from that ideal. But the mere fact that we can raise the question of
the worth of the ideal of our society shows that there is something in man
that is not altogether in slavery to his society, and therefore that we are
able, and hence obliged, to look for a standard with reference to which we
can judge the ideals of our own as well as of any other soicety."[10] Thus, the
ability to distinguish between one's own ideals and those of others presupposes that we possess a critical criterion antecedent to the various historical
forms of life and society. Modern social historians and cultural anthropologists paint an impressive picture of the wide spectrum of such forms,
which can be understood only within this comprehensive standard. Strauss

10. L. Strauss, *Natural Right and History,* Chicago and London 1953, p. 3.

explicitly includes among the universal, intercultural elements that we owe to the common nature of our humanity the possibility of making a distinction from one's own standpoint in history—i.e., within one's own society—between genuine and false human needs, thus achieving agreement about the obligatory hierarchy of basic human goods: "The problem posed by the conflicting needs of society cannot be solved if we do not possess knowledge of natural law."[11]

These reflections by an historian of philosophy show that even a societal utopia that would permit a critical distance vis-à-vis the contemporary forms of our society remains dependent on the guidance of an anthropology that informs us about human life and the fundamental goods that are needed if this life is to develop aright. These reflections also show the deepest concern of all theories of natural law, no matter how various, indeed contradictory, and occasionally incompatible their goals may be: namely, the yearning to learn how to understand the essence of the human person and to use this insight to formulate prescriptive statements about the goals in life that are appropriate to his essence and about the political-societal conditions that mark the parameters of a truly human existence. This yearning also explains why the idea of the natural law surfaced especially in the intellectual breakthroughs that accompanied times of crisis and the transition to new epochs. When the old order breaks down, along with the criteria of law and morality that were valid hitherto, one is compelled to ask whether there exists something that goes beyond what is posited by human persons, a law with a lasting validity "based on nature."

The problem of natural law always breaks out anew in such times of crisis, and it must be posed each time with a fresh acuteness. We recall here above all the awakening of the philosophical spirit in the Greek enlightenment of the fifth century before Christ; the cosmopolitical ideal of humanity that arose among the Stoics in the face of the decline of the classical world; the disintegration of the medieval structures of life in the transition to the early modern period; the development of the traditions of human rights in the aftermath of the French Revolution and the American independence movement; and, finally, the new world order based on the idea of human rights after the end of the Second World War. With the exception of the twentieth century, in which the natural law knew only a brief renaissance after the collapse of the Nazi tyranny, the beginnings of

11. Ibid.

these new epochs were high points of natural-law thinking and promoted its development.

A look back to such historical constellations allows us from a theological perspective to assess correctly the significance of the reception by early Christianity of the classical thinking about natural law. The adoption of Stoic-Roman doctrines of natural law by patristic theology is certainly not to be equated with a renunciation of the messianic radicality of the Gospel; rather, this was the necessary presupposition, in terms of the history of ideas, which permitted Christianity at the beginning of a new epoch to unleash the power of the Gospel to make its mark on culture and to shape the world. This is why its importance in the field of ethics is comparable to the decision by the first apologists to adopt the Greek concept of *logos* when they argued for the significance of the incarnation for the whole human race. The Protestant theologian Ernst Troeltsch is correct to see the adoption of the Stoic idea of natural law by the early church, which made possible the elaboration of a Christian ethics embracing all the private and political-social spheres of life, as one of the "foundational facts of world history" that have left their imprint on our modern world.[12] Although one can recognize in his typology of Christian doctrines of natural law a certain preference for the revolutionary sectarian type (since the radicality of the Gospel lives on in it with fewer compromises; the same evaluation can be seen later in Ernst Bloch), this does not affect the comprehensive judgment that Troeltsch makes from an historical perspective: it was basically the "main embodiments of the Christian idea" in the great *Volkskirchen* and their doctrines of natural law that made possible an impact in the history of culture on the political-social forms of human life and allowed the Gospel to bring a real historical influence to bear upon the life of the peoples.[13] It is scarcely possible to overstate the relevance of such a conclusion, drawn from the perspective of cultural history, to our contemporary reflections on the basic issues of theology and ethics. We can reverse it, to show the significance Christian ethics would lose if it were to abandon the claim it makes, on the basis of natural law, to address the entirety of human existence and to offer a normative evaluation of the forms of human life; for all it would offer, then, would be a moral theology valid only within the sphere of the church or a morality appealing only to the authority of scripture.

12. E. Troeltsch, "Naturrecht, christliches," *RGG,* first edn., Tübingen 1913, V, cols. 697–704, at 697.

13. E. Troeltsch, *Die Soziallehren der christlichen Kirchen und Gruppen* (Gesammelte Schriften, I), Tübingen 1919, p. 811.

However, Troeltsch's summary of the course of historical events also includes the sobering recognition that, until now, every success of natural law has turned out in retrospect to be a Pyrrhic victory.[14] For one thing, the subsequent cultural systems (themselves in turn justified in terms of natural law) refuted the claim of the previous cultural systems to supratemporal validity. Indeed, it has been asserted that Western ethics has a self-destructive nihilism, inherent in the idea of the natural law.[15] Another factor was the subterranean contrary current of another natural law, whose waves of protest continually broke the surface and joined battle under the banner of liberty and equality, autonomy and human dignity against the misuse of the doctrine of natural law by theocratic systems of government and absolutistic theories of the state.[16] Ultimately, the idea of natural law itself became obsolete, thanks to the use made of it by such worldviews. The suspicion arose that it was necessarily an easy prey to ideological misuse, which would thus be a characteristic of all theories of natural law; no theory would be able effectively to immunize itself against this risk. Thanks to the growth of historical thinking in the nineteenth century among historians of the law, and to the objections made by dialectical theology in the twentieth century, the basic historical, juridical, and theological problems that had been inherent from the outset in the natural-law tradition emerged with ever greater clarity.

2. The dilemma of justification

All these factors have generated a deep crisis for natural-law thinking in recent decades. It is required to justify itself against the background of a general questioning of the fundamental possibility of thinking in these terms. Philosophical and theological tendencies that otherwise have scarcely anything in common agree in the sphere of ethics, i.e., in their cautious reserve vis-à-vis the natural law. In the sphere of political and social sciences, the rejection of the natural law unites intellectual trends that are very different and have antithetical political goals, e.g., the decisionist doc-

14. E. Troeltsch, *Der Historismus und seine Probleme* (Gesammelte Schriften, III), Tübingen 1922, p. 127.

15. Cf. S. Breuer, *Sozialgeschichte des Naturrechts* (Beiträge zur sozialwissenschaftlichen Forschung 42), Opladen 1983, pp. 598ff.

16. On this, cf. E. Bloch, *Naturrecht und menschliche Würde* (Gesamtausgabe, II), Frankfurt second edn. 1991.

trine of the state and modern legal positivism on the one side and the critical theory of society on the other. The furthest reaching attempt to abolish natural law completely is made by a functional theory of systems,
which denies any relevance of the concept of natural law to genuinely significant problems in complex modern societies, which are articulated in
partial systems; all it can see in this concept is "an unthinking continuation of a lofty traditional title."[17]

The verdict seems crushing, yet the very fact that it does not apply to
natural law alone makes one pause. The natural law shares this fate with
most theories concerning ethics and the philosophy of law, as well as with
every question in the humanities that is formulated in such a way that it
claims to help clarify what these intellectual disciplines themselves call "the
question of truth." Once one has detected this resentment—which in fact
serves no function in the way of looking at things proper to a theory of systems—it becomes clear that the various theories offered by the humanities
as explanations of the phenomena of justice and morality are merely competing descriptive formulae that serve the system's own self-description,
each from its own standpoint. This standpoint can be recognized only on a
second- or third-order descriptive level, where it can be seen that it is arbitrarily interchangeable with other perspectives. This shows the allegedly rational justification of justice and morality to be an illusion; on these higher
levels of observation, all the claims to validity of the partial systems are dissolved. The idea of a legal or moral obligation ceases to bedazzle the reason;
as each science progresses to ever complexer levels of description, this idea
is finally unmasked as what it in fact always was, viz. the "tautological sym-
bolization" of the concept of normativity, which is identical with what can
be expected in societal terms. In this precise sense, the idea of legal or
moral obligation is identical with the fact of societal acceptance.[18]

This objection to the natural law feeds on many sources, but its attack
follows one direction only. There has scarcely been any investigation of the
background to this astonishing alliance in the history of ideas or of its political and ideological motives. It is, however, also true that the very plurality of voices raised in criticism indicates that the natural-law tradition of
the past was a melting pot for a variety of tendencies in ethical thought;
this tradition is a burden that weighs down on the examination of all the
specific problems posed by these tendencies. Instead of the ensemble of in-

17. N. Luhmann, *Das Recht der Gesellschaft*, Frankfurt 1993, p. 517; cf. pp. 538–43.
18. Ibid., p. 502.

dividual pieces of anthropological, historical, and theological knowledge, which reinforced one another to form a general tendency and converged in the basic presuppositions of the individual systems of natural law, today's discussion faces a hopeless accumulation of difficulties. These may not be insuperable when examined singly, but when taken together, they form a problematic layer that seems impermeable. Anyone who wishes to come to grips with the natural law must first break through this layer, unless he is content merely to lament his loss.

2.1. The semantic ambiguity of the natural law

a. "Natural law" as a theory of moral philosophy One reason for the widespread reserve vis-à-vis the concept of natural law is the unclarity with which it has been applied in various academic contexts. In the tradition of Catholic moral theology, "natural law" denotes primarily a theory of *moral philosophy* that insists, against an ethical non-cognitivism and relativism, that it is possible for ethical judgments to express the truth and to be universally valid. This kind of ethics bases its normative affirmations neither on emotional positions (emotivism) nor on an intentional feeling of value on the part of the will (philosophy of value), nor on a merely procedural process of the reason (discourse ethics), but on an objective foundation in the "ethics of Being" that exists antecedently in the nature of the human person and in those existential ends that are in accordance with his essence. The concept of natural law is widely employed here as a synonym for the concept of the natural ethical law. Thomas Aquinas does indeed make a distinction in his *Summa theologiae* between the *ius naturale* (the specific sphere where justice is to be exercised) and the *lex naturalis* (the participation of the practical reason in the eternal law), but later Thomistic tradition seldom retained this differentiation.[19] Rather, "natural law" extended its claims to every morally relevant sphere of the life of the individual, the society, and the state. For a long period, this concept served within Catholic theology as a bracket embracing statements about individual morality, social doctrine, and political ethics; but it appears less well suited to encompass that distinction between law and morality in the

---

19. The early Thomas still employs the concepts of *ius naturale* and *lex naturalis* in precisely the same sense (e.g., *In IV Sententiarum* d. 33, q. 1, a. 1). On the significance of the distinction, cf. J. M. Aubert, "Pour une herméneutique du droit naturel," pp. 466ff., and L. Oening-Hanhoff, "Mensch und Recht nach Thomas von Aquin," *PhJ* 82 (1975), pp. 10–30, esp. 16f.

sphere of individual ethics that must be made under the conditions of the modern period or the functional articulation of society, economics, and the state in the public political realm.

Another aspect of the semantic ambiguity attaching to the term "natural law" is that its use within the church largely parted company with the development of the history of concepts in the last hundred years. Whereas the controversy between the voluntaristic and rationalistic natural-law doctrines of the late Middle Ages was still carried on among the great theological schools with their various orientations, and the "autonomous" natural law of the early modern period came into existence on foundations prepared by the most important theologians of Spanish scholasticism in the Baroque period,[20] the neo-scholasticism of the nineteenth century no longer pays any attention to the discussions of the natural law that had taken place within German Idealism. The concept of "natural law" means completely different things in Fichte's *Grundlage des Naturrechts* (1796), in Hegel's early essay on the natural law (1802), and in the neo-scholastic handbooks that were written half a century later. There are no intellectual points of contact between philosophy's transcendental-historical law of reason and neo-scholastic theology's essentialist natural-law ethics. Both employ the same concept, but with different contents, and "never the twain shall meet."

b. "Natural law" as a theory of legal philosophy In jurisprudence and the political doctrine of the state, "natural law" designates a theory of *legal philosophy* distinct both from legal positivism and from the theory of systems. This theory maintains that individual rights to freedom and fundamental principles of law have a supra-positive validity antecedent to the formation of specific states. While natural law as an *ethical theory* shows little interest in the differentiation between law and morality, the question posed by natural law in legal philosophy necessarily presupposes the distinction of these two spheres. In the context of *legal* theory, one can inquire into the ethical foundations of law and into the moral acknowledgment of the demands made by the law only if the differentiation between law and morality is first understood as a specific question of legal philosophy, rather than as a question of fundamental ethics. On the other hand, the nineteenth-century school of legal history and the pure doctrine of law

20. On this, cf. R. Specht, "Naturrecht. Mittelalter und frühe Neuzeit," *HWPh* VI, 571–82.

in the twentieth century forced the natural law to withdraw its claim to be "law," since they regarded historical validity and the possibility of compelling obedience to the demands of the law as essential elements in the very concept of "law." The specific tension between idea and reality, which was immanent to the idea of natural law from the very outset, now points to a decisive deficiency. Natural law embraces only one part of the concept of law, that is, its ideal-normative aspect, but it is impossible by definition for the natural law to have the authority to compel obedience or the power to ensure its enforcement—elements that are necessary for the demarcation between law and morality.

The concept of "natural law" is often employed very vaguely, as a generic term for all those positions in legal philosophy that in some way or other maintain the non-arbitrary character of the law, without however referring to the concept of "nature."[21] Thus it is possible to employ this concept in legal philosophy and the history of law even without those ideas that are linked to it in ethical discussion, viz. the ideas of a "nature of things" immanent to the various spheres of societal life and of an ideal essential nature of the human person.

2.2. *The anthropological ambiguity of the natural law*

The unclarity about the second part of this term, that is, about the meaning of the natural *law,* is serious enough; but even more serious is the polysemy attaching to the first part. As the term itself indicates, *natural* law is based on the idea that the principles of the ethical life and of the legal order are related to the specificity of human nature. This in turn presumes that the common nature of human beings, as far as its ethical and legal relevance is concerned, is a stable and knowable reality, with an extent and contents that can be clearly defined—or at least that it is a regulatory idea that cannot meaningfully be called into question from any position. This presupposition, however, leads to the real crux of all doctrines of the natural law, since the concept of "nature" is not in the least unambiguous.

a. The idea of "a life in accord with nature" Etymologically, the fundamental meaning of the word "nature" (from *nasci,* "to be born") indicates

---

21. On this, cf. F.-X. Kaufmann, "Wissenssoziologische Überlegungen zu Renaissance und Niedergang des katholischen Naturrechtsdenkens im 19. und 20. Jahrhundert," in: F. Böckle and E.-W. Böckenförde (eds.), *Naturrecht in der Kritik,* Mainz 1973, pp. 126–64, at 131.

an *origin*. This, however, tells us nothing about a permanent ordering of human existence that would be in keeping with human nature. Even where the concept of nature is understood on the basis of the myth of a paradise where all is primordial and fresh, the formula of "a life in accord with nature" can serve completely antithetical purposes, from a pessimistic, backwards-looking analysis of the present day, to the forward-looking social utopias that have left their mark across the entire spectrum of the political-social history of ideas in the modern period. A good example of the first possibility is the classical philosopher Seneca, who dismissed all the civilizing achievements of his times, from the building of houses, agriculture, and cattle-breeding to the possession of land and private property as "unnatural" ways of life into which the Roman people had fallen when they turned their backs on the happier circumstances of former times.[22] We find the utopian variant at the end of the *Ancien Régime* in Rousseau's *Social Contract* (1762), where the Arcadian idyll of nature embodies the serene and tranquil atmosphere in which free *citoyens*—according to the fictional social contract—establish for all future times, in the fundamental act that constitutes bourgeois society, their individual rights, which include above all the right to personal safety and private property.[23]

A similar contradiction can be seen in classical ethics: in the name of nature, the Stoics reject precisely the way of life that the Epicurean philosophers recommend as in keeping with nature and beneficial for the health of body and mind. Whereas the Epicureans concentrate their attention on the human person in his empirical nature as a being with needs, Stoic ethics seeks to employ spiritual exercises to guide the human person to establish the sovereignty of his rational nature over the world of his instincts and passions and to recognize this as the true end for which the human person is destined.[24] This antithesis between the human being as an empirical nature with needs and as an ideal rational nature—which returns in the modern period in Kant's ethics as a radical dichotomy, and is one-sidedly resolved in Hobbes' reduction of the human person to a mechanism driven by antagonistic forces[25]—is the first fundamental alternative that faces all doctrines of natural law.

---

22. Cf. esp. the descriptions in his ninetieth Letter (cf. *Epistulae morales* 90,4; 90,44ff.); on this, cf. F. Flückiger, *Geschichte des Naturrechts*, I: *Altertum und Frühmittelalter*, Zurich 1954, pp. 215–18.

23. On this, cf. E. Bloch, *Naturrecht und menschliche Würde*, pp. 76–79.

24. On this, cf. P. Hadot, *Exercices spirituels et philosophie antique*, Paris 1981.

25. On this, cf. L. Honnefelder, "Natur als Handlungsprinzip. Die Relevanz der Natur

b. The teleological interpretation of nature A third possibility, which became significant above all in the Aristotelian-Thomistic tradition, considers the human person in his physical-intellectual existence and interprets him as a psycho-physical vital unity under the primacy of the reason. This conception became available to philosophical thinking after Aristotle had transformed the aprioristic contemplation of essences in the Platonic doctrine of ideas into a teleological metaphysics that made it possible to give the idea of natural law its place within an interpretation of the world as a whole. This interpretation in turn supplies the natural law with substantial contents applicable to all spheres of reality. According to the basic principle of the Aristotelian contemplation of nature, every living being has a "form" appropriate to its own essence; this exists as a potential in the material substratum and is actualized by means of a teleological process of coming into existence. In the case of animals and plants, this coincides with their organic growth, which allows them to attain their own "entelechy," that is, the perfection of form that serves their specific function. In the case of the human person, the definition of his "nature" appropriate to his species, that is, his specific telos (end), also includes the development of his reason, which belongs to the essential definition of what it is to be a human person. This is because the "end" of an existent always denotes the development of its nature in its highest possibilities; for Aristotle, it is not the original state that is "in keeping with nature," but rather the finished form, that is, the best possible condition of a thing or of a living being. "Nature is the end of every object. We call the condition which it displays at the end of the process of its coming into being, its 'nature'—whether of a human person, a horse or a house. The purpose and the end are that which is best."[26]

This means that one cannot simply discover the nature of the human person by looking at his external reality; nor is this nature identical to the ensemble of the empirical conditions of his existence. Rather, it is a nature constituted in a teleological sense, orientated towards an end, designed in keeping with a plan and a definition. The concepts of nature or being on the one hand and function, form, and shape on the other refer to one another; indeed, they converge to such an extent that the teleological con-

---

für die Ethik," in: Idem (ed.), *Natur als Gegenstand der Wissenschaften,* Freiburg 1992, pp. 151–83, esp. 162ff.; and G. Wieland, "'Secundum naturam vivere'. Über den Wandel des Verhältnisses von Natur und Sittlichkeit," in: B. Fraling (ed.), *Natur im ethischen Argument,* Freiburg and Vienna 1990, pp. 13–31, esp. 28f.
    26. *Politics* I, 2 (1252b); cf. also I, 5 (1254a).

templation of nature is from the very outset defined in qualitative terms. This contemplation interprets the reality of individual objects and living beings on the basis of individual values that belong to each individual existent as such. Our modern philosophical conceptuality would say that the teleological contemplation of nature does not make any purely descriptive judgments: its judgments are "mixed," containing both observable contents and a value-related statement about the meaning of these contents. Unlike the modern investigation of nature, which is orientated to the quantifiability of matter and the repetition of experiments, the teleological way of looking at nature is a movement of thought that goes beyond the standpoint of empirical observation to make value-statements about the perfection appropriate to objects and things, plants, and animals, and about the existence of the human person and the ends appropriate to his essence. This is why the modern accusation of a naturalistic fallacy completely fails to do justice to the basic idea of all teleological doctrines of the natural law; the same is true of the failure to distinguish between the natural law's qualitative, meaning-orientated interpretation of reality on the one hand and an allegedly metaphysical biology on the other.[27]

c. The risk of arguing in a circle The close link between "nature" and "end," which subsequently allowed Christian theology (against the background of its belief in creation) to elaborate a material doctrine of natural law applicable to all spheres of life, does however contain a dangerous ambiguity, which subsequently developed into the gravest problem inherent in the idea of natural law. On the one hand, the ahistorical character of the teleological interpretation of nature—in which we can discern Aristotle's true contribution to the elaboration of the idea of the natural law—favored from the outset an abstract understanding of "essence" that paid

---

27. Even the main representative of American neo-Aristotelianism, A. MacIntyre, was unable to free himself from this prejudice, which it seems impossible to eradicate from the history of philosophy. His accusation that Aristotelian ethics posits a "metaphysical biology" (*After Virtue. A Study in Moral Theory* [Notre Dame 1981]) is based on two false evaluations of history. First of all, it overlooks the point that the Aristotelian teleology of nature always intends to speak of the pattern of the individual form and the immanent functionality of an individual living being; unlike the Stoic universal teleology, it does not subordinate this functionality to a total function of nature (on this, cf. W. Theiler, *Zur Geschichte der teleologischen Naturbetrachtung bis auf Aristoteles*, Berlin second edn. 1965, p. 91; and K. von Fritz, "Teleologie bei Aristoteles," in: G. A. Seeck [ed.], *Die Naturphilosophie des Aristoteles*, Darmstadt 1975, pp. 246f.). The second misunderstanding consists in projecting this artificial idea of an "Aristotelian" teleology of nature into the *Nicomachean Ethics* and using it to govern the exposition of this work (cf. R. A. Gauthier, *L'Ethique à Nicomaque*, I: *Première Partie: Introduction*, Louvain 1970, p. 243).

more attention to the ideal, ontological nature of the human person than to his concrete, historical reality. This tension between an "ideal" and an "existential" understanding of natural law[28] has left its mark on documents of the church's magisterium, including the most recent social encyclicals.[29] More serious than this, however, is the second ambiguity of the teleological conceptions of natural law: the identification of nature and purpose, of "true" essence and highest end, entails the risk of a circular argument. The resolution of this circular argument devalues the insights of natural law, so that these become empty formulae—whatever substance they have comes from the succession of anthropologies and understandings of society. The legal philosopher Hans Welzel has described this circular structure of justification as the fundamental hermeneutical problem of the natural law: "The Protean form of human nature takes on the shape that each natural-law thinker wishes. He has already tacitly imported into his 'concept of the nature' of the human person everything that he himself finds correct and desirable: he then brings this forth anew to justify his own conviction about what is correct and in keeping with nature. The 'nature' of the human person is a concept so open and malleable that absolutely everything can be included in it, and can then be brought out again for the purpose of justification."[30] Aristotle himself is the best example of this procedure, since he is unable to have recourse to nature in order to discern what is to count as rational (and therefore natural to the human person); instead, he points to the judgment of wise men, that is, to the traditional morality that was already valid in his own period.[31] This means that he does not make nature the criterion of what is ethically good. On the contrary, he accepts the criteria of value supplied by traditional morality as the standard of what is to count as the natural end and essentially correct perfection of the human person.

The history of theories of natural law is full of examples that impressively confirm the suspicion that their normative insights into values are based on premises that had previously been read into the structure of the world or the nature of the human person. Plato can serve as a prominent witness in the sphere of political ethics. He derives his justification of the

---

28. On this distinction, cf. H. Welzel, *Naturrecht und materiale Gerechtigkeit,* pp. 10f.

29. On this, cf. U. Nothelle-Wildfeuer, *'Duplex ordo cognitionis'. Zur systematischen Grundlegung einer katholischen Soziallehre im Anspruch von Philosophie und Theologie* (Abhandlungen zur Sozialethik, 31), Paderborn 1991, pp. 136 and 315f.

30. H. Welzel, *Naturrecht und materiale Gerechtigkeit,* p. 16.

31. On this, cf. *Nicomachean Ethics* VI, 8 (1141b16–20).

best *political constitution* from a consideration of the parts of the soul and their "just" mutual relationship—a relationship that he has previously defined in precisely that hierarchical manner that corresponds to his ideas of an ordered political entity.[32] In the soul, the reason rules over the desires with the help of the will and brings about an ordered life of justice, while the rebellion of the desires against that part of the soul that is capable of government leads at once to a "purposeless multitude of occupations" and ultimately to anarchy, which is the supreme injustice. In the same way, the philosophically educated leaders of the state are to dominate the lower sections of the populace with the help of the soldiers and to maintain the entire republic in a condition of order. We should note that Plato calls such an ordering "just" precisely because it reflects, in the external sphere of political life, the situation within the human person, where justice "establishes the inner components of the soul in keeping with nature."[33] Similarly, one could interpret the mutual relationship of the parts of the soul in keeping with the model of a democratic assembly of citizens, so that democracy would necessarily be seen as the natural constitution of a state, based in the very essence of the human person. We may indeed hold, on the evidence of our historical experience, that democracy is the form of government that has best proved its worth, but the circularity of such a natural-law argumentation would be obvious. The same fundamental pattern would also permit a totalitarian ideology such as social Darwinism to justify its dislike of democracy: first, it would present the idea of the everlasting struggle for survival and the idea of a natural selection of the strongest as a natural law found in the whole of sentient nature; then it would project this back onto human society and the forms taken by the political struggle in this society.[34]

In the same way, we find in the history of political ideas natural-law arguments for the original *equality* of all persons, alongside other arguments intended to justify as natural an *unequal treatment* that would correspond to the natural differences among human persons. Thus, we find in Plato the idea that natural justice demands that all be treated equally—this can be inferred from the *Republic,* where Thrasymachus unsuccessfully tries to establish that justice is whatever is useful to the one who is strong. On the other hand, Callicles attempts in the *Gorgias* to unmask precisely this affir-

32. On this, cf. *Republic* IV, 443C–445D.
33. Ibid., IV, 444D.
34. On this, cf. E. Topitsch, "Restauration des Naturrechts?," in: Idem, *Sozialphilosophie zwischen Ideologie und Wissenschaft,* Berlin 1961, pp. 53–70, esp. 62.

mation of equality as a resentment on the part of the weak, who rebel against the natural right of those who are stronger and appeal to the laws of the state for help.[35]

In the case of the institution of *slavery*, the doctrines of natural law in the classical period also arrived at contradictory conclusions. While Aristotle (followed later by Thomas Aquinas and most writers in the Christian Middle Ages) maintained that some persons are determined by nature for a life of subordination,[36] the Stoics rejected this supposition on the basis of their doctrine of *oikeiôsis* and the consequent idea of humanity; indeed, Chrysippus taught explicitly that no human being is by nature a slave.[37] On this point, the church fathers up to Augustine generally followed the religious ideas of the Stoa about equality and interpreted slavery as a consequence of sin, something originally alien to human nature.[38] However, under the influence of a Neoplatonic idea of order, a quite different conception of nature made its way into the church's thinking about the law: the fundamental ontological structure of the world was increasingly explained in terms of a hierarchical structure of ordering. The zenith of this development came with the mediaeval theologian Bonaventure, who presented the *ordo hierarchicus*—a divinely-intended descent from the highest angelic hierarchies down to the gradated social ranks among human beings—as the natural ordering for human life in all its spheres. Thus, the obedience of the inferior to the superior (the secular ruler, the abbot in the monastery, the ecclesiastical prelate who exercised jurisdiction, or one's own husband) was elevated to the rank of a strict natural-law commandment, which in turn was intended to reinforce the acknowledgment of the hierarchical principle of order in daily life.[39]

In view of such disparate value judgments about the natural ordering of political-social life, it is not surprising that a natural-law consideration of important moral questions of private life also arrived at contradictory conclusions. Here, one need only point to the different attitudes taken by pa-

35. Cf. *Republic* I, 336B–344C; *Gorgias,* 482D–484A.
36. Cf. *Politics* I, 5 (1254b16–1255a2); on this, Thomas Aquinas, *STh* I, q. 96, a. 4; *In IV Sent.* d. 36, q. 1; *Summa contra Gentiles* III, c. 81 (nr. 2569).
37. Cf. Chrysippus, *Stoicorum Veterum Fragmenta (SVF)* III 353.
38. The sources (Theodoret, John Chrysostom, Augustine) are collected by F. Flückiger, *Geschichte des Naturrechts,* I, pp. 345–47.
39. Bonaventure, *De perfectione Evangelica,* in: *Opera omnia* (Ed. Quaracchi), V, p. 180: "The natural law dictates the hierarchical order which descends from the highest hierarchy by means of the angelic hierarchy to the human hierarchy, and it is in keeping with the hierarchical order that the inferior obeys the superior."

gan antiquity and the Christian Middle Ages to *abortion* and to the *killing of unwanted children,* indeed to human *sexuality* as a whole. In particular, the varied evaluation of female and male homosexuality shows that conduct that was abhorred throughout the Middle Ages as a *peccatum contra naturam* could be accepted in another societal context, under specific conditions, as a natural form of the human sexual instinct. The most interesting divergences, however, are the antithetical conclusions drawn by natural-law patterns of argumentation in the sphere of *married life.* According to the Platonic ideal of the state, it is not only slavery that counts as a just and natural institution; promiscuity on the part of the Guardians and the common education of their children are regarded as equally just and natural.[40] Thomas Aquinas later appeals to Aristotle when he arrives at precisely the opposite evaluation—on the basis of the same natural-law argument. Since the task of educating children, unlike the raising of progeny in the animal realm, demands a very long period of time and the atmosphere of security created by the fidelity of the marriage partners, Thomas concludes that monogamous and indissoluble marriage, which according to his understanding of the Christian faith possesses the dignity of a sacrament, is also a necessary institution of the natural law.[41]

A look through the list of the various normative value judgments that have been linked to the idea of the natural law in the course of its history compels the sobering conclusion that this idea seems an empty shape that can be filled with varying contents, providing no help in situations of genuine perplexity when one would like to know what is right and how one ought to behave. The kaleidoscopically changing pictures of this idea show that natural-law insights are based on premises found elsewhere. Like the blind spot in the eye of each particular worldview, one is unaware of these premises as long as the worldview remains viable; but when the background presuppositions change or the implicit interpretation of the world loses its historical validity, the natural-law patterns of thought cease to be of service. When the system of coordinates of the underlying understanding of the world and of the human person collapses, they no longer offer any ethical orientation.

It is in periods of anthropological disorientation that one most keenly notices the dilemma that the circular conclusions of the natural-law forms of argumentation keep leading back to the initial foundations, and that

---

40. Cf. *Republic* V, 449C.
41. Cf. Thomas Aquinas, *In IV Sententiarum,* d. 26, q. 1, a. 1.

their normative conclusions lead no further than the inherent possibilities of the insight into meaning that they presuppose. Just when one most needs the natural law, it displays its own helplessness. When other insights into meaning have dried up, the natural law has no further information to give the human person about the hierarchy of his needs and of the fundamental goods of his life. When the teleological view of human nature is itself called into question, and the human person is no longer capable of recognizing his own true ends, the old affirmations of the natural law take on the appearance of nostalgic imprecations, reminding one of certainties that have been lost.

2.3. The theological ambiguity of the natural law

The basic philosophical problem—i.e., whether statements of the natural law refer to the ideal rational nature of the human person or to his empirical structure as a natural being with needs—recurs in analogous manner on the theological level. At first sight, theological ethics does indeed seem to have the advantage, vis-à-vis philosophical ethics, of starting out with indications about meaning supplied by biblical anthropology, which provide essential fundamental affirmations, such as the human person as image of God, the equal dignity of woman and man, the significance of the fact of two genders, or the anthropological meanings of human sexuality. The biblical faith in creation gives theological ethics a clear point of reference for natural-law thinking, and this would seem to free it from the main difficulty posed by all philosophical theories of natural law, that is, that their substantial values must be borrowed from the disputed constructions of a speculative cosmology or a metaphysical anthropology.

This presupposition may be taken for granted from a theological perspective, but it already contains the first catch. If natural law is to make possible the justification—independently of every religious confession of faith—of moral commandments and of laws antecedent to the formation of any state, it is not possible simply to take creation theology's interpretation of reality and make this the unshakable foundation that is to do justice to this claim. It is indeed true, within the framework of the questions posed by theology, that the category of "creation" denotes that which is common to all human beings; this is in principle accessible to the natural reason of the human person and can therefore supply an appropriate point of contact for statements of the natural law. But this point of contact does not permit an instant connection, devoid of all presuppositions and logically independent of every confession of faith; for in the eyes of the "pure" natural reason, the fundamental affirmations a biblical anthropology makes about the theology of creation remain linked to the meaningful knowledge imparted by the Christian faith—especially as regards the material-substantial aspect of these affirmations. Critical self-reflection on how the church's moral proclamation has employed the formula of "Christian anthropology" quickly shows that this formula has been scarcely any more impervious to ideology than similarly comprehensive essential affirmations made in the sphere of philosophical anthropology.[42] Besides this, the very absoluteness of the claim made by the basic meaning, guaranteed as it is by divine revelation, confronts ethical thinking with new questions that have led, in the history of the Christian theories of the natural law, to answers that are no less contradictory than the alternative between an "ideal" or an "existential" natural law in the sphere of legal philosophy.

If the idea of natural law is based on the notion that law and morality are to be related to the specificity of human nature, this necessarily entails a number of further questions. How is this nature to be defined theologically? How does it disclose itself to the human person? How can he recognize it clearly and unambiguously? One does not dispose of this sixty-four-thousand-dollar question posed by all theories of natural law by simply referring to the biblical revelation or to the interpretation of the world offered by the Christian theology of creation. When we ask in a theological context about the nature of the human person, this question leads us straight to the heart of all theological thinking, to the intersection of the problems of creation theology, christology, soteriology, and the theological understanding of sin. The ultimate reason for the disagreements about the natural law, both in the ecumenical context and within Catholicism, is the difficulty of locating the question about the nature of the human person correctly within the network of other fundamental theological questions.

Where, then, does a theological ethic find the true image of the human person—in the garden of paradise or on Golgotha, the hill of crucifixion? Where does theology discern the true nature of the human person—in the original human being, as God had intended him to be in creation; in the fallen human being, marked by sin, who thwarts God's plan; or in the hu-

---

42. On this, cf. J. Ratzinger, "Naturrecht, Evangelium und Ideologie in der katholischen Soziallehre," in: K. von Bismarck and W. Dirks (eds.), *Christlicher Glaube und Ideologie,* Stuttgart 1964, pp. 24–30; D. Mieth, "Das 'christliche Menschenbild'—eine unzeitgemäße Betrachtung? Zu den Wandlungen einer theologisch-ethischen Formel," *ThQ* 163 (1983), pp. 1–15.

man being renewed by Christ, in whom the disfigured image of God shines out anew? Ought a theological ethics and a theological justification of human rights look at the human person as he is, or ought theological affirmations paint a picture of the human person as he could be, if he were to open himself to accept his true destiny and recognize his true being? The history of Christian theories of the natural law has been characterized from the beginning by this double perspective of a concrete look at the human being in the perspective of the history of salvation and a reflection on the essential structures of the "natural" human being that prescinds from the radical existential changes entailed by creation and sin, redemption, and perfection.

a. The christological natural law of the church fathers   In his monograph on the history of natural law (1954), conceived on a grand scale but never finished, the Reformed theologian Felix Flückiger transformed this double meaning of the theological concept of nature into a fundamental antithesis and interpreted the history of the Christian doctrines of natural law in keeping with this explanatory structure (which was indebted to the dialectical theology of his period). Here he distinguishes between two basic forms of the Christian idea of natural law and claims that these are in principle contradictory, defying all theological attempts at reconciliation (despite the historical existence of transitional forms). The first type of natural law theory is born of early Christian reflection on the history of revelation and eschatology. Its high points are Irenaeus' theory of recapitulation, Origen's theory of the *apokatastasis*, and Augustine's theology of history.

The basic idea of this "biblical" or "Christian" natural law builds on the presupposition that the question about the true nature of the human person can be posed in a theologically legitimate manner only with reference to the integral nature of the primal state: this was destroyed by Adam's sin, but renewed by Christ's salvific deed and re-established in the kingdom of God.[43] This is why God's original will is hidden from the natural human reason; it is no longer possible to discern this will by studying the wretched state of the de facto human nature, which is utterly corrupt. However, God has not abandoned the human person to the law of sin and death, but has revealed his original will in the law of Moses and renewed it in Christ, so that the human person can return to the integrity of his first nature if he submits himself in obedience to the historical proclamation of the divine will in the law and the Gospel. The substance of the formula "law and

43. Cf. F. Flückiger, *Geschichte des Naturrechts,* I, pp. 286–28; 301ff.

Gospel" is made explicit above all by the Ten Commandments of the Mosaic Decalogue and by Jesus' commandment to love. Both of these are substantially identical with the natural law, which in its pure form can be thought of only as a protological or an eschatological reality: it was imparted at the beginning, and it will once again be observed perfectly at the end, when the kingdom of God is fully established. In Christ, however, we have already been shown the image of the true human being who is totally in harmony with the will of God. He was already the prototype of the first Adam; now, through his incarnation, the shattered image of God has once again become visible. In the life of the incarnate Logos, in the figure of Jesus Christ, the fallen human person can discern anew the true meaning of love and freedom, of justice and mercy, and know how he may fulfill God's commandments.

Flückiger sees the soteriology of Irenaeus of Lyons as pre-eminently valuable evidence of the correctness of his historical reconstruction. This is where the christological natural-law thinking of the fathers emerges for the first time with full clarity: "Christ recapitulated in himself the entire history of the human person when he became a human being through the incarnation. In this recapitulation, he gave us salvation, in that we regained in him what we had lost in Adam—the image and likeness of God."[44] Since the re-establishing of the human person in the likeness of God also means the re-establishing of his fallen nature, Irenaeus has no difficulty in assuming the idea of natural law into the basic salvation-historical structure of his doctrine of recapitulation. When Christ renews nature and elevates it to its original perfection, this *restitutio in integrum* also exposes the knowledge of the natural law, which had hitherto been hidden: "The natural commandments of the law, by which the human person is justified, were observed, even before the law was given, by those who were justified by faith and pleased God. The Lord did not abolish these, but perfected and fulfilled them, as one may learn from his own words . . ."[45]

Irenaeus' formula *non dissolvit, sed extendit et implevit* hints at an interlocking of creation and redemption, and this points to an analogous intellectual form of the early Christian doctrine of natural law, rather than to the allegedly antithetical fundamental structure for which he is supposed to be the main witness. A similar conclusion is reached in individual historical studies of Augustine's christological conception of the natural law, according to which the perfect knowledge of the requirements of the natu-

44. *Adversus haereses* III, 18,1.
45. *Adversus haereses* IV, 13,1.

ral law depends on the knowledge of Christ. This is why these requirements find their historical *locus* in the *civitas Dei,* the historical sphere
where the renewed nature can blossom.[46] Despite the necessary corrections
to the historical picture, I am happy to agree with the positive evaluation
of the early Christian doctrine of natural law on which Flückiger's study is
based. The fundamental idea that "the Gospel means the re-establishing of
the *humanum,* of the human person in his true and original nature" must
be seen as an abiding insight of every theological natural-law ethics.[47]

  b. The rational natural law of the Middle Ages   In the first half of the
twentieth century, this same insight led to a temporary renaissance of
theonomous and christocentric intellectual forms within Catholic moral
theology; naturally, these abruptly lost their influence after the Second
World War, in the wake of new reflection on the methodology appropriate
to this discipline.[48] The weakness of the antithetical structure lies above all
in the theological dismissal of the second type of Christian natural law theories, which can first be seen—according to the rough outlines of the reconstructed history of decadence—when the Greek Logos-speculation is
adopted by Alexandrine theology. Thanks to Clement, and above all to
Ambrose, it becomes increasingly important in ethics too, until finally the
Aristotelian concept of nature invades mediaeval theology and suppresses
the biblical natural-law thinking of the early church. According to this reconstruction, we can see the dominance achieved by elements of the Greek
speculation on natural law (originally alien to biblical thought) above all in
the way in which the formula "law and Gospel" increasingly came to be
understood from early scholasticism onwards: while the identification of
the natural law with the Mosaic Decalogue was retained, Jesus' commandment to love tended to disappear from the natural law, and was finally replaced by the Golden Rule and the highest principle of the practical reason, that is, "one must do good and avoid evil."[49] From this perspective,
the influential definition of the natural law by the Decree of Gratian, often
quoted in mediaeval writings on canon law, can be understood as merely
the first step of a regrettable false development that holds the natural law

---

46. On this, cf. K. Demmer, *Ius Caritatis. Zur christologischen Grundlegung der augustinischen Naturrechtslehre,* Rome 1961, pp. 114ff., 151ff.
  47. F. Flückiger, *Geschichte des Naturrechts,* I, p. 321.
  48. On this, cf. P. Schallenberg, *Naturrecht und Sozialtheologie. Die Entwicklung des
theonomen Naturrechts der späten Neuscholastik im deutschen Sprachraum (1900–1960),* Münster 1993, pp. 180–252.
  49. Cf. F. Flückiger, *Geschichte des Naturrechts,* I, p. 423.

to be whatever is found in the law and the Gospel in accord with the
Golden Rule: one must treat one's neighbor as one would wish to be treated by him, and not do anything to another that one would not wish done
to oneself.[50]

This negative evaluation of the whole process of reception of the fruits
of classical thinking about the natural law into Christian theology does,
however, presuppose that the Golden Rule is a priori irrelevant to a theological ethics. But the Golden Rule is not in the least a mere "late Jewish
aphorism"[51] or the quintessence of popular wisdom doctrines in the classical period;[52] on the contrary, it is attested in the Bible itself in its positive
form (cf. Tb 4:15; Lk 6:31). The fact that Matthew's Sermon on the Mount
sees it as an appropriate exposition of Jesus' commandment to love (cf. Mt
7:12) is a weighty exegetical objection to the thesis that the biblical natural
law was replaced by a natural law of the reason in mediaeval theology. The
broad discussion that ensued upon the publication of Flückiger's book
pointed to several other errors of historical interpretation that we need not
discuss in detail here.[53]

c. The double order of knowledge Despite its historical deficiencies, this
presentation of the history of the theological doctrines of natural law,
which we have followed up to this point in order to set out the fundamental theological problems associated with natural-law thinking, has one indirect merit. By over-accentuating the ambiguity inherent in the theological concept of nature and allowing this to decompose into two contrary
clusters of meaning, it touches a sore spot in the Catholic natural-law tradition: for the problem of theological foundations, or more precisely the
problem of the mutual relation of natural reason and biblical revelation,
has been discussed hitherto in a less than satisfactory manner, systematically speaking. Even the phrase *duplex ordo cognitionis,* in common use since
the First Vatican Council, resolves the basic hermeneutical question of theological natural-law thinking only on the level of a formula. While the
dogmatic Constitution *Dei Filius* does define precisely the application of

50. "The natural law is that which is contained in the law and in the Gospel, where each
one is commanded to do to another what he wishes to be done to himself, and is forbidden
to inflict on another anything that one does not wish to be done to oneself" (*Distinctio* I, 1).

51. F. Flückiger, *Geschichte des Naturrechts,* I, p. 402.

52. On this, cf. A. Dihle, *Die Goldene Regel. Eine Einführung in die Geschichte der antiken
und frühchristlichen Vulgärethik,* Göttingen 1962.

53. Cf. the critical review by H. Reiner, "Zu Flückigers 'Geschichte des Naturrechts I',"
Archiv für Rechts- und Sozialphilosophie 41 (1955), pp. 528–61.

this formula to the problem of the natural knowledge of God, its meaning in the sphere of social-ethical or moral-theological affirmations remains very unclear.[54] Since the two orders of knowledge are distinct both in terms of their epistemological *principle* (natural reason or divine revelation) and in terms of their potential *object* of knowledge (natural, rational truths or supernatural mysteries of the faith), the formula of a "double order of knowledge" poses more problems in ethics than it solves, especially since the church's moral proclamation has not in the least made it clear up to now what might be meant by the "mysteries hidden in God" and inaccessible to the practical reason. We are given little help towards an understanding of the substantial meaning of this formula in the ethical sphere by the metaphor of two water courses flowing in the same direction and springing from the same source in God, which Pope Pius XII employed in a radio message on the fiftieth anniverary of the encyclical *Rerum novarum*, or by the image (very common in the church's social teaching) of the two arrows of natural-law argumentation.

We see how unclear this question basically remains from the recent discussion about the "theologization" of the church's social teaching (what E.-W. Böckenförde has called the "supplying of new foundations") and the alleged failure of Pope John Paul II to appeal to natural-law arguments for support in his most recent social encyclicals.[55] Although one does not find anywhere in the texts of the church's magisterium a negative position vis-à-vis the natural law or a conscious turning away from this, one can speak cautiously of a "broadening of natural-law argumentation,"[56] thanks to the christological-integral starting point in the concrete salvation-historical reality of the human person. When the personal humanism which already

54. Vatican I, *Dei Filius* 4, in: Henricus Denziger (ed.), *Enchiridion Symbolorum: Definitionum et Delarationum de Rebus Fidei et Morum*, Rome 1965, nr. 3015: "*Hoc quoque perpetuus Ecclesiae catholicae consensus tenuit et tenet, duplicem esse ordinem cognitionis non solum principio, sed obiecto etiam distinctum: principio quidem, quia in altero naturali ratione, in altero fide divina cognoscimus; obiecto autem, quia praeter ea, ad quae naturalis ratio pertingere potest, credenda nobis proponuntur mysteria in Deo abscondita, quae, nisi revelata divinitus, innotescere non possunt.*" ("And the perpetual consensus of the Catholic church has held and continues to hold that there is a double order of knowledge, distinct not only in terms of its principle, but also of its object: in terms of its principle, because in the one case we know by the natural reason, in the other by divine faith; and in terms of its object, because apart from those things to which the natural reason is able to attain, mysteries hidden in God are put before us, and unless these were revealed divinely, it would be impossible to know them.")

55. On this, cf. the critical appraisal by U. Nothelle-Wildfeuer, "*Duplex ordo cognitionis*," pp. 735–63.

56. Nothelle-Wildfeuer, "*Duplex ordo cognitionis*," pp. 747–50.

marked the Pope's first encyclical, *Redemptor hominis*, no longer bases the dignity of the human person exclusively (in natural-law terms) on the endowment with reason and the capacity to know but rather on the total salvation-historical reality of creation, incarnation, and redemption,[57] the encyclical is in keeping with contemporary theology's salvation-historical thinking, which had already left its imprint on the Pastoral Constitution of the Second Vatican Council. This christological-soteriological deepening was certainly a great improvement on the philosophical overloading of the neo-scholastic doctrines of natural law with their abstract thinking in two "stories," which had often been criticized. This gain does not, however, dispense theological ethics from the task of expounding the anthropological meaning of the theologically more substantial fundamental statements of the church's moral teaching and presenting these in a way that communicates their intention and makes it possible for people to grasp what is being said; for if the theological gain were purchased at the price of removing the rational basis for argumentation, little would ultimately be gained for ethics by thinking in terms of salvation history.

While one may welcome this departure from a primarily deductive mode of argumentation that was orientated towards abstract statements about the essence of the human person, one should not play down the danger inherent in the unmistakable theologization of social-ethical thinking, viz. the insidious evacuation of the claims to validity of natural-law statements. At any rate, such a danger must be taken more seriously in today's intellectual climate—where universal truth claims are on the retreat in philosophy and theology, and the societal plausibility of Christianity is crumbling—than at the time of the Council, when the dawning of a definitive reconciliation between church and society, between Gospel and culture, appeared for a brief moment on the horizon of theological hopes.

Thanks to the insidious evacuation of the sphere of validity of doctrinal statements based on the natural law, things could go in the opposite direction, just as happened at the beginning of the modern period with the elaboration of a rational natural law independent of revelation.[58] At that point in history, marked both by the internal dissolution of the *orbis christianus* and by the discovery of the New World, the Spanish theologians of

---

57. On this, cf. C.-J. Pinto de Oliveira, "Die theologische Originalität von Johannes Paul II.," in: O. Höffe et al. (eds.), *Johannes Paul II. und die Menschenrechte*, Freiburg i.Ue. 1981, pp. 60–91.

58. On this, cf. H. Welzel, *Naturrecht und materiale Gerechtigkeit*, pp. 95–99; K.-H. Ilting, "Naturrecht," cols. 270–73.

late scholasticism saw the chance of an escape route from the crisis of validity of the traditional Christian doctrinal tradition: they attempted to loosen the link between the knowledge of ethical-legal norms and divine revelation and to justify the fundamental demands of ethics and the validity of the norms of international law in dealings with other nations without recourse to the *lex evangelii,* that is, with the aid of reason alone. Since the Thomistic distinction between the principles of natural law and their application by means of *determinatio* and *inventio* tended more and more to be forgotten, and finally even the logical inferences from these principles were subsumed under the heading of "natural law," the late scholastic doctrines of natural law took on a rationalistic and deductive character. The intention of satisfying in rational terms the claim to validity of fundamental affirmations of Christian ethics thus joined forces with the dominance of a logical deductive process that cast a shadow on natural-law thinking as a whole.

d. The authoritative exposition of the natural law by the magisterium   For this reason, the history of natural-law thinking in the sixteenth and seventeenth centuries has often been interpreted as an erroneous development and as the decline of mediaeval natural law.[59] Research into individual aspects would no doubt require the modification of such an evaluation;[60] but, quite apart from this *historical* question, the danger to which natural-law thinking is exposed *in principle* emerges with particular clarity in the deductive natural-law systems of the early modern period. This became even more acute thanks to the attempt, characteristic of the twentieth century, to construct a comprehensive body of natural-law doctrine on the basis of church authority. From Leo XIII onwards, the popes have claimed that the church's religious salvific mission authorized them to give an authoritative exposition of the natural moral law in all its aspects and to submit to their own judgment all questions of societal life, to the extent that

59. This tendency characterizes above all the panorama of theological history offered by J. Th. C. Arntz, "Die Entwicklung des naturrechtlichen Denkens innerhalb des Thomismus," in: F. Böckle (ed.), *Das Naturrecht im Disput,* Düsseldorf 1966, pp. 87–120.

60. For example, D. Deckers argues for a much more positive judgment in the case of one theologian, in his well balanced monograph *Gerechtigkeit und Recht. Eine historisch-kritische Untersuchung der Gerechtigkeitslehre des Francisco de Vitoria (1483–1546)* (Freiburg i.Ue. 1991), though he does not fail to point out the "system-immanent dilemma" of the attempt to avoid both Thomistic intellectualism and a theological positivism. This leads him to point out the "lack of intellectual rigor" in Vitoria's thinking on the natural law (pp. 95; 123f.).

these are ethically relevant.[61] Since then, the arguments adduced to justify natural-law commandments vary between metaphysical affirmations about the essence of human nature, the affirmation of a necessary unity of the order of creation and the order of redemption, and (derived from this) the competence of the church's magisterium to provide authoritative exposition.

The results have been a strange kind of positivism and an ecclesiastical moral doctrine that is both deductive and authoritative. On the one hand, theologians sought to confirm church teaching by demonstrating its binding character in terms of natural law. On the other hand, where this binding character was not convincingly obvious, they appealed for support to the authority of the church's magisterium. Josef Ratzinger, at that time a Council theologian, pointed out this inner dichotomy of ecclesiastical natural-law doctrines in an article that made a great impression: "Such deductions were made with the intention of demonstrating that doctrines of the faith were binding even on the basis of pure reason; but since such deductions are not in the least obvious to everyone, appeal was made to the authority of the church in support of the rational character of these inferences. Hence, on the one hand, the demonstration of rationality was meant to strengthen a vacillating faith; while on the other hand, the authority of faith was meant to complement an uncertain rational certainty."[62] In a sense, this vicious circle of logical justification repeats on the theological level the same begging of the question that has already proved to be the Achilles' heel of philosophical natural-law thinking. "The 'natural law' which was meant to guarantee the positive law of the church was itself supported by the positive law of the church. In this remarkable distortion of natural law and positive law of faith lies the problematic aspect of the church's situation in the modern period, in the transition from a purely ecclesiastical society to one containing a variety of worldviews."[63]

These reflections by Ratzinger have lost none of their significance. They indicate the risk of a similarly unfortunate distortion in the post-conciliar period. The circumstances of church and theology may be different, but the danger remains that a moral doctrine based increasingly on the positive witnesses of faith (revelation, tradition, and magisterium) may contin-

61. On this, cf. J. Schuster, *Ethos und kirchliches Lehramt. Zur Kompetenz des Lehramtes in Fragen der natürlichen Sittlichkeit,* Frankfurt 1984, pp. 100–113.
62. J. Ratzinger, "Naturrecht, Evangelium und Ideologie in der katholischen Soziallehre," p. 26.
63. Ibid.

ue to claim to occupy the wide sphere of validity which belongs to the natural law—though the natural law itself would long since have become
emptied of meaning. In such a situation, the idea of natural law would
supply only the claim to universal validity but not the intellectual means
to establish this by means of argumentation, while the substantial contents
of ecclesiastical moral teaching would be guaranteed by authorities internal to the faith that provide certainty. Even if such an under-nourished
theological doctrine of natural law were to receive the formal support of
the highest authority of the church's magisterium, it could not supply precisely what theology sees as the real strength of the idea of natural law, that
is, a rational justification of the fundamental affirmations of the church's
moral proclamation and social teaching, with the possibility (at least in
principle) of universal plausibility. It may be possible for theological ethics
to escape this dilemma by a transformation of natural-law thinking. But
first it must ask: which of its normative conclusions can plausibly lay claim
to a universal obligatory character? It must also ask how this narrow sphere
of fundamental affirmations with validity in terms of the natural law is distinct from the specific meaning that the Gospel lays down in advance for
Christian ethics.

2.4. The historical ambiguity of the natural law

If one follows the development of natural-law theories from their origins in the classical period and in early Christianity, through their reception in the Middle Ages and their transformation in late scholasticism, to
the systems of an autonomous rational law in the modern period, one will
be surprised to note how long it took for the question of changes in law
and morality in the course of *history* to be posed against the background of
the problem of natural-law thinking. The "Copernican revolution" to a
self-sufficient natural law was not a catalyst here, since human nature was
interpreted in essentialistic terms and the modern conceptions of reason
were ahistorical; indeed, the result of this "revolution" was initially to suppress the insight (already acquired in the Middle Ages) into the historical
mutability of natural-law affirmations.

The early Christian and mediaeval writers were aware that, after the irruption of sin, the original commandments of the natural law made necessary an historical adaptation of the divine will. They expressed the partial
withdrawal of natural-law commandments and the accommodation of the
divine legislation to the changed salvation-historical situation of the hu-

man person by means of a distinction between primary and secondary (or absolute and relative) natural law. Thomas Aquinas attempted to understand the contingent course of history in his theological structure by basing it on the scheme of *exitus* and *reditus,* which encompasses the entire history of salvation from its two poles, that is, the proceeding of creatures from God and their return to him. He linked this basic salvation-historical outline with the Aristotelian concept of the practical reason and its gradated ethical judgment, relating this judgment to the nature of the human person—teleologically structured, yet at the same time open to specific projects. Thus he found no difficulty in accepting the idea that the commandments of the natural law are subject to historical and societal change in keeping with the changing existential situations of human beings and the mutability of their nature.[64] Even the natural-law theories of the late Middle Ages, which transposed the reason for the validity of the moral commandments from the inherent rationality of the divine will back onto the will of God itself, preserved their awareness of the historicity of the *lex naturalis,* in that they thought of the de facto moral order, with the natural-law commandments of both tables of the Decalogue, as the result of a free *ordinatio* by God. Nothing more would be heard of such a contingency in the history of theories of the natural law in the modern period until historicizing criticism begins in the nineteenth century.

a. The study of history as a support to moral theology Nevertheless, the fact that practices and customs, forms of ethos, and systems of law change in the course of history is as old as human society itself. From Socrates and Plato onwards, natural-law thinking, indeed philosophy as a whole, sees itself as the attempt to establish a firm stance by means of persuasion and education in the crisis of orientation that characterizes every historical period. Thanks to these origins, the idea of a law "based on nature" aims to preserve in times of epochal changes the knowledge that there is an objectively valid moral law over which no human person holds sway, a law that

64. *In IV Sententiarum,* d. 26, q. 1, a. 1: "According to the Philosopher in *VII Ethics,* human nature is not immobile like the divine nature. For this reason, those things that are established by natural law vary according to the various stages and conditions of human beings." *De malo,* q. 2, a. 4, ad 13: "It is otherwise in terms of substance: the same things are not just and good everywhere and for all persons: they must be determined by law. This is because of the mutability of human nature and the various conditions of human beings and things, according to the diversity of places and times." On this, cf. L. Honnefelder, "Naturrecht und Geschichte. Historisch-systematische Überlegungen zum mittelalterlichen Naturrecht," in: M. Heimbach-Steins (ed.), *Naturrecht im ethischen Diskurs,* pp. 1–27, esp. 8–16.

must be defended against the law made by the human person and "posited" by arbitrary human actions. However, the objectively valid moral law
need not be defended against history as such; it took a very long time for
humanity's ethical consciousness to see a threat in the sphere of history
and its cultural, religious, and political phenomena. From the beginnings
of classical historiography until well into the modern European period, the
historians and poets of the peoples tended rather to see history as a majes-
tic schoolmistress of life and a lofty school of virtue. According to Cicero's
classical instruction about the employment of history in rhetoric, history
relates the great events of the past, the exceptional deeds and moving fates
of historical persons, primarily because of their exemplary significance for
the present.[65] The view that the study of history helps one recognize the
common element of the one human nature and the bond uniting the various periods and peoples was long a dominant factor in the church's theories of the natural law. Even as late as the twentieth century, Pius XII
recommended the usefulness to moral theology of a broad historical education, since the study of history showed that the demands of morality
"have always basically been the same, for human nature essentially remains
always the same."[66]

According to this understanding, the histories of past epochs relate how
the inidvidual existence is embedded in the existential transgenerational
interconnections in peoples, nations, and states, and also in the church.
(We should note that "history" as a collective singular is a creation of the
universal-historical conceptions of the eighteenth and nineteenth centuries.) The historical high points reveal the unity of that human nature
that individuals share at all points of history and geography. Thus, history
is at the service of the common ends of human existence and of the human
nature that is still thought of as a teleological unity. It is the trustworthy
school of life and the sure guide through life's vicissitudes. Just as the mir-
acle—the narrative about an extraordinary occurrence in nature—is regarded as the chief delight of faith, so history—the recollection of the exceptional element in the lives of important human persons—becomes the
strongest support of moral theology, thanks to its exemplary significance.
As long as people are firmly anchored in the event of transmission, which
has been called "history" in an emphatic sense since the beginnings of
the modern consciousness of history, the historical transformation of the

---

65. Cf. Cicero, *De oratione* 2, 36; 2, 51.
66. Quoted from A.-F. Utz and J. F. Groner (eds.), *Aufbau und Entfaltung des
gesellschaftlichen Lebens*, nr. 6286.

forms of their ethos and of the social institutions of their lives do not *per se* give cause for alarm.[67]

The emergence of an historical consciousness did little to change this. Its first great witnesses in Italian humanism (Vico) and early German historicism (Herder, Humboldt, Goethe) continued to see the variety of historical phenomena as something thoroughly positive, an indication of the richness of human nature; it is only in the course of historical development that the complete variety of this nature becomes visible.[68] History does not alienate the human person from himself. As the subtitle of Vico's *Scienza Nova* indicates, the social nature of the peoples is revealed in history; it can be known only in the action of human beings and in the experience of what they do in history. Herder's idea of "humanity" is also marked by a similar interlocking of nature and history, in which the conception of an historical anthroplogy seems to be brought into harmony with belief in human nature as something perennially the same in an ideal unity of human history. The high rank accorded here to the individuality of the specific historical phenomenon remains subject to an idea of unity that encompasses the history both of nature and of the human person; this also involves a polemic attack on the monistic conceptions of the reason in rationalism. This idea of a history of nature that reaches its end in the human person and then branches out in his higher cultural development allows Herder to historicize nature itself, thus freeing the natural conditions of human life for a variety of cultural articulations; but this does not lead in Herder to a further relativism in the moral foundations of life, since he likewise naturalizes history, in a certain sense, and sees it as a coherent "natural" event. Thus, in a kind of rivalry between the popular spirit of the various cultures, an increasingly noble, purified, and mature idea of humanity emerges.[69]

b. Historical awareness as a threat to moral theology   The discovery of historical mutability as a fundamental category of the modern world sets off powerful tremors. Historical thinking becomes aware of the depth of these tremors only when it abandons belief in the unity of human nature and replaces this with a radical historicization of all forms of life. The historical school of law sees a conceptual Procrustean bed when it contemplates the distinctions made between absolute and relative natural law, pri-

67. Cf. R. Koselleck, "Geschichte, Historie," in: *GGB* II, cols. 593–717, esp. 641f.
68. Cf. G. Bauer, *Geschichtlichkeit. Wege und Irrwege eines Begriffs*, Berlin 1963, p. 10.
69. Cf. W. Schulz, *Philosophie in der veränderten Welt*, Pfullingen 1972, pp. 486–90.

mary and secondary natural law, or immutable and mutable natural law. All this is far too narrow, since the universal validity (which is exempt from the limitations of time and space) leaves only a modest space for the historical specificity of natural-law affirmations. Nevertheless, even the historical thinking of the nineteenth century maintains that the objective spirit displays an articulated order and a meaningful connected structure in all the variety that it generates in the sphere of customs and law, morality and religion, state and society; it is the task of historical knowledge to understand this structure. But a threatening undertone can already be heard in the admiration expressed for the variety of historical forms and in the enthusiasm for an individuality liberated from the metaphysical bonds of the natural law. From the perspective of the historical changes they have undergone, the life of the peoples, their historical institutions and cultural achievements, but above all their various conceptual systems in the field of morality and law soon appear as a confusing plethora of infinite configurations that can no longer be made sense of from any higher common standpoint.

An obligatory teleology built into human nature is now replaced by individuals who act in history with specific goals. Historical consideration shows not only that these goals simply coexist without any mutual links, but also that they often contradict one another; and it is not possible to resolve in the historical consciousness the seething "chaos full of harmonies and dissonances" that characterizes the real course of history, thanks to the intentions and actions of the individuals who stand behind these events.[70] As a secularized eschatology's aprioristic constructions of history lose their persuasiveness, so too there disappears the hope that ultimately all the dissonances might make their contribution to a higher harmony or an ideal goal of the development of history.

Not only is the historical moment so transitory that the individual human life is submerged in the epochal waves of the historical stream of life, but also the values that can be experienced simultaneously have a "confusing, unending plurality." Wilhelm Dilthey remarks in a fragment about the recognition of universal-historical interconnections that this variety flows over the individual: "It is like looking down at evening on some great foreign city. Its lights gleam up towards us, get stronger, disappear, vanish into a distance that we can no longer see."[71] The founder of the modern

70. W. Dilthey, *Der Aufbau der geschichtlichen Welt in den Geisteswissenschaften,* in: *Gesammelte Schriften,* VII, Stuttgart and Göttingen eighth edn. 1992, p. 236.
71. Ibid., p. 256.

intellectual sciences employs the metaphor of a ship adrift on the waves and the image of the illumination of a great city to express the precarious situation of the human person, who has woken up to the historical consciousness of his own historicity. He knows about the variety of historical life, since his study of history has disclosed this wealth to him; but at the same time he senses that the radical "historicization" of existence tips the human person down into a bottomless pit, should he fail to find a firm foothold on the path of self-appropriation in history.[72] It was precisely Dilthey, who saw the impossibility of attaining total historical knowledge and considered the plurality of the results of historical study as something in principle positive, who was supremely aware that the task of a critique of historical reason includes a philosophical response to the danger of relativism, which is present everywhere after the demise of the natural law. In a speech of thanks on his seventieth birthday, Dilthey looked back on his life's work as a philosopher and faced squarely up to the risk that the historical worldview, after liberating the human being from the spider's web of metaphysical thinking, could then submerge him in the chaos of a relativization of all substantial values: "The historical worldview frees the human spirit from the last chain that neither natural sciences nor philosophy have yet been able to tear asunder—but where are the instruments that will overcome the anarchy of convictions that threatens to inundate us?"[73]

The sense that even fundamental moral values and social institutions that had previously been firmly established on the basis of the natural law, such as marriage, the family, and the state, are subject to historical change, has not merely been the expression of a philosophical worldview since the end of the eighteenth century; in every area of life, this feeling could find support in historical facts and biographical experiences that expressed the basic feeling of an entire epoch. After the collapse of the bourgeois world in the First World War, Ernst Troeltsch wrote that people did not learn historical relativism as a theory in the history of philosophy—rather, they felt it in every fiber of their bodies, since it had altered their daily lives.[74] Although social change has considerably speeded up since then, it is no longer experienced today as an existentially threatening phenomenon to

---

72. The concept of *Vergeschichtlichung* [translated here as "historicization"] was coined by Graf Yorck and has been used in contemporary philosophy (above all by W. Schulz) to designate epochal tendencies of the present day. On this, cf. G. Bauer, *Geschichtlichkeit*, p. 48.

73. W. Dilthey, *Gesammelte Schriften*, V, p. 9.

74. E. Troeltsch, *Der Historismus und seine Überwindung*, Berlin 1924, p. 4.

the same degree. Clearly, it is possible to become accustomed to the profound functional change in primary social institutions that have a very direct impact on daily living, and this makes it easy to underestimate the extent and speed of the changes that have taken place.

c. Historical changes in ecclesiastical moral teachings In the period of historicism, the ability of the Catholic church to stand firm commanded respect from a distance.[75] But even here, a profound change has taken place since the mid-twentieth century, as if it were the most natural thing in the world. This affects not only the external form of the church's organization, but also the heart of its theological self-understanding, penetrating even its binding doctrine of faith, its liturgical life, and central affirmations of its moral proclamation. In order to grasp correctly the significance of these historical processes of transformation for the ecclesiastical understanding of the natural law, it is imperative that we recall the individual stages of this development, in a series of snapshots. The cases chosen here can be presented only very briefly, but they have an exemplary character. The review of a longer continuous period makes it clear that the problem of the historical relativism of moral judgments occurs in all its acuteness even within the church and its tradition of natural law.

From our modern point of view, one of the more curious events in church history was the protest by the theological faculty of the Sorbonne in Paris against smallpox vaccination, as late as 1785; the same faculty also tried to have the assembly of bishops forbid a public prayer of thanksgiving for the unexpected recovery of the Dauphin from illness. No less strange is the reason given by those in church circles in the first decades of the nineteenth century in many places, when they tried to prevent gas lamps from being set up in public places (these lamps were first erected in Paris and had spread from one European city to another): this new lighting technique was considered an invasive attack on the divine order of creation, which had laid down with sovereign wisdom the natural alternation of day and night and had ordained that only the moon and the stars might give the night their scanty light. The *Kölnische Zeitung* wrote in 1819: "We may not rebel against this, we may not ourselves determine the plan for the world in our wish to turn the night into day." A final outstanding example of erroneous historical judgments is Pope Gregory XVI's resistance

75. Cf., e.g., the judgment by W. Dilthey, *Einleitung in die Geisteswissenschaften. Versuch einer Grundlegung für das Studium der Gesellschaft und der Geschichte,* in: *Gesammelte Schriften,* I, Stuttgart and Göttingen eighth edn. 1990, p. 65.

to the introduction of railways into the papal state. Relying on contemporary reports by medical experts, who estimated that the human body could not tolerate any speed higher than thirty kilometres per hour, and inspired by a French play on words *(chemin de fer—chemin d'enfer)*, the pope held that passengers on the railway were unwittingly taking the direct road to hell![76]

It is easy, from a distance, to laugh at such mistakes. More serious is the fact that the church's magisterium opposed the modern idea of freedom from the very outset. A number of popes believed themselves obliged to castigate the fundamental rights of freedom in democratic states (freedom of religion, freedom of conscience, freedom of opinion, etc.) as a pernicious error.[77] Although we see more clearly today that the popes of the nineteenth century were reacting to a liberalistic distortion of religious tolerance and freedom of conscience, their scanty sensitivity to the significance of the fundamental political freedoms and to the genuine value of democratic plurality remains disturbing.[78]

If one includes the Middle Ages and the early modern period in this look back at the past, the justification that theologians at that time found in the Bible and in the natural law for the prohibition of interest, the use of violence in the struggle against heretics, and the toleration of pogroms against the Jews makes it impossible to close our eyes to the fact of change in the church's moral teaching. We arrive at the same result if we look at history *e silentio*, that is, if we ask why the church said nothing for centuries about societal practices that it attacks today as infringing human rights.

76. On these examples, cf. the information in A. Auer, "Die Erfahrung der Geschichtlichkeit und die Krise der Moral," *ThQ* 149 (1969), pp. 4–22, esp. 13.

77. Cf. Gregory XVI, *Mirari vos* (1832): "an absurd and erroneous opinion, which indeed rather ought to be called a madness," quoted in A. F. Utz and B. von Galen (eds.), *Die katholischen Sozialdoktrin in ihrer geschichtlichen Entfaltung*, I, Aachen 1976, pp. 136–59, at 148 [English translation: "*Mirari vos*," in: *The Papal Encyclicals 1740–1878*, edited by Claudia Carlen (Raleigh 1981), 235–41]; cf. also Pius IX, *Quanta cura* (1864), *Die katholischen Sozialdoktrin*, I, pp. 162–79, at 164 [English translation: "*Quanta cura*," in: *The Papal Encyclicals*, 381–86]; Leo XIII, *Libertas praestantissimum* (1888), *Die katholischen Sozialdoktrin*, I, pp. 180–223, at 194 [English translation: "*Libertas*," in: *The Papal Encyclicals 1878–1903*, edited by Claudia Carlen, IHM (Raleigh 1981), 169–81].

78. On this, cf. J. Isensee, "Die katholische Kritik an den Menschenrechten. Der liberale Freiheitsentwurf in der Sicht der Päpste des 19. Jahrhunderts," in: E.-W. Böckenförde and R. Spaemann (eds.), *Menschenrechte und Menschenwürde*, Stuttgart 1987, pp. 138–74; W. Kasper, *Wahrheit und Freiheit. Die "Erklärung über die Religionsfreiheit" des II. Vatikanischen Konzils* (Sitzungsberichte der Heidelberger Akademie der Wissenschaften), Heidelberg 1988, pp. 1–14.

It would be easy to add to these accounts of the historical relativity of ecclesiastical moral doctrines and their dependence on socio-cultural factors. The teaching of the church's magisterium has silently abandoned most of these historical evaluations; in a few cases, they have been explicitly revoked. Thus, when the Second Vatican Council acknowledged freedom of religion, offered a positive evaluation of human sexuality, and taught that all are called to holiness, it confirmed on the highest level of the magisterium the retreat from centuries of tradition. Similarly, the *Catechism of the Catholic Church* (1993) undertakes at a number of points an implicit correction of previous teachings, although the critical reaction to the *Catechism* scarcely noticed this. For example, the church's magisterium under Pius XII had appealed to natural-law arguments in its decisive rejection of the ethical acceptability of the voluntary donation of organs. The *Catechism* states: "Organ transplants conform with the moral law and can be meritorious if the physical and psychological dangers and risks incurred by the donor are proportionate to the good sought for the recipient" (par. 2296). This text declares the acceptability of an evaluation of goods (provided that the donor freely consents or that his legal representatives give permission) that previously was judged absolutely unacceptable, since the obligation in natural law to preserve the integrity of one's own body was considered to admit of no exceptions.[79]

As this example of the different evaluations by the church's magisterium of the voluntary donation of organs shows, even the innermost sphere of actions that are "intrinsically" evil—the sphere that reminds us of what we are never allowed to do—is subject to the possibility of change in history. This is indirectly confirmed by the passage from the pastoral constitution of the Second Vatican Council that the encyclical *Veritatis splendor* (1993) quotes as evidence of the continuity of teaching about the objective validity of the natural law and about intrinsically evil actions:

The varieties of crime are numerous: all offenses against life itself, such as murder, genocide, abortion, euthanasia and wilful suicide; all violations of the integrity of the human person, such as mutilation, physical and mental torture, undue psy-

79. Cf. Pius XI, encyclical *Casti connubii* (1930), in: A. Rohrbasser (ed.), *Die Heilslehre der Kirche*, Freiburg i.Ue. 1953, nr. 1702 [English translation: "*Casti connubii*," in *The Papal Encyclicals 1903–1939*, edited by Claudia Carlen, IHM (Raleigh 1981), 391–414]; Pius XII, discourse of September 13, 1952, in: A. F. Utz and J. F. Groner, *Aufbau und Entfaltung des gesellschaftlichen Lebens. Die Soziale Summe Pius' XII.*, Freiburg i.Ue. 1954, nr. 2281 [English translation: *Moral Limits of Medical Research and Treatment* (Washington: National Catholic Welfare Conference, 1952)].

chological pressures; all offenses against human dignity, such as subhuman living conditions, arbitrary imprisonment, deportation, slavery, prostitution, the selling of women and children, degrading working conditions where men are treated as mere tools for profit rather than free and responsible persons: all these and the like are criminal: they poison civilization; and they debase the perpetrators more than the victims and militate against the honor of the Creator.[80]

This conciliar text speaks with all desirable clarity. Crimes against the personal dignity of the human person and his physical and psychological life are condemned in unmistakable words. The pastoral constitution consciously avoids technical theological language here; still less is there any trace of the school terminology of neo-scholasticism. It calls the many infringements of human dignity "criminal" *(probra quidem)* and says that they "poison civilization" *(civilisationem humanam inficiunt);* they are the fruit of a debasement of one's own person and of an attack on the honor of the Creator. No exhaustive catalogue is given, but there is an obvious attempt to provide an exemplary list *(haec omnia et alia huiusmodi)* of infringements of the personal dignity of the human person in the various spheres of his life, thus supplying "a kind of negative proof that the various dimensions of human existence are linked in a unity."[81]

Despite its unmistakable goal, however, this conciliar text poses a number of problems when it is read in the light of the doctrine of instrinsically evil actions; as in other cases, here too the Council itself did not wish to have recourse to the patterns of argumentation used by professional theologians. The text does not speak only of intrinsically evil acts, but of infringements of human rights through *individual* actions (murder, abortion, euthanasia, torture), *societal situations* (inhuman living conditions, unjust working conditions, trade in human persons, slavery, prostitution), or crimes committed against the *international* community of peoples (genocide). The most important point, however—and it is only here that this solemn conciliar text becomes an eloquent document of change in the church's moral teaching—is that these actions have certainly not all been condemned as *intrinsece malum* at all times and in the same way. The early church arrived at a consistent affirmation of the value of life on the basis of the fifth commandment and condemned murder, abortion, euthanasia, and voluntary suicide as opposed to the dignity of the human person; but

80. *Gaudium et Spes*, nr. 27; on this, cf. John Paul II, encyclical *Veritatis splendor,* nr. 80.
81. O. Semmelroth, "Kommentar zur Pastoralkonstitution 'Gaudium et Spes'," in: *LThK*, supplementary Vol. III, col. 366.

she displayed greater tolerance in the first centuries vis-à-vis the classical institution of slavery. Indeed, most mediaeval theologians held that slavery was permissible. Gallus M. Manser, a Thomist social ethical philosopher, explained this as late as 1947 by saying that slavery was *not* intrinsically evil, so that it could be justified in other historical circumstances in order to ward off greater evils (e.g., the collapse of the economic order and the impoverishment of the entire populace).[82] In the same way, theologians and canon lawyers accepted for centuries torture and the extortion of confessions as a legitimate means of uncovering the truth in judicial cases.[83] Not only did the church tolerate this praxis in the Middle Ages and the early modern period; the church too made use of it in the fight against heretics. It is precisely when one endeavors to evaluate this historical fact without prejudice and anachronistic accusations that one is compelled to see it as evidence of the degree to which the moral consciousness of Christianity is dependent on the level of insight attained by historical-social reason in each period.

This list of individual witnesses documenting the historical transformation of ecclesiastical moral doctrines in each epoch and the patterns of justification that appealed to the natural law is not, however, intended to give the impression that the church was always content merely to adopt the dominant ethos of a period and sanction it by means of an additional religious legitimation. The interaction between church and society, between Gospel and culture, with its long historical periods of latency, must not be reduced to a one-sided dependence understood on the model of an historical basis and an ideological-religious superstructure. At any rate, the distinction between mutable and immutable natural law proves to be too narrow, if one is to do justice to the extent of the historical transformation; for this cannot be limited to a peripheral forecourt surrounding the immutable kernel of the natural law, a forecourt constructed of contingent adoptions of particular worldviews, non-moral descriptions of factual situations, and at most a few secondary conclusions. On the contrary, central

82. Cf. G. M. Manser, *Angewandtes Naturrecht,* Freiburg i.Ue. 1947, p. 66. It was only in 1888, with Leo XIII's encyclical *In Plurimis* (nr. 25), that the church's magisterium fundamentally condemned slavery (text in: A. F. Utz and B. von Galen (eds.), *Die katholische Sozialdoktrin in ihrer geschichtlichen Entfaltung,* I, p. 414 [English translation: "In Plurimis," in: *The Papal Encyclicals 1878–1903,* 159–67]).

83. On the role played by torture and physical punishments in the mediaeval law governing criminal proceedings, where circumstantial evidence was not yet admitted and a confession had to be presented, cf. W. Wolbert, *Der Mensch als Mittel und Zweck. Die Idee der Menschenwürde in normativer Ethik und Rechtsethik,* Münster 1987, pp. 96–100.

affirmations of the church's moral teaching are also affected by the inherent historicity of the Christian ethos. This is why a theological-ethical justification of the universal validity of ethical norms may not limit itself to interpreting the fact of their historical transformation as an external phenomenon of a "nature" which is conceived of as a trans-historical reality. Rather, historicity is a dimension of the human person and of his nature, with the consequence that the common element of human existence, which transcends all particular times, is found only in historical concretizations. It must be possible to demonstrate within the horizon of history itself the universal claim of a law "on the basis of nature," of a criterion of good and evil applicable to all concrete systems that order human existence, so that one may conceive of the growth of insight into the natural law as the epistemological process of an historical reason.

☒ II. *The problem of ethical relativism*

T
HE EXAMPLES given in the previous chapter—slavery, torture, lending at interest, or the voluntary donation of organs—show that the moral judgment of the church in these questions has always depended on the specific stage of development of societal circumstances and of historical-social reason. Within the course of European history, this historical relativity of the Christian ethos can be understood on the model of the interaction between the Gospel and culture, which includes what might be called phases of latency and periods of incubation. This attempt at an explanation breaks down, however, when we look across the boundaries of European Christianity to include also the non-Christian world religions and the non-European cultural spheres. As well as the pluriformity of the Christian ethos, an indisputable fact along the *diachronic* longitudinal section through the epochs of European church history, we find a plurality of moral conceptual systems along the *synchronous* latitudinal section through the cultural and religious history of humankind.

1. The discovery of the cultural relativity of our moral ideas

It was only after the *orbis christianus* had begun to show increasing signs of internal dissolution in the late Middle Ages, and after the Reformation had set the seal of an external confessional division on this disintegration, that Christianity had contact on a large scale with non-European cultures. At this point, it had already lost its unquestioned position of intellectual leadership within the European cultural sphere, so that it was no longer possible to understand the contact with foreign conceptual worlds only as an encounter between European Christianity and other religions. The discovery of new continents and the beginning of missionary work and colonization across the seas confronted European civilization as a whole with the ways of life of foreign peoples at a time when this civilization itself was already beginning to dissolve into heterogeneous political, economic, and cultural historical spheres. The sailors and traders of the national states in the early modern period reacted to the encounter with foreign cultures in the same way as those who stayed at home: partly with curiosity and admiration, but partly also with disgust and revulsion. We find both these antithetical patterns of perception in the first of those travel narratives of the seventeenth and eighteenth centuries which allowed an educated European class to come into contact with the unknown New World for the first time.

These oscillating intuitive reactions gave way to a scientific attitude only in the nineteenth century, when the systematic investigation of foreign cultures began. The scholars directed their attention now to the total character of cultures, inquiring not primarily into special deviant norms, but into the orientation achieved by foreign cultures in the various sectors of personal and societal life. It was soon discovered that "primitive" societies, poor in culture, who knew nothing of European moral principles such as the idea of altruism or the responsibility to care for one's children, or of particular sexual taboos, nevertheless possessed functional equivalents which could be the equal of European moral ideas, if seen from a sociological standpoint. The reciprocity among adults which is necessary for the survival of a society, the social integration of children, the ordering of sexual conduct—all these are achieved in these societies in a different manner than in Europe, without a collapse into general lawlessness.

The pioneers of scientific ethnology, from Edward Westermarck (1862–1939) and Bronislaw Malinowski (1884–1942) through William E. Sumner (1840–1920), to Franz Boas (1858–1942) and the generation of students whom he influenced (Ruth Benedikt, Margaret Mead, Melville Herskovits), all agreed in the protest against an ethnocentric model which would dismiss foreign cultures. Although they did not arrive at a unanimous position on important questions of the theory of culture, they felt themselves united in a common scholarly interest. They disagreed about fundamental premises such as the acceptance of a higher cultural development, the special status of the European cultural sphere, or the existence of transcultural criteria of rationality and science; nevertheless, their work contributed to deepening the shock of relativism in the European consciousness.[1] The results of this descriptive investigation of morality were widely perceived as empirical confirmation of the philosophical critique of

---

1. Cf. the overview of scholarship in K. P. Rippe, *Ethischer Relativismus. Seine Grenzen, seine Geltung*, Paderborn et al. 1993, pp. 11–63.

a universal view of history that left too little space for the plurality of cultural interpretative patterns and ideas about moral value.

It seems that even today the radical historicization of knowledge by the historical worldview and the discovery of the plurality of moral ideas in the field work of ethnographers meet on a common level. Many social scientists and cultural anthropologists, and a number of contemporary spokespersons for the history of ideas, take a relaxed, "common-sense" standpoint based on the tacit presupposition that the entire codex of societal regulations, including the moral convictions of a society, rests on mere conventions which developed in keeping with the fundamental economic conditions, the sociocultural living situations, or even the climatic and geographical conditions of each particular historical sphere. Moral or legal norms are likewise given their place in the societal rulebook, which determines the de facto existential attitudes of human persons and thus constitutes the only "real" stratum of social reality which is accessible to scientific investigation. Where the question of the normative validity of moral norms is posed, this is limited a priori to a specific cultural sphere, or to a social group whose members have implicitly or explicitly agreed to acknowledge these norms. In this perspective of empirical research, moral norms are never envisaged as anything other than relative phenomena; thanks to this a priori methodological conception, no attention is paid to their potential transcultural significance or to a validity which might transcend their empirical diffusion.

Moral philosophers were quick to voice their concerns about such an interpretation, which levels down the specific claim of moral norms and neutralizes a priori the problem of their universal validity. The first dialogues, which authors such as John Dewey, Richard B. Brandt, Max Scheler, and Marcus G. Singer attempted to initiate between the empirical investigation of cultures and the various schools of moral philosophy in the first half of the twentieth century, did not, however, lead in the short term to a broader interdisciplinary dialogue. To a great extent, accordingly, there was no contact between the systematic questioning which investigated the logical forms of justification and the modes of argumentation of ethical propositions on the one hand, and the cultural-anthropological and social-historical investigation of the various ideas about moral value on the other.

Because of its philosophical simplicity, professional philosophers long looked on the ethical relativism on which many empirical studies are based (consciously or unconsciously) as a fad of popular science; Bernard

Williams was the spokesman for all his colleagues when he called it the typical "anthropologist's heresy."[2] On the other hand, the ethnologists had the impression that contemporary philosophy failed to perceive the practical significance of the problem posed by the historical-cultural relativity of our moral ideas. In the first post-War debate about the philosophical foundations of international law, ethnologists and representatives of empirical cultural sociology frequently accused the systematic intellectual disciplines of simply ignoring the question of the universal application of declarations about human rights, since they could not answer it.[3] Since then, the search for the elements of a planetary ethos common to the various cultures has increased philosophers' awareness of the unanswered questions connected with the fact that convictions about moral value depend on specific cultures. Some philosophical tendencies which turned up their noses at ethical relativism a few decades ago now accept it. There is a broad consensus that philosophers must take seriously the problems generated by the starting point of ethical relativism, viz. empirical research; at present, however, the philosophical discussion shows no sign of a definitive solution to these problems.[4]

The answer to the questions posed by ethical relativism is so intimately linked to the self-understanding of ethics as a philosophical discipline that it scarcely seems possible to arrive at a genuine agreement, which would have to include a consensus on basic questions of methodology and substance. At most, there is the prospect of an agreement in view of a *negative* demarcation vis-à-vis unsatisfactory starting points for questions: this would exclude a priori two defective forms of an ethical theory which are based on a one-sided perspective and therefore cannot truly advance the moral-philosophical debate about ethical relativism. In her introduction to practical philosophy, Annemarie Pieper (from the University of Basle) describes both false paths against the background of the important distinction between *Moral* (the de facto existential conduct of human persons) and *Moralität* (the ethical system of reflection on *Moral*):

2. B. Williams, *Morality. An Introduction to Ethics,* Cambridge 1972, p. 34: "This is *relativism,* the anthropologist's heresy, possibly the most absurd view to have been advanced even in moral philosophy."

3. Cf. the statement by M. J. Herskovits, "Statement on Human Rights," *American Anthropologist* new series 49 (1947) 539–43.

4. Cf. the presentation of recent relativist positions (S. Toulmin, K. Nielsen, B. Williams, and P. Foot) in K. P. Rippe, *Ethischer Relativismus,* pp. 223–55. His conclusion is that: "At the present stage of the discussion, ethical relativism cannot be proved—but neither can it be refuted" (p. 268).

An ethics which merely investigates phenomena of *Moral* without considering the principle of *Moralität* loses its path in relativism. It is concerned only with variables; but the constants, a stable system of coordinates which would impart order to these variables, are missing. On the other hand, an ethics which studied only the principle of *Moralität* and lost sight of the phenomena of *Moral* would be unreal, remaining in the realm of abstract speculations, with no reference to what human beings actually do—even if in an extreme variety of ways—when they posit moral [*moralisch*] acts and judgments. Thus, the object of ethics may not be either *Moral* or *Moralität* in isolation, but only the relationship between *Moral* and *Moralität* in the context of human praxis.[5]

According to this methodological presupposition, a philosophical examination of ethical relativism must find a way between two extreme positions which (for opposite reasons) fail to do justice to the complexity of the question. As we shall see from the various attempts at an answer which this chapter will present and examine, moral philosophy in the twentieth century seldom succeeded in avoiding both these defective forms or in moving on beyond the unfruitful alternative of merely rejecting or merely confirming ethical relativism.

2. Types of philosophical argumentation in the encounter with moral relativism

Twentieth-century moral philosophy elaborated four basic forms of argumentation in order to engage in the philosophical encounter with ethical relativism. We may mention first of all the attempt to prove empirically the universal diffusion of general ethical principles, thus employing its own positivistic methodology to refute cultural relativism (1). An opposite form of argumentation begins with the accusation of the naturalistic fallacy, in which (it is alleged) every empirical theory of ethics gets entangled in one way or another (2). We also find the logical objection that it is no more possible to formulate a fundamentally relativistic stance, without contradictions, in the sphere of morality than it is in the sphere of our theoretical knowledge of the truth (3). Finally, a further reflection demands a sharper distinction within the intercultural spectrum of ethical phenomena between non-moral facts and specifically moral value judgments, and

5. A. Pieper, *Ethik und Moral. Eine Einführung in die praktische Philosophie,* Munich 1985, p. 38. [Translator's note: The English words "morals" and "morality" do not adequately reproduce the distinction made in the original text. This is why the German words are not translated in this quotation.]

between ethical principles and concrete norms (4). Unlike the first three types of argumentation, which reject a relativistic position in ethics as fundamentally unrealizable, this last objection has the more modest goal of describing more clearly the sphere and the level of de facto moral disagreements, in order to do justice to the basic structure of moral consciousness which is common to all cultures.

2.1. Denial of the empirical foundations

An obvious possibility of pulling the rug from under the basic thesis of ethical relativism consists in directing the methodology of ethnological comparison against this thesis and calling into question its empirical foundations. This procedure adopts the rule, often found in other confrontations, that one simply reverses the sharp lance of criticism and strikes the enemy with his own weapons on the battlefield that he himself has chosen. It is indeed true that the comparative material which has emerged thanks to the study of cultural history and ethnology is not at all unambiguous *per se*. In many cases, it can also be explained in non-relativistic terms. When the first relativistic "cultural shock" in the encounter with other peoples has been overcome, why may not an ethnographic investigation present proof of a universal diffusion of moral principles and ideas about values? This means that the study of the history of culture is inspired by the hope of ending up with moral-philosophical conclusions which run contrary to those that an ethical relativism would like to draw from the empirical facts.

The neo-scholastic moral philosopher Viktor Cathrein followed this path at the beginning of the twentieth century, in his three-volume work *Die Einheit des sittlichen Bewußtseins der Menschheit*. He worked through all available accounts and contemporary sources about the life of the peoples of the earth, both primitive and culturally developed, in order to verify empirically "the fact of the unity and universality of the ethical consciousness of humankind."[6] He does not intend to suppress the plurality of the ethical phenomena to which the history of humanity up to that date bears eloquent witness, and he acknowledges that there is scarcely any vice "which has not been accounted a virtue among some people or other."[7] Unlike contemporary ethnographers such as E. Westermarck, to whose book *The Origin and Development of the Moral Ideas* (1906) his own monumental

6. V. Cathrein, *Die Einheit des sittlichen Bewußtseins der Menschheit. Eine ethnographische Untersuchung*, I, Freiburg 1914, p. V.
7. Ibid., p. 11.

work is in many ways a counterpart, Cathrein does not accept the de facto spectrum of ethical views as sufficient evidence of the moral-philosophical thesis that all moral concepts are based ultimately only on different ethical feelings. If emotivism were correct, we would have to deny that our own moral judgments contained any objective substantial truth; these judgments would be nothing more than the generalization of individual emotional reactions to particular factual situations which provoked us to rage or to approval.[8] Cathrein wishes to argue against such inferences—which would abandon the cognitive claim of ethics—by asking the ethnographic "facts" whether, under the surface of manifold deviations and differences, "they do not bear witness to a basic stock of ethical concepts and principles which have been acknowledged by all peoples at all times" and therefore may count as "the inalienable common possession of all human persons."[9] He accepts "ethnography, when questioned with respect and honesty," as the authority that may decide this question; the aim of his investigation is "to construct a body of facts that embraces as many peoples as possible," appealing to cultural history to be the judge of his thesis that "the principles of the Decalogue are in their essence the common possession of all peoples known to us both in antiquity and at the present day."[10]

Cathrein has sometimes been accused of naively trusting sources chosen more or less at random, but this is not correct. He goes cautiously to work in pursuit of his grandiose goal. He wishes to draw on all accessible information and to question his sources in accordance with consciously chosen criteria for comparison; some of his methodological reflections meet the standards of modern research. His reflective methodological consciousness can be seen in the preference he gives to accounts by missionaries who had lived for a long period among the tribes in question, in his skepticism vis-à-vis spectacular travel narratives, and in his endeavor to go back to old sources which document the life of culturally undeveloped peoples before their encounter with European civilization. Other premises, such as the sharp distinction between cultured and primitive peoples on the sole basis of literacy, have been superseded by the advances of research in cultural anthropology. Cathrein shows himself superior to leading representatives of ethnography in his own period when he chooses not to order the ethnographic material in sectors according to contents (property, life, marriage,

8. Cf. E. Westermarck, *The Origin and Development of the Moral Ideas,* London 1908, p. 738.
9. V. Cathrein, *Die Einheit des sittlichen Bewußtseins der Menschheit,* I, p. 1.
10. Ibid., p. 18.

sexuality, veneration of gods), but rather to present together all the narratives about one particular ethnic group. This allows him to compare the orientations achieved by the various cultural systems.

One of the fundamental methodological considerations governing the individual portraits of all the ethnic groups which were known at that time is the insight that an empirical investigation of the ethical-religious facts presupposes a guiding concept of good and evil; otherwise, it is quite impossible to set boundaries to the object of study. This is why the objection that the validity of ethical norms cannot be determined by the quantitative fact of their geographical diffusion and temporal acknowledgment does not apply in this general form to Cathrein's endeavors. He does indeed conclude by pointing to an unclarified ambiguity in his own argumentation;[11] but he begins by vehemently opposing the widespread tendency in the cultural sociology of his day to equate the observation of factual ethnographic situations with an assertion about the truth claims of ethical judgments, so that ethics was conducted not as a systematic discipline, but only as an academic field within the history of culture. This is why he begins with a fundamental reflection on the validity and significance of ethical affirmations, before he presents the individual ethnographic and cultural-historical analyses which are meant to confirm his thesis of the unity of human moral consciousness:

The moral philosopher is no mere speaker who intends through the art of his rhetoric to win people for his own ideas and fill them with enthusiasm. Nor is he a mere historian who contents himself with recording what people have counted as good and evil at various times and places. Rather, the aim of his research is to discover what is naturally good and evil, deserving of praise and rebuke, and is accordingly to be acknowledged as such always and everywhere, and by all unprejudiced persons. He claims universal validity for the results of his research. For example, when he puts forward the proposition that murder, adultery, betrayal of one's fatherland, or perjury is wrong, he does not intend merely to assert that this is the case in Germany or France, or only at the present time and in the case of the civilized peoples; rather, he asserts that these actions are *per se*—hence, always and everywhere—wrong and abominable. If, however, nothing is good or evil in terms of its nature, if every distinction of this kind is the product of chance development, so that betrayal of one's fatherland, false testimony, adultery, etc. could become good and praiseworthy at some later date, then ethics is bankrupt. It has lost its occupation.[12]

11. Cf. W. Korff, *Norm und Sittlichkeit. Untersuchungen zur Logik der normativen Vernunft,* Mainz 1973, p. 65.
12. V. Cathrein, *Die Einheit des sittlichen Bewußtseins der Menschheit,* I, p. 5.

Against the theory that ethical judgments have their origin in human sentiment and then are subsequently generalized, Cathrein proposes the thesis that they have an a priori rational justification and a universal validity which is strictly logical. His aim is to prove that the concepts of good and evil are spontaneously formed by every rational human being, who, thanks to the very structure of his reason, understands the highest rule of morality (viz. that one must aim at good and avoid evil) and its immediate inferences (which are substantially identical with the Ten Commandments).[13] But why then does he go to the enormous trouble of writing a book that is hundreds of pages long and wearies the reader, weighing down the evidence with innumerable repetitions that this insight into objective ethical truths has in fact always existed in all peoples? It is clear that Cathrein believes that it must be possible to provide empirical verification of the a priori structure of the *one* reason shared by all human individuals by tracing the course of cultural history and presenting the ethnographic evidence for the *factual* unity of human ethical consciousness.

If empirical study revealed a fragmented ethical consciousness which could no longer be traced back to any unified forms of thought, this would be an important methodological decision in a scientific atmosphere marked by evolutionism and positivism; for this would mean that both the metaphysical thesis of the unity of human reason and the insistence that all human beings were descended from one first pair of parents (an affirmation already the object of sharp controversy among theologians) would appear to be refuted de facto. On the other hand, the empirical demonstration that human persons of all peoples and times agreed at least on the basic moral principles could be seen as a strong indication for the moral-philosophical thesis which attributed strict logical universal validity a priori to our moral judgments. Cathrein rejected the contemporary positivistic concept of knowledge; but the great weight which he attached to the empirical verification of the ethical affirmations contained in ethnographic testimonies reveals—unintentionally and indirectly—how far he himself was dependent on this concept.

Within the framework of the present investigation, it is of course impossible to study all the details of this ambitious attempt at an empirical refutation of ethical relativism, or to give a comprehensive account of the material which Cathrein assembled. We must be content here with a methodological analysis of the result which he presented. We begin by

13. Ibid., pp. 8–12.

looking at his own description of the fruits of his research, and then we ask whether such a result can in fact be justified via an empirical comparison. Cathrein summarizes his investigations as follows in the conclusion to his third volume:

> Everywhere, the good is recognized and approved as something one should strive after, whereas evil and vice count as abominable. The good is praised and rewarded, evil is rebuked and punished. We find in practice everywhere the universal principles that one should do good and avoid evil, that one should not do anything unjust, that one ought not to inflict on another that which one would not wish to suffer, and so on. Similarly, the universal commandments that one should not kill unjustly, commit adultery, steal, or bear false witness, are known everywhere in their general form.[14]

When he looks back on what must be called a literary journey around the world, which has led him to the primitive and cultured peoples of all continents and epochs of human history known at that time, Cathrein claims that he has completely furnished the "inductive proof" of his thesis.[15] Has he genuinely succeeded in doing so, or did he expect too much of the empirical methods of ethnography, so that his grandiose attempt failed?

Cathrein's work made little impression on cultural anthropologists, although scholars today recognize that he endeavored to study all the ethnographic sources which were available at that time, and that he compared these with one another in a manner that even modern criteria must acknowledge to be critical and unprejudiced.[16] He refused to level down the obvious differences in morals and customs, in lifestyles and legal systems, among the peoples of whom his sources spoke; but he tried to explain these differences in a manner that remained compatible with his thesis of a deeper unity of the moral consciousness of the peoples. For example, he pointed out that the widespread transgression of a moral law does not allow the inference that this is completely unknown: "People do many

14. Ibid., III, p. 563. In his *Moralphilosophie* (1911), Cathrein describes the knowledge of ethical norms as a syllogistic conclusion in which the general principles are the major premise, and the factual characteristics, which are empirically demonstrable in their universal diffusion, are the minor premise. Here, however, cultural history presents proof of the universal validity of the minor premise, not of the general presuppositions of the major premise. On this, cf. S. Leher, *Begründung ethischer Normen bei Viktor Cathrein und Wahrheitstheorien der Sprachphilosophie,* Innsbruck and Vienna 1992, pp. 88–91; 116f.

15. V. Cathrein, *Die Einheit des sittlichen Bewußtseins der Menschheit,* III, p. 563.

16. W. Dupré, "Kultur und Ethos. Zum Problem der Sittlichkeit in Primitivkulturen," in: C. H. Ratschow (ed.), *Ethik der Religionen,* Stuttgart 1980, p. 109.

things, not because they think they are good, but despite the fact that they think they are bad."[17] Referring to the divorce rate, which was already high in the United States and Europe, he noted that there is not the slightest difference here between the civilized peoples with a high culture and those ethnic groups whose "primitive" lifestyle moved many of his contemporaries to indignation. Cathrein also maintains consistently the distinction between fundamental ethical concepts and the more remote inferences drawn from these. Divergent inferences may be drawn in individual cases without harming the unity in basic ethic principles. Finally, he became aware in the course of his ethnographic studies that it was necessary to make a distinction between moral value judgments and non-moral situations, although he did not yet possess the precise terminology required to do this. In his view, the practices of killing children, abandoning sick and elderly persons, and killing one's own parents are no indication of a lack of altruistic feelings or caring bonds within the family; rather, these practices, which we find so alien, can be explained on the basis of the concrete existential situation of the nomadic hunters. "What most of us find a cruel custom can in reality be an act of mercy which the old persons themselves praise and indeed demand."[18] These interpretative principles command fundamental assent even today; or at least, they are seen as an explanatory model worth discussion (although it may not be possible to employ it to understand the example of killing one's parents: cf. section 4 of this chapter).

The scanty attention paid in the moral-philosophical debate about ethical relativism to Cathrein's great work is due less to his methods of dealing with his sources than to the epistemological presuppositions of the entire project, which remain strangely unclear, despite all his declarations of fidelity to his principles. Above all, the relationship of the attempted empirical verification to the alleged a priori validity of our fundamental ethical principles is unclear from the very start. The very fact that he calls his own mode of argumentation a complete inductive proof expresses a problematic closeness to the mechanistic worldview of the physics of his age, since this kind of language implies that one can demonstrate the fundamental ethical principles of humanity in the same way as the physical regularities of nature. Besides this, Cathrein loads down his thesis of the common rational origin of our universal fundamental ethical principles with the sci-

17. V. Cathrein, *Die Einheit des sittlichen Bewußtseins der Menschheit*, I, p. 31; III, p. 565.
18. Ibid., I, p. 15; cf. also III, pp. 567f.

entifically dubious theory of a common biological origin of humanity; the outcome is a peculiar cross between the theory of biological descent and a rationalistic epistemology. At the end of this ambitious attempt to destroy the relativistic foe with his own weapons, we are left with the hybrid of a biological-positivistic rationalism, which at best might have some use as an *argumentum ad hominem* in response to the representatives of one contemporary ideal of science. In the long term, the ambiguous attempt at a positivistic triumph over ethical relativism necessarily collapsed because of its own inconsistencies.[19] The strategy of turning empirical moral investigation against itself and compelling it to acknowledge eternal truths in the sphere of natural morality could not succeed, because Cathrein underestimated the tribute that he himself unwittingly had to pay to the positivistic understanding of science.

Nevertheless, his failure can be very instructive, since it invites both moral philosophy and cultural anthropology to make a more precise distinction than had been usual hitherto between the levels of empirical facts and statements of ethical meaning. Historical investigation can demonstrate neither the existence nor the non-existence of eternal values that were or are acknowledged in every society known to cultural history, for the simple reason that the written or paleographic evidence available to us permits us to know only a small section of human history as a whole and to study this scientifically. But even if (as Cathrein had intended) it were possible to find in our sources the complete empirical evidence of moral universals, this would be no philosophical proof that our moral judgments can possess universal truth and validity. On the other hand, of course, it is equally true that one cannot give empirical proof of the opposite, since this transcends in principle the competence of the historical investigation of morality. And this is why the fact that one cannot verify empirically the existence of universally accepted moral values and fundamental ethical convictions says very little about their significance for the academic discipline of ethics. This is because the relativity of ethical phenomena itself requires an explanation; this relativity does not refute the assertion that there is a universally valid criterion of good and evil, but on the contrary demands a point of reference which will permit the understanding of the mutually "relative" facts.[20] The impossibility of a positivistic refutation of

19. On this, cf. W. Dupré, "Kultur und Ethos," p. 110; S. Leher, *Begründung ethischer Normen bei Viktor Cathrein*, p. 116.

20. On this, cf. J. Morel, "Soziologische Wertrelativierung. Thematisierung eines

ethical relativism does not mean that this position is correct—for it is equally impossible to furnish proof of *its* correctness. The failure of empirical moral theories of every kind leads rather to the recognition that the problems connected with universally valid moral judgments must be decided on the level of a metaphysical question. The second type of argumentation which the philosophical ethics of the twentieth century developed in the debate with ethical relativism seeks to comprehend correctly the logical level on which ethical judgments are valid, as distinct from the level of the empirical description of facts.

2.2. *The accusation of naturalism*

The discussion of the naturalistic fallacy, which has been revived in contemporary moral philosophy by the influential trend called intuitionism, had initially only an indirect effect on the ethnological debate about cultural relativism. If, however, cultural relativism is understood as a moral-philosophical theory which affirms the equal value in principle of all the moral ideas of value that are attested in the course of human history up to now, it lays itself open to the same verdict that was originally applied in a broader sense to a number of naturalistic moral theories. In the history of philosophy, this accusation of naturalism is often called "Hume's law," with reference to a passage from his *Treatise* on *Human Nature* (1739–1740). This is in fact not completely apposite, since the Scottish philosopher did not intend to formulate a general law here, but only to draw attention to a problem: he had noticed, while reading the works of many respected moral philosophers, that sentences linked by "is" or "is not" often changed imperceptibly in these books into sentences with an "ought" or "ought not" as predicate.[21] This transition from an observation in the indicative to a nor-

Anliegens," in: W. von der Ohe (ed.), *Kulturanthropologie. Beiträge zum Neubeginn einer Disziplin* (Festschrift for E. K. Francis), Berlin 1987, pp. 217–29, esp. 225–29.

21. Cf. D. Hume, *Treatise of Human Nature* III/1 (1740), edn. Oxford, 1978, pp. 469–70: "In every system of morality, which I have hitherto met with, I have always remark'd, that the author proceeds for some time in the ordinary way of reasoning, and establishes the being of a God, or makes observations concerning human affairs; when of a sudden I am surpriz'd to find, that instead of the usual copulations of propositions, *is,* and *is not,* I meet with no proposition that is not connected with an *ought,* or an *ought not.* This change is imperceptible; but is, however, of the last consequence. For as this *ought,* or *ought not,* expresses some new revelation or affirmation, 'tis necessary that it shou'd be observ'd and explain'd; and at the same time that a reason should be given, for what seems altogether inconceivable, how this new relation can be a deduction from others, which are entirely different from it. But as authors do not commonly use this precaution, I shall presume to recommend it to

mative regulation involves a logical leap which is not immediately explicable, and which must therefore count as impermissible until a reason is given for it.

This correct observation is intended to do more than simply express Hume's astonishment at the careless way many philosophers treat the laws of logic; rather, he wishes to deprive such arguments of any justification once and for all, since they are based on a basic mistake that crops up again and again. They wish to infer what *ought* to be from what *is*, i.e. to derive *normative* conclusions from *descriptive* statements. This inference is, however, logically impermissible, since affirmations about facts and propositions about obligation lie on different levels. It is impossible to join these together to form a correct chain of argumentation. After the philosophy of linguistic analysis investigated the propositions of our moral language and attempted to elaborate something like a logic of moral argumentation, it became customary to say that no imperatives flow from indicatives, since the inference from the descriptive level to the moral order is generally illicit.

As a citizen of the most powerful maritime nation of his day, Hume could not fail to be aware of the variety of moral ideas which existed at that time. We do not know whether he had this in mind when he made his ironic remarks, which later led to the formulation of the law that bears his name. If the prohibition on deducing "ought" from "is" does in fact have the rank of a law of logic, then it applies not only to those naturalistic variants of the classical natural-law doctrines which Hume chiefly envisaged, but equally to relativistic moral theories. No moral value-judgments follow from descriptions of nature, irrespective of whatever deductions such theories might wish to make from the factual descriptions on which they rely. Before Hume's time, the French mathematician and theologian Blaise Pascal (1623–1662) had recognized that one can employ the accusation of naturalism to construct an argument *for* the universal validity of moral judgments (and thus *against* ethical relativism). In a celebrated fragment of his *Pensées,* he bitingly mocks the view that all laws and moral prescriptions are derived from the moods of a corrupt reason, the profit of vacillating rulers, or the changing customs of each age. It is completely irrelevant to the inherent truth of our moral laws where they were first acknowledged; what is good, true, and just on this side of the Pyrenees cannot be bad,

the readers; and am persuaded, that this small attention wou'd subvert all the vulgar systems of morality, and let us see, that the distinction of vice and virtue is not founded merely on the relations of objects, nor is perceiv'd by reason."

false, and unjust on the other side. Equally, it is irrelevant whether the moral laws came into force yesterday, or only today, for "anything else would mean that there is neither justice nor injustice that would not change its essence in keeping with the change of climate."[22] Moral laws and norms are in fact justified only by their inherent accord with reason and their agreement with the highest moral principle, in which the idea of an absolute moral obligation is anchored. However, the human reason is so thoroughly corrupt that it would like to avoid the knowledge of this origin of our moral laws; it devises every trick conceivable in order to bend the demands of justice and right in keeping with its own fancies, until finally only one thing is certain, that is, that "according to pure reason, nothing is just *per se.*"[23]

It is only when one overlooks the tone of mockery in these words and underestimates his skeptical recourse to the incurable corruption of the human reason, that one can read the concluding sentences of this fragment in such a way that one attributes the opposite meaning to Pascal— that is, so that he would appear to concede that the truth of law and morality was originally based on a "lawless foundation" and at one time had no justification. Now, however, since this truth has been in force for a long time and is universally considered to be reasonable, the reason commands that one conceal the true origin of law and morality, since reason with its intrigues would put an end to all law and morality if it once discovered the truth.[24] These final considerations show that the entire fragment is nothing but a philosophical parody of the inventiveness with which the human reason tries to extricate itself from the claim made by the moral laws. This is why we must set Pascal's reflections (only the first part of which is usually quoted) alongside Hume's critique of naturalistic ethics; they must be read as an early document of the ironic distance taken by many moral theories of the Enlightenment vis-à-vis the basic relativistic tendency of Pascal's age.

In the twentieth century, George E. Moore and Richard M. Hare attempted to define more exactly the logical error which they identified as the *prôton pseudon* of all moral debates. Hare formulated Hume's law more precisely by specifying that the logic of moral argumentation does not absolutely forbid drawing imperative conclusions from indicative presuppositions. Rather, it can be logically correct to infer concrete imperatives

22. B. Pascal, *Pensées,* Fragment 294.   23. Ibid.
24. Ibid.

from a given collection of premises, provided that these include at least one imperative premise. This means that there is a general prohibition only on inferences which wish to derive imperatives exclusively from indicative presuppositions and to make these presuppositions bear the burden, not only of the the specifying definition (which is logically subordinate), but also of the real justification of the imperative conclusion.[25] While Hare analyzes the logical form of our moral judgments, Moore begins his investigations one stage lower, that is, with the logical status of the basic moral word "good." In his *Principia Ethica* (1903), he demonstrates the simple meaning of "good," which is not constructed out of any further individual characteristics. We cannot explain the contents of this concept by dissecting it into descriptive components, as we could describe the meaning of the concept "horse" by listing the characteristics that make a horse a horse. The decisive difference is that "good" displays no kind of semantic complexity. It is a simple basic word of our language, which we cannot use other words to explain: "My point is that 'good' is a simple notion, just as 'yellow' is a simple notion; that, just as you cannot, by any manner of means, explain to any one who does not already know it, what yellow is, so you cannot explain what good is."[26] It is completely impossible to give any definition of the meaning of "good," because a definition always implies a logical process through which we understand a complex whole on the basis of its individual elements: "and in this sense 'good' has no definition because it is simple and has no parts."[27]

Moore coined the celebrated concept of the "naturalistic fallacy" to characterize the vain attempt to trace the independent meaning of "good," which can be grasped only by intuition, back to empirical characteristics. This refers, not to a "naturalistic false deduction," but to a simple "naturalistic error," the kind of mistake on which our false moral deductions are based when we derive an "ought" directly from an "is," because we unwittingly presuppose that we could define the good which ought to be by means of the "extra" characteristics that it would possess (so to speak) "in

25. Cf. R. M. Hare, *Die Sprache der Moral*, Frankfurt 1972, p. 49f. [English translation: cf. R. M. Hare, *The Language of Morals,* 1952]. A. Anzenbacher, *Einführung in die Ethik,* Düsseldorf 1992, p. 270, uses a simple example to illustrate the possibility of inferring a concrete imperative from a mixed collection of premises which also include indicative presuppositions. *Imperative premise:* you ought to return stolen goods to the owner. *Indicative premise:* the fur coat you are wearing is stolen goods. *Imperative consequence:* you ought to return to the owner the fur coat you are wearing.

26. E. G. Moore, *Principia Ethica* (1903) I, 7: edn. Cambridge 1971, p. 7.

27. Ibid., I, 7: ibid. p. 9.

addition to" the fact that it is good.[28] However, as Moore shows in exemplary fashion in his critique of Spencer's social-Darwinist ethics, this error does not remain limited to the semantic level.[29] Many moral systems are based on substantial propositions about value which de facto occupy the rank of a supreme moral principle, although there is no clarity about the logical status of these propositions. When he criticizes an erroneous use of the word "good," Moore intends at the same time to attack the attempt to justify such propositions about value by means of a surreptitious recourse to the meaning of "good," which can be grasped only by intuition. This practical interest links the accusation of the "naturalistic fallacy," as far as its consequences for moral-philosophical argumentation go, with Hume's law. Like the latter, it forbids the leap from an empirical-descriptive to a normative-prescriptive level, though of course with the difference that Moore takes exception to this illicit leap already in his analysis of the significance of fundamental moral words or highest propositions of value, not only on the level of moral inferences.

The result, however, is always the same, since a great variety of moral systems which otherwise have no recognizable similarities in their substantial premises may in fact be based both on the naturalistic fallacy and on the logically impermissible inferences drawn from this. For example, Marxist ethics succumbs to this kind of impermissible inference from the descriptive level to the level of moral evaluation when it calls a mode of conduct "good" because it is in accord with the dialectical historical process and serves the interests of the working class. In the same way, Moore's objections to Spencer's Darwinism also apply to modern sociobiology, since this seeks to infer the moral quality of behavior from the historical advantages it offers a tribe in terms of survival. They may diverge very widely in terms of substance, but all naturalistic doctrines of natural law, a revolutionary morality of social classes, and the evolutionary ethics of sociobiology commit the same logical error when they justify their assertions: they infer an "ought" directly from an "is." It is completely irrelevant, in terms of the validity of this kind of moral-philosophical argumentation, whether the state of affairs which is described concerns the

---

28. This is why F. Ricken, *Allgemeine Ethik,* Stuttgart et al. second edn. 1989, pp. 48f., makes a distinction between a broader and a narrower meaning of "naturalism" and "naturalistic theory." Hume and Hare are placed in the broader category of those interested in conclusions, while Moore is placed in the narrower category of those interested in the semantic significance of basic moral words.

29. Cf. Moore, *Principia Ethica,* II: pp. 45–54.

observation of biological regularities of human nature, the situation of historical antagonisms between classes in a particular society, or the best starting position in the gene-pool of a biological species. Thanks to the universal logical claim that they make, such considerations are also significant for the debate about ethical relativism. Hence, the attempt to justify the normative thesis of a fundamental ethical relativism by means of the empirical description of the historical relativity of our moral ideas is necessarily affected by Hume's law or by Moore's objections to naturalistic moral theories.

Nevertheless, the accusation of the naturalistic fallacy does not offer a definitive (or more precisely, an *exclusively* valid) answer to the problem of the historical relativity of moral value judgments. This is not only because of the moral-philosophical criticism of Moore's assertion that the term "good" is an absolutely indefinable concept (a word may be indefinable as a basic term of one language, S; but it may be possible for us to agree in a language of reflection, S^1, about its use)—nor is this only because he fails to distinguish sufficiently between the moral and the non-moral significance of "good" (a good knife, a good footballer, etc.).[30] These justified objections indicate weak points in Moore's critique, but they have no decisive significance in the debate about ethical relativism, since the accusation of the naturalistic fallacy is logically irrefutable, at least in the more precise form which Hare gave to Hume's law. This means that this accusation can be made against every moral theory which is defined in terms of its contents and is constructed on empirical foundations. This universal validity, which makes the accusation logically irrefutable, is its great strength. One must however ask whether the abstract form of a strictly logical universal validity, in which a great variety of moral systems are reduced to one single basic logical error, does not conceal a remarkable weakness of this argument.

The intellectual structure of the naturalistic fallacy dismisses the empirical level on which research into cultural anthropology poses its questions as irrelevant to moral philosophy, because it finds it unacceptable to make the inherent claim to validity of a norm dependent on the quantitative data of its historical and geographical diffusion. As far as the normative foundations of our moral judgments are concerned, this criticism is justified; but an argumentation which is interested only in the logical status of

---

30. On this, cf. F. von Kutschera, *Grundlagen der Ethik,* Berlin and New York 1982, pp. 52ff.; F. Ricken, *Allgemeine Ethik,* pp. 49ff.;-A. Anzenbacher, *Einführung in die Ethik,* p. 268.

the validity of moral norms deprives itself of the possibility of reflecting philosophically on the problem posed by the empirical plurality of our moral ideas, and of formulating a response to ethical relativism which carries the discussion further. If this question is rejected a priori, it is no longer possible to have a meaningful discussion of the problems it poses below the level of normative validity. Besides this, an excessively hasty transposition of the accusation of naturalism to the descriptive-historical investigation of morality overlooks the point that human reason—whose non-contradictory character ultimately decides about the specific contents of every historical moral system—is not a capability opposed to history, or something absolutely transhistorical. Reason cannot operate beyond history or outside the course of history: as concrete human reason, it can operate only in history. This is why it necessarily operates as a finite and historical reason. This means in turn that historical relativity, in the sense of an inescapable relatedness to one's specific standpoint in history, is a dimension of the reason itself, which cannot carry out its critical function vis-à-vis the concrete expressions of one particular ethos otherwise than within a shared historical parameter which determines a priori its possibilities of knowledge, in keeping with the "non-arbitrary logic" of the reason itself.[31]

There need be no necessary contradiction between the inherently historical character of the moral recognition of value on the one hand and its absolute validity and its origin in the practical reason of the human person on the other. As Max Scheler's debate with historicism shows, this historical character can also be explained within the framework of intuitionist moral theories which maintain the a priori validity of moral values, principles, and norms. This debate does indeed involve special presuppositions on the part of the philosophy of value, with its phenomenological orientation, since it postulates, alongside the reason, a specific intuitive capacity as the organ which perceives values. But Scheler's reflections on how one can combine the *successive* historical *discovery of values* with the *a priori validity* of moral values are very suggestive for rational theories of ethics too, which take their starting point in the structure of the human reason, with its innate capacity to recognize the highest moral principles. This is why it is worth analyzing these reflections in greater detail, even if one does not share the epistemological and ontological presuppositions of the philosophy of value and rejects the idea of an ideal sphere in which eternal values exist.

31. On this, cf. especially W. Korff, *Norm und Sittlichkeit. Untersuchungen zur Logik der normativen Vernunft*, Mainz 1973, pp. 62–75, esp. 65.

Scheler finds no cause for alarm in the fact that a variety of historical and geographical standpoints opens up a variety of paths to the comprehension of moral values. Accordingly, he would not find it particularly significant if the ethnological thesis were to be confirmed that particular insights into value were limited to single peoples or cultural families, or even to a group of individuals within such groups, but were initially hidden from others. The historical fact that particular peoples or epochs lag behind the moral knowledge of others does not contradict the objective obviousness and "validity in terms of Being" of the understanding of value; for as soon as humanity in one place has grasped the essentially necessary interconnections of the realm of value, this breakthrough acquires universal significance for all times and places.[32] Once the criteria of value which apply to the human person *qua* human person have emerged, the validity of this insight holds good for all of humanity, even if it is not attained everywhere and by everyone, empirically speaking. Otherwise, it would be impossible to provide a real explanation of the growth of our moral knowledge or of the phenomenon of the sudden opening-up of whole areas of value; Scheler finds examples of the latter in Jesus' Sermon on the Mount or the life of St Francis.[33] This is why the phenomenological ethics of value does not take a fundamentally antagonistic position vis-à-vis the theses of cultural relativism, as long as the latter understands itself only as an ethnographic theory about the empirical variety of views about value, and does not deny the objective evidential character of values that have in fact emerged. The philosophy of value does not wish to dispute or refute the ethical phenomena on which ethical relativism is based, but wishes rather to integrate these into a developmental logic of the understanding of value which would do justice both to the different substantial moral values and to the gradation among these. This means that ethical relativism, as an empirical theory, does not need to be "overcome." Rather, in today's situation within the history of science, it can be seen as an explanation which is a priori highly probable, given our knowledge of the polycentric origins of humankind.[34]

Thus we must assume from the outset that the horizon of ethical value is disclosed only in successive stages. Each period has its own structure for

32. Cf. M. Scheler, *Der Formalismus in der Ethik und die materiale Wertethik* (*Gesammelte Werke* [*GW*] II), Berne and Munich sixth edn. 1980, pp. 276–79.
33. Cf. Scheler, *Der Formalismus in der Ethik*, p. 309; Idem, *Wesen und Formen der Sympathie* (*GW* VII), Berne 1974, pp. 98–103.
34. Cf. Scheler, *Der Formalismus in der Ethik*, p. 277.

the experience of value, which makes possible or impossible a deeper penetration of the realm of value, thanks to the ways in which one epoch experiences (or else obscures) its evidential character. In accordance with this
fundamental principle, Scheler's critique is really addressed, not to an historical way of looking at morality, but to the absolute standpoint of a formal ethics which remains blind to the essentially historical character of our
perception of value. But as long as ethical relativism only wishes to make
the case for "the inherent history of the *ethos* itself, this central history *in*
all history," it does not yet contradict the assumption of an objective order
of value.[35] Scheler holds that ethical relativism becomes incompatible with
his own presuppositions when it takes the moral values to be mere symbols
of the convictions acknowledged in one particular cultural sphere and interprets the historical development of the ethos in other regions of the
earth as a growing assimilation to its own relativistic standpoint on values.
In Scheler's eyes, such a mistaken form of relativism fails to do justice not
only to the objective givenness of moral values, but also to the idea of a
genuine historical relativity of our perception of values, since it surrepti-
tiously holds the consciousness of our own age or our own cultural sphere
to be the culmination of historical development, thus absolutizing one section of the entire process.

Scheler has perceptively recognized here that even a moral skepticism,
despite the widespread historical phenomena to which it appeals, can become a special philosophical path which (paradoxically) draws its nourish-
ment from precisely the same feelings of cultural superiority which it
criticizes in others as making unattainable claims to absoluteness. His significance for the philosophical dialogue with ethical relativism lies above
all in the fact that he can take the historical relativity of our moral views
just as seriously as this relativism, but without being obliged to interpret it
in the sense of a fundamental equality in rank.On the contrary, he himself
has shown how the inherently historical character of the perception of values is compatible with the objective evidential character of the validity of
these values, so that moral skepticism does not supply the only explanation. Since he is able to integrate empirical-historical investigation into the
questions posed by moral philosophy, his approach proves superior also to
Moore's intuitionism and to the sheer rejection of naturalistic moral theories by analytic ethics. Above all, in his debate with ethical relativism,
Scheler recognized the necessity of making a more precise distinction be-

35. Cf. Ibid., p. 309.

tween values, principles, and norms than had hitherto been the case in most ethical theories. We need not take up this question here, however; we shall return to it in a later section of the present chapter.

2.3. The accusation of logical inconsistency

A third strategy employed in the philosophical debate with ethical relativism goes further than the accusation of a logical error or an illicit inference, that is, of confusing the descriptive plurality of our moral ideas with an equal normative value of these ideas. This strategy disputes the very possibility of making a consistent formulation of ethical relativism, where this is considered a normative theory. This argumentation is based on a development of the classical objections presented by Walter T. Stace in 1932 against the thesis of descriptive cultural relativism (viz. that there exists no common criteria for the evaluation of the divergent moral standards of different societies). If one accepts this, it is no longer possible to compare *with one another* the ethical aspects of the moral ideas of different societies and epochs. The consequence of this, however, is that it is no longer possible to question the moral standards acknowledged *within* one sociocultural group. This in turn means that we must banish the concept of moral progress to the realm of illusionary wishes. It would not be possible for us within our own historical and cultural sphere to make any judgment about the moral ideas of past times or to criticize the ethos accepted in contemporary society by appealing to a better future ethos. If there is no non-relativistic standpoint which permits the comparison of the moral code of one cultural sphere or of a smaller sociocultural entity with that of other groups, it becomes meaningless to see the abolition of slavery, of torture, the persecution of witches, or of the Inquisition as moral progress. Nor may one continue to speak of a higher development of the religious ethos within the Judaeo-Christian tradition: one may no longer see the social criticism of the prophets, the command to love one's enemies, or Jesus' Sermon on the Mount as the expression of a further development of the ethical consciousness, when compared with the *lex talionis,* the punishments envisaged by the laws governing purity in Leviticus, or the Ten Commandments of Moses.[36] One might indeed speak of changes within the biblical traditions, of charismatic new beginnings, or even revolution-

36. Cf. W. T. Stace, *The Concept of Morals,* London second edn. 1932, pp. 46–49; on this, K. P. Rippe, *Ethischer Relativismus,* pp. 190–95.

ary new approaches; but it would no longer be possible to compare these
with one another from an ethical point of view, or to evaluate them as
progress.

This is not all: a consistent ethical relativist could no longer be certain,
even within an existing society, about which moral standards another person accepted for himself. Not all the members of a given group share its
social system of norms; it may contain further sub-groups or individuals
who follow their own deviating group moralities or their personal private
morality. Under the given presuppositions, we cannot undertake a moral
evaluation of these—indeed, in many cases, we cannot even know what
they are. This makes it impossible to predict with any degree of certainty
what other people will do. And this in turn entails significant consequences for the cohesion of a society, which Stace dramatically illustrates
by means of the example of rival criminal gangs in Chicago. If it is not
possible to predict other people's reactions, a society very soon collapses in
chaos. But even apart from this specific American urban milieu of the
1930's, any society would gradually disintegrate if its members had no reliable expectations of each others' behavior and no established structures for
the non-violent resolution of conflicts.

This is why the critique of ethical relativism leads to the conclusion
that it is incapable of explaining its own starting point, viz. the cohesion of
one single social system of norms.[37] Naturally, this objection contains an
insinuation, in its practical consequences for the cohesion of human societies, which runs counter at least to the intentions of relativistic positions.
Further, this type of argumentation is more interested in the *methodological* problems involved in making a consistent formulation of a relativistic
theory than in the *practical* difficulties involved in living consistently with
such a theory. It therefore seems more helpful to reconstruct the fundamental affirmations of ethical relativism in such a way that they end up in
a self-referential contradiction as soon as one stops looking only at the levels of the individual statements and identifies the relationship between
them. Bernard Williams and Markus G. Singer take this route to a philosophical refutation of ethical relativism by dissecting its basic position into
a number of theses which cannot simultaneously be maintained. The following consideration reveals the inconsistency of an ethical relativism
which is understood in a normative manner: there is a contradiction between thesis A ("There is no moral norm which is universally valid in all

37. Cf. W. T. Stace, *The Concept of Morals*, pp. 51–53.

cultural spheres") and thesis B ("Each individual ought to follow the norms accepted in his own cultural sphere, without condemning the moral views of other peoples"), since universal validity is claimed at least for the demand of tolerance implied in thesis B—and this is directly antithetical to the presupposition established in thesis A.[38]

This conclusion seems compelling if one accepts the initial formulation of these two theses as the direct reproduction of the basic logical form of relativistic theories. If the validity of moral norms is based *only* on their acknowledgment within one particular group, it is no longer possible to explain why different groups ought to respect one another and acknowledge the otherness of their moral rules. Singer makes this false conclusion of ethical relativism clear by means of a simple consideration:

On this assumption, one could organize a group of thieves, who, by the mere fact that they like or want to steal, would be justified in stealing. On this assumption the members of 'Murder Incorporated' were perfectly justified in murdering whom they pleased, since they had no scruples against it. Indeed, on this view once could justify oneself in doing anything whatsoever merely by refusing to recognize any rule against it or by inculcating a taste for it. I have already pointed out how this is self-contradictory. No one is justified in violating any moral rule, or in violating the rights of another, simply because he wants to or finds it convenient, or simply because he has no scruples against it; and no one would be justified in this simply because he is a member of a group with similar dispositions.[39]

Such a reflection is too obviously absurd to require any specific refutation. On the other hand, one will scarcely find anyone who is ready to agree to such implications of relativistic theories. This means that one who wishes to defend ethical relativism against such objections must choose another path. For example, Gilbert Harman, one of the few moral philosophers who employ philosophical arguments in defense of ethical relativism, rejects the logical reconstruction of the basic relativistic thesis. He argues that the introductory formulation of the relativistic position already contains a "dissuasive definition."[40] It presents ethical relativism from the outset as a crazy construction which need not be taken seriously as a scholarly hypothesis. Even if one agrees with the logical refutation of ethical relativism, one must have a certain sympathy with this objection: it is possible to give a distorted reconstruction of the positions of other authors, espe-

---

38. Cf. B. Williams, *Morality: An Introduction to Ethics,* New York 1972, pp. 20f.; M. G. Singer, *Generalization in Ethics,* London 1963, pp. 328–34.

39. Singer, *Generalization in Ethics,* p. 332.

40. G. Harman, "Moral Relativism Defended," *PhRv* 84 (1975), pp. 3–22, at 3.

cially when one's aim is to refute them. In order to exclude this avoidable source of errors, it seems better to put to the proof of consistency a text written by a leading representative of ethical relativism, which therefore reproduces its fundamental thesis in authentic formulations.

An obvious choice here is the reaction by the American ethnologist Melville Herskovits to the Declaration of the United Nations on Human Rights. This position was officially supported by the American Anthropological Society at that time. If there exists something like a "relativistic creed" of descriptive cultural anthropology, we hear its original voice in this manifesto. Thus, the reconstruction of the logical process of argumentation which underlies ethical relativism can find support here in an unfalsified textual basis which excludes every possibility of erroneous definitions. This text also makes the analysis of its logical construction easier by emphasizing three fundamental theses embedded in the flow of thought:

The *first* is: "The individual realizes his personality through his culture, hence respect for individual differences entails a respect for cultural differences." One may deduce a *second* thesis from the fact that the cultures which have disappeared in the course of human history include both highly complex cultures with an extraordinary substantial richness and "modest," less highly articulated cultures: "Respect for differences between cultures is validated by the scientific fact that no technique of qualitatively evaluating cultures has been discovered." Finally, a *third* thesis accompanies this affirmation. It is a strong attack on the idea of absolutely valid norms and values, as this has been elaborated in the cultures of Western Europe and North America: "Standards and values are relative to the culture from which they derive, so that any attempt to formulate postulates that grow out of the beliefs or moral codes of one culture must to that extent detract from the applicability of any Declaration of Human Rights to humankind as a whole."[41]

If one compares these three principles, it is obvious that they express the thesis of relativism on different levels. Although their formulation builds on one another, they are not logically deduced from one another. Besides this, Herskovits does not distinguish between moral principles and the rules or norms derived from these; he makes no differentiations when he exalts the postulate of relativity vis-à-vis ethical principles and individual norms with a defined substance. The omission at this stage exposes his argumentation to criticism (cf. the fourth section of this chapter), and many critics agree with Scheler in seeing here the basic error of ethical relativism.[42] In this context, however, the question is whether it is at all possi-

41. M. J. Herskovits, "Statement on Human Rights," pp. 541–42.
42. Cf. M. G. Singer, *Generalization in Ethics*, p. 329.

ble to make a consistent formulation of a fundamentally relativistic position, that is, whether it is possible to maintain Herskovits' three theses simultaneously and without contradiction. Here we must examine more closely the logical status of each thesis, and the extent of their validity.

The first thesis, concerned with equal respect for the cultural diversity of all peoples, formulates the intention of a *cultural* relativism which is often referred to today as *descriptive* relativism. This thesis describes an indisputable fact, but it does not provide any theoretical explanation on this level for the existence of different moral ideas, or for the inference that they must all be respected without any distinctions. The second thesis wishes to justify the respect due to all cultures by appealing to the fact that we do not possess any scientifically sure methodology for making intercultural comparisons. This thesis must be called *ethical* relativism in the narrower sense (or *metaphysical* relativism); its fundamental concern is not the plurality of moral ideas itself, but the possibilities for a scholarly ethics to understand these comprehensively and to judge them in keeping with certain and logically justifiable evaluative criteria. Thus, ethical relativism in the narrower sense does not make any affirmations about the correctness of individual moral views, nor does it evaluate the concrete actions of members of another cultural sphere; rather, it contains a skeptical thesis about the scope of our moral judgments, seeing all moral ideas as "relative" in the sense that they reflect the standpoint of one particular group and are based on a conscious or unconscious agreement among the members of this group.[43] Ethical relativism need not dispute here that there is a "hard core of *similarities*" between cultures or something akin to "universals in human conduct."[44] But it refuses to accord these de facto agreements the status of obligatory criteria of value, still less to acknowledge the existence of an impartial and objective valid criterion which would make possible a binding evaluation of different moral ideas.

Herskovits formulates his main concern in his critique of the United Nations' catalogue of human rights in the third principle, and it is only here that we find a legal-ethical requirement addressed to the community of states as a whole: this community is obliged to guarantee each individual and all peoples the freedom to live in agreement with their own cultural traditions, and to follow their own legal traditions in establishing the political-legal ordering of human living in society as a part of their own

---

43. This "definition" is also accepted by defenders of ethical relativism such as G. Harman: cf. "Moral Relativism Defended," p. 4.

44. M. J. Herskovits, "Statement on Human Rights, "pp. 540, 542.

cultural system. According to the meta-ethical principle of the second thesis, however, it is no longer possible to justify this postulate of a *normative* or *a priori* relativism. If all our moral judgments are equally valid, and we possess no common transcultural criteria for the qualitative evaluation of these judgments, what permits us to make a moral judgment about the demand for tolerance and about its alternatives (such as feelings of hegemony, xenophobia, or a Eurocentrism with a "missionary consciousness")?

If *no* moral ideas can in principle claim a validity that embraces more than one specific group, and there exists *no* standpoint from which one can evaluate them objectively, why should respect and empathy vis-à-vis foreign cultures be morally better than the rigorous oppression of such cultures? If these presuppositions are correct, why should people in a cultural sphere where xenophobia and cultural isolation are deep-rooted accept the commandment of tolerance and the idea of multicultural openness? An adequate answer to this question presupposes that one can prove to every cultural stance that tolerance and respect for the otherness of that which is different are objectively valid and rationally justified demands. This does not, however, mean that it would be impossible to formulate a relativistic theory which dispensed with the principle of tolerance, and would demand moral attitudes such as universal respect, mutual consideration, non-violence, and respect for creatures in need of protection only from those in whose cultural sphere of reference such attitudes were already at home.[45] The commandment to be tolerant would then obligate only those in whose society it is morally acknowledged, whereas the members of another society would be permitted to treat others with impatience, persecution, and disrespect, if their own moral ideas gave them the right to do so.

In his defense of ethical relativism, Harman explains this point by taking the example of extraterrestrial beings who land on earth and torture and harass human beings without any consideration for us. To hurt or even kill a human individual has no meaning for them, since this is completely compatible with the implicit agreements which hold sway among them and determine their inherent moral judgment. This is why Harman holds it to be completely meaningless to demand that extraterrestrial beings "ought" not to treat us with cruelty, or to assert that they infringe a moral commandment when they do so. In the same way, in our eyes a

---

45. K. P. Rippe, *Ethischer Relativismus*, pp. 201f., makes this objection to the assertion that it is impossible to formulate ethical relativism in a non-contradictory manner, where this is understood as normative.

tribe of cannibals acts in a primitive and barbaric manner when they eat the sole survivor of a shipwreck; but according to Harman's ethical theory, we cannot say that they "ought" not to have eaten their victim, since the meaning of this word, in the strict moral sense, can be defined only in terms of the agreements which hold sway in their own group. These agreements permit a tribe of cannibals to enjoy eating human flesh—and we (who might be personally affected by this) cannot formulate a moral judgment about this that might be significant for the cannibals themselves. In this context, Harman also accepts the example of "Murder Incorporated," whose members unite in order to carry out jobs as professional killers: we may regret this and think it wrong that so many gangs of mobsters engage in their terrible business, but we cannot justify the moral judgment that they "ought not" to murder their victims—nor is it meaningful to assert that it is wrong to act thus. If, however, we do in fact sometimes say that such crimes "ought not to be," then we are using the term "ought" in an imprecise, somewhat general sense: it can be used in a *moral* sense only with reference to the internal judgments by the members of particular groups, who make these judgments on the basis of explicit agreements or of an implicit consensus among themselves.[46]

What are we to make of these strange reflections about extraterrestrial invaders, cannibal tribes, or bands of murderers? The first thing that these remarkable examples show is merely that these groups clearly believe that modes of conduct which offend our ideas about morality are compatible with the convictions of their own consciences and with the consensus which holds sway among them; although even this much can be doubted in the case of the members of "Murder Ltd" (it is no doubt easier for us to empathize with their supposed feelings than with the sentiments of extraterrestrial beings and cannibals). However, these examples do not in the least demonstrate that it would be a hopeless endeavor, still less something logically impossible, to confront them with the principle of equality or of mutuality and to bring them by means of such a confrontation to acknowledge moral rules that are equally valid both for them and for us. Here, we need only consider a similar occurrence, which Singer presents in confirmation of his thesis that malicious aggression and the torture of other persons out of sheer cruelty are always morally wrong, irrespective of the circumstances: "After the Indians in the Hudson Bay territory had obtained guns, it is reported, they 'used them to hunt Eskimos for sport, as

---

46. Cf. G. Harman, "Moral Relativism Defended," pp. 6–10.

we hunt bear or deer . . . when eventually the Eskimons got guns, the Indians left them alone'."[47] It may be that the custom of hunting Eskimos quickly spread among the Hudson Bay Indians at that period, and it is even possible that there existed a tacit consensus among them about the "rules" to be followed in this unequal contest. But it cannot be asserted that such rules were morally justified by the agreement among the Indians. If they had truly been convinced that they had a moral right to engage in this kind of pastime, they would not have abandoned their pleasure in the hunt at the first sign of resistance, but would have defended it to the hilt—in good conscience.

These three examples ultimately indicate nothing more than the possibility of formulating a relativistic position in such a way that it grants all groups—even those whose moral rules are compatible with intolerance and the use of force vis-à-vis others—the right to act in accordance with the moral standards that enjoy validity among them. But if we bear in mind the logic of language, with which this third type of argument confronts the position of ethical relativism, we see that not even this kind of theory is exempt from the accusation of self-contradiction: although it concedes to the members of particular groups the right to a deviant praxis, this thesis too makes the claim of universal validity—it is meant to be valid for people in all cultural spheres, irrespective of whether or not they accept the requirement of tolerance. This means that its logical form asserts something that it denies on the level of its substantial affirmations, thus entangling itself in a so-called "self-referential" contradiction. At any rate, a relativistic thesis understood in this way is incompatible with the position proclaimed by the third thesis of the manifesto of the American cultural anthropologists. The fundamental reason for the untenability of this kind of "moderate" ethical relativism, which refuses to give up a normative demand for tolerance, is its own incoherence. It is impossible to formulate it in a manner free of contradiction, because its central affirmation presupposes a universally valid moral principle of tolerance which remains exempt from the relativization of all other moral ideas.

The third argumentative strategy for the philosophical debate with ethical relativism thus distinguishes among the various kinds of relativistic moral theories and uncovers the inherent difficulties involved in the attempt to justify these,[48] which can be described as a triple dilemma from

---

47. M. G. Singer, "*Generalization in Ethics,*" p. 333.

48. For a more precise conceptual demarcation of the various kinds of relativistic theories, cf. K. P. Rippe, *Ethischer Relativismus*, pp. 209–22.

which there is no escape. First, *cultural* relativism finds a broad descriptive point of departure in cultural history, which can be seen as the main source of relativistic moral theories. However, this empirical foundation—which, as we shall see, can also be interpreted differently—does not necessarily imply an *ethical* relativism in the *normative* sense that all moral judgments would be equally valid. Secondly, while a *fundamental* relativism of this kind, which rejects every qualitative criterion of evaluation that goes beyond specific cultural boundaries, remains conceivable as a theoretical variant, it contradicts the theoretical considerations of most cultural and ethical relativists, who insist on retaining a universal requirement of tolerance. Thirdly, however, the attempt to combine the *principle of tolerance* with a relativistic position (understood in a normative sense) leads to the self-contradiction which has been exposed above. This variant of ethical relativism, with which most of its representatives consciously or unconsciously agree, collapses because of its own incoherence. It is impossible to formulate it in a manner free of contradiction, because it requires at least one non-relative element, that is, the principle of tolerance, which calls its own presuppositions into question.

From the standpoint of transcendental pragmatism, Jürgen Habermas and Karl Otto Apel have pointed out a self-referential contradiction in the "rebellion against the unreasonable assertion of universal moral principles" which they locate above all in neo-Aristotelian ethics and in contemporary post-modern thinking.[49] According to their diagnosis, humankind today is in a revolutionary situation which poses the alternative of agreeing to recognize universal moral principles and norms or else fragmenting into heterogeneous group moralities which exclude a common response to ecological, political, and military threats. In this situation, discourse ethics explicitly understands the reflexive demonstration of the validity of a universal principle of reason as an argument against the ethical relativism of empirical sociology and of a cultural anthropology which is in thrall to the methodological approach which characterizes the research drawn from this sociology.[50] Habermas and Apel have recourse to Kohlberg's concept of moral-pedagogical stages, which bases the development of the capacity for moral judgments on invariable structures and assumes that the basic moral capacity of human beings has a common intercultural foundation. Their discussion centers on two groups of problems, in which an alternative to

49. Cf. K. O. Apel, *Diskurs und Verantwortung. Das Problem des Übergangs zur postkonventionellen Moral,* Frankfurt 1988, p. 156.
50. Ibid., p. 311.

the difficulties of justifying relativistic moral theories can be seen. One of these groups may be called the program of applying universal rational principles with reference to history, the other the transition on the world scale to a post-conventional morality.

We need not discuss here the details of the arguments they present against the self-affirmative tendencies of specific small groups and cultural subsystems, especially since the persuasive force of these arguments is also drawn from the analysis of potential global risks which unmistakably threaten all peoples in today's world. In our context, the demand for a future macro-ethics of the non-violent resolution of conflicts and of universal willingness to achieve consensus merits attention above all because of the *reflexive* character of its justification. By transposing the question of the possibility of objectively valid knowledge to the deeper level of the question of the transcendental conditions of intersubjective consensus, the attempt is made to show that every argumentative discourse acknowledges a priori the validity of the rational principle, and that we are able to think as individual subjects only in such a way that we simultaneously respect all human persons as beings endowed with reason. These transcendental conditions of an *intersubjective* discourse are the *a priori* structures of every communication which aims at consensus, and hence they also apply to the *intercultural* dialogue and to the encounter between different sets of moral concepts. A dialogue that is serious and includes the search for common ethical ground can proceed only on the basis of a universal rational ethos if all the participants agree in acknowledging the goal of a shared consensus. Here, the transcultural validity of the principle of reason does not appear as the expansion of the European philosophy of consciousness, but as the presupposition of a "planetary macro-ethics of responsibility" and of the intercultural willingness to achieve consensus. Without a universal acknowledgement of human reason, it is impossible to think of these goals in a manner free of contradictions.[51]

2.4. The necessary differentiation between ethical principles, rules, and norms

One final form of the philosophical debate with ethical relativism attempts to discern a meaningful structure within the culturally-dependent

---

51. Ibid., p. 108. Cf. the earlier study by J. Habermas, *Zur Rekonstruktion des historischen Materialismus,* Frankfurt 1976, p. 83.

variability of the ethos itself. We have frequently encountered the distinction between principles and norms, or between fundamental moral principles and individual judgments, in connection with the forms of argumentation analyzed above. However, we wish to conclude by studying this objection on its own, since it is an autonomous form of the debate with ethical relativism. It can help to carry the discussion further on a level below that of the problems connected with logical justification, since, unlike the three other types, this type of argumentation recognizes that a description of the plurality of our moral ideas in some way also implies the normative problem of the various claims to validity on the part of these ideas, although it denies that these claims are contradictory on the level of moral principles or of fundamental ethical attitudes to value. This means that it interprets intercultural plurality as a surface phenomenon which is assuredly compatible with a universally valid depth-structure of the ethical consciousness.

Max Scheler made a distinction in this sense between variations of the *ethos*, understanding this to mean the historical discovery of moral values and of their hierarchical relationships; variations of *ethics*, that is, of the religious and cultural conceptual systems of the various peoples; and variations of *types of conduct*, which have a common structure that is valid despite all the cultural differences.[52] The concept of "types of conduct" proves especially helpful here, since we can use it to discern a common depth-structure among the many individual actions which count as deviations from the moral order or as transgressions of this order. Although the concrete substance of individual areas of action such as theft, adultery, or murder may be defined variously from one culture to another, and (along one historical axis) from one epoch to another, the basic value judgment entailed in this classification remains constant. There may be a considerable difference between the modes of conduct which count as adultery in polygamous and in monogamous societies, but this does not affect the ethical disapproval of adultery. In the same way, even regulations concerning property which do not privilege private possessions have a concept of "theft," although they may not interpret this as the infringement of an individual claim to possess something.

According to this scheme, the various exceptions to the prohibition of killing (the fifth commandment) are compatible with a transcultural rejection of murder, since this is defined as the conscious destruction of the

52. Cf. M. Scheler, *Der Formalismus in der Ethik,* pp. 303f.

personal value of another human being.[53] The traditional praxis of burning widows on the pyre in India, and the right of the Roman *pater familias* over the lives of all who lived in his house, could last only as long as women, slaves, and children were not acknowledged to possess any personal dignity apart from the personhood of the man: if (as in the case of suttee) the woman is considered as completely subsumed under the personal value of the man, it appears wholly plausible that she should follow her husband into death, once his person has been extinguished.

Nor must the death penalty be evaluated as murder, as long as it follows the idealistic theories of expiation by presupposing that even when the state imposes its most extreme penalty, it still respects the person on whom this punishment is inflicted.[54] Today, we disapprove ethically of the physical annihilation of a human being at the orders of the state, since the modern state with its established legal system has effective alternative ways to protect the legal order; capital punishment takes on the character of murder only when it denies the criminal his dignity as a legal subject, or where it is perceived to be incompatible with this dignity. The logic of this distinction also makes it possible to understand killing in war—an action tolerated by the religious traditions of many peoples, and indeed often held to be a meritorious deed—as something that does not contradict the universal prohibition of murder. It is precisely the fact that another human being is perceived, not in his *individual* personal quality, but only as an impersonal member of a hostile collective or as an anonymous "unbeliever," that makes war an inhuman exception to normal life; yet even under the exceptional conditions of martial law, one who kills a personal foe for reasons inherent in the individual relationship to him (e.g., jealousy or revenge) is considered a murderer. Only when his personal value is blotted out does the enemy become an anonymous representative of the hostile power—and killing him remains compatible with the ethical disapproval of murder.

This explanation of why killing in war is not considered murder seems more plausible than the traditional justification of the exceptions to the prohibition of killing. If one agrees with a long tradition of European moral philosophy in restricting this prohibition in such a way that only

53. On what follows, cf. ibid., pp. 313–19.

54. On the classical form of these idealistic theories of punishment, cf. I. Kant, *Metaphysik der Sitten,* A198–205 (ed. by W. Weischedel, VIII, Frankfurt a.M. 1968, pp. 454–59), and G. W. F. Hegel, *Grundlinien der Philosophie des Rechts,* 100 (Theorie Werkausgabe, VII, Frankfurt a.M. 1970, pp. 190f.).

the killing of an *innocent* person is absolutely forbidden, then one can at most legitimate killing someone in self-defense, or carrying out a death penalty inflicted in keeping with the law; but one cannot legitimate killing in war, since the only exception allowed by this rule is *individual* guilt incurred by one person vis-à-vis another. The mere fact of belonging to one of the two peoples at war does not involve the members of the hostile armies in guilt in this *individual* sense. But the theory of the extinction of the personal dignity of the military foe can at least explain the psychological mechanism on which martial law is based, although this naturally does not even begin to identify the circumstances under which killing in war can be justified. In the context of the debate with ethical relativism, the exceptions to the prohibition of killing are relevant primarily because they indicate how individual actions are understood in substantial terms and are given a different moral evaluation from other actions with a similar external object ("killing"). The consequence for the meta-ethical level of questioning—concerned with the affirmation or contestation of the existence of moral judgments which are capable of being universally true—is that, even when we have considerable reservations today about the doctrine of a just war in our own tradition, or the idea of a holy war in the Islamic tradition, such doubts do not refute the thesis that fundamental types of conduct such as theft, adultery, and murder meet with moral disapproval in all cultures (even when the matter denoted by these terms in each case may be described by means of other factual characteristics).

According to this objection, therefore, a relativistic moral theory which generally contests the existence of universal moral ideas acknowledged in all cultures is based on an unacceptable confusion of the levels of our moral consciousness. This argument, first developed by Cathrein and later taken up by Scheler, recurs frequently in the modern philosophical debate about ethical relativism. In its simplest form, this objection urges the necessity of a clearer distinction between *principles, norms,* and *rules,* as well as consideration of the specific *degree of universalization* which these possess at the various stages of cultural development. Where we do in fact discover contradictory moral norms and rules in the world's religions and cultures, these must be reduced to a few principles which are antecedent to all subsequent variations and hence constitute as it were a moral grammar common to the individual ethical linguistic families. The American moral philosopher M. G. Singer affirms that these fundamental common points include the negative principle *neminem laedere,* a positive precept of generalization (the substance of which has of course been interpreted in a variety of ways), and the principle that one must bear responsibility for the consequences of one's actions. Thus he distills a threefold principle from the descriptive plurality which uses a variety of moral norms to evaluate specific individual situations in the various cultures. This principle—concerning suffering, justification, and the consequences—is universally acknowledged on a deeper level of our moral consciousness.[55]

It is of course possible for unclear transitions to exist between moral principles and norms, and this can make it difficult to assign specific ideas to one or other principle or norm. For example, it seems doubtful whether the often quoted praxis whereby the members of an Eskimo clan kill their parents when these have grown old should be considered a subsidiary exceptional norm which puts into practice—under the exceptional conditions of life in the Arctic—the general principle that one should spare one's parents unnecessary suffering.[56] If such a principle were universally acknowledged, it would have to lead in all cultures to exceptional norms which would allow one to kill one's parents as soon as their suffering became ineluctable. This, however, is not in the least the case: on the contrary, there is a virtually universal prohibition of killing one's parents. This means that we cannot understand the behavior of the Inuit clan in keeping with the simple rule of distinction between universal principles and individual deviant norms.

On the other hand, the fact that a tribe in the kingdom of Tonga in the south Pacific is apparently ignorant of a commandment to keep one's promises can help to clarify this distinction. Even without the societal institution of the promise, the inhabitants of Tonga have developed forms of cooperation in their mutual relationships which are able to guarantee a lasting fulfillment of rights and obligations. Without the principle of the predictability of actions by others and by oneself, a society would disintegrate; but this principle is preserved in their society, even without the institution of the promise which is essential in other societies. Clearly, Tongan morality is familiar with functional equivalents to the norm that one must keep a promise, and these equivalents are sufficient even where there is no fixed verbal affirmation of what one intends to do in the future.[57] Although they do not know the otherwise universal norm that one must

55. Cf. M. G. Singer, *Generalization in Ethics,* p.104–6.
56. This argument, which has been common among ethnographers since V. Cathrein, is defended in contemporary moral philosophy above all by G. Patzig, *Ethik ohne Metaphysik,* Göttingen 1983, pp. 80f. For a critique, cf. K. P. Rippe, *Ethischer Relativismus,* pp. 108f.
57. On this, cf. the account by K. P. Rippe, *Ethischer Relativismus,* pp. 158f.

keep a promise, they acknowledge a subsidiary exceptional rule which serves the same principle that the reliability of human relationships must be guaranteed beyond one specific moment in time.

In the same way, the restrictive condition which the Quran applies to the prophet Muhammad's toleration of polygamy can help clarify the distinction between moral principles and norms or rules. We read at Sure 4:3, "And if you fear that you are not behaving correctly in the matter of (female) orphans (entrusted to your care), then each one of you should marry the number of wives you are permitted, two, three, or four. And if you fear that you would not treat (so many) aright, then marry one, or the same number of wives (as you have slaves)! This will be the best way for you to avoid wrongdoing." An older interpretative tradition understood this passage as limiting the number of legitimate wives a man might have to four at most; this was a progressive step, when compared with the preceding historical period, in which a man could have as many wives as he wished. Most Islamic legal scholars, however, interpret the text differently: although it is permitted in principle for a Muslim to marry up to four wives, the necessary condition is that he treat all of them with the same respect. This, however, entails a psychological demand which can scarcely be fulfilled in practice. This is why this "modern" interpretation understands the Quran as advertising that a man should renounce the possibility (*per se* legitimate) of marrying other wives, because this would constitute unjust behavior vis-à-vis the one wife to whom he is already married.[58]

Accordingly, although the Islamic regulations concerning marriage at least admit polygamy as an exceptional norm, they serve the same principle as the strict obligation to monogamy that has developed in our European cultural sphere. This means that the requirement of marital fidelity and the exclusivity of a personal relationship of love, which Christians from the very beginning have understood as a reciprocal obligation on both husband and wife, represent an insight with which Islamic consciousness has long been familiar on the level of principles. If we recognize the monogamous ordering of marriage as the expression of an ethos of human dignity which corresponds to the fact that both wife and husband are subjects,[59] we need not limit this recognition to our European tradition which

58. Cf. P. Antes, "'Ethik' im Islam," in: C. H. Ratschow (ed.), *Ethik der Religionen. Ein Handbuch,* Stuttgart 1980, pp. 202f., and Idem et al. (eds.), *Der Islam. Religion—Ethik—Politik,* Stuttgart 1991, p. 75.

59. On this, cf. P. Mikat, *Ethische Strukturen der Ehe in unserer Zeit: Zur Normierungsfrage im Kontext des abendländischen Eheverständnisses,* Paderborn et al. 1987.

is influenced by Christianity. The fact that monogamy is prescribed by law in most Islamic states today is not only evidence of the acknowledgment of the same moral principle; it also shows that the institutional elaboration of this recognition in view of a normative ordering of the relationship between the sexes has taken a path in the Islamic cultural sphere similar to the development in our own culture.

The examples of the killing of one's parents among the Eskimos, of the lack of an institution called "promise" among the inhabitants of Tonga, and the de facto limitation by Islamic legal scholars of the polygamy which is conceded in the Quran make it clear that, even on the descriptive level, the spectrum of our moral ideas is a very ambiguous phenomenon, which often allows an interpretation in a non-relativistic sense. This is why today's cultural anthropologists take for granted the demand that, when ethnographical data are to be evaluated, one must begin by asking on what level the differences in moral views actually lie. Genuinely different criteria of moral value exist only when cultural divergences cannot be explained on the basis of a different factual situation or of a different form of organizing the satisfaction of the same fundamental human needs. The majority of the remaining divergences are due to the application of the same moral rules to different groups of persons; in this case, the differences affect not the *substance* of moral norms, but the *sphere of their validity.* Finally, the impression of a striking plurality of moral views separating the various cultures is further weakened when we bear in mind that these are at different historical-societal *stages of development.* It is virtually impossible to avoid a false total picture if an artificial synchronization of the levels of comparison compares cultures which are only just beginning to explore their possibilities with cultures that can look back on a long history of development.[60]

In this way, the distinction between principles, norms, and rules and the consideration of the degree of universalization which these have at the

60. On these methodological considerations, cf. above all the study by Westermarck's student M. Ginsberg, "On the Diversity of Morals" (1953; quoted from the author's collected essays with the same title, London second edn. 1962, pp. 97–129), who distinguishes the follow six groups of different moral views: (1) variations generated by the application of the moral rules to a different group of persons; (2) variations due to a different assessment of the facts; (3) variations based on the different significance of individual actions in different situations and social institutions; (4) variations derived from the divergent weight attached to the individual elements of a moral system; (5) variations determined by the different ways in which fundamental needs are met; and (6) variations caused by a different degree of development of morality (pp. 101–6).

various degrees of development of a culture lead to an important method-ological postulate addressed to the empirical investigation of morality: if it is to be substantially appropriate, a proposed interpretation must not only take seriously intercultural plurality, but must also be able to understand the transcultural common elements. It becomes all the more urgent to ex-plain the agreement in many central areas of ethics—in itself, an astonish-ing matter—when one attempts to interpret it from the perspective of a relativistic theory of ethics. Concentration on what is singular can suggest a wrong methodology which would attribute disproportionate weight to deviations rather than to the rule. If the total picture is constructed from peripheral phenomena and exceptional developments, neglecting the com-mon denominators of the cultural systems which one is investigating, it will be incapable of understanding either the intercultural plurality or the common elements which exist.

A cultural-sociological investigation of our moral ideas which intended to refute the universal claim of moral principles and norms on the model of physical regularities, by poking around in cultural history until it found the contrary example of a deviant particular norm which has been accepted at *some time and place on earth,* would necessarily lead astray. Analogies from natural science are helpful here at most in the sense that the historical-cultural variability of our moral ideas can be understood on the basis of a model of living systems borrowed from biology. The occurrence of individ-ual deviations or the formation of irregular patterns is not evidence against the existence of a universal species-specific program, according to which all the examples of a particular species display a core of common characteris-tics; in exactly the same way, isolated special developments in individual tribes do not refute the universal acknowledgment of a core of common moral ideas.

The philosophical objections to a purely numerical methodology of in-tercultural comparison, which juxtaposes individual specific norms with-out inquiring into the rank which these enjoy in the total ethical system of the culture in question, may not however be allowed to obliterate the dis-tinctions, indicated above, between the levels on which *empirical* and *nor-mative* affirmations are valid. Moral norms and rules do not owe their nor-mative validity to the de facto acknowledgment which they possess; rather, from a logical perspective, they are justified by the moral principles which they must make concrete in circumstances which may in fact change, and their ultimate justification is derived from the highest moral principle, in which the difference between good and evil and the unconditional de-

mand of moral obligation are anchored (cf. Chapter IV, section 2). Nevertheless, the de facto diffusion of moral convictions is not irrelevant to the
science of ethics. From the beginnings of cultural-anthropological research, the theory of ethical relativism has claimed to do best justice to the
plurality of moral convictions and to the divergences which exist between
individual moral systems. This makes it particularly significant that the
fourth type of argumentation, which we have traced from Scheler via a
number of Anglo-Saxon moral philosophers to the methodological discussion in contemporary ethnology, calls into question the *empirical* factual
basis that is one of the main sources of the plausibility of this explanatory
model. This type of argumentation recalls the attention of the interdisciplinary dialogue to the fact that the work of comparative moral research
need not in the least end with the observation that the material is disparate
and intrinsically contradictory. On the contrary, if it interprets the ethnographic testimonies in the light of the differentiations set out above, it can
present evidence of an astonishingly wide diffusion of moral universals
which have been, or are, acknowledged in virtually all societies known to
cultural history until now. The conclusions which the analysis of sources
suggests in historical research are also supported by the empirical researches of modern developmental psychology and the theories of moral pedagogy based on these studies. The description of the moral developmental
processes through which children and young persons in all cultures pass,
and which influence the growth of attitudes to moral value even in adult-
hood, offers a synchronous cross-section attesting to a high degree of convergence of universal basic moral norms and identical modes of judgment.[61]

It was a commonplace of cultural sociology in the past to assert that this
area of overlap covered only the taboo on incest and the disapproval of
murder; but the shared sector of fundamental ethical convictions includes
more than this, covering moral prohibitions and rules concerning obligation both in the private sphere of life and in society. According to the list
of potential moral universals drawn up by Klaus Peter Rippe in his study

61. Here we must refer above all to the theory of the invariable stages of moral development, which the American developmental psychologist L. Kohlberg elaborated on the basis
of the answers his test-persons gave to questions involving so-called moral dilemmas, and
which his collaborators then checked by means of control groups from a great variety of cultures. Kohlberg gives a summary of his results and of their moral-philosophical implications
for the debate with ethical relativism in *Moral Stages: A Current Formulation and a Response
to Critics*, Basle et al. 1983, pp. 71–75.

of ethnographic literature, this core sector includes both obligations vis-à-vis one's relatives (sexual taboos, the rejection of adultery, the precept of exogamous marriage, reciprocal obligations between parents and children, solidarity vis-à-vis one's progeny, an obligation to regulate inheritance) and obligations of solidarity in relation to society as a whole (readiness to cooperate within the group, care for the poor and disadvantaged, duty to obey the leaders). Within the clan of one's relatives, one's own society, or human society as a whole, there exists a universal acknowledgement of the prohibition of murder and lying, the condemnation of rape and of deliberate aggression in general, the duty of *pietas* to the dead, the precept that promises must be kept, and a universal obligation to mutual help which goes beyond cultural boundaries. As well as these moral precepts which regulate personal attitudes, expectations of loyalty, and obligations of solidarity among individuals, we also find social-ethical obligations derived from the various economic parameters of existence (regulations concerning property, prohibition of theft, ideas concerning justice).[62] It may be necessary to correct this list, which says little about the substantial elaboration of the individual ideas; nevertheless, it shows that the sector of intercultural common elements is larger than a superficial glance at the cultural history of humanity might initially suggest.

62. Cf. once again K. P. Rippe, *Ethischer Relativismus,* pp. 110–12.

III. *The significance of history and the historicity of morality*

THE PHILOSOPHICAL and cultural-anthropological debate with ethical relativism leads to a double conclusion: this discussion can both demonstrate the inherent difficulties entailed in justifying a relativistic theory of morality and at the same time show that the empirical facts on which such a theory wishes to base itself can also be interpreted in a non-relativistic sense. But more is needed than this refutation of ethical relativism if we are to explain what a transcultural ethic means and to demonstrate its universal claim to validity in an historical world. It is impossible to refute logically the transcendental reflexive arguments against skepticism and the accusation of the naturalistic fallacy. On the gnoseological level on which these arguments move, there are no exceptions to the principle that a rational insight, once attained, is necessarily always true; it must make this claim in ahistorical abstraction and is accordingly obliged to disregard the historical-genetical presuppositions of ethical knowledge. From this point of view, it is correct to prescind from questions concerning the cultural, social, or religious conditions in which our moral consciousness comes into existence; but one may not simply jump over such questions in the debate with ethical relativism, because otherwise the particles of truth contained in this position—viz. the insight into the inherent historicity both of the lived ethos and of ethical reflection—can easily appear a concession granted a priori. The philosophical strategies of refutation which we have presented do not indeed question, still less deny explicitly, the historicity of ideas about moral value. However, if the very question about the historical origin of our moral concepts is regarded as inappropriate, there is no possibility of seizing the chance offered by this historicity to demonstrate the universal claim to validity of moral principles and norms in a manner that is related to history.[1]

1. On this, cf. M. Heidegger, *Sein und Zeit,* Tübingen 9th edn. 1976, pp. 228f., and H.-G. Gadamer, *Wahrheit und Methode. Grundzüge einer philosophischen Hermeneutik,* Gesammelte Werke I, Tübingen 6th edn. 1990, pp. 350f.

Nor can the descriptive evidence that a large sector where moral ideas overlap is acknowledged in virtually all societies and cultures amount to a genuine proof of the transcultural claim to validity of moral norms; for such a demonstration presupposes an intercommunication between *reason* and *nature* on the one hand, and *history* and *culture* on the other. This undertaking can succeed only when the formal-abstract refutation of ethical relativism and the material-empirical demonstration of moral universals is complemented by a theory of the historical reason which, when applied in practice to the sphere of ethics, law, and politics, leads to a developmental logic of the moral consciousness in history. Such a logic will be sketched in this chapter, in the debate with the hermeneutical philosophy of history of the twentieth century and with the attempts at a renewal of natural-law thinking. Our first step is an historical inquiry into the philosophical intention which prompted the discovery of historicity in the last century. We shall then present a systematic discussion of the anthropological significance of history in dialogue with these approaches.

1. The philosophical intentions of historical thinking

There are two reasons for going further back than Karl Jaspers and Ernst Troeltsch and concentrating above all on *Wilhelm Dilthey.* First of all, Dilthey is considered the real discoverer of the historicity of the human person and of his world. His reflections on the logic of the historical and social sciences and on the foundations of an autonomous methodology appropriate to the intellectual sciences have pointed the way for all subsequent scholarship, even though Dilthey himself in his later years questioned whether it was truly possible to derive all historical knowledge from the interior experience of the individual, who experiences in his spirit the substance of what was expressed by others. This means that Dilthey's significance for the methodological self-justification of the modern anthropological sciences that investigate meaning is comparable to the significance attributed in general to Kant in the field of the natural sciences. Whereas Dilthey's work had a great impact from the very outset on the intellectual study of language and history, and has often been the object of sociological studies in recent decades, philosophical ethics has paid strikingly little attention to it until now.[2] This is all the more remarkable when we bear in

2. An exception is the valuable study by T. Herfurth, *Diltheys Schriften zur Ethik. Der*

mind that the thematic richness of the perspective in Dilthey's writings, which embrace philosophical anthropology, law and morality, and literature and pedagogy alike, could have provided a varied stimulus to the reflection on the foundations of ethics.

The second reason for taking a fresh look at Dilthey is the duality which characterizes his position on the natural law and his essays on ethics and political philosophy, a duality reflected in the divergent interpretative models found in the philosophical critique and the study of Dilthey until the present day. Some accused Dilthey, shortly after the publication of his posthumous writings, of promoting an historical skepticism by means of his anti-metaphysical attitude and his doctrine of the "worldview" with its typologies. Others celebrated him as the one who had overcome precisely this skepticism: he had challenged relativism by appealing to knowledge of the "historical creative power" of life, thereby freeing human existence to accept its historicity and to dedicate itself to the great objectifications of life.[3] A third trend, following the critical social theory of the Frankfurt School, accuses him of betraying his own claim to have brought Kant's transcendental philosophy to its completion: by making "life" the fundamental category, he has introduced a concept contrary to the reason, and the philosophy of history misuses this concept in order to justify the existing order of things. According to this interpretation, one will look in vain in Dilthey's writings for an historical-critical analysis of the bourgeois society of his period, or for the inclusion of utopian thinking in the concept of history. The heart of Dilthey's philosophical self-reflection, that is, the doctrine of the worldview, is a betrayal of the discovery of the historical relativity of all philosophical systems and claims to normative validity, because it pretends to use the postulate of an all-embracing meaning amid all historical uncertainty in order to accomplish something that the death of metaphysics has removed from the agenda.

Such an interpretation of Dilthey's thinking about history leads, how-

---

Aufbau der moralischen Welt als Resultat einer Kritik der introspektiven Vernunft (Epistemata 119), Würzburg 1992.

3. We find the first interpretation among the neo-Kantians, e.g. in H. Rickert, *Die Philosophie des Lebens. Darstellung und Kritik der philosophischen Modeströmungen unserer Zeit*, Tübingen 2nd edn. 1922, pp. 27f., 46–50; and especially in E. Husserl, "Philosophie als strenge Wissenschaft," *Logos* I (1910–1911), pp. 323–41. The opposite interpretation, in terms of the philosophy of life, began with Dilthey's editor, G. Mich (Editor's foreword, in: Dilthey, *Gesammelte Schriften (GS)*, Stuttgart and Göttingen eighth edn. 1992, V, pp. VII–CXVII). Thanks to O. F. Bollnow, this became for a long time the dominant interpretation: *Dilthey. Eine Einführung in seine Philosophie*, Stuttgart 2nd edn. 1955, pp. 11–32.

ever, to a dichotomous judgment of his work as a whole, for it requires the supposition that Dilthey ultimately lost his skeptical courage to resist the brittleness of those orderings of life that had come into existence in the course of history—in other words, he would have yielded to a contemplative reconciliation with the contradictions of the de facto course of history, a reconciliation that did not shrink even from a hidden resumption of metaphysical traditions of thought.[4] This accusation may fail to do justice to the seriousness of Dilthey's analyses in the field of the philosophy of history; like the claim laid to him by the proponents of the philosophy of life, it represents a misinterpretation of the intentions of his thinking. Nevertheless, it reflects the nature of his thinking, many-faceted and rich in motifs. As we have seen, the presence of these two poles in his thinking is disputed—yet it is precisely this duality, a passion for enlightenment curbed by historical self-doubts, that makes it once again profitable to study him, in an age in which the concepts of "history" and "historicity" threaten to become nothing more than the empty formulae of a fashionable philosophical jargon.

1.1. The historical worldview of Wilhelm Dilthey

The discovery of historicity as a fundamental category of human life is accompanied by the rejection of a priori historical constructions which seek that which is truly real not in the de facto course of history, but in a "concept" realized in this course of events, or in an "idea" which would become manifest therein. The foundations of the intellectual sciences laid down by *Wilhelm Dilthey* (1833–1911), and his entire theory of historical knowledge, reject from the outset every "empty" metaphysics of history, whether in the form of an historical plan that replaced the Christian belief in providence, or in the form of a teleology immanent in the historical process, or a general idea of progress.[5] For Dilthey, there is no onward progress of history as a continuous higher development of justice, morali-

---

4. This kind of critical interpretation, accusing Dilthey of an imperfect liberation from Idealistic metaphysics in the sphere of his critical philosophy and of a restorative tendency in the field of ethics, especially as regards the philosophical study of law and the state, replaces the interpretation drawn from the philosophy of life from the 1960's onward. Cf., e.g., H. J. Lieber, "Geschichte und Gesellschaft im Denken Diltheys," *Kölner Zeitschrift für Soziologie und Sozialpsychologie* 17 (1965), pp. 703–42, esp. 706–10, 731–39; and the cautious summary by F. Bianco, "Dilthey und das Problem des Relativismus," in: E. W. Orth (ed.), *Dilthey und die Philosophie der Gegenwart*, Freiburg and Munich 1985, pp. 211–29, esp. 223–29.

5. Cf. W. Dilthey, *Der Aufbau der geschichtlichen Welt*, *GS* VII, p. 284.

ty, and culture. One may speak of such a progress only in the sense that the "moral-political experiential sphere" of human action, which we call society or the historical world (as distinct from the external history of nature), is constructed by the intertwining of succeeding generations and the interactions of individuals who act in history. This is why the attempt to obtain a panoramic view of the totality of history can never claim more than an heuristic-problematic value: in other words, all it does is specify the problems that must be resolved by means of individual historical research.[6] But no matter from what position or at what point of time the total sum of individual historical pieces of knowledge is added up, it always leads back to an insight into the many-sidedness of life and the brittleness of forms of life in the historical world. One of the fundamental insights of Dilthey's thought is the acceptance of this knowledge; for one can act within history only when this insight is accepted. It is no longer possible to conceive of the methodological consciousness of the modern humanities and the self-exposition of the human person in today's philosophical anthropology without this insight.[7]

a. Historical knowledge and the epistemology of the humanities   Individual historical research into the "text" of life—which in Dilthey's view includes not only the historical source material in the narrower sense, but also the testimonies to the human spirit found in poetry, music, and pictorial art, as well as the achievements in law and morality, science and politics in the great cultural systems—is, however, only one aspect of historical knowledge. We can indeed never possess a complete overview of the interaction of individuals with one another and with the historical objectifications of life (as opposed to quantitative causal relationships in the realm of nature). This, however, does not mean that history decomposes into an unrelated aggregate of individual developments, events, and situations which are mutually indifferent or even hostile. The many-sidedness of life (with its inexhaustible creative force which dissolves forms that have come into being in the course of history in order to produce new forms) becomes an antagonistic contradictoriness only when the metaphysical systems each attempt to objectify one aspect of the living nexus.[8] The task of

6. Cf. Dilthey, *Über das Studium der Geschichte, der Wissenschaften vom Menschen, der Gesellschaft und des Staates, GS* V, pp. 44f., 48, 60f.

7. On this, cf. O. F. Bollnow, *Dilthey,* p. 32; H. Ineichen, "Wilhelm Dilthey," in: O. Höffe (ed.), *Klassiker der Philosophie,* II, Munich 1981, pp. 187–202, esp. 192f.

8. Cf. W. Dilthey, *Weltanschauungslehre. Abhandlungen zur Philosophie der Philosophie,*

historical knowledge is to reconstruct the "context of life and of history in which each part has a significance," thus forming a counterpoint to the anarchy of systems which remains insuperable in the field of metaphysics.[9] This means that the historical concepts of *typos* and of structure, which replace the "eternal" truths of reason of an earlier metaphysics in Dilthey's doctrine of the worldview, certainly envisage a new form of universality. Like the words of a sentence or the sequence of notes in a melody, they stand in an effective universal context which makes it possible to describe their meaning and significance, when one attempts to understand these.

Even the later Dilthey—who finally recognized the failure of his attempt to attain an immediate certainty by means of recourse to inner experience as the fundamental fact of the historical world—wishes to remain open to the possibility that "meaning and significance are generated only in the human person and in his history."[10] This means that the hermeneutical change in his later writings is not generated by a resigned compromise with the position of a relativism based on history,[11] but by a presupposition about meaning which he infers from the philosophy of history: "Like the letters of a word, life and history have a meaning."[12] The universal interest in knowledge, which can be glimpsed in such affirmations behind the scholarly will to arrive at knowledge of individual matters, leads to a latent juxtaposition in Dilthey's basic attitude to the philosophy of history; depending on the critic's standpoint, this can be described as a keener awareness of the problems involved and a positive bipolarity, or else as an inherent self-contradiction and an indecisive retreat from facing the ultimate consequences of Dilthey's own approach. It is certainly not unfair to Dilthey to interpret this lack of an ultimate synthesis in his thinking as a conscious renunciation of definitive solutions. Dilthey attempts to do justice to intellectual currents which run in opposite directions and to be fair to contradictory interests: he is indeed aware of the irreversible consequences of the historical consciousness for human existence, but at the same time he also wishes to stem the tide of profound changes and to

---

GS VIII, p. 87; and on this text, F. Bianco, "Dilthey und das Problem des Relativismus," pp. 224f.

9. Cf. W. Dilthey, *Der Aufbau der geschichtlichen Welt, GS* VII, p. 291.

10. Ibid.

11. According to T. Herfurth, the development in the later writings becomes possible when Dilthey abandons his "philosophical obsession," i.e. the supposition that the history of ideas can attain an immediate certainty: cf. Dilthey's *Schriften zur Ethik,* p. 127.

12. W. Dilthey, *Der Aufbau der geschichtlichen Welt, GS* VII, p. 291.

maintain that it is possible for philosophy to attain universally valid knowledge even in the midst of transformation.[13]

b. The meaningful coherence of the totality   The inherent complexity of historical thinking is well exemplified in the central concept of "structural context," which was initially elaborated to speak of the inner life of the individual as a teleological totality and subsequently took on a kind of bridge-function in Dilthey's system between psychology and the history of ideas. At this latter point, it was broadened to include the experience of what others had previously experienced and the understanding of larger existential units. Dilthey struggled all his life to establish the possibility of such an experiential transfer, but he did not succeed in clarifying all the problems involved.[14] His analyses always take the same starting-point: the structural context which the human sciences investigate (as distinct from the physical regularities studied by the natural sciences) is originally grasped in the individual experiences which make up our total inner experience. Although this immediate experience of the causal interconnectedness of life exists only as the individual experience of an individual form, there is more to it than this: the biographical context of the individual life in which it is experienced contains an excess of meaning which can be grasped only by the methods which the human sciences employ in order to reconstruct it. This excess of meaning denotes "a way of affirming something about the whole of reality" which subsumes under wider categories the relationships we can grasp among our inner experiences.[15] This is because the expressions of the individual's life, to the extent that it is possible to grasp their mutual relatedness and thus to see something of the teleological unity of the course of this life, are also "representations of something universal"; and it is only these "representations" that make it possible to take a retrospective overview of another individual life and experience what another person experienced.[16]

Similarly, the biographical understanding of the historical course of a person's life, which Dilthey sees as the methodological key to understanding historical contexts, points beyond the mere reconstruction of an indi-

13. Cf. F. Bianco, "Dilthey und das Problem des Relativismus," p. 215.

14. On this, cf. O. F. Bollnow, *Dilthey*, pp. 146f.; H. J. Lieber, "Geschichte und Gesellschaft im Denken Diltheys," p. 718.

15. W. Dilthey, *Der Aufbau der geschichtlichen Welt, GS* VII, p. 195; cf. also Idem, *Ideen über eine beschreibende und zergliedernde Philosophie, GS* V, pp. 174f., 179; and Idem, *Das Wesen der Philosophie, GS* V, p. 373.

16. Dilthey, *Der Aufbau der geschichtlichen Welt, GS* VII, p. 219.

vidual experiential structure; this is why the larger context of the individual's historical world is always included a priori in the context created by his existential experience. The structure of the individual experience forms part of a larger totality which can be seen as the higher structure governing the story of a human life, that is, as the biographical universe within which the inner experiences take on a unique personal character. And this biographical-psychological universe in turn forms part of a larger segment of individual existential totalities which correspond structurally to one another and hence are located within a meaningful context. This makes the idea of structure as a totality with its center within itself, characterized by the recurrence of inner experiences or historical meanings which remain constant and by their relation to their specific centers,[17] a formal connecting link which unites such disparate circumstances as psychological experiences, individual persons, communities which transcend the individual, societal institutions, and historical matters to one great causally interconnected complex. Since the same structure is found in the smaller and in the larger units, comparative historical thinking is able to make a synthesis of more and more realities, which coalesce as parts of an ultimate existential unity which can then be understood as the context of meaning of the societal-historical world.

This entire chain of reasoning presupposes the relatedness of individuals in their inner experience and their interaction with the segment of their specific historical world; this was already presupposed (in a somewhat naïve and unhistorical manner) when people spoke of the unity of human nature as a whole, and it remains exceedingly important for historical consciousness. It is this relatedness that permits one to take the step from the context of individual experience to the objective structure of a segment of the historical world, thus making it possible to attain synthesizing judgments or general affirmations about meaning in the field of historical science.[18] Naturally, Dilthey must pay a price for this possibility: he is obliged to strip the idea of historical individuality of the substance that the individual could experience—it is dematerialized to such an extent that it is equally applicable to works of art, persons acting in history, or epochs of world history. Hence, the historical world which is constituted by the intentional goals of individuals who act in history and their mutual interactions ultimately appears to be a strangely abstract causal interconnection

17. Cf. Ibid., p. 237.
18. Cf. Ibid., pp. 138 and 155; on this, O. F. Bollnow, *Dilthey,* pp. 165f.

of general forces and power relationships, in which the individuality of specific historical events and the differences between individual lives risk being eradicated.[19]

But does not this contradict the privileged role which Dilthey assigns to the *biography* of significant persons, and especially to their literary reflection on their own lives in the form of *autobiography*, when compared with all other sources of historical knowledge? As long as Dilthey kept to his plan of providing a *psychological* basis for the human sciences, this preference was certainly an obvious idea. Written biographies are an excellent aid to the study of an historical epoch, since they make it possible today to experience the life of a person who lived in the past, and this life is an exemplary reflection of the historical development of an age. However, once Dilthey turns to a *hermeneutical* understanding of history, it becomes increasingly problematical to accord a privilege to autobiographical sources, although he still maintains their importance in fragments of his later works. As Hans-Georg Gadamer has shown, this can in fact prevent the move from chronologically later psychological experience of another's experience to insight into the given context of historical meaning. This is because history transcends the existential context of the individual. This context is either experienced immediately, or else experienced at a subsequent date in the mirror provided by biographical testimony to another person's life.[20]

Historical contexts are not *per se* the object of inner experience. They are constructed from experience (whether one's own, or that of other persons), but exist in the objectifications of life which historical knowledge must endeavor to understand. This is why Dilthey's late works see the transition from a purely psychological subsequent experience to an understanding of intellectual constructs as the only path that can overcome historical skepticism.[21] The starting point in the philosophy of life is linked here with an interest in universal history which is consciously deployed as

---

19. On this, cf. P. Hünermann, *Der Durchbruch geschichtlichen Denkens im 19. Jahrhundert: Johann Gustav Droysen, Wilhelm Dilthey, Graf Paul Yorck von Wartenburg: Ihr Weg und ihre Weisung für die Theologie*, Freiburg 1967, p. 234; H. J. Lieber, "Geschichte und Gesellschaft im Denken Diltheys," p. 726. Lieber accuses Dilthey of accepting individuality only as a "singular variation of the universal structure," with the consequence that history is reduced to formal structure of spirit, which remains identical in its variations and congeals into "the continually-renewed preservation and repetition of that which is identical in the process of its variation" (p. 727).

20. Cf. H.-G. Gadamer, *Wahrheit und Methode*, pp. 226–29.

21. Cf. W. Dilthey, *Der Aufbau der geschichtlichen Welt*, *GS* VII, p. 260.

a counterweight to all the inevitable relativization which is the fruit of historical knowledge. History, we now learn, is "nothing other than life itself, grasped from the perspective of the totality of humanity—a totality which constitutes a context."[22] As the course of an individual life possesses a unifying center point, so too history as a whole generates a meaningful context: the meaning can be seen in the creative products of this life, that is, in society, the state, and the family, as well as in the cultural systems of law, morality, and science.[23]

This transition from psychological subsequent experience to a hermeneutical position of historical understanding does however presuppose a parallel between the individual existence and humanity; Dilthey postulates such a parallel, but does not genuinely demonstrate its possibility. The supposition of an analogous correspondence between the individual life history and the course of universal history is a methodological move with an importance that can scarcely be exaggerated, since it leads Dilthey to insight into the *anticipatory structure of historical understanding,* which is presupposed equally in the knowledge of meaningful contexts of individual and of universal history. This thesis, which Dilthey develops as it were *en passant,* is one of the most important services he rendered to theological ethics, and to theology as a whole; it has lost nothing of its validity today, and indeed it is only today that we can genuinely grasp its consequences, thanks to Wolfhart Pannenberg's universal-historical christology. Knowledge of life is meant to disclose the objective meaning of life; in a celebrated fragment, published only after Dilthey's death along with sketches for a continuation of the *Aufbau der geschichtlichen Welt,* he writes as follows about the relationship between the parts and the whole in this knowledge of life:

This relationship never exists in a completed form—one would have to wait for the end of life, since it would be impossible before the hour of death to have an overview of the totality which allows one to determine the relation between its parts. One would have to wait for the end of history, for only then would one possess all the material necessary for a definition of its meaning. On the other hand, we have access to the totality only because the parts allow us to understand it.[24]

The reference to the significance of death is made more specific, so that the parallel between the course of the individual's life and the universal

22. Ibid., p. 256.
23. On this, cf. W. Dilthey, *Das Wesen der Philosophie, GS* V, p. 409.
24. W. Dilthey, *Der Aufbau der geschichtlichen Welt, GS* VII, p. 233; cf. also pp. 237, 267.

historical context can be understood more exactly. Death is not only the temporal end of the trajectory of the individual existence; it is also the conclusion of the individual life history, the final synthesizing act which bestows totality, meaning, and coherence on his life. When this idea is transposed to the historical course of "humanity" as a total subject, or to universal history as a whole, it suggests an important difference: in the case of the death of the individual, the real end point allows us to grasp the total meaningful coherence of his history. In the case of universal history, however, this is possible only by anticipating its metahistorical end point. Thus the *retrospective* panorama of past history changes into an all-embracing *anticipation*—otherwise, it is not possible to understand the meaning of universal history.

It is not possible to test empirically the application to universal history of the proposition that each part has significance for the totality and expresses something of this totality, just as it derives its own meaning precisely from this totality, since we never have access to the full significance of the totality. This means that Dilthey's reflections on the hermeneutics of history in his later writings have a problematical affinity to the historical constructions of the speculative Idealism about which he himself wrote.[25] This is, of course, not a decisive point when we inquire into the philosophical intention which generates his reflections on the historicity of the modern world. The transition from a psychological subsequent experience to a hermeneutical standpoint in history may remain somewhat unclear, but these very difficulties show how intensely Dilthey struggled in his later works to establish the possibility of "absolute" knowledge and to understand objective historical contexts of meaning.

c. Meaning, purpose, and value Of all the areas studied by the human sciences, it is above all the sphere of law, morality, and ethics which makes it clear that the historical self-knowledge of the human person, which leads him from one historically relative point to the next, is also the path which confronts him with the question about the absolute. In order to demonstrate the coherence of the historical world, which reveals itself in the mutual dependence of partial historical knowledge and a necessary anticipation of the meaning of the totality, Dilthey has recourse to fundamental concepts of classical ethics such as the *ultimate end*, the *highest good*, and a *supreme value*. He reinterprets these concepts by relating them

25. On this, cf. H.-G. Gadamer, *Wahrheit und Methode*, pp. 228–34.

to the structural-psychological analysis of inner experience, which remains for him the starting point of all historical knowledge even after he makes the transition to a hermeneutical understanding of history. Accordingly, meaning, purpose, and value are not data or characteristics inhering in objects independently of the subjective experience of active individuals; rather, they are the way in which the inner experience of active individuals is rendered visible in its temporal extension.[26] *Meaning* discloses retrospectively the unity of the course of a life, when the individual experiences, which followed one another in the succession of time, take on their own inherent connectedness. The category of *value* describes the contemporary experiences of value, that is, the reality of the historical world, which is experienced only in the present moment as positive or negative. Finally, *purpose* (or ideal) indicates how the human person, acting on the basis of these experiences of value, reaches out towards his own future.[27] Thus, these three categories encompass the fundamental temporal modes of life, as regards the inner experience and the external action of the human person. The decisive point here is that Dilthey fundamentally insists on the priority of *meaning*, since it is only in recollection that the mere disparate juxtaposition of our experiences comes together to form one unified course of life. On the other hand, he also emphasizes that none of these categories— meaning (past), value (present), or purpose (future)—can be subordinated to the others, since "each of them, from its own particular perspective, makes it possible to understand the totality of life."[28]

The structural similarity between the existence of the individual and history as a whole allows Dilthey to employ these basic historical concepts not only to reconstruct the unity of the course of history, but also to understand this historical context of meaning as the historical-philosophical foundation of an ethical system. Since they presuppose the mutual acknowledgement of these experiences, which initially exist as separate juxta-

26. Cf. W. Dilthey, *Der Aufbau der geschichtlichen Welt, GS* VII, p. 242; on this, T. Herfurth, *Diltheys Schriften zur Ethik,* pp. 198f.

27. Cf. W. Dilthey, *Der Aufbau der geschichtlichen Welt, GS* VII, p. 201.

28. Ibid., pp. 201f., cf. also pp. 233–36. The primacy of meaning and recollection, which Dilthey saw as the "most basic category of historical thinking" (p. 202), is a matter of dispute among scholars. While O. F. Bollnow (building on a suggestion by G. Mich) argues that Dilthey in his later writings suppresses the original priority of recollection and places a stronger emphasis on the dynamic aspect of the creative construction of unity (cf. Dilthey, *Der Aufbau der geschichtlichen Welt,* 127–32), H. J. Lieber accuses him of a "retrospective tranquillization of historical thinking" ("Geschichte und Gesellschaft im Denken Diltheys," p. 732).

posed elements, these individual experiences of value and purpose coalesce
to form a "region of values"[29] in which a "structural connectedness of feelings about value" emerges; this in turn leads to a "kind of objective universal system of value."[30] Just as the investigation of individual facts leads
historical knowledge to insight into a universal totality of meaning and
a "teleological interconnectedness of the world," so practical thinking's
analysis of the actions and purposes posited by our will ceases only when it
reaches a supreme value, a supreme good, or a supreme rule of conduct.
Clearly, Dilthey presupposes here that when individuals empathize with
others' experiences and feelings about value, their freely posited purposes
will lead ultimately to the acknowledgement of an objective hierarchy of
values—a hierarchy based on the subjective feeling of mutual respect.
Dilthey takes a significant step beyond Kant when he deduces the moral
feeling of respect, not only from the rational nature of the human person
in general, but also from a shared structure of the feelings experienced. He
does not merely postulate the necessity of respect for every other rational
being; he is also able to explain how the fundamental moral feeling of respect is generated by the feelings one experiences and by empathy with the
feelings of others. The assumption that the classical concept of a teleological understanding of behavior, along with its axiological presuppositions,
can be harmonized with the modern idea of autonomous esteem and purpose in the framework of universal-historical thinking, leads decisively beyond Kant's formalism.[31]

   d. The person's own value and the acknowledgement of the other   Dilthey
identifies the supreme value which provides the criterion for the examination of all historical realities (which *per se* are relative) as the value proper
to the *individual* or *person*.[32] Although he is aware how much his own biography owes to German culture, and his analysis is initially limited to the
sphere of human history in Europe, Dilthey regards the doctrine of the
value of individuality and of personal existence (two concepts which he
employs as synonyms) as a "social and ethical truth which must never be
lost to sight."[33] This fundamental ethical truth is the basis of all moral convictions, all legal norms, and all pedagogical models; it is in a sense the

29. W. Dilthey, *Das Wesen der Philosophie, GS* V, pp. 400f.
30. W. Dilthey, *Der Aufbau der geschichtlichen Welt, GS* VII, p. 60.
31. On this, cf. T. Herfurth, *Diltheys Schriften zur Ethik*, pp. 170, 193–95.
32. W. Dilthey, *Der Aufbau der geschichtlichen Welt, GS* VII, pp. 242, 256–58.
33. W. Dilthey, *Ideen über eine beschreibende und zergliedernde Psychologie, GS* V, p. 228.

quintessence of the historical development to which such diverse philosophical movements as classical Greek antiquity, Christianity with its
teaching about the human person as God's image, the philosophical skepticism of the modern period, and the transcendental philosophy of the European Enlightenment have made their contributions. The systems of the
various worldviews offer contradictory justifications for their positions,
but these are merely "unprovable metaphysical interpretations of the ethical fact";[34] no matter what position one takes, there is no alternative in
practice to the acknowledgement of the person's own proper value. The
idea of a contractual state of law corresponds to this supreme moral insight
in the field of social ethics; this idea in its turn presupposes a kind of fundamental norm, that is, the obligation to honor legal obligations and to
carry out contracts.

In his lectures on ethics, Dilthey formulated more clearly the mutuality
of this common acknowledgement, from which the validity of all moral
norms derives. In his view, the highest moral commandment, or the fundamental rule of ethical conduct, can be elaborated in two directions, that
of faithfulness to one's own self and that of respect for the value proper to
others; from the perspective of individual ethics, faithfulness to one's own
self has the priority, while acknowledgement of others has the priority
from the perspective of social ethics:

If one considers the individual empirically, the faithfulness of the person to his or
her own self—which is identical with the selfhood or identity—constitutes the
fulfillment of the obligation, when another person or group of persons, likewise
equipped with a value of their own and capable of faithfulness to their own selves,
enters a relationship with this individual. Thus there emerges a consciousness of
unity, which has its basis in fidelity to one's own self and in respect for the value
proper to the other person.[35]

Respect for one's own personal value thus generates not only the task of
moral self-education and formation of one's own character, but also the
obligation to acknowledge others. In terms of social ethics, this basic
moral norm becomes concrete in the historical validity of specific norms of
societal life which correspond to the various stages of development of the
historical-social reason. Dilthey does not provide an exhaustive list of such
social-ethical norms, but the manuscript of his lectures readily suggests

34. Ibid.
35. W. Dilthey, *System der Ethik, GS* X, p. 102; cf. also Idem, *Der Aufbau der
geschichtlichen Welt, GS* VII, p. 262.

what such a list would have to include. According to the summary by Thomas Herfurth, Dilthey basically adopts here the ideas of his own period about legal ethics and politics, above all the rights to work, to social justice, to free development of one's personality, to private property, to possession of the means of production and to inheritance, to form free associations of persons, and to marry freely and establish a family.[36] While such a list makes it clear that Dilthey did not belong to the avant-garde of his period, it certainly demonstrates his openness to the concerns of social reformers during the reign of Wilhelm II, thus qualifying the accusation that he was a proponent of a backward-looking historical utopia in the field of social politics.

Ultimately, Dilthey was convinced that he had brought Kant's transcendental philosophy to its completion, as far as its practical application was concerned. He believed that he had been able to overcome its two great weaknesses and to free the categorical imperative from its one-sided link to the ideal rational nature of the human person. This decisive step beyond Kant made it possible in Dilthey's eyes to anchor the fundamental rule of ethical conduct *psychologically* in a theory about the interior life of feelings, and to link it in terms of the *philosophy of history* with a comprehensive scheme of the development of the historical-social reason:

One may develop as follows the insight attained by Kant when he spoke of the categorical imperative: there exists only one absolutely firm principle in the ethical world, viz. that the mutual union of wills in an explicit contract, or in the tacit acceptance of the fact of reciprocity, possesses absolute validity in relation to every consciousness. This is why honesty, uprightness, fidelity, and truthfulness form the stable structure which supports the moral world. All the ends and all the rules of life—even kindness and the striving for perfection—are subordinate to this structure. There is a hierarchy of obligation here: one must descend to kindness and the gift of oneself to others, and from there one must descend yet again to the concern for one's own perfection.[37]

Thus, Dilthey's achievement in the field of ethics consists not only in his recognition of the significance of historicity for the validity of moral and legal norms; this had already been realized in the historical legal school. Although he vacillates between a psychological basis and a hermeneutical understanding of history, and tends to return without sufficient reflection to problems which had been posed by the philosophy of life and had already

36. W. Dilthey, *System der Ethik, GS* X, pp. 89f.; on this, cf. T. Herfurth, *Diltheys Schriften zur Ethik,* pp. 167f.
37. W. Dilthey, *Das Wesen der Philosophie, GS* V, pp. 410f.

found a solution, he succeeded in achieving a reconciliation of reason and history which was not based on a priori constructions but on the recognition of a demand which genuinely emerges in the course of history.

For Dilthey, the historical world is the product of a liberation from the fetters of a metaphysical order of things, and is thus indebted to a fundamental relativization of the modern worldview, but he emphasizes, vis-à-vis historicism, that this process of emancipation itself aims at establishing a new form of the validity of moral values and non-arbitrary norms *within* history; only the recognition of these values and norms will allow the historical consciousness to develop.[38] What counts as ethics, customs, and the established ethos in the various epochs of cultural history varies from one historical unit to the next; nevertheless, it is possible for historical knowledge to work through the field of these relative forms and to arrive at a "single ideal system" of ethical conduct: the ways in which morality is understood by the different peoples are merely historical "modifications" of this single system.[39] When historical investigation of the individual cultural systems compares their morality, law, and ethical understanding, it is forced to ask whether they might possess some kind of historically-related objectivity, despite the relativity of their specific forms. Here, Dilthey has recourse to the fundamental concepts of the ethical tradition (supreme value, supreme good, supreme purpose) in order to conceive of a relationship between the finite and the absolute which would be available at every standpoint within history, and thus would be immanent to history. "Our task is to show how [the relative concepts of value in the various periods of history] have broadened to become something absolute"—this is how he summarizes the goal of all historical knowledge, near the end of his life.[40]

Knowledge of the absolutely valid ethical values and norms proves thus immanent to historical consciousness. Acknowledgement of this knowledge indicates that there are, so to speak, places where one may pierce the barrier to the absolute, places where the meaningful connectedness of the historical world can be perceived. When it is freed from the hierarchical interconnections which establish order in a metaphysical worldview, the acknowledgement of the dignity and the value in "every individual, when considered as a human person" remains a criterion for historical conscious-

38. Cf. W. Dilthey, *Der Aufbau der geschichtlichen Welt, GS* VII, p. 262: "These truths possess universal validity, because they make a regulation possible at every point in the historical world." Cf. also pp. 256f.
39. W. Dilthey, *Einleitung in die Geistewissenschaften, GS* I, p. 61.
40. W. Dilthey, *Der Aufbau der geschichtlichen Welt, GS* VII, p. 290.

ness and a guarantee of objectivity in relation to history.[41] When the world is historicized, ethics does not lose its foundations; rather, Dilthey takes up the fundamental ethical concepts of the tradition, interpreting these as regulative ideas which allow the universal-historical context to become visible and which make it possible once again to conceive of the unity of history.

1.2. Historical consciousness and cultural ethics in Ernst Troeltsch

The greatest contribution in the twentieth century to the philosophical illumination of our historical consciousness was made by the penetrating questions and inexorable analyses of the Protestant theologian, philosopher of religion, church historian, and social ethicist Ernst Troeltsch (1865–1923). These have traditionally been separate academic disciplines; their combination here indicates the wide-ranging, interdisciplinary scholarly interests that prompted Troeltsch's voluminous writings on ethics and the philosophy of culture. His most important book is the great work *Die Soziallehren der christlichen Kirchen und Gruppen* (1912). Its typological analysis of Christian doctrines of the natural law, showing how these dovetail with the great historical social forms of Christianity, indicated the path that was to be taken by research in cultural sociology and the religious sciences; but we already find a chapter on "the concept of historical relativity and its relation to the establishing of norms" in his programmatic work on the philosophy of religion, *Die Absolutheit des Christentums* (1902), in which he first set out his thesis about the supreme validity of Christianity in history. In the space of a few pages, Troeltsch formulates the basic thesis of the philosophy of history which all his later work seeks to maintain in the field of social and cultural sciences, that is, that the questions generated by historical thinking are not characterized by "the either/or of relativism and absolutism," but by "the mixture of these two. The problem of history is how to explain the emergence, from a relative starting point, of tendencies that develop in the direction of absolute ends."[42] In the short work

---

41. Ibid., p. 262.
42. E. Troeltsch, *Die Absolutheit des Christentums und die Religionsgeschichte,* Tübingen 3rd edn. 1929, p. 47. On the place of ethics in Troeltsch's basic religious-philosophical concept, cf. G. Becker, *Neuzeitliche Subjektivität und Religiosität. Die religionsphilosophische Bedeutung von Heraufkunft und Wesen der Neuzeit im Denken von Ernst Troeltsch,* Regensburg 1982, pp. 331–44; G. Droesser, *Freiheitspraxis im Prozeß. Zur geschichtsanthropologischen Grundlegung einer Theologie des Ethischen,* Frankfurt 1992.

Der Historismus und seine Überwindung (1922), published by his friend
Friedrich von Hügel shortly before his death, Troeltsch gives a retrospective account of the development of his own thought and claims that the
"idea of an abiding and definitive system of values" is the heart of his
scholarly confrontation with the historical science of the nineteenth century and the aprioristic doctrine of values of the twentieth century.[43]

   a. Between historicism and value ethics   The struggle with historical relativity, to which his entire life's work as a Christian theologian and philosopher of culture was dedicated, led Troeltsch between these two philosophical antipodes in such a way that he never genuinely made contact with
either of the two sides. Despite his disinclination to accept Scheler's value
ethics and his reservations vis-à-vis Neo-Kantianism's transcendental logic
with its new justification of a system of absolute values,[44] his own abiding
philosophical aim is to overcome historicism. He believes that this is possible only on the basis of the manifold articulations of historical cultural
phenomena, although Troeltsch was more skeptical of the chances of success at the end of his life than at the beginning of his academic career. At
any rate, Troeltsch is certain that one cannot do justice to the problems
caused by the radical historicization of modern culture, as long as one refuses to accept this complexity of the historical consciousness. Attempts to
reverse the autonomy of history by means of an aprioristic construction
lead nowhere. Nevertheless, Troeltsch insists throughout his work—from
the early work on religion to his final lectures in London—that moral values have their own origin, which cannot be derived from the psychological-
historical process by which they come into existence. On this issue, which
determines the starting point for ethical questioning, he completely adopts
the aprioristic position of Kant and of his contemporary Neo-Kantians: "It
is not the manner of their genesis, but the fact of the substantial contents
of the logical links, that is decisive."[45] Once the idea of the personality as
the highest ethical end has emerged from all its natural and psychological
roots, it develops autonomously, following its own epistemological regularities, irrespective of *when, where,* and *how* this breakthrough first occurred.
   Troeltsch moves beyond this insight into the formal a priori of the prac-

43. E. Troeltsch, *Der Historismus und seine Überwindung,* Berlin 1924, p. 3.
44. Cf. E. Troeltsch, *Der Historismus und seine Probleme,* I: *Das logische Problem der
Geschichtsphilosophie,* Gesammelte Schriften III, Tübingen 1922 (reprint Aalen 1961), pp.
605–9.
45. E. Troeltsch, *Der Historismus und seine Überwindung,* p. 4; cf. also pp. 15f.

tical reason as the initial point of departure for ethics: he clearly rejects the theological Kantianism of Wilhelm Herrmann when he emphasizes that neither philosophical nor theological ethics may be understood as a "doctrine about the subjective determinations of the acting will."[46] Rather, ethics must go beyond concentration on the formal interior dispositions of the individual to include a "doctrine about the ultimate ends and purposes of human existence"—and this doctrine must be related to history.[47] The primary characteristic of ethical behavior in Troeltsch's eyes is that it is understood as the realization of *purposes* and *goods*. Accordingly, it cannot be simply independent (as the Neo-Kantianist a priori wrongly presupposed) of the historical process, whereby values are grasped and these purposes and ends are recognized. It is indeed true that the unity of ethics can be discerned only in "the purely formal concept of an absolute, necessary purpose which is valuable *per se*," not in the historical process whereby values are formed; nevertheless, one cannot dispense with this process if one wishes to come to know the specific ethical contents and evaluations.[48] Although history is not an instrument for the straightforward realization of values and norms, it is "the humus from which they grow."[49] He makes the same point even more clearly when he writes: "History does not exclude norms. Its true work is the production of norms and the struggle to make a synthesis of these norms."[50] But the very fact of this unending historical conflict discloses a deeper convergence towards a common unity. The process whereby values are posited in history is conceivable only because "values with a common fundamental direction and the capacity of mutual confrontation emerge in these individual constructions. In this confrontation, these values generate an ultimate decision based on inherent truth and necessity."[51]

Behind the assumption that the historical process of the formation of values also provides a criterion for the evaluation of the individual norms in this process lies the principle—already encountered in Dilthey—of the subsequent experience of other persons' feelings, a principle which Troeltsch

46. E. Troeltsch, *Grundprobleme der Ethik, GS* II: *Zur religiösen Lage, Religionsphilosophie und Ethik,* Tübingen 2nd edn. 1922 (reprint Aalen 1962), pp. 564, 570f. On the critique of W. Herrmann's ethical conception, cf. B. A. Gayhart, *The Ethics of Ernst Troeltsch: A Commitment to Relevancy* (Toronto Studies in Theology 53), Lewiston 1990, pp. 125–34.
47. E. Troeltsch, *Grundprobleme der Ethik, GS* II, p. 552.
48. Ibid., p. 616.
49. E. Troeltsch, *Die Absolutheit des Christentums,* p. 64.
50. Ibid., p. 47.
51. Ibid., pp. 46f.

extends to the various human systems of values. We are able to experience other persons' inner states and understand what they mean only because of an original common ground which enables us—or, more precisely, compels us—to compare other persons' values and value systems with our own. The postulate of a unity of ethical consciousness underlying the historical process of differentiation does however indicate an unclarified presupposition which generates an ambiguity in Troeltsch's thinking. When he wishes to identify the ultimate reason for the unity of this historical process, he appeals to an original common ground and similarity of the human spirit, seeing here the reason for the autonomous validity of moral purposes and objective goods vis-à-vis historically relative value systems. This proximity to a formal apriorism in ethics tends however to obscure the real distance from Kant's ethics which results when Troeltsch derives moral action from the autonomous intellectual ends and purposes of human existence. Although he occasionally calls his own historically-related cultural ethics the continuation of Kant's ethics, and says that his intention is to complement Kant's ethics of subjective ends by means of an objective ethics of goods in Schleiermacher's sense, he seems insufficiently aware of the significance of his own approach and of the distance from Kant to which this necessarily leads.[52]

b. The ultimate eschatological goal of history Troeltsch wished to show that all intellectual purposes and the ultimate ends posited by moral action are derived from an original unity of the human spirit; but even as early as *Die Absolutheit des Christentums,* he found total consistency impossible in this area, since this intention conflicted with the religious-philosophical and theological intention of conceiving of an increasing convergence on the part of humanity's moral convictions (which would, however, finally converge only at a point beyond history). To the eye of an unprejudiced historian, the multiplicity of moral value systems in the course of human history up to now does not in the least seem to be an "unlimited mob . . . of conflicting values," still less a "dense chaos."[53] On the contrary, it is astonishing to see how few are the fundamental ethical and religious ideas

---

52. This is the assessment of W. Pannenberg, "Die Begründung der Ethik bei Ernst Troeltsch," in Idem, *Ethik und Ekklesiologie: Gesammelte Aufsätze,* Göttingen 1977, pp. 70–96, at pp. 73f.: "The consequence of this lack of clarity was that Troeltsch believed his own teleological basis for ethics, with its emphasis on the objective societal goals alongside the subjective goals of the ethics of personality, to be merely an 'extension' of Kantian ethics. In reality, what we have here is a completely different approach."

53. E. Troeltsch, *Die Absolutheit des Christentums,* p. 55.

that have nourished human life up to the present day; and this empirical fact forces an initial *quantitative* limitation of historical relativism. In addition, the comparison between the various values and ideal conceptions discloses a common *qualitative* criterion of evaluation which can be recognized as valid from every single position, even if the various approach-roads to this criterion remain individually distinct. This means that the historical mode of thinking does not forbid the "mutual comparison of the great values and substance of the life of the mind, evaluating them by means of a criterion, i.e., subordinating them to the idea of a common goal."[54] Troeltsch no longer sees this common goal as something based in the original unity of the human spirit, but interprets it "as the ultimate end which is now in the process of realization"[55] and is not exhaustively realized in any of its individually different approximative forms.

Troeltsch agrees with Schleiermacher in employing the idea of an ultimate end to establish a teleological ethics, but he parts company with Schleiermacher when he interprets it eschatologically. This no longer represents a real ultimate ethical end for humanity, but functions only as a preliminary, innerworldly substitute for a common, metahistorical end. Obviously, the idea of the kingdom of God—understood along the lines of contemporary exegetes (above all J. Weiss) as an eschatological gift belonging purely to the realm beyond history—lies behind this theological employment of the fundamental ethical cipher of a supreme purpose. More significantly, however, Troeltsch follows the school of "consistent eschatology" in seeing the kingdom of God as something radically above this world and beyond time, and he applies these attributes to the idea of an ultimate ethical end. The convergence of the basic trajectories in the historical process towards a "universally valid, normative end which indicates the direction that everything is to take" points beyond all the preliminary common characteristics and constructions of unity to an absolute end which (according to Troeltsch) can lie only beyond history.[56] The price he pays for this assumption is that the complementary idea—that is, that the multiplicity of individual definitions of purpose finds a synthesis in the unity of the human spirit—no longer has any function, and there is no resolution of the tension between present and past, that is, between the eschatological end and the shared past.[57] By declaring the afterlife to be the

54. Ibid., p. 52.
55. Ibid., p. 56.
56. Ibid.
57. Cf. W. Pannenberg, "Die Begründung der Ethik bei Ernst Troeltsch," p. 89.

eschatological "location" of a growing convergence of all definitions of moral value, he is able to hold together both the universal validity of the moral ends of humanity and the individually various and historically relative forms in which these ends have been realized. This means that he has transported into the future the idea of a universal ethical a priori, which was his starting point. This idea no longer leads to the concept of a "de facto universal which is completely present in its human realization," but is transformed into the idea of "an end which gives direction to everything; in history, the orientation is not always uniformly strong and clear, but this end always points the way ahead."[58]

Troeltsch began with the idea of an original unity of the human spirit, but he later abandoned this concept in order to make space for the cultural-historical investigation of the various value systems which had developed in the course of history. Clearly, he assumed that only an end which lay ahead of the historical process could "be common, yet at the same time be truly comprehensible only in the mode of individual history."[59] He provided no substantial justification of this assumption, which is indeed not immediately obvious—since even a unity which is already realized, or an a priori shared spirit, must be appropriated and realized by each specific individual. However, the spectrum within which the play of historical forms can unfold is incomparably wider when it is only the future that can set limits to its open possibilities.

 c. The idea of personality, the ethics of culture, and the ideal of rational humaneness Troeltsch broadly follows Dilthey's model in the formal basic structure of ethics and its division into individual and social ethics, agreeing with him in seeing the *biographical* unity of a life as symbolizing the *moral* unity of the overarching societal forms. It follows that the highest end of the personality, in which the unity of action is displayed, is realized in two directions. On the one hand, all the ethical demands which concern "the behavior of the subject in relation to himself and to all other subjects," that is, ethics in the intimate interpersonal sphere, are derived from the a priori valid idea of the personality;[60] on the other hand, this supreme idea also entails the requirement that one "esteem and aim at objective values of the family, the state, society, science, art, and religion."[61] These

58. E. Troeltsch, *Die Absolutheit des Christentums,* p. 57.

59. Ibid.

60. E. Troeltsch, *Grundprobleme der Ethik, GS* II, p. 618; cf. Idem, *Der Historismus und seine Überwindung,* p. 10.

61. E. Troeltsch, *Grundprobleme der Ethik,* p. 618.

material and cultural values are "obligatory values" and "objective ends," which Troeltsch "understands as substantial values possessing a universal validity which transcends all that is arbitrary and individual."[62] Unlike the commandments of formal personal morality, these cannot be developed from the a priori end of reason, but must always be first "inferred empirically from history" and only at a secondary stage be reduced to a classifying system. In agreement with the highest end of morality, the criterion of this system is "the contribution it makes to forming the personality in profundity and strength."[63]

There always exists an analogy between the subjective ends posited in individual ethics (which Troeltsch also calls "morality" in the narrower sense of the word) and the objective ends posited in social and cultural ethics (which he correspondingly calls "ethics" in the broader sense). The main reason for this analogy is that dedication to the objective material world of goods also helps perfect the individual, and thus is subordinate to the aprioristic idea of the personality.[64] However, the two main areas of ethics point in different directions, since subjective personal morality "thanks to its formal character, leads out of history into that which is atemporally valid," whereas the objective ethics of goods "locates us directly in history and development."[65]

d. The historical logic of development of the moral consciousness   This means that the object of ethical investigation is not individual morality in the immediate interpersonal sphere; according to Troeltsch, the demands of this kind of morality are subject only to "relatively small historical variations."[66] Historical thinking is confronted with incomparably harder problems when it wishes to understand the major constructions of ethical

62. E. Troeltsch, *Der Historismus und seine Überwindung*, p. 22.

63. E. Troeltsch, *Grundprobleme der Ethik*, p. 622.

64. Cf. Ibid., p. 617: The highest ethical goal "is nothing other than the goal of formation of the personality, since 'personality' means the kernel of a higher inner life which is the antithesis of the mere life of the soul, individuality and subjectivity, and is superior to these. This kernel emerges from subordination to absolutely necessary goals. This entails the development of the individual and societal aspects of this goal: the former is the elaboration of the value of one's own personality, while the societal aspect is the mutual acknowledgement and support of the value of the personality of others. It is obvious here that individual and social morality presuppose and determine one another."

65. E. Troeltsch, *Der Historismus und seine Überwindung*, p. 30.

66. E. Troeltsch, *Grundprobleme der Ethik*, p. 623. Cf. also ibid.: "Since all that is involved here is the universal validity and necessity of the ethical goal and these very general fundamental conditions for the formation of the personality, the ethical is by its very nature basically ahistorical; its fundamental traits are identical everywhere."

thinking and the logic of its development in each epoch in the various fields of the super-individual world of goods (family, state, production fellowship, science, art, religion, etc.). Troeltsch has a wider perspective than Dilthey here, since he goes beyond the parameters of European history to take in the entire history of humanity; for this reason, the process of historical understanding is even more complex in his eyes than it was for Dilthey. For Troeltsch, the second pole of ethics, antithetical to the formation of the individual character, is no longer limited to the construction of a national ethics embracing the state and society, or a European ethics of science and culture; rather, the complement to personal morality demands the elaboration of a collective ideal of rational humaneness for all human beings, an ideal that is (so to speak) a super-individual personal value under which the historically relative value systems of cultural history can be subsumed. Troeltsch holds that the enigmatic idea of a collective ideal of the personality supplies the link whereby the individual social groups form the unity of their own nation and the nations form the moral unity of humankind. This extension of the idea of personality allows him to develop the moral concept or ideal of humanity, which is quite different from the anthropological or geographical concept of "the inhabitants of our earth" or the biological category of "the supposed blood relationship of all those creatures that bear a human face."[67] In keeping with the postulate of a supreme ultimate end of morality, this supreme ideal of humaneness binds together all the specific ethical ideals, from love of one's own neighbor to the acknowledgement of human rights and of international justice in dealings between states.

Once the breakthrough to this highest stage of the development of moral consciousness has taken place at some point, it remains valid for all time, and the highest end of the ethical world issues its demands of its own accord, without needing renewed confirmation or a continuous ratification from empirical human beings which would make these demands valid. As he struggled to solve the problems of historicism, Troeltsch saw with increasing clarity that the logic of this independent validity is the weakness of the idea of a supreme ethical world-end in terms of the philosophy of history: for the historical realization of the idea of humaneness in the individual sectors of the super-individual material world does not occur by means of a continuous process of formation which slowly canalizes the stream of life in history. Rather, one is left with the insight that the re-

67. E. Troeltsch, *Der Historismus und seine Überwindung*, pp. 13f.

alization of the ethical end in history can take place only along the difficult path of struggle and compromise, and that each age must set out on this path anew.[68] The inevitable necessity of a compromise between the highest rational end and the specific historical-social developmental conditions entails that the concrete forms of social and cultural ethics never possess a validity beyond their own epoch—for otherwise, they would lose their ethical obligation in their own historical period.

The rejection of all aprioristic historical constructions compels one to make a sharp conceptual distinction in the sphere of ethics between the formal morality of the conscience, based exclusively on the acknowledgement of the supreme ideal of the personality, and the many various ethical cultural values which the historical meanderings of the stream of life has brought forth. Troeltsch looks for connecting lines back from the formal morality of the conscience, with its claim to supratemporal validity, to the great variety of cultural spheres of peoples and states, of law, and of science; such connecting lines would guide the individual constructions of the stream of life in history in a common direction. It proves impossible to elaborate a unified substantial ethics of culture which would be capable of describing the practical elaboration of the individual sectors of social, scientific, and religious life under the claim made by the idea of the absolute personality. The formal morality of the conscience and the specific substantial cultural ethics may indeed have common roots in the ethical consciousness, but it is impossible to understand their interconnection as a systematic ethical science that would be valid for all times. "All these attempts to deduce a system of values, whether from the essence of the reason or from society, from the world-process or from the religious end, prove incapable of dealing with the variety and power—not to mention the tensions and intersections—of cultural values in real life."[69]

e. The concept of cultural circles Troeltsch discerns a way out of this dilemma when he endeavors, from his own historical standpoint, to make a cultural synthesis of the confusing variety that has emerged in the course of history. Once one abandons the attempt to understand foreign historical realities of the past on the basis of an overarching unity of meaning which would link those epochs to one's own history, a skeptical philosophy of culture is able to make a synthesis, at least of the multiplicity of historical life *within* one cultural circle. The historical individuality of each cul-

68. Cf. Ibid., pp. 18f.
69. Ibid., p. 36.

tural circle discloses how a "special variety of the reason has come into existence here, in this place,"[70] and challenges the ethical consciousness to purify this, freeing it from historical ballast and concentrating it on its own center. The individual cultural circles cannot be classified in terms of one unified tendency or one single pattern of historical progress, and this means that one cannot evaluate them by means of some criterion that would exist antecedent to their elaboration in history. Hans Georg Drescher, Troeltsch's biographer, is, however, right to say that these cultural circles are not to be thought of as closed monads without any "windows."[71] Since the breakthrough to the perennially valid values of the morality of the individual conscience can take place in any cultural circle, the various paths of the reason in history—despite the genuine contradictions in which their historical expressions get entangled—do possess something like a common point of convergence. Troeltsch's researches in the philosophy of history and cultural anthropology end by confirming the main thesis of his philosophy of religion, which transposes into the sphere beyond history the common end of the whole development that makes it possible to conceive of a unity of humankind in the truth. "The absolute, immutable value, which is not conditioned by anything that lies within time, is not found within history, but in the sphere beyond history which is accessible only to presentiment and to faith."[72]

Nevertheless, the concept of "cultural circles" is more than merely the expression of a resignation on the part of the philosopher of history: it occupies an intermediate postion between the acknowledgement of historical individuality and the postulate of transhistorical meaning. It denotes "an individual reality with a universal tendency,"[73] although such realities cannot direct the course of history towards a unified center which would take on historical form in human conduct. Hence, the concept of cultural circles signals the end of the initial attempt to overcome historicism by means of the philosophy of history. At the same time, it shows that Troeltsch wants to retain a hope in history—albeit a hope that is buffeted and broken—even as he rejects claims to ultimate absoluteness; at the end

---

70. Ibid., pp. 39f.

71. On this, cf. H. G. Drescher, *Ernst Troeltsch: Leben und Werk*, Göttingen 1991, pp. 508f. The idea of "cultural circles" can also be understood on the basis of Dilthey's interpretation of the "epochs" which represent mutually-open historical parameters of meaning, but cannot be fitted into any overarching pattern of development. On this, cf. P. Hünermann, *Der Durchbruch geschichtlichen Denkens im 19. Jahrhundert*, p. 255.

72. E. Troeltsch, *Die Absolutheit des Christentums*, p. 47.

73. H. G. Drescher, *Ernst Troeltsch*, p. 508.

of his life, he questioned anew the idea that Christianity possessed the supreme validity in history.

1.3. Historicity and the interpretation of existence in Karl Jaspers

The preceding sections have set out the various stages in the debate about ethical relativism among philosophers and cultural anthropologists since the 1930's. This discussion attracted little attention outside the spheres of moral philosophy and the empirical study of culture, but the topic of historicity and of the historical mutation of ethical norms became once more the focus of philosophical inquiry after the Second World War. The philosophy of existence posed the question of the historical validity of moral values and norms on the basis of the great existential questions of human existence, rather than on the basis of the historical individuality of specific cultural circles. We shall now discuss this fundamental ethical problem in the light of the philosophical interpretation of existence offered by *Karl Jaspers* (1883–1969), who includes both the universal norms of morality and the historical powers of the state, of religion, and of culture among the "objective forms" in which the individual experiences the claim an obligation makes on him. "The one true ethical behavior, which is acknowledged in its *universal* rules by *all* human persons, remains *objective:* you shall not lie, kill, steal, commit adultery, etc. These propositions are extrinsically comprehensible. They do not vary in an arbitrary manner in the course of history; within the limitations of their own modifications, they give valid expression to something universally human."[74] The fact that moral norms are often denied, or not acknowledged equally in every place, does not refute their universal validity. The *objective* obligation which they express is not derived from the phenomenon of universal historical diffusion, but from an ideal universality of Being which finds historical expression in these supra-individual powers.

a. Objective and existential obligation   Existing ethical laws for conduct in the world remain, however one-sided and abstract, in their pure objectivity, since the fact that something is universal and possesses its general validity does not suffice to make it absolutely true.[75] The individual encounters the absoluteness of an *existential* obligation only in the challenge

74. K. Jaspers, *Philosophie* II: *Existenzerhellung,* Berlin et al., 4th edn. 1979, p. 360.
75. Cf. Ibid., p. 130.

to become himself in history—and it is this challenge which decides whether the objective obligation will be acknowledged. In pure objectivity, however, which finds expression in the universally valid moral norms, all that is guaranteed is the correctness of conduct: this becomes "true" only when the individual encounters in this objectivity the challenge to become himself, so that the moral obligation can be seen as an expression of the absoluteness of existence. Historical consciousness is fulfilled when freedom takes hold of the individual existential possibilities and investigates whether the universal norms of the moral law and the objective powers which govern existence in history are "the true expression of the existential path for this subjectivity."[76] Hence, authentic existence means that one demands objectivity from one's own historical standpoint, and that one acknowledges objectivity wherever it enables one to enter the freedom of one's own selfhood. Objectivity on its own remains restricted to mere correctness, while subjectivity on its own remains restricted to sheer arbitrariness; but objectivity serves to make historical existence authentic, when this authenticity reveals itself in the foundations of subjectivity and is assimilated by this subjectivity in free selfhood.[77]

In Jaspers' view, the historical consciousness is not fulfilled by means of the "realization of something that exists in perennial validity" or the continuous "approximation to a type," but only by a process whereby the forms of objectivity in the moral world are investigated and are adopted as paths to the existential authenticity of one's own selfhood.[78] This is why the "universal" dimension involved in a claim to objective obligation—a dimension which makes itself known in the norms and individual precepts of the moral law—can never express the whole truth about human existence, even when these norms and precepts enjoy universal recognition in all times and places. Nevertheless, this objective dimension remains a

---

76. Ibid., p. 355.

77. On this, cf. F.-P. Burkhard, *Ethische Existenz bei Karl Jaspers* (Epistemata: Reihe Philosophie 13), Würzburg 1982, pp. 67–70.

78. K. Jaspers, *Philosophie* II, p. 132; cf. also p. 124. Jaspers also makes a terminological distinction between the "historical" *(geschichtlich)* consciousness and a "purely historical" *(historisch)* consciousness: the latter is limited to the kind of knowledge of history which is appropriate to an academic science, whereas *geschichtlich* consciousness means that knowledge in which the self becomes aware of its own historicity. In keeping with the primacy of illumination of existence vis-à-vis orientation to the world, *geschichtlich* consciousness is more important than *historisch* consciousness. On this, cf. F. Linares, "Jaspers' Geschichtsdenken," in: Idem, *Beiträge zur Staats- und Geschichtsphilosophie*, Hildesheim et al. 1988, pp. 119–45, esp. 119f.

"path" and "form of communication" in all the negations, indissoluble rec-
iprocities, and inexact realizations, and is thus a necessary counterweight
to subjectivity.[79] The claim made by historical truth is recognized only in
the confluence of universality and selfhood, of moral norm and personal
freedom, of objective and existential obligation, for it is only in this way
that "the depth of one's own being is present . . . in a manner unmistakably its own . . . in the unique temporal reality."[80]

Jaspers does not explain in detail how the existential truth which is
grasped in the decision to be one's own self (a truth that can never be anything other than my own truth) can unite with the truth of the other person (which is equally the object of a completely personal choice) in such a
way that the outcome is the recognition of a universal truth which encompasses both of us. We are left with the postulate that "absolute validity and
relativity do not rule one another out," since an absolute claim cannot be
posited otherwise than in relation to the historical existence of individuals.[81] It is not possible for philosophy to resolve the "primal paradox" of
ethical thinking, that is, that "truth exists as individual truth and yet is related to other truths; that there appear to exist many truths, and yet there
is only the one truth."[82] One can only accept this paradox; it cannot be
comprehended by the reason. We recognize that we exist together with
other persons and that we must acknowledge ethical demands together
with these persons, but there is never any end to the process of making
mutual demands. Philosophical inquiry can illuminate the movement involved in making a demand, but not the objectively valid substance of this
kind of absolute demand—moral norms, rules of conduct in society, social
institutions, mutual legal obligations. Ethical thinking is continually challenged to give a systematic account of this process of making mutual demands and to indicate "those meaningful demands which are . . . unconditional, and hence true, at this particular place in history," but it is
impossible to avoid entanglement in irresoluble difficulties and conflicts
when one attempts to answer such questions.[83] In his most important
work, the *Philosophie,* Jaspers grasps ever more clearly the dilemma of giving an account of morality in terms of the philosophy of existence and

79. K. Jaspers, *Philosophie* II, p. 132.   80. Ibid., p. 122.
81. Ibid., p. 419.   82. Ibid.
83. Ibid., p. 380. On this, cf. H. Welzel, *Naturrecht und materiale Gerechtigkeit: Problemgeschichtliche Untersuchung als Prolegomena zu einer Rechtsphilosophie,* Göttingen 4th edn.
1960, pp. 189f.

demonstrating the absolute validity and the historical relativity of ethics, but he does not succeed in resolving this dilemma.

b. The unity of humankind in evil Jaspers returned after the Second World War to the problem of ethics in the historical world, in his book *Vom Ursprung und Ziel der Geschichte.* Although this study does not explicitly discuss historicism or the theses of ethical relativism which continued to dominate cultural anthropology at that period, it engages at least implicitly in the debate with relativistic positions, since it attempts to provide an answer, from the perspective of the philosophy of history, to the horrors of the recent world war, whose destructive power had attained truly "planetary" dimensions for the first time thanks to the employment of modern techniques of mass annihilation. It was only the experience of the universality of terror that forced people to realize that they shared a common fate, and this challenges Jaspers to inquire whether the unity of history—already realized in evil—also contains positive potential for the future of humanity. His starting point is the affirmation that "humankind has a single origin and a single end." This is a philosohical "profession of faith," since neither of these ideal points of unity can be demonstrated empirically; they exist only as history's "boundaries."[84] Against the arbitrariness of a purely aesthetic historicism—for which everything has an equal value, so that ultimately nothing is of any value—Jaspers maintains that a philosophical reflection on history must inquire, in the chaos of chance events, about the meaning and structure of world history, for it is this meaning and structure that can give birth to the unity of humankind.[85]

If we use the term "universal history of the earth" in the strict sense, it is only in very recent years that we can speak of a genuine "world history." Even if we include the preparatory stages from the period of the great discoveries onwards, this "world history" embraces only a tiny section of the total course of human history up to now. World history is no older than one or two centuries; the preceding "history" amounts to roughly the five thousand years in which the ancient high cultures of China, India, the Near East, and Europe came into being. The period before the first emergence of historical cultures, when human beings emerged as a species in

84. K. Jaspers, *Vom Ursprung und Ziel der Geschichte,* Munich 3rd edn. 1952, p. 17; cf. also pp. 316, 326.
85. Ibid., p. 332. On this, cf. F. Linares, *Jaspers Geschichtsdenken,* pp. 140–45. He draws attention to the "high ethos" that forms the basis of an historical-philosophical conception where we are taught to consider all human persons as brothers and sisters.

the course of natural history and the various linguistic and racial groups were formed, must be seen in this perspective as the immensely long "prehistory." The tracks of an answer to the mystery of the human person and the origin of his freedom are lost in this prehistory.[86]

c. The concept of axis time After setting out this chronological structure, Jaspers now looks at a cross-section of history, in the hope that this will help to answer the questions about the meaning of human existence which remain open in an exclusively diachronic perspective. Here he encounters a remarkable fact which had indeed often been noticed, but had never been made the starting point for a reflection on history as a whole: the parallel emergence in three different geographical regions of intellectual movements with great significance for world history within a relatively brief period of time, which he accordingly calls the "axis time" of human history. It is scarcely possible to exaggerate the importance for the emergence of the historical consciousness in human beings of this space of roughly five hundred years between 800 and 200 BCE, as we see from a glance at the dates of the great founding figures of the pre-Christian world religions and schools of philosophy in this period. Confucius and Lao-Tze lived in China; the Buddha lived in India, where the Upanishads were composed; in Iran, Zoroaster taught the dualistic image of the world, with its central ideal of the struggle between good and evil; at the same period, the prophets worked in Israel, from Elijah, Isaiah, and Jeremiah to Second Isaiah; in Greece, the great poets and philosophers from Homer, Parmenides, and Heraclitus to Plato composed texts which even today hold a foremost place in world literature. Jaspers holds that the coincidence of these events in the wide geographical regions of China, India, and Europe in a narrow historical corridor of only five hundred years is a uniquely significant historical phenomenon which allows us to grasp the structure of human history as a whole. In his philosophy of history, the concept of the ideal "axis time" replaces the theological image of the "center" of time, on which our calendar with its enumeration of the years *post Christum natum* is based; the difference, in his eyes, is that the idea of "axis time" is based on empirically demonstrable facts, whereas the event of God's incarnation is accessible only to faith.

Jaspers summarizes his philosophical understanding of history in four points. In view of the fact that these are only partially accessible to scientif-

---

86. K. Jaspers, *Vom Ursprung und Ziel der Geschichte*, p. 98.

ic historical *research*, one is entitled to ask whether the theoretical academic status of his concept of axis time is not in fact closer than he realizes to a division of history into theologically significant periods and the patristic theological concept of the *praeparatio evangelii*. The church fathers too interpreted historically accessible facts such as the extension of the Roman empire, the intensified "yearning for redemption," or the availability of universal intellectual categories in Greek philosophy in the light of a universal *interpretation* of history—and all of this is structurally similar to Jaspers' idea of axis time. At any rate, Jaspers' reflections on history likewise involve an overlapping between the historical events which he records and the significance which he attributes to these events; and this is possible only on the basis of a comprehensive philosophy of history, as we see when we ask whether Jaspers' four basic assumptions are the fruit of historical research or of a philosophical interpretation of history. *First,* the beginning of the axis time coincides with the end of the high cultures which had existed in these historical periods for millennia. *Second,* Jaspers infers the abiding significance of the axis time for all history from the fact that humankind still lives on the basis of what happened then. *Third,* despite the geographical limitation, the effects of those events embrace the totality of history. *Fourth,* although the three worlds involved emerged independently and in different historical spheres, a common understanding and a mutual recognition is possible in the questions common to human existence: "In their encounter, they acknowledge that the others share their own concerns."[87] This fourth point is the most important consideration in Jaspers' eyes.

 d. The ethical meaning of history   During the axis time, the decisive revelations of human existence occurred in China, India, and Europe, giving the human person insight into his own self and his position within his world and its boundaries. Unlike Hegel, Jaspers conceived of the relationship between these three worlds, where the origin of today's humankind lies, not as a dialectic succession in the development of the human spirit, but as a parallel "multiplicity of the same reality in three forms" leading along different paths to a common end.[88] While his emphasis on the equal originality of these historical worlds recalls Troeltsch's concept of cultural circles, Jaspers underlines more strongly the converging tendency of a total

87. Ibid., p. 27.
88. Ibid., p. 30.

development which generates the history of our contemporary age as a universal world history: "These are three autonomous modes of a history which later—indeed, only in our own days—became one single unity."[89] In its common axis time, humankind anticipates in the life of the spirit the unity which is the end that still lies ahead of the actual course of history; with the beginning of the epoch of modern world history, this unity takes a decisive step closer to its realization. "The new dimension in this age in all three worlds is the human person's consciousness of Being in general, of himself, and of his limitations. He experiences absoluteness in the depths of his selfhood and in the clarity of transcendence."[90] Precisely this transition from the particular to the universal was the beginning of the historical movement towards unity, for at that time "the fundamental categories in which we still think emerged, and the foundations of the world religions by which people still live were laid."[91]

In keeping with the struggle against myth and the awakening of the logos, there was a consistent tendency to "make religion an ethical matter,"[92] so that the axis time "revealed" in ethical terms "what would later be called reason and personality."[93] Since then, humankind cannot forget natural law and human law: and even when this memory is continually betrayed by lapses into barbarity, it nevertheless prompts a consciousness of the unity of all human persons.[94] The basic religious-philosophical tenor of Jaspers' theory about philosophical faith means that he holds that such a consciousness cannot be objectified and reduced to a definitive synthesis on the level of systems of thought or religious symbols. This insuperable barrer should not lead one to despair of the possibility of achieving mutual understanding on a level below that of verbal objectifications: Jaspers holds that everyone is under the ethical obligation—perhaps the only truly universal obligation that exists—of believing, in every historical situation, that human existence contains still-unexplored possibilities of communication, even when such residual human possibilities often appear to be "impossible at the present moment."[95] The profoundest demand inherent in human existence is common to all persons; however, since it does not manifest itself in historical objectifications which possess an obligatory character, it will not in fact lead to a real historical unity in which all the positive potential of human existence is definitively safeguarded.[96]

89. Ibid.
90. Ibid., p. 20.
91. Ibid.
92. Ibid., p. 21.
93. Ibid., p. 22.94. Cf. Ibid., pp. 66, 325.
95. Ibid., p. 326.
96. Cf. the closing section, where Jaspers writes: "The unity of history, in the sense of

Hence, the unity of history finally remains for Jaspers a necessary postulate of reason (in Kant's sense), but one that cannot in fact be achieved. If we are to conceive of political-moral conduct as still meaningful in an age of technological-scientific world civilization, we must accept the idea of a world unity which takes specific form on the level of international action as the concept of "a legal order which liberates from distress and brings the happiness of the greatest possible number of persons."[97] Nevertheless, we know that the genuine course of history is not determined by a continuous approximation to this idea, but by the successive growth of unity and the no less passionate destruction of unity.

2. *The anthropological meaning of history*

It is not easy to subsume under one heading the philosophical intentions on which the development of historical thinking in the twentieth century was based. The analyses of the historical worldview of Dilthey, the cultural philosophy of Troeltsch, and Jaspers' philosophical interpretation of existence have revealed common intellectual motifs, but also ambiguities which accompany the most important stages of historical thinking from the very outset. Dilthey postulates the transition from the subsequent psychological experience of the context of individual experience in an individual biography to the hermeneutical insight into the objective structural context of history as a whole; he does not really demonstrate that it is methodologically possible to make this transition. Troeltsch can maintain the universal validity of objective moral norms only at the price of an unbridgeable gulf which makes impossible any historical mediation between the sphere of the formal morality of the individual conscience on the one hand and the substantial cultural ethics of the various peoples on the other hand, such that objective knowledge would be possible. In Jaspers, the question of the total context of history is transposed to the problem of historicity as an existential-ontological characteristic of human

---

the unification of humankind, will never be completed. History lies between its origin and its goal, and the idea of unity is at work in history. The human person takes his great path through history, but he does not bring this path to a conclusion by realizing his final goal. Rather, the unity of humankind is the boundary of history. This means that the achievement and completion of unity would be the end of history. History remains movement, guided by unity, i.e. by means of concepts and ideas of unity" (*Vom Ursprung und Ziel der Geschichte*, p. 326).

97. Ibid., p. 325.

existence, with the consequence that the philosophical interpretation of existence reduces the hermeneutical meaning of history to a necessary contribution which allows human subjectivity to understand itself in the encounter with the forms of objectivity.

With regard to the historical demonstration of a universal ethics and the philosophical understanding of the forms this ethics has taken in each specific culture, the most important point is not to determine the extent to which these ambiguities in historical thinking can be explained within the individual intellectual positions and their prominent representatives; what counts here is that the primary intention of these philosophical reflections on the process of historicization of the modern world is not to relativize modern norms and objective ideas about values, but rather "to free the human person for history and in history."[98] These scholars do not seek to fashion universal historical constructs or defend a meaning immanent to history: their goal is insight into the anthropological meaning of history. Behind the destruction of aprioristic-speculative or smoothly harmonizing views of history lies a deeper intellectual intention, that is, the desire to understand how the historical world exists for us and how we can understand ourselves as moral agents in this world. This interest in the *anthropological* historical question opens up the possibility that historical thinking can become an important dialogue partner of contemporary theological ethics. The philosophical analyses that we find in Dilthey, Troeltsch, and Jaspers in the context of specific questions (on the basis of the human sciences, the understanding of individual cultural circles, or the interpretation of human existence) help theological ethics to understand the significance of history for the success of human life and the meaning of moral action.[99]

98. H. J. Lieber, *Geschichte und Gesellschaft im Denken Diltheys*, p. 740. Dilthey himself confirms that his thinking aims at a liberation "for" history, when he writes, towards the end of his life: "The last word of the spirit, when it has examined all the worldviews, is not their relativization, but rather the sovereignty of the spirit vis-à-vis each one of them, and at the same time the positive awareness that the one reality of the world is present for us in the various modes of conduct of the spirit" (*Das Wesen der Philosophie*, *GS* V, p. 406).

99. Because of an obvious practical interest, discussion among moral theologians about the historicity of Christian ethics has concentrated hitherto on the change in meaning of individual ethical norms, underestimating (with the exception of K. Demmer's hermeneutical approach) the contribution of historical thinking to the construction of fundamental ethics. Among the many studies of aspects of this topic, the following deserve special mention: A. Auer, "Die Erfahrung der Geschichtlichkeit und die Krise der Moral," *ThQ* 149 (1969) pp. 4–22; K. Demmer, *Sein und Gebot: Die Bedeutsamkeit des transzendentalphilosophischen Denkansatzes in der Scholastik der Gegenwart für den formalen Aufriss der Fundamentalmoral,*

Unlike a prescientific *cosmological* interpretation, which pictures history in terms of space as the stage on which individual human beings play out their lives as one generation succeeds another, this *anthropological* understanding sees more in history than the external sequence of temporal successiveness. History is not reduced to a succession of actions, some earlier and some later, linked to one another merely by the temporal line on which they are strung out: rather, history denotes the total parameter of human existence and of the world, embracing all the individual parameters that bound the lives of individuals, states, and peoples. Only this boundary, which unites the various parameters, allows them to realize their own particularity vis-à-vis other individuals, states, and peoples. Accordingly, when history is understood as the total parameter of existence and of the world, it signifies more than the external course of time, which can be measured by a calendar and divided into years, months, weeks, and days; history is time as *formed, interpreted,* and also *endured* through human action. It acquires its meaning only through human existence; history takes place precisely as human action,[100] and the human person receives information about himself only *in* history and *from* history. If he has no understanding of his historical provenance, he is a stranger to his own present and his future is a closed book. Dilthey summarized the outcome of the irreversible process of the historicization of the modern world, which also reveals the anthropological meaning of history, in the famous words: "The human being is essentially historical."[101]

As a medium in which human freedom is expressed, history is the bridge between nature and spirit, between the world and the reason, which allows the human person to acquire genuine self-awareness. The abiding dialectic of history is based in this act of mediation, which is constitutive of human life: history is not only the *objectification* and *representation* of freedom, but also presents a *limitation* and *resistance* to freedom. As an expression of freedom, the construction of the historical world is an achieve-

---

Munich et al. 1971, pp. 120–68; Idem, *Deuten und handeln: Grundlagen und Grundfragen der Fundamentalmoral,* Freiburg 1985, pp. 52–58; W. Korff, *Norm und Sittlichkeit: Untersuchungen zur Logik der normativen Vernunft,* Mainz 2nd edn. 1985, pp. 62–75; H. Rotter (ed.), *Heilgeschichte und ethische Normen,* Freiburg 1984; G. Höver, *Sittlich handeln im Medium der Zeit: Ansätze zur handlungsorientierten Neuorientierung der Moraltheologie,* Würzburg 1988, pp. 200–273; K. Demmer, "Geschichtlichkeit," in: H. Rotter and G. Virt (eds.), *Neues Lexikon der christlichen Moral,* Innsbruck 1990, pp. 262–66; H. Weber, *Allgemeine Moraltheologie: Ruf und Antwort,* Graz et al. 1991, pp. 113–17.

100. On this, cf. above all K. Demmer, *Deuten und handeln,* pp. 52ff.

101. W. Dilthey, *Deutsche Geschichtsschreiber, GS* XI, p. 140.

ment of the inherent historicity of the human person, revealing his "essence" or his "being" in the dimension of time.[102] But history is not only an empty space in which the human person can portray himself; it is also a dimension that bears up the human person, in which he discovers himself, something that exists antecedently: "Truly, it is not history that belongs to us, but we who belong to history."[103] This inversion of things, which is meant to prevent an existentialist-docetic devaluation of history, reminds the human person that an abiding dialectic between *power* and *powerlessness* on his part corresponds to the dual aspect of history. On the one hand, the historical world is the work of the human person; he helps to form it as the medium whereby he interprets himself and comes to know himself, and the world is changed a priori by this unavoidable process. However, the human person is not *only* one who forms history: he is also subject to the continual flux of the circumstances in which he lives. By assimilating the given data of the tradition, he himself becomes a different person. Thus, he changes history and yet remains subject to it. This second aspect can give the human person safety and a sense of being at home, as long as he encounters in history the powers that support his life and give it its consistency; but this aspect often appears threatening, since he feels himself helplessly exposed to processes which relentlessly speed up the tempo of his existence.

This dialectic interlocking with human freedom makes history a universal interpretative category for the understanding of human existence, embracing both the traditional fundamental ethical categories of "nature" and "reason" and more recent philosophical themes such as "life," "world," or "experience." However, these concepts retain their necessary function within a theological ethics which is open to stimulus from historical thinking, since they prevent erroneous interpretations of the anthropological understanding of history. Hence, the attempt to understand the significance of history in its interaction with other fundamental ethical concepts does not aim to set a new limitation on history's ranking as the universal category for the interpretation of human conduct; but this attempt can help to neutralize the risks which accompany the development of historical thinking and to overcome the ambiguities which have characterized it since the beginning.

102. This aspect has been persuasively elaborated by K. Jaspers, *Philosophie II*, pp. 119–21.
103. H.-G. Gadamer, *Wahrheit und Methode*, p. 281.

2.1. History and the world

It seems at first sight obvious that the two concepts "history" and "world" belong together. I do not have in mind here the philosophical problem of universal history, which the Enlightenment designated by means of the noun "world history";[104] my starting point is rather the way in which we speak, with the historicism of the nineteenth century, of an "historical world." The addition of the concept "world" makes it clear that the term "history" (or "historicity") designates more than an existential of human existence which would be unaffected by the external course of real historical time; to speak of the historicity of our world is to give expression to the historicization process which is not limited to the radical historicization in human self-understanding but is also a fundamental structure embracing the real world of the human person in every sphere.

In his book *Erfahrung und Geschichte,* the Freiburg philosopher Max Müller calls the historical structure of all reality the decisive fundamental trait of contemporary philosophical thinking. History is not experienced as one single reality, nor as a plurality of specific events, but as the comprehensive parameter of Being, which alone permits the reality of all that exists. Hence, history embraces persons and institutions, everything produced by law and morality, art and science, the life of religion and philosophical thinking, industrial progress with its risks, the actions and the sufferings of individuals, as well as the victories and defeats of single peoples or of humanity as a whole. "History does not occur in the world. History is the world. It is not in Being. History is Being, the all-embracing course of reality from the beginning to the end."[105] This means that "history" and "the world" are correlative concepts, each describing the total parameter of human existence. They designate the total sphere, what B. Welte has called the "playing field" of human action. Since all that exists belongs to the total sphere of the human person and can become the object of human action, historicity and "the world" are interchangeable descriptions of all that exists. Here, the word "history" has an anthropological-ethical significance which particularly emphasizes the dynamic, transformative aspect of human existential reality, while the term "world" more

104. On this, cf. R. Kosellek, "Geschichte, Historie. V. Die Herausbildung des modernen Geschichtsbegriffs," *GGB* II, cols. 647–91, at 664.

105. M. Müller, *Erfahrung und Geschichte,* Freiburg and Munich 1971, p. 231. Cf. also B. Welte, *Geschichte und Offenbarung* (edited posthumously by B. Casper and J. Feige), Frankfurt 1993, pp. 25–27.

strongly recalls the given elements on which human labor in history works, changing and forming these. In view of the temptations of one particular kind of ecological thinking, one must therefore recall that the "world" is not restricted to what is supplied by nature.[106] The "world" also includes the traces left by the action of previous generations in history, that is, all that has been produced in the fields of culture, technology, science, and religion. In philosophical terms, this can be called (with Hegel and Dilthey) the sphere of objective spirit.

2.2. History and life

Thanks to its very origins, historical thinking is closely linked not only to the methodological self-reflection of the modern intellectual and cultural academic disciplines, but also to the philosophy of life. Although this was seldom the object of specific reflection, and the emphasis provided by the philosophy of life did not always help to improve the conceptual clarity of the historical analyses, there exist sufficient substantial points of contact to explain the often problematic closeness of these two fundamental intellectual tendencies. Both the category of history and the concept of life point to the temporal flux of all that is real; this is why their significance can be completely grasped only on the basis of the structural analogy they possess in the self-consciousness and experience of the human person, when philosophical reflection attempts to gain an overview of their speculative contents.

Despite these common elements, however, the concepts of "history" and "life" are not simply identical. The range of their meanings shows that historicity can be thought of only as a dimension of life, and that the concept of historicity cannot be formed independently of the concept of life: "Historical life is a part of life *per se*."[107] A further difference is even more important: unlike the historical action of the human person, the phenomenon of life itself needs no further justification. In all the variety of its spontaneous expressions, it "cannot be brought before the judgement seat of the reason."[108] Earthquakes and catastrophic floods are just as much a part of the natural history of life as those natural phenomena which human beings are capable of mastering. When we consider them as biological expressions of life, there is no distinction between cancer cells and healthy

106. On this, cf. G. Scherer, *Welt - Natur oder Schöpfung?*, Darmstadt 1990, pp. 16f.
107. W. Dilthey, *Der Aufbau der geschichtlichen Welt*, *GS* VII, p. 359.
108. Ibid.

cells in the body; like viruses and bacteria, they are part of the rich variety of life, and there is no authority of any kind within the total system known as "life" which we can call to account for the "harm" that these organisms inflict.

Without the use of reason, the inner achievement of the human consciousness in the historical dimension, it is impossible to grasp the causal interconnection which comes into being in history as a result of the progress of life through time and the conscious actions of human beings in time. This means that we can make a clearer demarcation between the two spheres of meaning by saying that the concept of history is closer to the reason than the concept of life (which it presupposes as its point of departure and overarching concept). Outside the original context in the philosophy of life, the term "life" reminds us today above all that human history, with all its technological, cultural, and artistic achievements, is only one segment in the natural history of a pulsating universe; the immeasurable variety of this universe involves far more than its anthropological function of providing a home for human beings. But although natural life has a value of its own, it too—like the human world in the narrower sense of the word—bears the traces of the activity of preceding historical generations in technology and agriculture, science and culture. This is why history denotes more than just one segment of life. Rather, history and the consequences of historical action are always an aspect of life *per se*.

2.3. History and experience

The anthropological meaning of history can be seen above all in its relationship to experience. Once again, the bridge between the two concepts is supplied by the phenomenon of the inherent historicity of the human person, which is the basis both of the construction of the historical world and of the self-appropriation and self-knowledge of the human person in this historical world. For historical thinking, "experience" denotes neither the totality of empirical facts which form the basis of our knowledge of nature, nor the privileged access to the mystery of another person which can be revealed in the intimacy of an "I-Thou" relationship. Rather, historical experience is the way in which the human person becomes conscious of an existential relationship to history, a relationship that has left its mark on him and that determines his present. "As an historical process, its model is not the ascertaining of facts, but the remarkable coalescing of recollection and expectation to form a single whole: we call this experience, and we acquire experience when we have experiences."[109] The world in which the individual lives forms the given "sounding board" which allows the personal experience of the individual to become historical experience. This transition to the hermeneutical experience of history involves much more than the simple knowledge of historical contexts; it occurs in the insight that the historical tradition in which I stand has something to say to me, something to which I must open myself, if I am to understand my own life.

In his critical reflection on what philosophy might be able to achieve in an historical world, Dilthey assigned philosophical reflection a double task. First, it must accompany critically the transition from the individual's unconscious experience of life to a conscious recognition of those values and ends which establish themselves in unconscious experience as livable and worth living for. At a second stage, it must accompany, by means of a methodical supervision, the further transition from this individual experience of life, which has now been raised into a considered awareness of values, to the common experiential potential of a whole generation. Dilthey writes, in a very important section about the relationship between philosophy and the experience of life:

> Life is the inherent relationship of the achievements of the mind in the context of the person. Experience of life is the growing consideration and reflection on life. This takes relative, subjective, arbitrary, and isolated aspects of the elementary forms of purposeful conduct and elevates these to insight into what is valuable and effective for us. What is the meaning of the passions in the totality of our life? What is the value of self-sacrifice—or praise and recognition by others—in a life which is understood in a natural way? The individual's experience of life does not work on its own to resolve such questions: it widens to include the experience acquired by society. Society is the general regulator of the life of sentiment and instinct. In order that individuals may live together in society, law and custom put boundaries to the passions, which of themselves know no rules. Through division of labor, marriage, and property, society creates the necessary condition for a regulated satisfaction of human instincts, thus setting people free from this terrible dominion. Life acquires a space for the higher sentiments and strivings of the mind, which are enabled to gain the upper hand.[110]

The experience of life is constructed from a multiplicity of individual experiences which may contradict or intensify and confirm one another. Through the total texture of human passions, instincts, and rational actions, these grow into a societal parameter of experience, which provides

---

109. H.-G. Gadamer, *Wahrheit und Methode*, pp. 225f.
110. W. Dilthey, *Das Wesen der Philosophie, GS* V, pp. 408f.

the background for assessments of value—and these in turn affect the interpretation of the individual experiences of life. Ethical knowledge is the fruit of experience which is interpreted in this way and consciously made one's own. The activity of interpretation and the element of reflection inherent in every experience empower the person to accept the values he has recognized, and to find in these the orientation for his life:

> The experience of life which society acquires in this kind of labor allows ever more precise definitions of the existential values, which thus take on a clearly regulated position, thanks to public opinion: in this way, society itself generates a hierarchy of values which conditions the conduct of individuals. Individual experiences of life come into their own on the humus of society. These come into being in many ways; their kernel consists of personal experiences, where these disclose a value. We receive other lives as onlookers who observe the passions of human beings—passions that can go so far that they destroy their own selves, and hence also their relationship to other persons—and the sufferings to which these passions lead. We supplement these experiences of life by means of history, which shows us human stories on a broad canvas, and by means of fiction, which reveals above all the painfully sweet tension of passion, its illusion, and its dissolution. Taken together, all these factors make the human person more free and open for the despair and the happiness that come from dedicating oneself to the great objectifications of life.[111]

It would be a subjectivistic misunderstanding were one to appeal to one's own experience to justify refusing the claims made by the existing state of affairs in marriage and the family, society, and the state. The experience of life is always more than merely the segment of the individual experiential world that exists in myself at any given moment; experience of life can be gained only by receptivity to the experience of other persons in similar existential situations. In other words, one may not refuse in principle to pay attention to the experiential potential of past generations. Only one who accepts the validity of history and confronts the claim it makes is capable of experience. This can be seen in the way one copes with personal existential situations: in the long term, more is required than improvisation from case to case, and one must always have recourse to typical solutions which have proved their worth in comparable situations.

The communicative elaboration of ethical judgments in face of new and unusual societal challenges must likewise be able to look to historical experience for support. The life of the individual, or of one single generation, is so short that it cannot succeed if it refuses to adopt traditions and

111. Ibid., p. 409.

to build on traditional experiences. On the other hand, people in every generation see their own existential situation as so new and different from that of their parents that they feel obliged to change traditional patterns of orientation as quickly as possible, so that these may provide them with orientation for the future. There is no way to avoid this tension between tradition and a new beginning, between the adoption of values and their transformation, since this tension corresponds to the dialectic unity between one's own experience and openness to the experience of others. Far from presenting a risk, it is a necessary presupposition for success in one's existence. The life of a human being may indeed be profoundly marked by his provenance, but it is never only the outcome and consequence of the past: rather, each person is a new beginning in which existence occurs anew in an unprecedented and unrepeatable manner.[112]

The tension between tradition and new beginning is immanent to the concept of experience. The original sense of the etymological root in German indicates that the "experienced" [*erfahren*] person is one who has traveled far and seen a great deal in his life: this is what it means to "experience" [*er-fahren*] the world. One who has learned how to travel—which does not mean simply letting oneself be transported to distant places—possesses a wide experiential horizon.[113] He remains open to the foreign element in all new experiences and does not succumb to the delusion that he already knows everything and hence requires no further experience. The experienced person faces up to new things and is conscious of his own limitations in the vicissitudes of life. Only the awareness of the limitations of every individual experience—whether positive or negative, life's high points or its disappointments—enables one to have other experiences and to learn from the new experiential element each time. This means that the process whereby the historical experiential potential of each period enters the ethical consciousness does not lead to an exhaustive knowledge, nor does it end in the dogmatic resentment of everything new (which is often confused with an historical consciousness of tradition). Rather, historical experience demands that one meet common challenges in exactly the same way as in individual life, that is, with an openness to what is new—for only this openness, which accompanies every genuine experience, prevents fidelity to one's own experience from congealing into a backward-looking

112. On this, cf. B. Welte, *Geschichtlichkeit und Offenbarung*, pp. 45ff.

113. On the original interconnection between "traveling" and "experiencing" and the risk posed here by modern systems of transport, cf. H. Rombach, *Strukturontologie: Der menschliche Mensch*, Freiburg and Munich 1987, p. 79.

rigidity. Preservation may indeed be a rational act which reminds our ethical consciousness of stages of insight which we have already attained; but historical experience also includes the knowledge that its fruit must prove its worth again in the future, so that it can never exist in an exhaustive form.[114]

2.4. History and reason

If history is the development of the human being in the medium of time, it also concerns him in his specific characteristic as a rational being who bears ethical responsibility. The idea of moral obligation does indeed transcend the sphere of history, since the ethical commandments demand recognition, irrespective of whether they are understood in their substantial elaboration as eternal truths or as time-conditioned specifications of the ethical requirement.[115] Nevertheless, the fact that the reason as such transcends history, with the consequence that the logical validity of ethics cannot be based on the facticity of its recognition within history, is only one aspect of the issue involved here. In virtue of the very reason which allows him to transcend history, the human person experiences himself as dependent on history. He is capable of developing an historical consciousness, discerning historical interconnections, and acquiring an experiential knowledge of history on which he relies in making ethical judgments. These are not meaningless restrictions imposed on the ethical reason, nor are they a harsh constraint which would keep the reason trapped in the fetters of history. On the contrary, traditions always contain an element of freedom and ethically relevant experience, which the reason must disentangle and set free from the flux of historical events.[116] Hence, the reason itself is situated within history. It is not bestowed on the human person in abstraction, but as a part and function of his historical being, and he can develop the reason only within time.

Reason, as the capacity to take a reflexive distance vis-à-vis one's own self, empowers the human person to rise above historical ties and to reflect on his own standpoint within history. He exists in time, yet he is superior to time, since his reason allows him to transcend history. Nevertheless, the

114. Cf. H.-G. Gadamer, *Wahrheit und Methode,* pp. 286, 361.

115. This aspect is often overlooked in the debate among theologians about the unconditional validity and the time-conditioned formulation of moral norms. On this, cf. W. Schulz, *Grundprobleme der Ethik,* Pfullingen 1989, pp. 406f.

116. On this, cf. esp. H.-G. Gadamer, *Wahrheit und Methode,* pp. 281–90, 352–68.

idea of an *absolute* reason, active beyond history on the abstract summits of the spirit, is not a possibility available to the finite human person who exists in spirit, soul, and body. His reason never acts otherwise than as an historical reason, since it remains dependent on many kinds of circumstances—experiences, wishes, actions, expectations, and disappointments —and is active precisely therein. The reason permits the human person to transcend history and to inquire into the moral principles and values which give his action normative validity; but even here, it remains the *concrete* reason of a being who acts in history and must reflect on his own historical path if he is to arrive at true knowledge. There is a dialectical relationship between the concepts of "history" and "reason," as far as their existential function of revealing reality is concerned. It is not history that makes the human person a rational being capable of ethical responsibility and true knowledge; but it is only *in* and *through* history that he can realize this rational capacity which is inherent in his finite nature.

If historicity is an inherent element of the reason, considered as the way in which the finite human being acquires knowledge, then this will also apply to the practical application of the reason in the spheres of ethics, law, and morality. This is why we may not think of historical change in the recognition of moral principles and norms as a contradiction of their validity (which is based in the reason) and of their claim to universal acknowledgement. A superficial equation of the historical transformation of our understanding of morality with a fundamental relativization of the normative value of such views ignores the decisive insight which motivated historical thinking in its most important twentieth-century philosophical representatives. If one takes historicity seriously as an inherent dimension of the reason, one will not interpret the path which led in the past to knowledge of the truth as a unified pattern of development, or a process which tended toward its end [goal] from the very outset; rather, one must assume that there were detours, breaks in continuity, and sudden jumps without any goal. Nevertheless, this path led to thresholds of practical insight and humane discoveries, and it is no longer possible for the reason to go back to a point in time before these thresholds were crossed. Accordingly, the fact that human knowledge is conditioned by history in many ways does not mean that the reason is incapable of discerning the truth; nor does it limit the validity of the affirmations of reason to the historical sphere in which these affirmations were first made. "Historicity" does, however, mean that the reason becomes capable of discerning the truth along a path in history. And it is possible for the reason, as it takes this path, to squander insights that have already been achieved, and thus fail to deploy its own capacities. Such thresholds—in keeping with the structure of the historical knowledge of truth—can be crossed only at one particular place and one particular (and contingent) point in time. But once such historical discoveries have entered the consciousness of the human spirit, wherever and whenever this takes place, they have the capacity to become the abiding possession of the reason, valid henceforth at all times and places. The reason discovers its own potential precisely in such paths and breakthroughs. Once this potential is grasped by the consciousness, the reason itself demands that one must hold onto the knowlege of the truth that has been acquired, even if this is not yet universally acknowledged, still less put into practice in the same manner by everyone.

It is easy to see what this means for the rational justification of the norms of natural law, or for the idea of universal human rights. The structure of every historical insight into the truth, as set out above, means that the path such insights must take before they can be acknowledged begins in specific instances: the fact that human rights cannot be acknowledged, and defended against specific threats to human existence, otherwise than from *one* particular standpoint in history is not an argument for or against their claim to universal validity. It is completely impossible in one specific historical-political constellation to formulate a definitive and exhaustive catalogue of human rights, for the concrete realization of such rights entails the anticipation of a totality which will never be grasped completely. This is why philosophy considers the belief that all human persons possess an underived right to be an idea of the reason, which became the common possession of all humanity as soon as it was uttered for the first time. Once the threshold to this truth has been crossed, no difficulties and defeats in the course of the historical-political realization of this idea can obliterate the *fact* that his reason allows every human being to grasp the demand that this idea makes on him.

If anything like a general rational interest on the part of humanity may be said to exist, expressing the will to collective self-respect, this can be seen today in international politics, in the field of human rights. Its lack of success does not refute the idea of a universal ethos of human rights; this merely reminds us that the process of the historical realization of such an ethos does not run so smoothly as the enlightened consciousness of progress would like to believe. The inevitable disappointment can quickly turn such expectations of progress to a fundamental resignation vis-à-vis the reason, as we can see in many places in the contemporary discussion of human rights. But although historical thinking has been accompanied from the outset by the temptation to this kind of skepticism about the reason, its philosophical intentions point in fact in a different direction: historical thinking did not aim to proclaim the end of reason, but to discover how the reason might be preserved in history.

2.5. History and nature

This brings us to a final pair of concepts, which link a hermeneutical consciousness of history with the classical idea of natural law and provide a transition to the question we shall study in the next chapter. Historical thinking shattered the assumption that the human person had an essential nature which was always the same, untouched by the passage of time; and this had been the basis of the traditional idea of natural law. Dilthey's famous assertion, "Only his history tells the human person what he is,"[117] is a decisive rebuttal of the program of every idealistic philosophy of consciousness which would seek to arrive at valid affirmations about the human person by means of introspection alone. More is required for genuine self-understanding than reflection on one's intrapsychical reality, that is, the reflexive consciousness of one's acts of thinking and the achievements of one's memory, experiences, and moods; it is only in history, in which one's actions and wishes, one's possibilities and expectations display themselves, that one can gain objective information about oneself. The totality of human nature in its whole richness, with its potential and capacities which are yet to be awakened, can be grasped only in history, not by an aprioristic affirmation about its essence or by a perception of its substance which remains limited to the consciousness.

This does not mean that the concept of human nature or the idea of natural law has no function within historical thinking. In order to emphasize how essential this idea is, recourse is had to the idea of an "historical natural law"—an idea chosen by the representatives of historical thinking themselves.[118] It is the inherent historicity of the human person that constructs the historical world: his reason and his nature enable him, as a being consisting of body and soul, to achieve this task. He does not possess the reason as an abstract capacity or external characteristic, but as a func-

117. W. Dilthey, *Die drei Grundformen der Systeme, GS* IV, p. 529; cf. also V, p. 180; VII, p. 279; VIII, pp. 166, 224.

118. Cf. W. Dilthey, *System der Ethik, GS* X, pp. 14, 92, 103; on this, G. Bauer, *Geschichtlichkeit. Wege und Irrwege eines Begriffs*, Berlin 1963, pp. 70f.

tion of his concrete human nature; in the same way (as the historian Johann Gustav Droysen puts it), history is basically possible because of a "remarkable charism of human nature, which is so fortunately imperfect."[119] Since we are finite rational beings, the only way for us to know and to will is in the medium of time: thus, the constitutive expressions of our life point us to history. This means that the human person is orientated to history by his very nature and is destined to have an existence in history. It is not his history that makes him an active being who shapes the world and leaves his imprint on culture: the constitution of his finite nature as body and soul gives him this character a priori.[120]

Thus, an anthropological understanding of history, which sees history as the time formed and endured by the human person, cannot do without the concept of human nature. When the human person encounters the objectivations of his freedom and his reason, his technical skill and his varied intellectual-cultural activity in his historical world, this presupposes his remarkable dual human nature, as well as the unavoidable boundary experiences which make him aware of his own finitude in all his historical activity. This means that, although historicity is understood in a radical manner in the modern period, it is not an exclusive characteristic of our own time, something that would make us fundamentally different from those who lived in earlier times. Rather, the historical consciousness is a reaction to the irreversible historical transformation which encompasses every sphere of life; and, as such, it is the manner *specific to our own epoch* in which the modern human person experiences the *essential finitude*, which he shares with people of every age.[121]

Despite a common misunderstanding, theological anthropology has never defined the human person—even under the influence of metaphysical thought—as an essentially ahistorical being. Rather, when it interpreted his inherent temporality and the constitutive fragmentary quality of his action as an essential element of his contingent nature as one who exists in body and soul,[122] it was aware of the anthropological structure which un-

119. Quoted by H.-G. Gadamer, *Wahrheit und Methode*, p. 217.

120. On this, cf. W. Korff, *Norm und Sittlichkeit*, pp. 65–72.

121. This is why A. Léonard is correct to emphasize the common dimension which links a Chinese from the age of Confucius with an Englishman of the Victorian age: *Le Fondement de la Morale: Essai d'éthique philosophique générale*, Paris 1991, p. 257. The fact that all historical transformations of human living conditions are only a change *within* this common metaphysical "nature" does not, however, refute the thesis that this nature can be perceived only *in* the specific form in which it appears in history, and that concrete ethical norms can be known only in a context related to history.

122. Cf. Thomas Aquinas, *Summa theologiae* I–II, q. 5, a. 1, ad 1; q. 5, a. 7.

derlies the phenomenon of historicity, although (naturally) the epochal historical experience of this phenomenon still lay in the future. This is why the historical presuppositions of theological ethics do not allow one to construct an unbridgeable antithesis between nature and history, or to understand these as mutually exclusive dimensions of human existence. Rather, the intellectual challenge is to accept historicity as one of the essential characteristics of modern life, in which the human person experiences his own nature as a finite being.

✣ IV. *The universal claim of natural law*

W E HAVE FREQUENTLY seen in the two preceding chapters
that it is not possible to discuss ethical relativism and the
analysis of the historicity of our moral consciousness from
some neutral standpoint, independent of any context. The discussion of
the philosophical problems posed to ethical thinking by the historical
transformation and the cultural variety of our moral ideas has been conducted up to now from a theological-ethical position which itself is based
on particular moral-philosophical presuppositions; irrespective of all differentiation in various directions and the dissimilarities in the formal argumentation, these presuppositions could be assumed as a common starting
point in the history of Catholic moral theology until a few decades ago.
These fundamental positions can be called essential philosophical *praeam-
bula fidei* in the field of moral theology. They include above all the presupposition that the practical reason is capable in principle of grasping the
truth, the assumption that universal moral principles exist, and the conviction that individual ethical norms do not owe their validity merely to a decisionist regulation (whether through the legislation of the divine will or
through an authoritative decision of the church), but can be justified in rational terms. The insight into the process of historicization of the modern
world has often gone hand in hand with the assumption that, while one
cannot reduce all the intercultural variety and historical change to a mere
surface phenomenon—the superficial transformation of a human "nature"
which *per se* would be immutable—it nevertheless remains incomprehensible, unless one postulates a fundamental identity of human existence.

We have not provided any justification hitherto for these two basic
moral-philosophical positions, viz. the thesis that the practical reason is capable of grasping the truth and the assumption that there is one structure
of human existence that underlies the historical process. These have been
presented only as possible alternative positions, which were not genuinely
affected by the objections we have discussed. This is why our next task is
to explore these positions in greater detail, developing them by means of
arguments and nuancing them so that they can be defended against the

misunderstandings which we have already mentioned. This too cannot be done on a *tabula rasa*. We build here on historical approaches which enlighten, correct, and develop each other. Because of the level of its philosophical reflection and its inherent capacity for differentiation, the theory of the practical reason on which *Thomas Aquinas* bases his doctrine of the ethical natural law seems a good historical starting point, which can provide substantial help towards a systematic justification of our two theses. Hence, we shall compare Thomas' natural-law ethics and the theory which it presupposes with the modern ethos of human rights and the idea of the inalienable dignity of the human person in order to obtain a viable basis for the claim to universal validity made by moral principles and the capacity of the reason to acknowledge ethical norms. Our intention is not an historical reconstruction of central elements in Thomas' ethics, but a productive confrontation in which our contemporary problems prompt the questions we put to this ethics. This can shed a new light on natural-law ethics itself, allowing us to see more clearly differentiations which have been overlooked in the past.

1. Preliminary hermeneutical reflections

In view of the accusations leveled against the idea of natural law—the alleged naturalistic fallacy, the logical circularity of the arguments employed to justify it, and its ahistorical character—it seems that philosophical or theological attempts to resuscitate it must be doomed to failure a priori. An additional difficulty in the case of Thomas' natural-law ethics is that this was seen for a long time as the basic historical form of all ecclesiastical doctrines of the natural law. Thomas' theory of the *lex naturalis* was seen as the historical prototype which supplied the function of legitimation exercised by the theological doctrines of natural law until well into the nineteenth century. The portrait of Thomas' ethics in Ernst Troeltsch's *Soziallehren der christlichen Kirchen und Gruppen* (1912) is a good example of this interpretative tradition, which reduced the historical difference between Thomas and his neoscholastic followers to a seamless continuity. This portrait is composed of three interpretative layers, a sociological level, a metaphysical level, and a specifically theological-religious level; together, these constitute an architectonically ordered whole, which is supposed to represent the inherent rationality and Christian character of the theocratic world order in the Middle Ages.

1.1. Thomistic natural law as a metaphysical idea of order

According to this interpretation, the *sociological* function of the mediae-val doctrine of natural law was the theoretical legitimation it provided to an ecclesiastical monoculture which corresponded to the church's claim to incorporate every aspect of political, cultural, and academic life into the "total life" of its religious concept.[1] This organism was crowned by the *metaphysical* construction elaborated by Thomist ethics, which understood the social ordering of the world as anchored in God's eternal reason. This means that Christian social philosophy—as we see in an exemplary man-ner in the natural-law ethics of Thomas Aquinas—is based on a transposi-tion of metaphysical-theological insights to the sphere of societal-cultural life. The practical reason which is at work here is not yet recognized as having an autonomous regulative function for these spheres; it is under-stood as a straightforward extension of the theoretical reason, that is, as the application of a universal metaphysics of *ordo* to the specific societal con-structions of human life.[2] Ultimately, the closely interwoven sociological-cultural and metaphysical-philosophical functions of the natural law are based on a *theological* reasoning which, according to Troeltsch, is meant to justify the inevitable compromising of the ethical radicalism of the Gospel. While the mediaeval doctrine of the natural law thus amounts "de facto to a relative Christianization of life in the world," this process never devel-oped so far that the various spheres of life in the world became completely Christian.[3]

The individual theological doctrines of the orientation of nature to grace, of the gradated hierarchy between the natural and the supernatural, and the organic distribution of individual roles, states in life, and min-istries under the overarching guidance of ecclesiastical authority obscure this break in continuity by declaring it to be a theologically necessary con-sequence of sin. This means that the idea of a Christian monoculture is purchased at the price of a "far-reaching relativization of the radical princi-ples of a genuine Christian ethics."[4] While the reality of societal life in the Middle Ages may appear to be the expression of the divine reason and at least an incipient assimilation to the ethical ideal of the Gospel, the truth is that it corresponds rather to patriarchal Old Testament ideas of social or-

---

1. E. Troeltsch, *Die Soziallehren der christlichen Kirchen und Gruppen, Gesammelte Schriften (GS)* I, Tübingen 2nd edn. 1919, p. 254.
2. Cf. Ibid., p. 257.   3. Ibid., pp. 270ff.
4. Ibid., p. 273.

der, or conservative Aristotelian notions, which are given a religious sanction by the identification of Stoic natural law with the biblical revelation. This process involves an unresolvable tension with the fundamental ethical message of the Gospel: on the one hand, the external Christianization of the Aristotelian ethics of virtues and ends and of the Stoic doctrine of the natural and rational law was possible only because of a certain affinity between the individual elements of this synthesis, but, on the other hand, Troeltsch discerns a gulf that will always yawn between the Gospel and social ethics, because "one can never draw on the New Testament to construct social doctrines."[5]

This theological interpretation of the moral compromise is based on the assumptions about the philosophy of history in Troeltsch's eschatology, which sees the kingdom of God as a metahistorical reality lying wholly beyond this world, contributing no input to the shaping of this world or to the ordering of human society on earth. This theological thesis evoked further discussion only within theological controversies about the possibility of a biblical natural law; it played no great role in the reception of Thomas' doctrine about the natural law in legal philosophy.[6] However, Troeltsch's presentation of the other elements which allegedly made up the ensemble of ecclesiastical doctrines of the natural law won broad assent. Apart from the question of the sociologically legitimatory function of these doctrines, scholarly interest centered on their deductive status as the application of metaphysical ideas of *ordo* and on the cosmological character of the practical reason, seen in its totality as a participation in the divine world-reason which penetrates nature through and through. This interpretation was followed not only in presentations of Thomas' thinking on the natural law by Max Weber and Hans Welzel, which had a great influence on the history of scholarship in the twentieth century;[7] it also agreed with the image that neothomistic moral theology and social philosophy had of themselves. Their understanding of the strict unity between theoretical and practical reason, between metaphysical-religious and ethical-political *ordo,* meant

5. Ibid., p. 254.

6. On the reactions of Catholic moral theology to Troeltsch's interpretation of Thomas' natural-law ethics, cf. K. Tanner, *Der lange Schatten des Naturrechts: Eine fundamental-ethische Untersuchung,* Stuttgart et al. 1993, pp. 6of.

7. On this, cf. L. Honnefelder, "Die ethische Rationalität des mittelalterlichen Naturrechts: Max Webers und Ernst Troeltsch Deutung des mittelalterlichen Naturrechts und die Bedeutung der Lehre vom natürlichen Gesetz bei Thomas von Aquin," in: W. Schluchter (ed.), *Max Webers Sicht des okzidentalen Christentums: Interpretation und Kritik,* Frankfurt 1988, pp. 254–75, esp. 257.

that they were de facto exposed to the accusation of a "Christian patriar-chalism."[8] Some exponents of Thomistic natural law went so far as to make the assertions—which we find bizarre today—that the idea that men and women enjoyed equal rights in marriage, or the demand that workers should have a share in decision-making in their places of employment, contradicted the fundamental principles of a natural-law *ordo* of marriage or property. Such scholars unintentionally provided eloquent examples of the dilemmas involved in establishing the affirmations of natural-law thinking, and of the ease with which this kind of thinking succumbed to ideology.[9]

Troeltsch was the first to apply the methodology of investigating the history of natural-law thinking not as a pure history of ideas, but in its in-terconnection with societal forms and the laws of cultural history, and this has proved extraordinarily fruitful ever since. It permits not only a critical interpretation of the integration achieved by the mediaeval natural law, but also a sociological and epistemological interpretation of the role played by Thomistic natural-law thinking in its nineteenth-century revival in connection with the distance from modern culture promoted by the restoration in the Catholic church and the construction of special ecclesi-astical miniature societies in German Catholicism.[10] Nevertheless, this re-construction of the mediaeval doctrines of natural law is based on mistak-en historical and systematic judgments, at least as far as the position of Thomas' ethics in this picture is concerned; such judgments include both the alleged sociological function of the natural law as a legitimatory frame-work for a universal monoculture and the theoretical presumption that metaphysical ideas of *ordo* hold the gradated architectonic structure to-gether. Mediaeval research in the last decades has corrected the romantic picture of *ordo* at many points, showing in a great number of individual studies of daily life in the Middle Ages that the monoculture of mediaeval life never existed in the form so often evoked. Similarly, investigations into the history of philosophy have raised doubts whether metaphysics was in

---

8. E. Troeltsch, *Die Soziallehren der christlichen Kirchen und Gruppen*, p. 260.

9. On this, cf. E.-W. Böckenförde, "Kirchliches Naturrecht und politisches Handeln," in F. Böckle and Idem (eds.), *Naturrecht in der Kritik*, Mainz 1973, pp. 96–125, esp. 116–21.

10. On this, cf. F.-X. Kaufmann, "Wissenssoziologische Überlegungen zu Renaissance und Niedergang des katholischen Naturrechtsdenkens im 19. und 20. Jahrhundert," in: F. Böckle and E.-W. Böckenförde (eds.), *Naturrecht in der Kritik*, pp. 126–64, esp. 139–41; A. M. Knoll, *Katholische Kirche und scholastisches Naturrecht: Zur Frage der Freiheit*, Vienna et al. 1962; S. Breuer, *Sozialgeschichte des Naturrechts*, Opladen 1983. All these scholars develop the approach first taken by Troeltsch.

fact the highest organizing framework among the forms of mediaeval knowledge, such that all the individual elements of academic knoweldge would have been "derived" from metaphysics.

We have known at least since Wolfgang Kluxen published his inter-pretation of Thomas—which is broadly accepted today, apart from the fundamental controversy among moral theologians about the relative im-portance of morality and the ethics of faith—that Thomas does not under-stand the relationship between metaphysics (as speculative insight), theo-logy (as knowledge derived from revelation), and ethics (as a practical science) as a deductive gradient which would allow one to apply meta-physical and theological knowledge to the subsequent sphere of ethics (and praxis). This challenges the metaphysical thesis in Troeltsch's interpre-tation of Thomas, according to which the ethical principles could be bor-rowed from metaphysics, and the entire material substance of the natural law could be inferred from the *lex aeterna*. This unity between metaphysics and ethics, between the theoretical and the practical reason (which Thomistic authors too maintained at that period), contradicts the original Aristotelian-Thomistic insight into the autonomy of the practical reason, which is recognized today precisely by those scholars who appeal to Thomas as the primary witness in their critique of dominant tendencies in contemporary moral theology.[11]

1.2. Competing interpretations of Thomas today

This means that the attempt at a new systematic reading of Thomas' doctrine of natural law is entitled to assume that this—in its original his-torical form—has not simply been disposed of by the critical objections to the rationalistic natural-law thinking of a later period or to the neo-thomistic doctrines of natural law in the nineteenth and twentieth cen-turies, although of course one must ask how a concept of natural law which is indebted to Thomas' model might meet these objections. Nevertheless, this attempt meets a methodological difficulty, thanks to the special status of Thomas' thinking within Catholic theology. Every inquiry into Thomas is accompanied by an interest in present-day issues: apart from historical

---

11. Cf., e.g., G. Grisez, "The First Principle of Practical Reason," in: A. Kenny (ed.), *Aquinas: A Collection of Critical Essays,* London 1969, pp. 340–82; J. Finnis, *Natural Law and Natural Rights,* Oxford 1980; M. Rhonheimer, *Praktische Vernunft und Vernünftigkeit der Praxis: Handlungstheorie bei Thomas von Aquin in ihrer Entstehung aus dem Problemkontext der aristotelischen Ethik,* Berlin 1994, pp. 40–43, 49–53, 147, 428, 526.

information about the position taken by Thomas himself, one hopes for enlightenment on the contemporary theological question too. There is no reason to be surprised that the self-understanding of the modern interpreter makes its contribution to understanding what Thomas meant; this is in accordance with the fundamental hermeneutical context of every inquiry into historical texts. This methodological starting point is, however, additionally complicated by the profound controversies in today's Catholic moral theology, where all the disputants hold that they may appeal to Thomas and lay claim to him more or less explicitly in support of their own moral-theological approach. This is why the fruits of an historical reconstruction of Thomas' natural-law ethics play a major role in the dispute about the methodological self-understanding of an entire theological discipline, even when the theologians are aware that one must attempt to preserve the clearest possible distinction between questions about historical knowledge and problems of systematic justification of modern theses.

This confused hermeneutical starting point, where one can never wholly exclude one's own interests when one investigates the texts, leads Catholic moral theologians and social ethicists today to plead for an exclusive concentration on the substantial ethical problems, and not to make the solution of these problems harder by an inquiry into Thomas which can never attain historically certain results.[12] So radical an historical abstinence is impossible, since every systematic consensus about substantial problems occurs within the parameter of questions that have already been posed historically, at any rate as far as the fundamental questions of philosophy and theological thinking are concerned; nonetheless, an historical interpretation of Thomas must certainly remain aware that the inextricable entangling of individual historical questions and fundamental contemporary problems makes the hermeneutical circle more acute. Before we turn to the texts themselves, we offer a typology of contemporary interpretations of Thomas, showing how varied and contradictory are the expositions of his doctrine of the *lex naturalis* and the *inclinationes naturales*, and of his theory of the practical reason.

Obviously, we cannot present a panorama of all the interpretations of Thomas' ethics and their various presuppositions. We content ourselves with inquiring into how the various types of exposition understand the relationship between the natural law and the practical reason, and the transition from the highest principles to the individual ethical judgments of the

---

12. Cf., e.g., C. Kissling, *Gemeinwohl und Gerechtigkeit: Ein Vergleich von traditioneller Naturrechtsethik und kritischer Gesellschaftstheorie*, Freiburg 1993, pp. 166f.

practical reason. If one assembles the various forms of interpretation along an imaginary line, with the formal structure of the reason at one end and the substantial concreteness of the natural law at its other end, we find that the various approaches form four basic groups.

For the *first* group, the concept of *lex naturalis* in Thomas is nothing more than a formal structural law of the practical reason, so that the doctrine of the natural law is merely an expression of the fact that the human person, as a rational being, ought to act rationally; this leaves open the question what this rationally-determined action amounts to in substance. A *second* group maintains an intermediate position: here too, the regulative character of the ethical law consists in a regulation of the reason. In its organizing activity, however, the reason depends on the de facto natural inclinations and tendencies of the human person, which present an outline of how the substantial regulation by the reason will turn out to be. A *third* variant agrees in emphasizing the normative authority of the reason, but does not limit this to a formal authorization: it assumes that the reason, in virtue of its own capacity to form judgments, is also capable of an unerring comprehension of the substance of the ethical law. This third type of interpretation differs from the second type above all in the kind of consent it posits between the authoritative character of the reason and the ends at which the natural tendencies aim: instead of an anticipatory outline, there is an unbroken identity. The substantial ends at which nature aims agree a priori—though as it were in a slumber—with that which the reason recognizes to be good. The *fourth* model scarcely plays any role today in the historical study of Thomas or in systematic ethics. Since it is largely isolated within recent exposition of Thomas, and overlooks the points of agreement reached among the proponents of the first three variants (e.g., the parallel between the theoretical and the practical reason, the methodological autonomy of ethics vis-à-vis metaphysics, the gradated character of ethical judgments, or the understanding of practical science as an outline), it must be said that this model is extremist. It corresponds to the traditional neothomistic view that the ethical law is an ontological order immanent to human nature, which the human person must realize in moral conduct. Here, the activity of the practical reason is broadly subordinate to the theoretical reason, and all it retains is the function of registering: it accepts the normative directives contained in the essential knowledge of human "nature" and transmits these to the active powers of the will.[13]

13. The social ethicist A. F. Utz is an outstanding German representative of this type of exposition: "The universal validity [of ethical norms] is a consequence . . . of the 'immov-

It is doubtful whether any researcher of Thomas or moral theologian seriously maintains the first form, which sees nothing more in the *lex naturalis* than the formal empowering of the reason to perform its own activity, that is, the acknowledgment of the autonomous structural regularity of the reason. When Martin Rhonheimer vehemently rejects the thesis that "the *lex naturalis* is completely indifferent in relation to possible 'substance',"[14] and refers in this context to a study by Karl-Wilhelm Merks,[15] he overlooks the fact that Merks does not intend to demonstrate the indifference of the reason in relation to its substantial contents, but rather the unity of all concrete substantial determinations in the fact that they are based in the reason. Besides this, Merks has made it completely clear in a subsequent study—no doubt impressed by the new esteem for a "natural life"—that concrete knowledge of good and evil is possible only in view of a "totality which is integrated by the reason" and pays due heed to the human person in his "total constitution," that is, in every dimension of his existence.[16]

The second interpretative variant occupies an intermediate position, since it sees the *lex naturalis* as entailing the rational determination of human conduct together with a substantial anticipatory outline of that which is ethically correct. This is the position taken by the majority of German-speaking moral theologians today. Despite other differences, philosophical and theological ethicists such as Wilhelm Korff, Klaus Demmer, and Ludger Honnefelder broadly agree in this interpretation of the *inclinationes naturales* and in their understanding of the practical reason.[17] This

---

able' essential structure, since only essential knowledge derived by a process of abstraction can form universally valid ethical norms. When the practical reason spontaneously utters the imperative in view of this essential knowledge, it supplies the ethical form to ontological knowledge": Idem, "Die Ethik des Thomas von Aquin," in: W. Ockenfels (ed.), *Ethik des Gemeinwohls: Gesammelte Aufsätze 1983–1997,* Paderborn et al. 1998, pp. 17–26, at 18. Despite his attempt to clothe his essentialist thinking in modern garments, A. J. Lisska too remains bound to this basically neoscholastic type of interpretation, since he derives moral philosophy (as a logically secondary discipline) from metaphysics, thereby ultimately undermining the autonomy of practical rationality: cf. *Aquinas's Theory of Natural Law: An Analytic Reconstruction,* Oxford 1997, pp. 55, 96, 125ff., 137, 152. See the critical review by F.-J. Bormann, *Theologie und Philosophie* 74 (1999) pp. 425f.

14. M. Rhonheimer, *Praktische Vernunft und Vernünfigkeitt der Praxis,* p. 545 n. 51.

15. Cf. K.-W. Merks, *Theologische Grundlegung der sittlichen Autonomie: Strukturmomente eines "autonomen" Normbegründungsverständnisses im Lex-Traktat der Summa theologiae des Thomas von Aquin,* Düsseldorf 1978, pp. 281–83.

16. K.-W. Merks, "Naturrecht als Personrecht? Überlegungen zu einer Relecture der Naturrechtslehre des Thomas von Aquin," in: M. Heimbach-Steins (ed.), *Naturrecht im ethischen Diskurs,* Münster 1990, pp. 28–46, esp. 39.

17. The same tendency can be seen in F.-J. Bormann's recent interpretation of Thomas'

position does, however, retain a certain ambiguity on the question of whether the natural predispositions of the ethical life denote only those areas for which the practical reason must issue a normative regulation, or whether these natural predispositions also indicate a substantial direction which must be taken by the reason when it gives specific directives; the image of a "basic outline" or "rough sketch" certainly suggests the latter alternative. In W. Korff's reflections on the "relational logic" between the practical reason and the natural inclinations, and on the role of prudence as the competence to make practical decisions, this question is answered unambiguously in favor of a normative relevance on the part of the ends of natural endeavor. Since those who hold this position are accused of simply following a purely formal understanding of the natural law, devoid of any "substance," it will be useful to present this clarification by means of a representative quotation:

> Thus, the *inclinationes naturales* too have an innate teleology. They are not mere *material* for the acting reason; on the contrary, they prevent the reason from acting in an arbitrary manner. Nevertheless, since they are regulative realities with an open potential, they too require an *ordinare*. They are not rules which directly guide action; they are not norms, but meta-norms. If they are to do what nature intends, they require a normative specification, and this is performed by the practical reason as 'prudence.' This must discover the appropriate ways and means, thereby ultimately giving a more precise formulation to each particular end.[18]

The third interpretative variant, found in scholars like G. Abbà, A. Léonard, and T.G. Belmans, presents a coherent position maintained with great intellectual consistency. Its foremost representative in the German-speaking world is M. Rhonheimer. I disagree at important points with his exposition of Thomas; nevertheless, since it has made a decisive contribution to the theory of the practical reason which I shall elaborate in the next section, I should like to present it in somewhat greater detail here.[19] According to Rhonheimer—and, as I have said, all contemporary interpreta-

---

doctrine of natural law in terms of the theory of action: *Natur als Horizont sittlicher Praxis,* Stuttgart 1999. Bormann attempts here to develop the interpretative model inspired above all by W. Korff.

18. W. Korff, "Der Rückgriff auf die Natur. Eine Rekonstruktion der thomanischen Lehre vom natürlichen Gesetz," *PhJ* 94 (1987) pp. 285–96, at 289. Cf. also F.-J. Bormann, *Natur als Horizont*, pp. 230–36.

19. I am grateful to M. Rhonheimer for allowing me to read the manuscripts of important essays in which he replies to misunderstandings of his position (including some of which I myself have been guilty) prior to their publication. I am also grateful to him for critical objections which have allowed me to complete and clarify my own position.

tions of Thomas apart from the neothomistic type agree here—the starting point of Aquinas' theory of the *lex naturalis* is the autonomy of the practical reason, which develops strictly parallel to the theoretical reason while having recourse to its own specific principles.[20] In the highest principle of the practical reason—viz. the requirement to do good and avoid evil—which is presupposed in every individual judgment, this interpretation (unlike the first two types) does not see a formal principle of judgment which would act autonomously to specify the contents of ethical insight. Rather, it sees here a principle which prompts action, a principle at work from the very outset in the natural inclinations of the human person to assign their proper rational measure to the fundamental human goods (self-preservation of the individual, survival of the human species, the life of the sexes, life in society, knowledge of truth). In the natural inclinations, the highest principle of the practical reason is differentiated in the various individual precepts of the natural law, which in turn embraces the totality of all inclinations and basic goods under the formal aspect of their "orientation to reason."

Hence, the substantial specification of the *lex naturalis* does not occur in an interplay between the reason and the natural inclinations; rather, it is the fruit of a self-development of the practical reason in the ensemble of natural tendencies and basic human goods.[21] According to Rhonheimer, there is therefore a reciprocal inclusive relationship between the natural inclinations and the practical reason, which tends towards a large degree of identity; he understands it as analogous to the unity of matter and form.[22]

Against the authors of the second group, and especially in his debate with G. Wieland, Rhonheimer defends the model of dynamic unity by drawing attention to two misunderstandings which (in his view) derive from an inadequate grasp of the unity of the human person as body and soul. The penetration and shaping of the natural inclinations by the prac-

20. Cf., however, the nuances in the observations by C. Schröer, *Praktische Vernunft bei Thomas von Aquin*, Stuttgart et al. 1995, p. 64. This scholar correctly points out that the justifications for action supplied by the practical reason always entail theoretical judgments about the relevant sphere of action.

21. Here, Rhonheimer follows the interpretation of Thomas by L. Lehu: *La raison, règle de la moralité d'après Saint Thomas d'Aquin*, Paris 1930. This was an original critique of the naturalistic justification of morality in Neothomism, which did not however receive much attention at that time.

22. On this, cf. M. Rhonheimer, *Natur als Grundlage der Moral: Eine Auseinandersetzung mit autonomer und teleologischer Ethik*, Innsbruck and Vienna 1987, pp. 94f. (Eng. tr.: *Natural Law and Practical Reason: A Thomist View of Moral Autonomy*, New York 2000.)

tical reason, which understands them as specifically human goods, does not make them the "substantial" element in contrast to a "non-substantial" element; nor is the practical reason a purely formal capacity, basically devoid of substance, which relates *ab extra* to the *inclinationes naturales*, working upon these as if upon a foreign object. Rather, the fact that the human person realizes himself as soul and body means that there is an indissoluble unity between the inclinations which come from his bodily dimension and the practical rational activity of the human spirit. On the one hand, the *inclinationes naturales* are a priori more than mere nature; on the other hand, the practical reason itself must be understood as an inherent component of human nature.[23]

This means that the natural inclinations are not only "matter" on which the regulative activity of the reason works; they are the strivings of a rational being, that is, the expression of the personal unity of the human being, even before they are "ordered." "The sphere of human goods is already delineated and formulated in terms of its contents"[24] before the reason grasps these as specifically practical goods and defines them more precisely as ends for action; however, the natural inclinations are intended to provide only an indirect criterion which cannot supply immediate directives for one's conduct, and can become the rule and criterion for conduct only through the ordering activity of the reason.[25] This is because the practical reason is located a priori in the dynamic striving of the person towards that which is naturally good for human beings, so that it progresses as it were infallibly to knowledge of all the individual precepts of the ethical law through its regulative activity *in* the natural inclinations; here, it is guided by its highest principle and accompanied by prudence.

Individual stages or steps can be discerned within this process of differentiation, such as the deduction of the "secondary precepts" from the *praecepta communia* or the ultimate "operative specification" of the universal principles in prudent judgment. Rhonheimer places special emphasis on the inherent unity of this entire process. The transition to the secondary precepts and to the practical prudent judgment about conduct is the crowning of one and the same practical reason, which exists first in the stage of its evidential character on the level of principles and then (though no chronological sequence is implied here) when it is put into practical opera-

23. Cf. the postscript to the English edition: *Natural Law and Practical Reason*, pp. 560–64.

24. Cf. M. Rhonheimer, *Natur als Grundlage der Moral*, p. 237.

25. Cf. also Ibid., p. 79.

tion. Thomas' theory about the ethical law can be seen as a theory about the practical reason, since it reflects on the self-unfolding of the practical reason, which comes into play in a completely autonomous manner and finds its crowning achievement when it arrives, in a normative dynamism of its own, at concrete directives for putting individual ethical insights into action. Rhonheimer does indeed say at one point that the discovery of the deduced precepts of the ethical law "is not possible without the discursive mediation of the reason, and (only) in connection with experience."[26] However, if I understand him correctly, this recourse to "experience" refers only to the inner self-experience of the moral subject, thanks to which the individual knows that he is "handed over" a priori to the infallible sentence of his reason.[27] Thomas thus differs from the Aristotelian theory of ethics as practical science, by conceiving of the practical principles and their operative realization by prudence—not by the conscience, which is in reality dispensable for the one who acts with prudence[28]—as habitual knowledge on the part of the individual acting subject, and hence as principles of the practical reason *itself*.[29]

The strength of this interpretation of Thomas is above all the way in which it expresses the autonomy of the practical reason vis-à-vis the theoretical capacity, the motive force of its highest principle, and its unity in itself. It can also understand the development of Aristotle's doctrine of the "excellent man" into a normative theory of the practical reason as a meaningful extension where Thomas does justice to the intention of his philosophical source and takes it further. However, such strengths conceal the remarkable difficulties in this interpretation, as we shall see in the following expositions of texts. The decisive question can be formulated thus: this interpretative variant attempts to maintain the same clear distance from two mutually incompatible interpretative tendencies, that of neothomistic ontological ethics and that of an "autonomous" ethics of the reason, which Rhonheimer discerns in the authors of the second group. He himself describes his position as somewhere "in a no man's land between two hostile battle lines."[30] Is this double distance in fact maintained, and what is its outcome in practice? On the level of the practical inferences and the nor-

26. M. Rhonheimer, *Praktische Vernunft und Vernünftigkeit der Praxis*, p. 553.

27. Ibid., p. 578.

28. Cf. Ibid., pp. 361f., 383ff.

29. Cf. Ibid., pp. 506, 552.

30. Postscript to the English edition, M. Rhonheimer, *Natural Law and Practical Reason*, p. 557.

mative individual judgments of the practical reason, one cannot discern the distance from the neothomist moral conception with the same clarity as one can on the level of theoretical justification.

There can be no doubt that Rhonheimer's impressive interpretation of Thomas is superior to that of neothomism when he follows W. Kluxen by analyzing the autonomous mode of realization of the practical reason and its independence from all metaphysical ontological knowledge. He also offers an impressive reconstruction—matched only by G. Abbà—of how Thomas' theory of the practical reason is embedded in a comprehensive ethics of virtue, which gives it the character of a morality of prudence.[31] But at one point, Rhonheimer remains closer than he realizes to the traditional neothomistic interpretation of Thomas when he argues that the ends of natural striving are elevated by the organizing activity of the practical reason on the level of concrete behavior in such a manner that they become normative ends for conduct, without undergoing any substantial transformation; these ends must be aimed at and realized in every single act. The transposition of the analogy between matter and form to the relationship between the practical reason and the *inclinationes naturales* leads him to dissolve the complementarity between these two in favor of an identity whose outcome is decided a priori, thus greatly reducing the scope of the practical reason or of prudence to define more specifically the ends of natural striving. A careful reading of the text gives the impression that, despite all his emphasis on the autonomy of the practical reason, Rhonheimer's exposition of Thomas shackles it to the *inclinationes naturales*, so that it basically appears to be a "trick" on the part of nature, which imposes its own standards on human activity—and even makes use of the reason to do so.[32]

The relationship between individual actions and the ends of natural striving remains likewise problematic. Must every individual action realize *in actu* all the ends immanent to the striving of the human person? Or is the "organization" carried out by the reason in these natural inclinations related to the totality of the relevant actions, such that these form a totality integrated by the reason, presenting as it were a "field of expression"

31. F.-J. Bormann agrees in emphasizing "the prudential character of Thomas' moral theory": *Natur als Horizont*, p. 291–95.

32. This means that Rhonheimer's interpretation comes unintentionally close to the position of A. J. Lisska, who finds in Thomas' doctrine of the natural law "a theoretically coherent and ontologically justified form of ethical naturalism" (op. cit. *Aquinas's Theory of Natural Law*, p. 67).

which allows the human person to realize his inclination towards the natural ends of striving? In the first case, each individual act of verbal communication with our fellow human beings would have to intend the communication of the whole truth, and every single act of sexual communion between marriage partners would have to be orientated to the procreation of children. In the first case, one can imagine conversational situations in which certain aspects of the truth might legitimately be withheld, and the sexual fellowship as such would remain open to children even if this orientation (which is an essential dimension of sexuality) is not intended in every individual act.

2. Natural law and practical reason in Thomas Aquinas

The typology of various interpretations of Thomas presented here began with the various definitions of the relationship between the practical reason and human nature, or more precisely between the organizing activity of the *ratio* and the *inclinationes naturales*. This may not have made it sufficiently clear what is being debated here, but that would not be remarkable, given the confusion which reigns among the interpreters of Thomas on this question. The various positions often approximate to one another, even overlapping verbally, so that it is not always easy to discern the substantial differences. One is surprised at the polemic directed by authors of the third group against occasionally imprecise references to the "creative reason," when one bears in mind the virtually limitless confidence these same authors put in the infallible dynamism of a reason that is supposed to unfold harmoniously and without any break in continuity in the process of a developing self-explication, which leads it to knowledge of the individual judgments which guide behavior. Do not these reservations vis-à-vis a "creative" reason suggest that this model embeds the reason so totally in nature that it appears only as the reverse side of nature? And is it not truly degraded to a merely formal authority, if its only task is to ratify the normativity of action which is decided in nature a priori?

In order to avoid such verbal confusion, let us look once more at the controversial problems of interpretation before we examine the individual texts. These problems constitute a heuristic framework which will remind us, as we read Thomas, of the neuralgic points which require special attention. The *first* disputed point is whether the fundamental evidential character or aprioristic insight of the practical reason applies only to its highest basic principle (i.e., that one should do what is good and avoid what is evil), or whether this primal moral evidential character extends to a number of principles which are linked to the highest principle; the contents of these principles might be described as roughly identical to the Ten Commandments. The *second* question is how the practical reason in its organizing activity is related to the natural inclinations and strivings. The disagreements on this point concern above all the extent to which these have a normative structure a priori, since (on the one hand) they are open to a more precise definition by the reason but (on the other hand) they themselves limit and guide this definition. Widely divergent answers are given to this question: while one position sees the natural inclinations of the human person only as "raw material" for the interpretative act whereby the reason makes the inclinations its own, another extreme position reduces the activity of the natural inclinations to the function of a "scanning organ" which has the tasks of registering as correctly as possible the laws which are inscribed in the natural foundations of human life and of elevating these laws to the rank of moral norms. A *third* controversy which has broken out anew among recent interpreters of Thomas is how one should conceive of the transition from the general principles of the ethical law to the specific individual judgments made by the practical reason, and how the individual elements of *conclusio* and *determinatio* overlap in this mediatory process. Behind this lies the question of the precise definition of the specific status of certainty attaching to the practical reason and the gradations of the judgments this makes.

2.1. The parallels between theoretical and practical reason

Bearing these interpretative problems in mind, we now turn to the investigation of Thomas' texts in order to analyze the central significance and the systematic implications of his theory of the practical reason. Our interpretation follows the structure of his discussion of the problem in the *Summa theologiae*, where we find the final version of Thomas' doctrine of the natural law and the theory of the practical reason on which this doctrine is based. We also draw on the earlier remarks of Thomas in his commentaries on the *Sentences* of Peter Lombard or the *Nicomachaean Ethics* of Aristotle and in his treatise on the soul, where these offer greater specifications or indicate the existence of unclear issues.

Our presentation need not take up individual matters which are explicable only on the basis of the *historical* development of the *lex* tractate in the Middle Ages, nor need we present in detail his statements about the promulgation of a law, the analogous unity and distinction among the different kinds of law, or the transition in salvation history from the law of the Old Covenant to the *lex nova* of the Gospel. From a *systematic* point of view, a fresh reading of Thomas' doctrine of the *lex naturalis* can presuppose the fruits of the reception of Thomas among philosophers, since there is a consensus today even among commentators who infer different consquences with regard to the regulative activity of the practical reason. These contradictory interpretations of Thomas concern the way in which the practical reason, as an epistemological capacity independent of the theoretical reason, develops its function of guiding conduct vis-à-vis the soul's potentialities of will and feeling; there is, however, no dispute today about the autonomy of the practical reason itself, which Aristotle's model of practical knowledge allowed Thomas Aquinas to rediscover, nor about the relationships among practical knowledge, the metaphysics of action, and the knowledge of revelation on the part of the *sacra doctrina*. Indeed, it has almost become a commonplace to assert that the doctrine of the eternal law intends to supply a subsequent speculative insight into the relationship between human and divine reason, although this insight does not aim at the immediate direction of conduct; despite all the variety of contemporary expositions of Thomas, no one seriously calls this into question.

Despite this unanimity in defining the basic relation between practical and theoretical knowledge, it remains a matter of dispute how precisely Thomas conceives of the function of the reason in creating order in the sphere of human activity. We find texts which are virtually identical with the neothomist subordination of the *intellectus practicus* to the theoretical reason—or, to use the term most common in Thomas, the speculative reason. For example, he can agree with Aristotle that the human intellect "expands" to embrace the fields of its practical activity or that the objects of its knowledge can be accidentally "ordained" towards activity.[33]

This, however, does not mean that something recognised by the speculative intellect becomes at a second stage the object of the practical capacity to act, in addition to the fact that it has already been recognised theoretically, for this would mean that the same piece of knowledge would first have to be grasped by the speculative intellect, before the practical reason could put it into action. Rather, what we have here are two distinct orien-

---

33. *STh* I, a. 79, ad 11: "*Intellectus speculativus per extensionem fit practicus . . . Accidit autem alicui apprehensio per intellectum, quod ordinetur ad opus, vel non ordinetur.*"

tations of the one single human intellect, which is fundamentally one single intellectual capacity, but which can be ordained to two different ends, i.e., to the contemplation of the truth for its own sake alone or to the contemplation of the truth for the sake of action.[34] Thus it is not on the level of the capacity itself that the difference between these two forms of activation of the one single intellect is revealed—for otherwise, they would be two distinct potentialities, like the reason and the will—but rather on the level of the *habitus* which perfects the rational capacity and empowers it to attain its own specific ends, that is, on the level of the *intellectus principiorum* in the case of the speculative epistemological capacity, and on the level of the *synderesis* in the case of the practical epistemological capacity.[35]

These habitual forms of knowledge of the human spirit are strictly parallel, and are based originally on one single intellectual capacity. Since the human spirit is open to Being in its totality, its unity (antecedent to the division into the speculative and the practical intellect) corresponds to the unity of the transcendental determinations of Being. This means that the true object of the practical intellect is not the good *per se*, but the good recognized under the aspect of truth; similarly, truth can be the end of the speculative epistemological capacity only to the extent to which it represents a desirable good for this capacity.[36]

The autonomy of the two human modes of knowledge is not compromised by the common origin of the speculative and the practical intellect in the one potentiality of the human spirit, nor by the fact that considerations of complementarity mean that each of these is also competent with regard to the specific object of the other—in the one case, that which is true; in the other case, that which is good. Rather, their unity of origin supports and justifies their parallel orientation to their specific epistemological goals and the dependence of each mode on specific epistemological principles which are not subordinate, but rather co-ordinated, one to the other. This allows Thomas to assert a genuine equality in origin of theoretical and practical knowledge, without deriving the latter from the former

---

34. *STh* I, a. 79, ad 11: "*Nam intellectus speculativus est, qui quod apprehendit, non ordinat ad opus, sed ad solam veritatis considerationem: practicus vero intellectus dicitur, qui hoc quod apprehendit, ordinat ad opus.*" Cf. Aquinas' remarks *In III De Anima*, lect. 15 (nr. 820): "*Intellectus practicus . . . differt a speculativo secundum finem. Nam speculativus speculatur veritatem, non propter aliquid aliud, sed propter seipsum tantum; practicus autem speculatur veritatem propter operationem.*"

35. Cf. *STh* I, q. 79, a. 12.

36. *STh* I, q. 79, a. 11, ad 2. On this, cf. E. Schockenhoff, "Personsein und Menschenwürde bei Thomas von Aquin und Martin Luther," *ThPh* 65 (1990) 481–512, esp. 488ff.

and reducing it to a mere subordinate sphere of application of theoretical knowledge. Thomas also gives this parallel a terminological expression. He avoids speaking of the practical epistemological capacity as something lying a priori on the lower level of the *ratio inferior* within the hierarchical structure of the intellect, and speaks rather of the *intellectus practicus*. Within its own sphere, this is in charge of subordinate acts of understanding and forms of realization which are equal in rank to the discursive activity of the understanding and the intellectual virtues of the theoretical epistemological capacity.

The primary expression of the parallel between theoretical and practical reason is the fact that every form of knowledge possesses its own unprovable principles, which it recognises naturally and presupposes as the primary foundation in all individual judgments. Like the theoretical reason, the practical reason too has its own point of departure. Its acts are not inferred from the judgments of the speculative reason, but are based on its own principles and derived from these principles in keeping with the norms of a practical epistemological logic.

We can see the great importance which Thomas attaches to the underived status of the judgments of the theoretical and the practical reason in the formal structure which he repeatedly employs to introduce his arguments. Here we find parallel terms: *sicut in ratione speculativa . . . ita etiam in demonstrationibus rationis practicae*. One example is the central article I-II 91, 3, which contains in a nutshell the theory of the practical reason:

The procedure of the practical reason is comparable to that of the speculative reason, since both depart from specific principles in order to reach specific conclusions . . . Just as the conclusions of the various sciences in the sphere of the speculative reason are inferred from indemonstrable, naturally known principles—not known on the basis of nature, but discovered by the activity of the reason—so must the (practical) reason too make the transition from the commandments of the natural law, as from common and indemonstrable principles, to arrive at more specific definitions taken in accordance with the human reason. Provided that they fulfill the other requirements of the concept of 'law,' these particular determinations are called human laws.[37]

These brief remarks already show us the entire line of argumentation which links the theory of the practical reason with the doctrine of the natural law. Thomas begins with the example of the theoretical reason, where the situation is exactly the same, and shows that the *principia communia et*

37. *STh* I–II, q. 91, a. 3.

naturaliter cognita of the practical reason are equally indemonstrable. The highest principles involved in making judgments (e.g., the principle of non-contradictoriness) are grasped intuitively when an object is comprehended. They cannot be inferred anew from presupposed principles of a higher order, since this would lead to an infinite regression that would dislocate the entire chain of conclusions.[38] This is why the highest forms of judgment are necessarily indemonstrable; their validity is due to their evidential character as principles, which can be perceived in the actual process of making a judgment, but cannot be proved on its own. Thus, everyone who grasps the meanings of the concepts "part" and "whole" understands at the same time the universal law of logic that the whole is greater than the part, but this does not mean that one would be able to demonstrate this law on its own.[39] If someone were to deny that each part is included in the whole, and is accordingly smaller than the whole, we would at once suspect that he had not correctly understood the meaning of the concepts "part" and "whole" which he was employing in the judgment he formulated; his assertion would provoke only misunderstanding and bewilderment. Nor could one help him with arguments, since he had alienated himself from the sphere within which our forms of logical argumentation are valid.

According to Thomas, exactly the same applies to the first principles of the practical reason, which are also the highest principles of the *lex naturalis*. We cannot err about these principles, since we already presuppose them in every practical judgment which intends to realize the good. The validity of the highest forms of judgment is based exclusively on the first primal insight into the meaning of the good, and every human being who thinks rationally is familiar with this meaning. One who grasps the *ratio boni* and knows that the good ought to exist has also grasped the highest principle of the moral law, that is, that one must do good and avoid evil; the practical reason makes all further judgments in the light of this principle,[40] which in fact is only the preceptive form of all the individual judgments of the practical reason, expressing in the form of gerunds those propositions by means of which the reason specifies how the good ought

---

38. *In VI Ethicorum*, lect. 5 (nr. 1177): *"Principia autem demonstrationum sunt indemonstrabilia, alioquin procederetur in infinitum."*

39. *In VI Ethicorum*, lect. 5 (nr. 1179); cf. also *STh* I–II, q. 94, a. 2.

40. Cf. *STh* I–II, q. 94, a. 2: *"Et ideo primum principium in ratione practica est quod fundatur supra rationem boni, quae est, 'Bonum est quod omnia appetunt.' Hoc est ergo primum praeceptum legis, quod bonum est faciendum et prosequendum, et malum vitandum."*

to be. The basic commandment—*bonum faciendum, malum vitandum*—is articulated, so to speak, in the universal principles of the practical reason. Thomas never gives an exhaustive list of these principles, contenting himself with indications. For example, he can illustrate his thinking by pointing to the individual principles *nulli (iniuste) nocendum esse* ("one may not do harm unjustly to another person"), *non iniuste agere* ("one may not act unjustly"), *medium tenere* ("keep to the middle course"), *rectitudinem servare* ("preserve righteousness"), or to the Golden Rule and the law of love of one's neighbor.[41] Thomas sometimes also mentions individual commandments from the law of the Old Covenant *(non furandum et similia)*, and he can identify the highest principles of the natural law with the Ten Commandments as a whole, above all in the early statements in his commentary on the *Sentences*.[42]

If one considers the list of these principles of action, one notices that (with the exception of the last-mentioned examples) these are universal imperatives which urge the adoption of a fundamental moral attitude, without however containing on this level a more precise definition of the correct measure to be preserved or of the damage to be avoided. Thus, the formulation of these highest principles is not highly defined in terms of their substance; all it does is indicate the sphere within which the basic moral distinction between good and evil is to be realized in accordance with the highest command of the moral law. Nevertheless, the general character of these highest principles and their lack of specific definition should not lead us to consider them as mere tautologies, completely devoid of substance.[43] On the contrary: they express fundamental insights of the practical reason, such as the absolute equality of all human beings, their equal dignity as persons, and the equal value of their goods, and the substance of these insights is extremely important. They find expression in a form which remains general on this level and therefore requires specification if they are to guide action. In this context, Thomas says nothing about the relationship of these universal principles to the one fundamental

41. Cf. *In V Ethicorum*, lect. 12 (nr. 1018); *In III De Anima*, lect. 14 (nr. 826). Cf. also *In III Sent.* d. 37, a. 2, qIa. 3, sol. 2, ad 2; a. 4, ad 2; *In IV Sent.* d. 33, q. 1, a. 1, ad 7 (= Suppl. q. 65, a. 1, ad 7).

42. Cf. *In III Sent.* d. 37, a. 1, vid. 1: "*Sed haec decem praecepta sunt naturaliter scripta in intellectu practico uniuscuiusque.*" Cf. also *In III Sent.* d. 37, a. 2, qIa. 3., sol. 1: "*decem praeceptis, quae sunt quasi prima legis initia.*"

43. F.-J. Bormann (*Natur als Horizons*, pp. 214–17) has pointed this out very clearly. He makes a strict distinction between the concepts "formal" (in the ontological sense) and "formalistic" (meaning devoid of contents); cf. also pp. 125, 212ff.

commandment of the moral law, or how individual moral commandments can be deduced from them; at this point, it is not yet necessary for him to investigate this question, since his argumentation is limited to showing that the practical reason has its own principles, which are naturally known and indemonstrable and are not inferred from the judgments of the speculative intellect.

Apart from this formal similarity, Thomas is also aware of specific differences between the speculative and the practical intellect. It is these differences which fully reveal what it means to affirm the autonomy of our practical epistemological capacity. One fundamental difference is connected to the specific orientation of the practical reason mentioned above: it does not investigate for the sake of knowledge alone, but comes to fulfillment when it realizes in action what it has come to know. This orientation to an end in action gives a specific direction to its conclusions too, different from that of the judgments of the theoretical reason. The latter have a counter-rotating circular structure, in the sense that the theoretical reason investigates its objects *ad extra,* evaluates what it has sought in the light of its own principles, and thus returns to its own self; but the practical reason does not remain within this circle. It must go beyond the mere recognition of its object to realize this object in action; only in activity do the potentialities of the will come to that rest which the speculative intellect attains when it returns to its own principles. Thus, the practical reason is not limited to the acts of seeking and evaluating: it comes to fulfillment only in the concluding function of *praecipere,* that is, in the act of issuing a command through which it sets in motion the realization of that which it has come to know.[44]

This final judgment on the part of prudence, on the threshold that leads to the activity of the will, is not something external to the practical reason, something merely assigned to it like the evaluation of our theoretical knowledge in view of some end or other. On the contrary, it belongs to the very structure of the practical reason that it leads to action. One and the same practical reason evaluates the ends of human praxis, selects the means and paths that will lead to these ends, and attains its definitive fulfillment as a practical epistemological capacity in the transition to the realization of these ends.[45] This is why *instigare ad bonum* and the correspon-

---

44. *STh* II–II, q. 47,a. 3: *"Ad prudentiam pertinet non solum consideratio rationis, sed etiam applicatio ad opus, quae est finis practicae rationis."* Cf. also *STh* II–II, q. 47, a. 8; and *In VI Ethicorum,* lect. 9 (nr. 1239): *"Non autem stat hic ratio practica, sed ulterius procedit ad agendum."*

45. Ibid.: *"Et ideo necessarium est tertium opus quasi finale et completivum, scilicet*

ding *murmurare de malo* denote more than a mere pedagogical appeal to realize in action what one has recognised to be right; such a division of the practical reason into one aspect concerned with pure knowledge and a subsequent paraenetic appeal to apply this knowledge would directly contradict the specific character of our practical epistemological capacity. Rather, it is one and the same reason that investigates what is correct for praxis in the light of its own highest principles and also, by the very fact of recognising this, issues the command to do it.[46]

Finally, the prescriptive role of the practical reason, which impels us to accomplish that which is good, leads to its own form of certainty, which is connected with the structure of the practical judgment about conduct. Unlike conclusions in the sphere of the theoretical reason, which always issue in particular substantial inferences on the basis of universal principles, the logic of the conclusions drawn by the practical reason also allows one to infer from particular premises conclusions which guide conduct in the light of principles which are recognised naturally. In the case of the *syllogismus operativus,* both the *minor* and the *conclusio* can consist of particular determinations, since there are usually a number of means and paths that lead to the ends in question. This is why the prudential judgment about conduct, when it makes a choice among these various and contingent means, can lead only to results which are correct in praxis, not to results which are strictly necessary.[47]

This special structure of the conclusions drawn by the practical reason corresponds exactly to its specific object, that is, human activity, which involves not only unshakable principles (which can be recognised by the practical reason just as infallibly as by the theoretical reason), but also mutable circumstances and the variety of existential conditions occuring among human persons; it must evaluate these in the light of these principles and regulate them in a way that accords with reason.[48] One must

---

praecipere quod procedatur ad actum: et hoc proprie pertinet ad prudentiam." Cf. also *STh* I–II, q. 91, a. 3; q. 94, a. 5; q. 95, a. 2.

46. *STh* I, q. 79, a. 12: "*Unde et synderesis dicitur instigare ad bonum, et murmurare de malo, inquantum per prima principia procedimus ad inveniendum, et iudicamus inventa.*"

47. *STh* I, q. 47, a. 1, ad 3: "*In speculativis medium demonstrationis, quod perfecte demonstrat conclusionem, est unum tantum: sed media probabilia sunt multa. Et similiter in operativis, quando id quod est ad finem adaequat, ut ita dixerim, finem, non requiritur quod sit nisi unum tantum.*" *STh* I, q. 82, a. 2: "*Sunt autem quaedam intelligibilia quae non habent necessariam connexionem ad prima principia; sicut contingentes propositiones . . . Et talibus non ex necessitate intellectus assentit.*"

48. *STh* I–II, q. 14, a. 1: "*In rebus autem agendis multa incertitudo invenitur: quia actiones*

therefore expect a priori that the judgments about practical conduct and the preceptive acts of the practical reason will have a different status of certainty than the logical conclusions drawn by the speculative intellect. Human knowledge must be content here with a degree of certainty which corresponds to the contingent object it has to regulate, for it is impossible for it to have the same infallible certainty in the sphere of mutable matters (typical of the situations in which human beings act) that it has in the realm of its theoretical application, where it is dealing with logical inferences.

However, this form of practical universal validity—specifically distinct from the validity of the universal laws governing the logic of thought, to which no exceptions are possible—is not to be considered a defective mode of the degree of certainty which can be attained by the theoretical reason. The fact that practical judgments are always valid *ut in pluribus* is completely in accordance with their own degree of certainty: as Thomas says (following Aristotle), these judgments envisage always the general run of cases, not every conceivable particularity (or particularities which are not conceivable in advance). Hence, even if they cannot appeal to absolutely infallible criteria, they are just as valid as the judgments of the theoretical reason with regard to speculative knowledge.[49]

2.2. *The practical reason as law*

The acts of the practical reason are distinguished from those of the theoretical reason by the power which sets in motion and directs activity, and this is the real reason why Thomas can call the directives of the practical reason a "law." Doubtless, historical reasons have their own significance here; it may also be relevant to note that he consciously elaborates his philosophical theory of the practical reason within a theological context in the *Summa theologiae*. From the perspective of the theological synthesis, which sees the human person subordinated to the eternal law of divine providence and confronted with the salvation-historical claim made on him by the *lex nova* of the Gospel, the human reason—if its preceptive character is to emerge clearly—must take on the character of a law capable of effectively guiding human activity under the eternal law of God and in

---

sunt circa singularia contingentia, quae propter sui variabilitatem incerta sunt." Cf. also *STh*
I–II, q. 91, a. 3; *STh* II–II, q. 47, a. 3, ad 1.
    49. *STh* I–II, q. 96, a. 1, ad 3.

relation to the various kinds of positive laws which have been established in the course of history.[50] The concept of the natural law is an obvious framework for philosophical understanding of the various laws which the theologian is to discuss: it is a kind of "mold" presupposed by each of these, from the *lex aeterna,* via the positive divine laws of the Old and New Covenants, to the ordinances of human legislators.[51] But apart from these external reasons which may have induced Thomas to transpose his theory of the practical reason into the doctrine of the natural law, one should not overlook the inherent affinity between these two concepts. The intellectual framework of the *lex naturalis* allows him both to retain the prescriptive character of the natural reason (as distinct from the speculative reason) and to emphasize the special manner in which the human being (as distinct from all other creatures) is led by the reason to do what is good.

In art. I-II 90, 1, Thomas deduces the concept of the law from an ordinance of the reason *(ordinatio rationis)* and explains this as an important element of his theory of the practical reason *(aliquid pertinens ad rationem; quoddam dictamen rationis).*[52] The intention of this passage is not only to demonstrate the rationality of the law, as distinct from a mere positing of the law by an act of God's will. Rather, Thomas sees the legal character of the practical reason as the expression of its specific nature: by means of preceptive acts (which nevertheless do not contradict the ethical autonomy of the human person), it moves us to do what is good and gives "commands" to the will. Not all the acts of the practical reason possess the character of a law, of course; this applies only to those *universal* propositions orientated to action, which the reflective reason either considers in specific acts or else knows in an habitual manner.[53] Once again, the distinction between these universal affirmative judgments of the practical reason— which have the same relation to the concrete actions as the contents of the speculative reason have to the conclusions—and the universal principles of our theoretical epistemological capacity is that the former expect not only

50. On this, cf. M. Rhonheimer, *Praktische Vernunft und Vernünftigkeit der Praxis,* pp. 535ff.

51. On this, cf. L. Honnefelder, "Naturrecht und Geschichte. Historisch-systematische Überlegungen zum mittelalterlichen Naturrecht," in: M. Heimbach-Steins (ed.), *Naturrecht im ethischen Diskurs,* pp. 1–27, esp. 10.

52. Cf. *STh* I–II, q. 93, a. 3, ad 2: *"Lex humana intantum habet rationem legis, inquantum est secundum rationem rectam."*

53. Cf. *STh* I–II, q. 90, a. 1, ad 2: *"Et huiusmodi propositiones universales rationis practicae ordinatae ad actiones, habent rationem legis. Quae quidem propositiones aliquando actualiter considerantur, aliquando vero habitualiter a ratione tenentur."*

assent, but also obedience in praxis, since assent to the judgments made by the practical reason always entails activity in accordance with what has been recognized.

Whereas the theoretical reason presents its judgments in the form of "affirmations" *(enuntiabilia)*, the acts of the practical reason summarized in the "law" *(lex)* aim at a directive which expresses the obligatory character of that which the reason has recognized.[54] This means that the practical reason does more than merely present affirmations on which the acting subject can reflect from the distance of a detached observer. Nor is it left to the arbitrary choice of the will whether or not it acknowledges the judgments taken by the reason. Rather, the specific acts of the reason entail the realization in practice of its own obligatory force and its character as criterion, letting a reflection of its light shine even in the affective strata of the human soul with the help of prudence and the ethical virtues.[55] As Aristotle and Thomas understand it, the practical reason intends not only to consider, evaluate, and argue, but also to "guide" *(dirigere)*, "lead" *(inducere)*, "lay down" *(ordinare)*, "direct or command" *(praecipere vel imperare)*, in order to evoke in the human potential for action a movement in conformity with reason.[56] And this is why Thomas can define the law as a kind of rule or a criterion for actions, leading a person to do or to avoid something, according to whether or not it appears to be in harmony with the rational character which is seen in the law. Thomas sees the reason as *regula et mensura* of human acts, not because it employs an external criterion for its evaluation of individual actions, but because it is in these actions that the reason realizes its own character. Hence, the etymological explanation of "law" in terms of the phonetic similarity between *lex* and *ligare* must be understood in the sense of a binding *to* reason and *through* reason. As Thomas expressly emphasizes in another text, the *vis obligandi* of the law does not denote some external coercive force, but rather the inherent rationality of the law's commands, which the acting subject recognizes.[57]

---

54. *STh* I–II, q. 92, a. 2: "*Sicut enuntiatio est rationis dictamen per modum enuntiandi, ita enim lex per modum praecipiendi. Rationis autem proprium est ut ex aliquo ad aliquid inducat. Unde sicut in demonstrativis scientiis ratio inducit ut assentiatur conclusioni per quaedam principia, ita etiam inducit ut assentiatur legis praecepto per aliquid.*"

55. *STh* I–II, q. 104, a. 1: "*Praeceptorum cuiuscumque legis quaedam habent vim obligandi ex ipso dictamine rationis, quia naturalis ratio dictat hoc esse debitum fieri vel vitari. Et huiusmodi praecepta dicuntur* moralia: *eo quod a ratione dicuntur mores humani.*"

56. On this, cf. J. de Finance, "Sur la notion de la loi universelle," in: *Idem, Personne et valeur*, Rome 1992, pp. 151–76, esp. 172.

57. *STh* I–II, q. 90, a. 1: "*Lex quaedam regula est et mensura actuum, secundum quam*

The second function of the concept of law in the context of the theory of the practical reason is the speculative clarification of the relationship between finite human reason and the divine reason. We may be slightly suprised to note that Thomas systematically discusses the question of the *congruus ordo* of human conduct in his *Summa contra Gentiles* in the course of his teaching about the special activity of the divine providence in rational creatures.[58] The structure of the *Summa theologiae* assigns this task to the newly-conceived tractate on the law, where it is investigated in one single article which asks *utrum sit in nobis aliqua lex naturalis*. As a theologian, Thomas is certain that the divine reason is universally present in all that happens; after acknowledging the law in the preceding article as a rational ordinance, he now investigates the relation between the directive function of the human reason and this divine reason.

The law can be present in an existent being as rule and criterion in two ways: first, as that which directs and lays down a criterion, and secondly in that which is directed and orientated to this criterion, since it is directed and evaluated to the extent that it participates in the rule and criterion. Since all those creatures that are subject to divine providence receive their rule and criterion from the eternal law, it is obvious that they also participate in some manner in the eternal law, since it is this that inspires in them the inclination towards their own actions and ends. More than all other creatures, however, the rational creature is subject in a pre-eminent manner to divine providence, since this creature itself participates in providence by exercising this providence for itself and for others. Thus it acquires a participation in the divine reason which gives it a natural inclination to the act and end proper to its own self. And it is precisely this participation in the eternal law by a rational creature that is called the natural law.[59]

In this line of argument, the concept of the law has a hinge function, since it can be affirmed in an analogous manner both of God and of his creatures. The law as rule and criterion can have both a transitive and an intransitive meaning, depending on whether it imposes itself on another or it itself bears the imprint of the rule and criterion. Since all creatures are subordinate to the divine governance of the world, they also stand under the eternal law which is at work in them, inclining them towards ends appropriate to their own species. This shows that the theological concept of

---

inducitur aliquis ad agendum, vel ab agendo retrahitur; dicitur enim lex a ligando, quia obligat ad agendum. Regula autem et mensura humanorum actuum est ratio, quae est primum principium actuum humanorum." Cf. also *STh* I–II, q. 104, a. 1 (n. 55 above).

58. Cf. *ScG* III, c. 78.

59. *STh* I–II, q. 91, a. 3.

the eternal law is completely congruent with the concept of divine providence. Seen from God's perspective, the substance of the *lex aeterna* extends equally to all creatures; but there is a significant difference in the manner in which it is effective in them. The rational creature attains an active participation in the eternal law by itself carrying out the task of the divine providence in its own sphere and for the other creatures *(ipsa fit providentiae particeps, sibi ipsi et aliis providens).* "Natural law" is the name given to this share in carrying out the work of divine providence, which falls to rational creatures alone. Its place within the structure of God's providence vis-à-vis his creation is discerned precisely when we speak of the special dignity of the human person and his pre-eminent position among the other creatures. This agrees with the total perspective disclosed in the prologue to the *Secunda pars,* where Thomas considers human action: unlike the other creatures, the human person will be considered, not only as *exemplar* of the divine goodness and wisdom, but also in his dignity as God's *imago,* on whom is bestowed free sovereignty over himself and over his conduct.[60]

At this point, Thomas specifies how the human person, as a rational creature, exercises sovereignty over his own conduct. He takes up the question of the psalmist: "Who lets us see what is good?," and replies with the psalm's own words: "The light of your face, O Lord, shines upon us" (Ps 4:7). From St. Augustine onwards, the exegesis of this verse had spoken of the illumination provided by the inner light of grace, but Thomas reads the psalm's reply as pointing to the light of the natural reason, which allows the human person to recognize good and evil *(quasi lumen rationis naturalis, quo discernimus quid sit bonum et malum).* It is not a directive of the insight (as in the animals) that allows the human person to attain the actions and ends that correspond to his essence and to which he is obligated in the ethical sphere *(ad debitum actum et finem),* but rather a functional equivalent to this insight, by means of which he participates to an special degree in the eternal reason of God; in the human person, this takes the place of the natural regulation by insight. Thomas speaks here of the light or the "weapons" of reason *(arma rationis),* which take the place of animal instincts in the human person.[61] The possession of this light, bestowed by God on the intellectual creature so that it is able itself to direct

---

60. Cf. Prologue to *STh* I–II: *"Restat ut consideremus de eius imagine, idest de homine, secundum quod et ipse est suorum operum principium, quasi liberum arbitrium habens et suorum operum potestatem."*

61. Cf. *STh* I–II, q. 95, a. 2.

its natural inclinations to those ends which are proper to it, is nothing other than the *lex naturalis*, whose speculative basis in the divine reason is the topic of this entire article.[62]

The concept of the natural law allows Thomas to identify the pre-eminent manner in which the human person is made a sharer in the divine reason. One would, of course, misunderstand this particular participation if it were thought of as a kind of "interruption" or "weakening" of the divine governance of the world, which includes God's rule over the human person; in the same way, the human reason's participation in putting divine providence into action is not a "loosening" or "detachment" of the human person from his ties to the Creator. The rational, regulative self-movement of the human person in accordance with the *lex naturalis* is indeed an *exceptional instance* within the graded order of the reality of our world, since it is only the human person who has the privilege of guiding his own self to the ends of his action by means of his insight into the commandments of God *(per intellectum divini praecepti)*.[63] However, this pre-eminence must be seen, from the perspective of the eternal law, as the supreme example of creaturely participation in God's reason: here, the share God grants his creatures in the divine reason (*participatio* in the sense of an active communication) takes on its full meaning. Only an intellectual and rational participation in the *ratio aeterna* does full justice to the concept of the law, since only this kind of participation corresponds to the double meaning of "law" which Thomas sets out at the beginning of the article: this includes not only a passive state of being regulated, but also an active element of regulation.[64] One first consequence for the controversies among present-day interpreters of Thomas is that the meaning of his doctrine of the *lex naturalis* would be narrowed down from the very outset if it were tied down one-sidedly to only one of these two aspects.[65]

---

62. Cf. also *In IV Sent.*, d. 33, q. 1, a. 1: "*Sed quia homo inter cetera animalia rationem finis cognoscit, et proportionem operis ad finem; ideo naturalis conceptio ei indita, qua dirigitur ad operandum convenienter,* lex naturalis *vel* ius naturale *dicitur.*"

63. Cf. *STh* I–II, q. 93, a. 5.

64. *STh* I–II, q. 91, a. 2, ad 3: "*Sed quia rationalis creatura participat eam intellectualiter et rationaliter, ideo participatio legis aeternae in creatura rationali proprie lex vocatur: nam lex est aliquid rationis.*"

65. The naturalistic interpretation of neo-Thomism flattens the distinction between the passive participation of irrational creatures in the divine reason which governs the world, and the actively regulating participation on the part of the human person, since it understands the goals towards which the created nature of the human person strives as a normative ontological order into which he inserts himself as active subject. However, the active and regulative element in human participation in the eternal law, which is the primary

2.3. The significance of the natural tendencies

This does not yet explain the relationship in the human person between the two elements of the natural law, the active self-regulating principle of the reason and the passive state of being regulated (according to which all created things are subject to providence). This is clarified only by the doctrine of the *inclinationes naturales*, which occupies a central position in contemporary investigations of Thomas' theory of the natural law (although the texts themselves cannot answer most of the questions which play a central role in today's discussion among moral theologians). The construction of article I-II 94, 2 shows how closely the natural tendencies are linked from the outset to the theory of the practical reason. This article, which offers a concentrated summary of the preceding line of argumentation, asks whether the natural law includes several commandments or only one. With its tripartite structure, this article has the appearance of an independent short tractate within the entire doctrinal study of the law, and it shows us with special clarity the unity of Thomas' theory of the practical reason and its interconnection with the other elements of his theory of conduct.

In the first part, Thomas recapitulates the parallels between the speculative and the practical reason, and explains once again the underivable status of their obvious principles. In the second part, he unfolds the highest principle of the practical reason: the fundamental moral difference between good and evil is an immediate inference from the evidential character of the good. The prescriptive power of the good is, so to speak, the primal ethical phenomenon which sets the practical reason in motion, just as, in the sphere of theoretical knowledge, astonishment vis-à-vis that which

---

concern of the concept of *lex naturalis*, is also reduced if one follows M. Rhonheimer (*Praktische Vernunft und Vernünftigkeit der Praxis*, pp. 539ff.) in limiting it to a mere recognition by the reason of these natural goals for human endeavor. When Thomas affirms that the natural law is active in the human person *sicut in regulante et mensurante* (*STh* I–II, q. 91, a. 2), this means more than that the human person recognizes the goals of his conduct "in an active, cognitive manner" (M. Rhonheimer, p. 539). Rather, in keeping with the Aristotelian model of the practical reason, this has a function of *creating* order; according to *In I Ethicorum*, lect. 1, the specific object of *moralis philosophia*, within the spectrum of philosophical sciences, is *ordo quem ratio considerando facit in operationibus voluntatis*. This is why the participation of the human person in the eternal law must also be seen as an active self-realization and a rational self-regulation of human praxis. On this, cf. esp. L. Honnefelder, "Natur als Handlungsprinzip. Die Relevanz der Natur für die Ethik," in Idem (ed.), *Natur als Gegenstand der Wissenschaft*, Freiburg 1992, pp. 151–83, esp. 178; F. Ricken, "Naturrecht I," *TRE* 24: 132–53, esp. 143.

exists is the beginning of all perception.[66] One who grasps the claim made by the good and the evidential obligatory character contained in the idea of the good has also grasped the absolute contradiction between good and evil. That which is good moves the active subject towards what ought to be, whereas that which is evil goes in the opposite direction and keeps him away from what ought to be. The force of the highest principle, which makes demands of the human person, impelling him to realize the good *(bonum est faciendum et prosequendum)* or keeping him away from evil *(malum vitandum)*, is transposed to the subsequent judgments made by the practical reason.

This means that Thomas has answered the first part of his initial question: all the commandments of the natural law are "based" on the one commandment to do good and flee from evil; in its turn, this commandment is based on the absoluteness which is a characteristic of the good.[67] However, this one commandment can unfold its power to direct action vis-à-vis the potentialities of the soul only when it is articulated in a plurality of commandments which follow the natural inclinations of the human person and dispose these to attain the end [goal] of an existence in keeping with reason:

All the other commandments of the natural law—viz. that everything that is to be done or avoided belongs to the commandments of the natural law, which the reason grasps in a natural manner as good things for the human person—are based on this [one law]. But since the good bears the character of an end, whereas that which is evil bears the opposite character, all [ends] to which the human person has a natural tendency are understood in a natural manner to be good and hence as something to be realized, whereas the opposite is evil and is consequently to be avoided. This is why the order among the commandments of the natural law corresponds to the order of the natural inclinations.[68]

66. *STh* I–II, q. 94, a. 2: *"Sicut enim ens est primum quod cadit in apprehensione simpliciter, ita bonum est primum quod cadit in apprehensione practicae rationis, quae ordinatur ad opus: omne enim agens agit propter finem, qui habet rationem boni."*

67. Ibid.: *"Et ideo primum principium in ratione practica est quod fundatur supra rationem boni, quae est,* Bonum est quod omnia appetunt. *Hoc est ergo primum praeceptum legis, quod bonum est faciendum et prosequendum, et malum vitandum. Et super hoc fundantur omnia alia praeceptia legis naturae."* The *persuasive* character of this highest principle, which is inferred directly from the contradiction between good and evil, has been convincingly set out by M. Rhonheimer, *Praktische Vernunft und Vernünftigkeit der Praxis*, pp. 547ff.

68. *STh* I–II, q. 94, a. 2: *"Et super hoc fundantur omnia alia praecepta legis naturae: ut scilicet omnia illa facienda vel vitanda pertineant ad praecepta legis naturae, quae ratio practica naturaliter apprehendit esse bona humana. Quia vero bonum habet rationem finis, malum autem rationem contrarii, inde est quod omnia illa ad quae homo habet naturalem inclinationem, ratio naturaliter apprehendit ut bona, et per consequens ut opere prosequenda, et con-*

The articulation of the one principle of the practical reason in the plurality of the commandments of the natural law thus occurs in accordance with the plurality of our natural inclinations and of the order which reigns among these tendencies. The argumentation of this entire article seeks to demonstrate that the highest principle of the practical reason—that one should do good and avoid evil—is articulated in a plurality of individual moral precepts. The plurality of the commandments follows the plurality of the human goods which the reason comprehends, and these in turn correspond to the plurality of the natural inclinations on which they are based. The brevity of Thomas' next remarks will disappoint a reader who might expect a more precise analysis of the articulation of the one commandment in many commandments and a detailed exposition of this process.[69] Thomas limits himself to distinguishing three levels of our human existence, on which our natural inclinations orientate us to ends which correspond to our essence as creatures with a body and soul. The first level, shared with all substances, concerns the basic self-preservation of our natural being; a second level, shared with other living beings, concerns the fellowship between the sexes, the procreation of our species and the education of children; the final level, which belongs specifically to human

---

traria eorum ut mala et vitanda. Secundum igitur ordinem inclinationum naturalium, est ordo praeceptorum legis naturae."

69. In his analysis of this article, J. Finnis regrets that according to Thomas, there is a "logical gap" between the ordering of the *inclinationes naturales* and the specific individual precepts of the natural law. This gap is not to be bridged by rational principles, but by further inferences and practical experiential knowledge; Finnis clearly holds this to be insufficient in a philosophical theory of ethics (*Fundamentals of Ethics*, Oxford 1983, p. 69). Consequently, he finds the doctrine of *inclinationes* an "irrelevant schematization" (Idem, *Natural Law and Natural Rights*, Oxford 1980, p. 95), and he would prefer to replace this with his own system of seven incommensurable, self-evident and equal "basic goods" (life, knowledge, the element of play, the beautiful, fellowship/friendship, practical rationality and religion: pp. 85–95). These basic goods lead, via a number of further intermediary principles (a starting point in a coherent plan for life, no arbitrary preferential treatment of individual basic values or persons, a balance between distance and dedication to the fundamental values, rational efficiency, respect for every fundamental value in every action, promotion of the common good, and obedience to one's conscience), to concrete norms of conduct (pp. 103–26). In our present context, we may prescind from the question whether this truly solves the problem which Aristotle, Thomas, and Kant allegedly failed to resolve, viz. the formulation of the bridge-principles which translate fundamental values into norms of conduct (on this, cf. the criticism by W. Mommsen, *Christliche Ethik und Teleologie*, Altenberge 1993, p. 118). Thomas, at any rate, does not intend to present a complete list of all the intermediary principles of the practical reason, but to discuss their necessary interplay with the natural ends of human striving, which alone allow one to recognize that which is good on the practical level.

existence, is constructed by the specific inclinations which correspond to the nature of reason itself. This includes above all the striving for rational knowledge, beginning with the yearning to know the truth about God and the desire for a life in human fellowship, with all the individual consequences for the human person (e.g., that one avoids uncertainty, and does not insult or harm others). This list need not contain more than hints and exemplifications; Thomas explicitly emphasizes its incomplete character, frequently inserting expressions such as "and similar matters" or "and others of the same kind."[70]

It is clear that Thomas does not intend to present a complete list of the many individual commandments of the natural law, or to justify each one specifically. Rather, he investigates the unity of the natural law in the plurality of its commandments, and discovers this unity in that which is common to all of them, that is, that they are all based on the highest rational principle.[71] The plurality of commandments corresponds here to the pluridimensional structure of our natural striving, since it is precisely the natural inclinations that make a continuous articulation of the natural law necessary. Thomas wishes, however, to show here that the ends of our striving, which have many ramifications on the level of nature, form an integrated whole under the primacy of the reason. The *inclinationes naturales* belong to the natural law only as a striving completely shaped by the reason; similarly, all wrong behavior by human persons contradicts nature to the extent that it resists integration on the part of reason.[72] Behind this lies the Aristotelian idea, which Thomas shares, that the human person himself can evaluate his own strivings and posit the ends for his own conduct. Since nature never shows us more than outlines of the perfected form of our human existence, we ourselves must employ reason to commit ourselves to concrete ends for conduct.

As has been demonstrated precisely by scholars of the second group (W. Korff, K.-W. Merks, K. Demmer, and L. Honnefelder), this event is char-

70. Cf. also *ScG* III, c. 129.
71. Cf. *STh* I–II, q. 94, a. 2, ad 1: *"Omnia ista praecepta legis naturae, inquantum referuntur ad unum primum praeceptum, habent rationem unius legis naturalis."*
72. *STh* I–II, q. 94, a. 2, ad 2: *"Omnes inclinationes quarumcunque partium humanae naturae, puta concupiscibilis et irascibilis, secundum quod regulantur ratione, pertinent ad legem naturalem, et reducuntur ad unum primum praeceptum"; STh* I–II, q. 94, a. 3, ad 2: *"Omnia peccata, inquantum sunt contra rationem, sunt etiam contra naturam, ut patet per Damascenum."* Thomas makes a distinction here in the case of the *vitium contra naturam* in the narrower sense, however (which refers above all to sexual errors). On the primacy of reason, cf. also *STh* I–II, q. 18, a. 8, ad 2.

acterized by a bipolar structure, and two equally underivable aspects must collaborate if this is to succeed.[73] This structure can be described *negatively* by excluding two extremes. The reason is not a mere source of ratification of the natural striving; nor does this striving offer an infinitely malleable raw material. The knowledge of good and evil does not simply follow the ends towards which nature strives; subordination to the commandments of the natural law does indeed correspond to the structure of our natural striving as a whole, but the normative substance of that which regulates human life is not yet fully formulated on this level. This is why the reason cannot be content with simply registering this substance as correctly as possible and then transposing it unaltered to the level of the ethical order; the reason's interpretative activity involves a greater degree of *forming*. In keeping with the active meaning of the Latin concept *informare*, it imprints a form on the ends of natural striving, until the reason recognizes the perfected form of possible human existence, thus laying down the normative and obligatory ends for human conduct.

This, however, means that we do not see on the level of nature, as such, what nature allows the human person to be; this is disclosed only in the mirror held up by the possibilities inherent in our human existence, and these are grasped and made available by the reason. In *positive* terms, the relationship between the natural ends of human endeavor and human reason could perhaps be compared to the image of a work of art which exists both as a preliminary sketch and in the stage of its execution and completion. Or, if one prefers to understand human life as a biographical text, it resembles on the level of nature a sketch which must be completed by means of the responsible moral self-education of the individual, that is, in a rational process which embraces the entire life history. Finally, one can perhaps discern in the natural dispositions of our conduct something like a basic melody of human existence: only the final composition produced by the reason can establish the overtones and undertones or the rhythm of the music.[74]

<hr/>

73. Cf. esp. W. Korff, *Der Rückgriff auf die Natur,* pp. 286–91; K.-W. Merks, *Naturrecht als Personrecht?,* esp. pp. 38–43; L. Honnefelder, *Natur als Handlungsprinzip,* pp. 154–61; K. Demmer, "Natur und Person. Brennpunkte gegenwärtiger moraltheologischer Auseinandersetzung," in B. Fraling (ed.), *Natur im ethischen Argument,* Freiburg 1990, pp. 55–86, esp. 57ff. For a summary, cf. P. Bubmann, "Naturrecht und christliche Ethik," *ZEE* 37 (1993), pp. 267–80; C. Kissling, *Gemeinwohl und Gerechtigkeit,* pp. 162–68.

74. F.-J. Bormann employs the structurally analogous image of "horizon" in order "to express both the limiting function of the *inclinationes naturales* . . . and the malleability of the spheres of action which are thereby opened up" (*Natur als Horizont,* p. 236).

These metaphors can help make clear the structure of the relationship between the reason and the natural ends of human striving, on which Thomas' theory of the ethical natural law is based. It is, however, noticeable that Thomas, in the context of his theory of the practical reason, has little interest in a discussion of the substance of individual normative affirmations of the ethical law. This is why we must emphasize once again that these texts offer no answer to most of the concrete questions that modern scholars pose to them—to the extent that these questions are posed in keeping with criteria that can be analyzed, and are not merely the product of vague, anachronistic associations. Nevertheless, the interpretation of Thomas' doctrine of the *inclinationes naturales* has a high symbolic significance in view of contemporary debates in moral theology—higher than in Thomas' own work.

One indication of this is the fact that most of the authors who follow the third interpretation and hold that the normative substance of the natural law is already decided on the level of the ends of human striving see this as a moral-philosophical justification for the prohibition by the church's magisterium of artificial contraception.[75] Independently of how one might wish to evaluate the correctness of the individual arguments adduced in support of this position, such an interpretation is possible only when Thomas' theory of the natural law is read in the light of subsequent doctrinal development in this question, so that the open-ended list of *inclinationes naturales* is filled out with a substance corresponding anachronistically to this development—in contradiction of the conscious reserve employed in the original texts themselves.

If, however, the natural given elements in human conduct are interpreted as a narrowing-down which imposes a prior structure on that which is ethically good, it becomes possible to recognize, on the level of the ends of our natural striving, something like a basic anthropological pattern which allows us to understand human sexuality. The ends of our natural striving have a pluridimensional structure, involving the levels of self-preservation

75. Cf. J. de Finance, *Sur la notion de la loi naturelle*, pp. 165ff.; M. Rhonheimer, *Natur als Grundlage der Moral. Eine Auseinandersetzung mit autonomer und teleologischer Ethik*, Innsbruck and Vienna 1987, pp. 113–39; G. Grisez, "A New Formulation of a Natural-Law Argument against Contraception," *The Thomist* 30 (1966), pp. 343–61; T. G. Belmans, *Les sens objectifs de l'agir humain: Pour relire la morale conjugale de Saint Thomas*, 1980; A. Léonard, *Le Fondement de la Morale. Essai d'éthique philosophique générale*, Paris 1991, pp. 252–54.; G. Grisez later provided another basis for his arguments, however, in the essay published jointly with J. Boyle, J. Finnis, and W. E. May, "Every Marital Act ought to be Open to New Life: Toward a Clearer Understanding," *The Thomist* 52 (1988), pp. 365–426.

and procreation, gender duality and personal authenticity; accordingly, while the essential substance of human sexuality is present in this basic anthropological pattern, it would not be possible to infer a normative and obligatory evaluation of every single sexual act from what is only an outline, a sketch. Rather, on this view, married life and the realization of sexual fellowship as a whole are called to realize the goods which the practical reason recognizes as naturally inherent in human sexuality (the complementary roles of man and woman, personal love, unconditional fidelity, procreation and education of children), and it is the practical reason which must judge here what kinds of individual actions can (or cannot) be integrated into the totality of this common striving on the part of the marriage partners—such a question cannot be decided on the level of an interpretation of historical texts. We shall return to this question when we discuss the problem of actions which are evil *per se*.

2.4. The gradations in the practical reason and the historical transformation of the natural law

As our analysis has shown, the articulation of the highest principle of the practical reason into the plurality of commandments of the ethical law is effected through an interplay between the reason and the natural inclinations which allows the former to integrate the latter into a rational totality. This is accompanied by recognition of good and evil in the hierarchical order among these inclinations. On this level, however, it is not yet possible to define the substance of good and evil: since they offer only the outline of those ends in which our human existence is realized, the concrete determination of what is ethically good by means of a definition of the means to be employed remains the task of the practical reason; and it is the perceptive acts of prudence which make the practical reason operational in specific fields. Since the natural law is concerned with universal commandments, knowledge of the natural law does not include the ultimate determination of conduct and the specific assessment of a given situation. Since, however, the concrete determination of conduct by the judgment of prudence and of the conscience is the work of one and the same practical reason which also comprehends the universally valid commandments of the natural law, there must be intermediary stages and transitional points in this practical reason where it can transmit its directive force to the individual behavioral potentialities. This gradation in the practical reason is not expressed only in the ultimate prudential judgment about the application of the law, nor in the reflective judgment of conscience about one's conduct; rather, it generates within the natural law itself a ramification of its commandments. Articles I-II 94, 4 and 5, in which Thomas concludes his theory of the natural law, analyze this gradual epistemological process in its various degrees of certainty.

Thomas has recourse once again to the specific structure of the judgments made by the practical reason, which realize in a specific context the human spirit's basic capacity for truth. Since the speculative reason is concerned with the knowledge of necessary and immutable things, it possesses the same absolute certainty on all the levels on which it makes judgments; it is always one and the same truth that is known in the same way in the various individual judgments. Thus, the object of the speculative reason is truth, to the extent that this is *per se* immutable, and this is why its judgments are universally valid, even if they are not recognized with the same measure of certainty by all persons—for example, an equilateral triangle always has three equal angles, irrespective of whether everyone is aware of this. Here, however, we see a decisive difference between the two epistemological forms of our rational capacity:

The practical reason, however, is concerned with contingent things, a category which includes human actions. Although a certain necessity does still hold sway in the common definitions, the practical reason displays more and more frequently a defect, the more it descends to individual matters. In the speculative sphere, the truth which is common to all holds sway both in the principles and in the conclusions, even if as a matter of fact some persons recognize it, not in the conclusions, but only in those principles which are called universal concepts. In the practical sphere, on the other hand, as far as individuals are concerned, the same truth and practical correctness *(rectitudo practica)* do not hold sway everywhere. This exists only in relation to that which is common; and even where the same correctness exists in the individual matters, it is not known in an equal measure by all persons.[76]

Unlike the errors of theoretical knowledge, possible divergences in the individual judgments of the practical reason cannot be explained solely on the basis of individual differences in the epistemological ability of human beings. In the practical sphere, the variety concerns rather the object of knowledge itself, for the reason is dealing here, not with immutable matters, but with the particularities of specific actions. Hence, divergences in the judgments of the practical reason are not to be attributed only to sources of error in the knowing subject that may be due to congenital de-

76. *STh* I–II, q. 94, a. 4.

fects or culpable failures; rather, they are rooted in the plurality and changes of the situations of human life, which in turn are generated by the mutability of human nature itself.[77] This is why it is not possible for a truth or a practical correctness shared by all persons to exist on the level of the concrete inferences drawn by the practical reason: individual actions in their singularity and contingency cannot be known by means of universal and necessary concepts. Rather, it is on the level of the highest principles and the basic rational capacity of every single human person that we must locate the practical truth which is common to all, and the infallible comprehension of this truth.[78] In its more specific judgments, the practical reason is subject to a law of diminishing certainty. This is why we must assume a priori that its outcomes on this level will display a broader spectrum.

Since the practical reason must not only recognize that which is absolute, but also direct the realization of the absolute in the contingent, its preceptive acts can vary according to time and place. This, however, does not mean that such divergences are generated by an error or some other functional defect on the part of the reason. Naturally, the practical reason shares with the speculative reason the general fallibility of finite reason, which can be the source of many errors. Apart from this customary source of error, which is rooted in an individual defect that can (in principle) be corrected, Thomas also discerns a constitutive defectibility of our practical epistemological capacity, which is commensurate with its object. This is why the diminishing degree of certainty in practical judgments and their strong tendency to error are not *per se* a defect; rather, they are the epistemological mode appropriate to our mutable nature, the mode in which the reason creates order in the sphere of human praxis—for it can discern

---

77. *STh* I–II, q. 97, a. 1: *"Propter mutationem conditionum hominum, quibus secundum diversas eorum conditiones diversa expediunt."* *STh* II–II, q. 57, a. 2, ad 1: *"Natura autem hominis est mutabilis."* *De malo*, q. 2, a. 4, ad 13: *"Et hoc contingit propter mutabilitatem naturae humanae et diversas conditiones hominum et rerum, secundum diversitatem locorum et temporum."* Thomas understands the mutability of human nature not in the sense that we, as human beings, could change into some other being and assume another nature (that of an angel or of an animal). When he speaks of the *natura mutabilis,* he means that human nature in itself displays a great breadth of forms in which it has been realized in the course of history; this presupposes that human existence possesses a fundamental identity. On this, cf. J. de Finance, "Réalité et normativité de la nature humaine," in Idem, *Personne et valeur,* pp. 176–204, esp. 189ff.

78. *STh* I–II, q. 94, a. 4: *"Sed quantum ad proprias conclusiones rationis practicae, nec est eadem veritas seu rectitudo practica apud omnes; nec etiam apud quos est eadem, est aequaliter nota. Apud omnes enim hoc rectum est et verum, ut secundum rationem agatur."*

only as much certainty in each sphere of reality as that sphere in fact offers. In practice, the use of reason also requires the capacity to discern the measure of certainty on the part of our finite knowledge which is appropriate to each specific case. The human reason can also err by expecting too much certainty, and this is why Thomas explicitly urges, in the field of human conduct, that "one should neither demand more certainty, nor be content with a lesser degree of certainty, than is appropriate to moral science."[79]

Thomas draws on an example which had enjoyed classical status since Plato and Aristotle when he explains why the reason must reach more divergent outcomes the further it descends into the sphere of the individual and takes into consideration the changeable circumstances of human conduct. The principle that one must restore to its owner property that he has left in one's charge is inferred from the highest principle of the ethical law *quasi conclusio propria* ("as a direct conclusion"), and must therefore be considered a universally valid principle of the natural law. Nevertheless, the reason may command one in certain circumstances to refrain from following ths universal law, for example, when a man insane with fury demands his sword, or when a traitor to his country demands the restoration of his property.[80] In such cases, reason itself recognizes the presence of a particular circumstance which prohibits obedience to its own universal commandment; such cases are readily recognized as exceptions which do not call into question the universal validity of the corresponding commandment in the natural law. In addition to this, other regulations involving questions of further detail, for instance the negotiation of more specific conditions for the return of property, cannot be covered by a universal commandment; here too, specific regulations are not deviations from the general rule. Indeed, they no longer come under the universally valid conclusions (with their possible exceptions), since they are the outcome of a specific procedure which is *not* based on simple deductions from principles. This more precise definition of general principles, leading to concrete regulations for conduct, is the work of an autonomous act of the practical reason, which Thomas calls *determinatio* or *adinventio*.[81]

Most of the judgments of the practical reason, especially in their daily

---

79. *In I Ethicorum*, lect. 3 (nr. 36).

80. *STh* I–II, q. 94, a. 4. Cf. *In III Sent.*, d. 37, aa. 3–4; *In V Ethicorum*, lect.12 (nr. 1023); lect. 16 (nr. 1085).

81. *STh* I–II, q. 95, a. 2: *"Sed sciendum est quod a lege naturali dupliciter potest aliquid derivari: uno modo, sicut conclusiones ex principiis; alio modo, sicut determinationes quaedam aliquorum communium."*

use, are particular regulations of this kind. They are not guaranteed by deductions from the highest principles, but supply more detailed specifications to fill the space which these principles open up. While the principles
of the natural law allow the inference that a crime deserves punishment, it
is human laws that regulate the fixed tariff of penalties: this is the classical
example of the *determinatio* involved here, but Thomas also draws on
analogies from manual work to make clear the necessity of specifying and
filling out the knowledge derived from the natural law. Thus, he underlines the reason's "creative" function in the process of *determinatio* and *adinventio* by drawing the comparison with a master-builder who takes the
general basic form of a house and elaborates it into the concrete plan of
this specific house. Finally, one can also discern the autonomous significance of *determinatio* for the knowledge of concrete rules of conduct from
the fact that (unlike all those conclusions which can be known without error) it presupposes a special experiential competence, such as one finds
above all in wise and outstanding persons.[82]

Thomas expounds clearly the significance for the theory of the ethical
law of the gradations of the practical reason with their increasing latitude
and diminishing degree of certainty. In the light of this nuanced theory of
the practical reason, the idea of natural law can no longer be understood as
a definitively fixed system of individual normative affirmations. The
specifically individual and historical state of human knowledge, as well as
the incalculable variety of circumstances in which human persons live, set
limits a priori to the detailed formulation of the natural law; and these
limits require more specific definitions and additions born of the historical
experience of human persons. This, however, means that natural law itself
contains neither a concrete ethos nor detailed regulations for conduct.
Rather, it defines what we might call a normative meta-framework and a
system of supreme coordinates, which is articulated into a concrete ethos
by the practical reason, bearing in mind the historical and contingent existential situations of human persons. This concrete historical ethos is mani-
fested in individual, historically mutable virtues, and is anchored in the
natural law, which contains its highest principles and the outline of its
ends; nevertheless, its substantial knowledge is not the product of immediate deduction, but is attained through this second procedure, with its own
forms of practical judgment.

An immensely complex epistemological process is involved in the elab-

82. *STh* I–II, q. 100, a. 11.

oration of rules for specific conduct, where both historical discernment *(adinventio)* and more precise definition *(determinatio)* play a decisive role.[83] Although Thomas uses the example of the *lex humana* to illustrate the gradated structure in which we give an account of our practical conduct, the ethical natural law too requires expansion, addition, and more precise definition, since its principles remain limited to the universal sphere and to those conclusions drawn immediately from this sphere. The decisive point of comparison is that the inferences from the highest premises of the *lex naturalis* must be filled out by an "inventive" activity on the part of the reason if they are to attain the real object of ethics, that is, specific conduct in the great variety of circumstances of human life. The progress of the reason towards ever greater specificity does indeed take place in the light and force of its highest principles, but the inherent logic of the orientation of such chains of practical argumentation means that, the more specific one becomes, the less certainty can be attained. This is why the *determinationes* and *adinventiones* by which the reason progresses towards knowledge of particular matters must be evaluated in the light of their own highest principles. Thus, ethical knowledge will be achieved on a trajectory from the universal to the concrete, and the affirmations made on the concrete level, supported by experience, will lead in their turn to a deeper grasp of the universal.[84]

When we say that Thomas' doctrine of the natural law has a dynamic, open character, this is not only because there can be exceptions to the universal commandments which derive from the highest principles; in Thomas' eyes, such justified exceptions are not only the necessary tribute that every ethical theory must pay to the inevitable abstraction of universally valid laws, but also reflect the fact that human nature itself cannot be

---

83. *STh* I–II, q. 91, a. 3: *"Istae particulares dispositiones adinventae secundum rationem humanam." STh* I–II, q. 94, a. 3: *"Multa enim secundum virtutem fiunt, ad quae natura non primo inclinat; sed per rationis inquisitionem ea homines adinvenerunt, quasi utilia ad bene vivendum."* I–II, q. 94, a. 5: *"Multa enim supra legem naturalem superaddita sunt, ad humanam vitam utilia, tam per legem divinam, quam etiam per leges humanas."* On this, cf. esp. W. Kluxen, *Philosophische Ethik bei Thomas von Aquin,* Hamburg 3rd edn. 1998, p. 235; L. Honnefelder, *Die ethische Rationalität des Naturrechts,* pp. 263ff.; F.-J. Bormann, *Natur als Horizont,* pp. 291ff.

84. On this, cf. C. Schröer, *Praktische Vernunft bei Thomas von Aquin,* pp. 202f.; M. Rhonheimer, Postscript to the English edition, p. 578. I cannot, however, understand why it should be illegitimate in this context to refer to *STh* I–II, q. 91, a. 3, where Thomas uses the example of the "inventive" activity of the *lex humana* to exemplify his discussion of the gradations in ethical judgments.

thought of as absolutely immutable.[85] In a certain sense, this is true of the simple fact that both women and men share the same biological nature. But it applies even more strongly when we consider our nature as a culturally elaborated reality and investigate the ordering of our social lives. In the first dimension of human existence, where it is (for example) natural that the human person has two feet, human beings do not display the same similarity as fire in Greece and fire in Persia, which are physically identical phenomena; although human nature in general entails that the right half of the body is better-equipped than the left half, there also exist left-handed persons. The spectrum of variety is even broader when we look at the cultural forms of human life, for example, the customary forms of clothing, which differ from country to country and change with the passing of time. This is trivial in itself, but it is very significant at this point in the text, because Thomas sees it as an analogy to the manner in which the universally valid prescriptions of the natural law are realized on the level of concrete conduct. It is an anthropological constant of human nature to use clothing to hide one's nakedness and shame; on the other hand, the custom of wearing a *tunica* is limited to one particular cultural sphere. In the same way, precepts which come under the heading of justice, such as the prohibition of theft, are absolutely immutable, but the precise regulations governing the realization of such precepts can be mutable under certain circumstances.[86]

Thomas makes a very exact distinction between the sense in which our nature is mutable, and the sense in which we must assume the existence of an immutable minimum which is termed "natural" in a stricter sense.[87] As there are some essential characteristics of our biological human existence which are always the same (e.g., the fact that we belong to the species of living beings), and it is impossible to imagine the concept of "human person" without these characteristics, so too with the moral order: we must assume the existence of immutable principles presupposed by the very idea of human co-existence in society. It is only these highest principles of the natural law *(prima principia communia; quaedam principia communissima, quae sunt omnibus nota)* that are strictly universal and necessary; they cover only what must be assumed true in all cases. For Thomas, apart from the highest principle of *bonum faciendum* and its equivalents, the only im-

---

85. *In V Ethicorum*, lect. 12 (nr. 1026): *"Sed apud nos homines, qui sumus inter res corruptibiles, est aliquid secundum naturam, et tamen quicquid est in nobis mutabile vel per se vel per accidens."*

86. *In V Ethicorum*, lect. 12 (nr. 1028–29).

87. F.-J. Bormann presents a penetrating analysis of Thomas' understanding of the "mutability" *(mutabilitas)* of the natural ethical law: *Natur als Horizont*, pp. 249–54.

mutable, universally known, and absolutely universally valid principles, where the human reason cannot err, are the Golden Rule and the command to love one's neighbor. In the case of the so-called secondary commandments of the natural law, which are directly inferred from the highest principles and are in effect their first and nearest conclusions *(quasi conclusiones principiorum communium; quasi conclusiones propinquae principiis),* he assumes that their universal validity can be limited either by particular circumstances or by a lack of knowledge in individual instances. Nevertheless, it is in general possible for all persons to know these secondary commandments on the intermediary level of the natural law, whose primary example is the prohibitions of the Decalogue; hence, Thomas regards these as the common property of all mankind. There may indeed exist fundamental divergences with regard to the understanding of justice, according to circumstances of time and place, but this is not because we lack any universal concept of justice; rather, this concept, which is anchored in human nature, may require a variety of specifications *propter mutationem conditionum hominum,* so that there is not universal agreement everywhere about what is considered to be good and just on the level where individual actions are evaluated.

Time and place are the most important factors influencing the variety of specifications added by divine and human laws to the commandments of the natural law. Hence, although the human reason can grasp the Ten Commandments with infallible certainty (even if this does not in fact always happen), we find within the biblical revelation the addition of explanatory prohibitions, expansions, or clarifications regarding the sphere within which these commandments are valid; and these are even more subject to historical change. For example, the priestly legislation adds the prohibition of blasphemy to the prohibition of false testimony in the Decalogue (Lv 24:15), and extends the commandment about parents to cover older relatives too (Lv 19:32). The precept not to hate one's brother or harm him in any other way is added to the prohibition of killing (Lv 19:16), the prohibition of adultery is expanded into a general prohibition of fornication, the prohibition of theft is completed by a prohibition of usury, etc. If the commandments of the Decalogue are to find acknowledgment in their basic substance in the course of history, they require further prohibitions which will surround them in the manner of a forecourt and thus complete them.[88] Since these necessary expansions have become a

88. Cf. *STh* I–II, q. 94, aa. 4–5, and I–II, q. 100, a. 1; q. 100, a. 5, ad 1; q. 100, a. 11.

part of history and are themselves subject to further changes, the natural law never attains validity in history otherwise than in a mutable form, even though its universal commandments are immutable *per se*. An absolutely immutable ethical law would be conceptually impossible for Thomas, since it would accord neither with the mutability of the circumstances of human life nor with the laws governing the activity of the practical reason. Since the reason can activate its motivating power only when it bears in mind the specific nature of human activity, an ethical law conceived in strictly ahistorical terms, which simply ignored the variety of conditions affecting human conduct, could have no real validity. Accordingly, it is only logical that Thomas limits the function of the principles of natural law to the preparation and justification of a framework of ethical order, while he follows the Aristotelian model of an ethics of virtue when he elaborates the concrete ethos in his *Summa Theologiae*.

3. Encountering the classical objections to the natural law

Modern research into the history of theology takes a very different view of Thomas' ethics from that of the neothomism which was long dominant. This saw the doctrine of natural law primarily as a transposition of metaphysical ideas of order to the realm of human life in society and of individual human conduct. The modern view is, however, also opposed to the interpretation of Thomas' thinking about the natural law found outside the Catholic sphere in the twentieth century, in such scholars as Ernst Troeltsch, Max Weber, Hans Welzel, or Ernst Topitsch. The doctrine of the natural law conceived by Thomas within the framework of his theory of the practical reason is not intended to provide theological legitimation for the alleged monoculture of mediaeval life; nor can one deduce from this doctrine a specific moral doctrine or a normative philosophy of society. Rather, the doctrine of the natural law, along with Origen's understanding of freedom, the patristic theology of the *imago Dei*, Augustine's idea of *dignitas*, and Abelard's concept of the conscience, belongs in the total context of reflection within the theological tradition on the ethical autonomy of the human person and his special dignity as a rational being capable of assuming responsibility for his own life. Thomas makes a close link between natural law and human dignity when he interprets the *lex naturalis* as that participation in the divine governance of the world which is appropriate to the rational character of the human person; and this link can be understood as the beginning of the process in intellectual history wherein the individual awakens to self-consciousness as a moral subject.[89]

If Thomas' own elaboration of the doctrine of the moral law in the context of his theological ethics is so different from the rationalistic and Thomistic systems of natural-law thinking which have been developed from the seventeenth century onward, one is entitled to doubt whether the classical objections to natural-law argumentation apply to Thomas himself. As we have shown in the first chapter, these objections envisage a pattern of argument which can indeed be found in some individual points in Thomas (e.g., when he justifies the order of monogamous marriage by appeal to natural law) but is *not* typical of his theory of the practical reason and his doctrine of the ethical law. This means that one should hesitate before subsuming Thomas' model of the *lex naturalis* under the customary constructions of natural law and assuming that the well-known objections have implicitly invalidated it. When Thomas elaborates his theory of the ethical law, he consciously distances himself from the metaphysics of conduct and from a consideration of the ethical law from the perspective of theology; hence, this theory is an independent approach to which these objections must be adressed specifically. If it emerges that Thomas' theory can withstand a critical analysis, this result would have more than merely historical significance as a corrective to erroneous judgments made by historians of theology: it would also have considerable systematic consequences. If Thomas' theory of the ethical law is *not* based on a naturalistic fallacy, does *not* succumb to a circular justification, and also leaves space for the development of historical forms of ethos, then it could provide a convincing explanation of the function that must be attributed to a universal ethics in our historical world.

3.1. The argument of naturalistic fallacy

The first accusation leveled at the classical doctrines of the natural law is that their judgments are based on an illegitimate inference from descriptive states of affairs to prescriptive consequences. Such a confusion between the levels of significance and evaluation presupposes, however, that the human reason in its practical application functions as an epistemological principle independent of the theoretical reason, transposing statements

89. On this, cf. L. Honnefelder, *Die ethische Rationalität des mittelalterlichen Naturrechts*, p. 271; J. B. Metz, *Christliche Anthropozentrik. Über die Denkform des Thomas von Aquin*, Munich 1962, pp. 43–52.

of fact known to the theoretical reason in the form of indicatives to the level of prescriptive regulations which lay down what ought to be the case; but we do not find this complete identification of the theoretical and the practical reason in Thomas. On the contrary, his whole theory of the *lex naturalis* is based on the strict inderivability of the practical reason with regard to its origin, its highest epistemological principles, and its consequent laws of realization. If one takes this threefold autonomy of the practical reason seriously, there is no reason whatsoever to pose the problem of deducing normative value judgments from theoretical affirmations about human nature; for the practical reason does not obtain its highest moral principle from the basic propositions of the theoretical reason. Rather, the normative premises from which it deduces its conclusions possess their own fundamental evidential character, which allows the practical reason to knows them. Accordingly, its judgments are not based on an illegitimate "application" of theoretical insights to the sphere of human praxis; rather, the imperative character of the moral principle, valid a priori, is transposed to the whole series of initial conclusions and subsequent specifications, and the final transition entails a diminishing degree of certainty in the prescriptive judgments.

The structuring activity of the reason, which lays down the *ordo praeceptorum,* does indeed follow the order of the ends of natural striving. These, however, become morally relevant only when they are structured by the reason, which takes on the character of criterion in these ends. Logically speaking, this argumentation is based on an *imperative* premise, that is, the axiomatic fundamental difference between good and evil which the moral principle maintains. In the light of this fundamental difference, more specific imperatives can be deduced from further *indicative* premises, viz. the ends and goods synthesized in the *inclinationes naturales.* The indicative presuppositions to which the judgment of the practical reason appeals on the intermediate stage are indications with a pre-moral character: they predispose the outcome from a substantial point of view, but the normative obligatory character of the concrete imperatives is generated only by the *ordinatio rationis* which becomes visible in these natural presuppositions of human existence. This means that the structure of judgment underlying Thomas' theory of the natural law does full justice to the "most difficult task" of ethical argumentation, that is, "arriving at substantial norms with an anthropological basis, without committing the naturalistic fallacy."[90]

90. F. Ricken, "Naturrecht I," p. 151; on this, cf. also A. Anzenbacher, *Einführung in die*

The logical status of this structure corresponds exactly to the precise formulation of Hume's law, which allows the deduction of more specific moral imperatives from a mixed group of premises which contain not only indicative propositions, but also at least *one* originally imperative starting point. This means that a natural-law argumentation which follows this pattern is not based on an illegitimate inference from an "is" to an "ought," but rather on a logically correct application of the specific law of consequences proper to the practical reason in its own underivable autonomy.

The epistemological possibilities offered to us today by the natural sciences allow us to define the limitation placed at the intermediate level on the ethical commandments by the structure of the natural dispositions of our human nature with greater precision than was possible for Thomas, with his brief remarks about the structure of the *inclinationes naturales*. This does not affect the basic idea, viz. that when the reason exercises its function of guiding action, it encounters non-arbitrary presuppositions and conditions which must be heeded in an exact manner if human praxis is to succeed. Without this insight, it is impossible for our human existence to develop its true potential. This insight is not based on special anthropological presuppositions, nor on ahistorical definitions of the degree of development of human nature which has been attained at any particular point in time. Rather, we are led to heed these natural presuppositions of our conduct by the recognition of the fundamental fact that the human person, even in his ethical autonomy, is a finite being who must follow the structure of his natural needs when he takes charge of his own life, and cannot arbitrarily alter his existential constitution. This is why natural-law patterns of thought enter every ethical argumentation in some form or other, if the attempt is made to arrive at substantial imperatives; this remains true even if most contemporary approaches in ethical thinking no longer make any explicit reference to the tradition of the classical doctrines of natural law.

In today's philosophical anthropology, however, we find many affirmations and avenues of research which could be considered as corresponding structurally to Thomas's doctrine of the *inclinationes naturales*, and indeed (to the extent that this is at all possible under the conditions of modern science) as an empirical verification of this doctrine. The first approach to be mentioned here, thanks to the claims it makes for itself, is the theory of

---

Ethik, Düsseldorf 1992, pp. 90–97; M. Rhonheimer, *Praktische Vernunft und Vernünftigkeit der Praxis*, p. 549.

"essential purposes of life" or "existential purposes" elaborated by Johannes Messner, an important natural-law ethicist, in his book *Das Naturrecht* (1958) with the intention of substantiating the *ordo bonorum*. His combination of inductive inference and the metaphysical interpretation of an objective order of goods and values found a broad echo in Catholic social ethics, although his implicit presuppositions provoked criticism.[91] We shall therefore look at three other approaches, which arrive at similar conclusions from different starting points.

The analysis of the basic triadic structure of human life presented by the social ethicist Wilhelm Korff refers explicitly to Thomas and elaborates his affirmations about a threefold basic pattern of human conduct: making use of things in practice, aggressive competition, and care for others. These fundamental human dispositions are related to one another in a structure which of its very nature is not open to the arbitrary choice of individuals, and this means that the ethically relevant "nature" of the human person must be understood as a "perichoresis" in which the *fulfillment of needs, self-assertion,* and *willingness to exercise care for others* mutually condition and limit one another. The practical reason can give normative regulation to the sphere of action of these natural driving forces in various ways, depending on the dominant cultural images and historical forms of the ethos in particular epochs; but the basic interactional structure presupposed in all human conduct is a non-arbitrary anthropological constant element. Korff differs from Thomas in that he does not limit himself to a speculative exposition of these anthropological matters, nor to a description which appeals exclusively to the constitution of the human person as body and soul. Rather, numerous empirical insights from behavioral research and human cultural history are presented as evidence of the existence of such a structural framework, establishing a certain basis for the supposition of an invariable predisposition of human conduct by natural motivating structures.[92]

---

91. On this, cf. G. Höver, *Erfahrhung und Vernunft. Untersuchungen zum Problem sittlich relevanter Einsichten unter besonderer Berücksichtigung der Naturrechtsethik von Johannes Messner,* Düsseldorf 1981, pp. 117–22; C. Kissling, *Gemeinwohl und Gerechtigkeit,* pp. 112–20.

92. On this, cf. W. Korff, *Norm und Sittlichkeit,* pp. 76–112, and Idem, *Der Rückgriff auf die Natur,* pp. 291ff. A cautious criticism is expressed by U. Zelinska, *Normativität der Natur—Natur der Normativität. Eine interdisziplinäre Studie zur Frage der Genese und Funktion von Normen,* Freiburg 1994, pp. 191–93. He suggests replacing the formula of perichoresis, which is orientated to the results of the classical research into behavior, by the "basic pattern of balance between one's own interests and those of society," which he adopts from sociobiology (p. 193).

The English moral philosopher Morris Ginsberg, whom we have already met as a critic of ethical relativism, analyzes the relationship between
fundamental human needs and ideas about moral value, translating the
concept of *summum bonum* (employed in the ethics of Aristotle and
Thomas to indicate the highest existential potential of the human person)
by means of the idea of an all-around excellent life, or all-around excel-
lence, in which all the moral ideals of an epoch have their origin. He follows Aristotle in emphasizing that the evaluation of the ends of human
conduct, and a fortiori their integration into a supreme existential end,
cannot take place by means of a quantitative measuring or a comparison
between the degrees of satisfaction attained by different individuals; rather,
this requires the intuitive (or as Thomas would say, the connatural) judgment of an excellent human being. In order to avoid the much-discussed
logical circle which threatens Aristotle here, Ginsberg requires that one replace the figure of the excellent human being with his special capacity to
formulate ethical judgments by a rationally checkable reconstruction of
the relationship between moral ideals and the fundamental needs of human nature. He sees a dialectical relationship of tension between these two
poles: while our moral ideals serve to protect fundamental human needs,
they also transpose and correct these needs by establishing a rational balance among them.

Human needs take diverse forms in individuals, and they are also
shaped in many ways by cultural factors. Ginsberg distinguishes between
ends which are instruments and ends which are their own end, and he
identifies three categories of needs which are basic constant forms of human desire. The first group embraces the needs of the body, the second the
needs of the mind, and the third our social needs; the ideal of health of
mind and body, the striving for truth, and the moral ideas of love, collabo-
ration, and justice correspond to these needs.[93]

A decisive point for Ginsberg's anti-naturalistic theory of fundamental
human needs is that our moral ideals can arise only on the basis of natural
goods and ends; at the same time, however, these ideals transcend such
goods and ends by a process of the constructive imagination, which integrates them into a rounded-off form of human life: "It will be seen that
these ideals, though rooted in human needs, imply obligations and make
demands which control and transform them. These demands are not arbi-

93. M. Ginsberg, "Basic Needs and Moral Ideals," in: Idem, *On the Diversity of Morals*,
London 2nd edn. 1962, pp. 130–48, esp. 132–34.

trary but are inherent in the structure of the needs and the ideals and are, so to say, necessitated by the structure. Each ideal generates its own norms and they appeal and constrain in varying degrees."[94] Ginsberg attributes the plurality of human lifestyles to the varied balance among those moral ideals toward which every human person is inherently disposed, thanks to the very structure of human needs, which is identical in every person (at least in its components). We need not discuss here whether his account of the genesis of our moral ideals is accurate; but even if his analysis has been superseded in some points (especially as regards the role of cultural formation in begetting "artificial" needs), the parallel between Ginsberg's three-fold basic structure of the needs of human nature and the structuring of the *inclinationes naturales* is surely remarkable.

The structuring of the natural goods and ends which Thomas postulates on the levels of the preservation of the individual and the species, of partnership between the sexes, and of a life in human society and the knowledge of the truth, also includes an inclination towards those natural ends which human beings share with animals. Nevertheless, the needs of the first two levels are structured in us in a specifically *human* manner. They find satisfaction, not in an instinctual manner, but by means of an interplay with the reason which is present even in the "animal" stirrings of the human person. Among contemporary anthropological approaches, we find this double character of human existence—in a sense, at the antipodes to Ginsberg's system based on fundamental goods—most clearly expressed in Erich Fromm's theory of the fundamental existential needs which must achieve a correct balance, if an autonomous ethical personality and a "productive" character-structure are to be formed. Fromm sees the human person as characterized by a strange split, an existential contradiction: as a natural being, the human person takes his place in nature with its physical regularities and its animal instincts, while at the same time transcending nature as a rational being whose life is entrusted to his own self. The human person is a part of nature, yet transcends nature. Indeed, he must transcend it, since he has received, not the animal's equipment of instincts, but the capacity to shape his own life in conscious response to the claim made by moral ideals.

Fromm supposes that the dichotomous structure of human life gradually developed in the course of phylogenesis. As dependence on instinct diminished, so consciousness increased, along with the ability to govern con-

94. Ibid., p. 136.

duct rationally. This capacity found externally visible expression in the growth of the brain, with a correlative elaboration of a specific category of existential needs in the interior experience of the human person. This is why Fromm distinguishes between two categories of fundamental human needs; when these come into conflict with one another, an extremely precarious situation can result. The human person shares *physiological* needs with the animals (hunger, thirst, the need for rest and sleep or sexual satisfaction), but he also has *existential* needs which characterize him specifically as a human person, viz. one in charge of his own life. Here we can see the human person not only as an instinctual being, but also as one who transcends this dimension in his search for meaning and his hunger for happiness, and as one who experiences a profound uncertainty in the conflict between his fundamental needs: "Hunger, thirst, and the sexual instinct may be completely satisfied, but this does not mean that the human person himself is satisfied."[95] Unlike the animal, the human person cannot find the solution to his most urgent problems in satisfaction of his instincts *alone.* The existential uncertainty remains even when his physiological needs are fully satisfied. The deep-seated biological and existential antinomy of the human person means that his real questions arise only when he thinks that he has solved the task of coping with life on the primary level.

Fromm sees the yearning for identity and orientation (i.e., a fundamental need for meaning) and for the conscious experience of his own self as the basic existential needs common to all human persons. When these are fulfilled, the result is psychological health and a positive attitude to life; if they are continually thwarted, however, this promotes the development of a destructive character. Other basic needs are the experience of being securely "at home" and the longing for unity, which counteract the existential contradiction of the human person, and the need to engage in creative activity, which encompasses everything from trying out one's own strength to the ability to transcend the world by means of reason and to set something in the world in motion. The need for transcendence is closely linked to the longing for devotion, which Fromm understands as the desire to subordinate one's life to demanding ideals.[96] Although Fromm offers a somewhat different presentation of such fundamental human needs, it is not difficult to grasp that this is an articulation of the two poles towards

95. E. Fromm, *Psychoanalyse und Ethik. Bausteine zu einer humanistischen Charakterologie* (*Gesammelte Werke* II), Stuttgart 1980, pp. 1–157, at 34.
96. E. Fromm, *Die Anatomie der menschlichen Destruktivität*, Hamburg 1974, p. 245.

which (in Thomas' view) the specifically human inclinations tend: life in society and the striving for truth.[97]

Like Ginsberg's list of fundamental human goods, Fromm's investigation of the anatomy of basic existential needs intends to uncover anthropological constants; this is indicated by his rejection of a relativistic interpretation of these needs. The concrete manner in which these are satisfied may indeed be dependent on a whole number of culturally specific factors, but this does not make this satisfaction arbitrary. Rather, it must take its bearings within the conditions of human existence, making possible a resolution of its antinomic conflict. The decisive point here is that each of the existential needs can be satisfied in one of two manners, either by love and tenderness, by striving for truth and justice, or else by hatred and oppression, destructive violence, and pleasure in cruelty. The antinomy of the fundamental existential human needs can be seen with special clarity in the danger that our aggressive potential poses to our own selves. Nature has equipped the human person with aggression, which may take the form of a tendency to self-assertion at the service of life, or of a healthy competition; on this level, aggression is as yet only a pre-moral phenomenon. Like the instincts concerning power, possessions, sexuality, and care of others, therefore, the aggressive potential must be cultivated by means of moral self-education, where one learns how to behave in society. Only the development of this kind of productive character-structure allows the human person to find a response to the existential contradiction of his existence which will go beyond the ebb and flow of momentary experiences of pleasure.

Fromm's anthropology can also be understood as a contemporary presentation of central themes of Thomas' ethics when he interprets the true end of human life as the highest degree of happiness. Both thinkers see the human person's happiness as the achievement by which he finds a lasting respose to the basic existential conflict posed by being a part of nature, yet orientated to truth and goodness in a manner that transcends nature. They agree that the idea of happiness involves more than a sensuous state in the human person, or the capacity "to experience some kind of pleasure" in

---

97. In the chapter on Fromm in his dissertation, S. Wirz discerns five fundamental existential needs: first, the need to experience identity; second, the need to engage in creative activity; third, the need to be "at home" and have security; fourth, the need for a framework which provides orientation and an object for one's devotion; fifth, the need to enter relationships with other human beings. Cf. *Vom Mangel zum Überfluß: Die bedürfnisethische Frage in der Industriegesellschaft,* Münster 1993, pp. 121ff.

any arbitrary way.[98] Since the human person's real questions arise only when his physiological needs have been met at least to some extent, the idea of happiness aims at a quality of the person and his character which will allow the existential contradiction in the human person to be overcome.

3.2. *The argument of circular justification*

Our historical overview of the numerous and sometimes contradictory inferences which have been drawn from the "nature" of the human person in the history of ethical thinking led us to the second objection to the classical doctrines of natural law, viz. the accusation of a concealed question-begging, or—to make the same point more drastically—of the employment of a circular argumentation to arrive at the concrete affirmations of such doctrines. It is alleged that the substance of a "life in accord with nature" was first transposed as an anthropological description onto the concept of "nature," and then deduced as normative consequences from the "nature" which was understood in this manner: the idea of "nature" would be nothing more than a hollow mold here, available to be filled with a variety of anthropological, metaphysical, or social-philosophical contents, which were then clothed with an ethical dignity on the basis of their alleged conformity with nature—thus concealing their origin in arbitrary affirmations. This last point makes this argument against the natural law a critique of ideology: the aim is above all to reveal the way in which "natural law" has been abused as a legitimation of forms of societal domination or patriarchal gender-relationships. A classical example of the undeniable susceptibility of classical natural law to ideology from its earliest period would be Plato's derivation of the existing constitution of the state from a hierarchical model of the degrees in the human soul; in the twentieth century, examples would be the refusal to allow employees to participate in decision-making in their workplaces or the exclusive power of the man to take decisions in all matters concerning the marriage in which he was only one of the partners (allegedly deduced from the very nature of marriage itself).

Although there is a close connection between the last objection to

---

98. E. Fromm, *Psychoanalyse und Ethik*, p. 121. On the rejection of a relativistic interpretation of human needs, and on the interpretation of happiness as an objective achievement which the human person must realize, cf. S. Wirz, *Vom Mangel*, p. 129.

Thomas' theory of the *lex naturalis* (concerning the possible naturalistic fallacy) and this present objection, it is not so easy to reply to the charge of a circular justification. To begin with, we must recall that Thomas explicitly reckons with the mutability of human nature and the diminishing certainty of individual normative judgments; the closed circle of justification is broken a priori by the fact that different degrees exist in the application of the practical reason. Nevertheless, the theory of the practical reason, and especially the doctrine about the ends of natural striving, have anthropological implications which are not established within Thomas' ethical theory by means of argumentation, but are simply presupposed. Despite its autonomous basis in the self-realization of the practical reason, Thomas' ethic—like every system of moral philosophy—has an inherent and necessary relationship to anthropology and to metaphysics, which of course may not be understood as a subordination to these or a deduction from them. Until we have clarified the precise status of these anthropological implications within the course taken by the ethical argumentation, we cannot give a definitive reply to the accusation that Thomas' theory begs these questions.

There is a significant anthropological presupposition in the very starting point of Thomas' ethics: that the human person is a rational being who bears responsibility for his own life and therefore has the capacity to know that which is good and necessary for his human existence as a whole, that which brings human existence to its integral fulfillment.[99] All the more does this apply to the supposition that this good, which is recognized by the reason and is true of the human person in his entirety, is sketched in advance by the structure of his natural motive forces. The two basic anthropological presuppositions which form the background to Thomas' theory of the practical reason and to the doctrine of the natural law can be summarized in two affirmations: the human person acts as a free and responsible rational being, that is, as a person, and he develops his personal existence, in keeping with the constitution of his existence as body and soul, in a necessary relationship to his own self and to others, as well as in the transcendence of his spirit in the direction of that which is true and good.

99. *In IV Ethicorum*, lect. 4 (nr. 1162): *"sed circa ea quae sunt bona et utilia ad hoc quod tota humana vita sit bona."* Ibid. (nr. 1166): *"Prudentia est habitus cum vera ratione activus, non circa factibilia, quae sunt extra hominem, sed circa bona et mala ipsius hominis."* In *De virtutibus in communi*, a. 9: *"Nam bonum hominis inquantum est homo, est ut ratio sit perfecta in cognitione veritatis, et inferiores appetitus regulentur secundum regulam rationis: nam homo habet quod sit homo per hoc quod sit rationalis."*

These anthropological implications are not in the least arbitrary suppositions or adventitious definitions, in the sense that the normative consequences inferred from them would be completely different if other presuppositions had been chosen. Rather, the relationship between anthropology and ethics is exactly the opposite, when we consider ethics as a practical science: ethical reflection begins with the self-realization of the practical reason as its initial datum, and then asks about the anthropological conditions which might account for the underivable phenomenon of the rationality of human praxis. Only thus can ethical reflection uncover the implications entailed by the ethical responsibility of the human person and by his fundamental moral capacity. The anthropological thesis required by Thomas' doctrine of the natural law does not extend beyond the irrevocable conditions of moral self-determination and responsibility for shaping one's own life; these are, so to speak, the minimum requirement if we are to conceive of a concept of moral behavior which would be valid for the human person as such. In short, the demands of the natural law in the strict sense refer to a basic stock of existential conditions and possibilities of expression which belong to human existence as such and make ethical conduct possible.

At this point, we can see a differentiation within natural-law thinking which follows the differentiated degrees of the practical reason. Just as the latter is strictly universal only in its highest principles and the conclusions drawn immediately from these—since these are recognized by every human being with a priori necessity—so the substantial sameness which the concept of the natural law discerns in human existence at all times and places is restricted to the inalienable basic presuppositions without which ethical existence is impossible. On this first level of natural-law argumentation, the human person is not yet considered in the dimension in which he can attain his highest fulfillment and realize the fullest potential of his being, but in the dimension which *initially* makes his human existence possible. This is also the reason why the *negative* precepts of the natural law, which protect the inviolable sphere of freedom proper to the human person, claim a strictly universal validity, whereas the *positive* precepts, which point the path to a life which is genuinely meaningful as a whole, have only that general validity which attaches to the judgments made by the practical reason on each specific level.

This differentiation between the two levels of argumentation in favor of the legitimacy of natural-law norms means that we must understand the concept of "nature" on the first level as a *minimal definition* which envisages only the most basic requirement for human existence, not the authentic realization of this existence. No matter what comprehensive life-project a person follows, and whatever he may do in order to realize this project in specific detail, he needs the basic possibility of developing himself as a being consisting of both body and soul, of seeking fellowship with other like-minded persons, of striving to know the truth, and so on. The natural motive-forces of his existence, which Thomas summarizes in the doctrine of the *inclinationes naturales*, indicate an external a priori framework for every attempt to discover happiness and a meaningful life and to lead a life which is successful as a whole. Accordingly, reflection on the indispensable minimum conditions for human existence, on which the theory of the *lex naturalis* is based, resembles the process of reduction in the contemporary discussion of human dignity and human rights, whereby we take the variety of ideas about anthropological meaning which human persons follow and distill from these that normative kernel of human dignity which the idea of inalienable human rights seeks to protect.[100]

When the modern concept of human rights takes as its critical criterion the element in human existence which is always and everywhere the same—what Aristotle calls "that which is naturally right" φύσει δίχαιον —it presupposes a modest, "culturally neutral" anthropology (to use Otfried Höffe's term). Like the Aristotelian-Thomist idea of the natural law, this anthropology can be employed on its first level only in a critical manner: in other words, all we can do is note the infringements of that which is naturally right. This is because this "modest" anthropology deals, not with the comprehensive realization of individual personal existence, but only with the "initial conditions" of human existence.[101] It is open to interpretations on a higher level, but it does not yet supply a criterion for them. It is precisely this that allows the anthropology of human rights, reduced to the absolute kernel of human existence, to claim a validity that embraces every historical epoch and can be proposed to every culture. This anthropology, however, points beyond itself to an idea of human dignity which it cannot completely analyze or expound. Hence it is not unrelated or indifferent to the systems of anthropological meaning which offer us the image of successful human existence; rather, it is essentially open to anthropologies with a greater degree of substance. However, when such com-

100. On this, cf. E. Schockenhoff, *Ethik des Lebens. Ein theologischer Grundriß*, Mainz 1993, pp. 177ff.

101. On this, cf. O. Höffe, "Ein transzendentaler Tausch. Zur Anthropologie der Menschenrechte," *PhJ* (1992), pp. 1–28, esp. 7–13.

prehensive interpretations of life, and the plausible directives that a lofty ethics issues against the background of these interpretations, aim at universal validity (as in the case of the Judaeo-Christian tradition), this occurs on a different level than that on which the universal validity of the principles of natural law or the universal acknowledgment of natural-law prohibitions is postulated.

Let us return to the question with which this section began. We can now give a summary answer: a logical justificatory circle is excluded by the laws governing the activity of the practical reason and its inductive procedure in the realm of the concrete, as Thomas presumes in the case of the *determinatio* and *adinventio* of the ultimate imperatives which guide conduct. Instead of a circular deduction, we have a justification on various levels: the *first* consists of the natural law in the stricter sense of the term, containing only a reduced anthropology which is required by the concept of human existence as such. On this level, ethics is not deduced from anthropology; on the contrary, the intention is to discover the anthropological implications which are necessarily presupposed in the self-realization of the practical reason and in the other phenomena of the ethical realm. On the *second* level of the natural law, concerned with the comprehensive success and ultimate potential of human existence, the relationship between ethics and anthropology is reversed. Here, against the background of various anthropological systems of meaning and the *maximum conceptions* of humanity which each of these proposes, the practical reason can arrive de facto at specific directives of a lofty ethical character, with a universal claim that goes beyond the absolute validity of their negative prohibitions.

It is true that Thomas does not distinguish between these two levels of the natural law with the clarity that we would desire today, since he was not as conscious as we are of the question of the cultural variability of human existence. In the theological context within which he develops his theory of he natural law, the obvious step is to place greater emphasis on the union of the two aspects; for us, when we wish to justify the natural law, it seems urgent to distinguish them clearly. Since the affirmations about anthropological meaning contained in the lofty ethical directives of the biblical-Christian tradition claim to perfect human nature, they necessarily belong within a comprehensive concept of the *lex naturalis*; and the substance involved here is not without any relation to this concept even at its reduced (and hence "neutral") level. From our perspective, Thomas' failure to reflect explicitly on the distinction between the two levels—that of an absolute minimum presupposition of human existence, and that of its integral perfection—must be considered a weakness in his exposition of the theory of the natural law. If, however, this distinction is substantially plausible, it indicates an indispensable residuum of natural-law thinking which is not affected by the standard accusation made by modern criticism of the natural law.

3.3. The argument of an ahistorical understanding of nature

Now that our exposition of Thomas' texts has shown clearly that mutability is a specific characteristic of human nature, a brief discussion of the third main accusation leveled against the classical doctrines of the natural law will suffice. There is a general consensus among contemporary historians of philosophy that the conception of a "self-sufficient" natural law, which originated in late scholasticism and reached its high point in the early modern period in the treatises on law of Spanish baroque theology, is based on the presupposition that the essential nature of the human person is unchangeable.[102] However, a comparison with Thomas' theory of the *lex naturalis* shows that this development within the tradition of natural-law thinking entails a transformation of the original approach; many later criticisms of the idea of natural law are in fact made possible only by this transformation. Within his theory of the natural law, Thomas himself envisaged a reflection in a number of distinct steps which can account for what we now call the historicity of morality. In order to sense how closely these arguments are linked to his entire theological-ethical project, it suffices once again to recall briefly the difference between the theoretical and the practical reason, the various degrees in the laws of application of the practical reason, the openness of human nature to receiving a form, and the multiplicity of the conditions of human life.[103]

For Thomas, the idea of *natura mutabilis* does not mean that the "na-

---

102. On this, cf. H. Welzel, *Naturrecht und materiale Gerechtigkeit. Problemgeschichtliche Untersuchungen als Prolegomena zu einer Rechtsphilosophie*, Göttingen 1960, pp. 95–99; K.-H. Ilting, "Naturrecht II," *GGB* IV, 270–73; J. T. C. Arntz, "Die Entwicklung des naturrechtlichen Denkens innerhalb des Thomismus," in: F. Böckle (ed.), *Das Naturrecht im Disput*, Düsseldorf 1966, pp. 87–120, esp. 100–112.

103. The significance of these factors for our understanding of the historicity of morality has been set out with especial clarity by L. Honnefelder, *Naturrecht und Geschichte*, pp. 8–16. Cf., however, also P. M. Hall, *Narrative and the Natural Law. An Interpretation of Thomistic Ethics*, Notre Dame and London 1994, pp. 94–105. She centers her interpretation on the internal "history of discovery" of the practical reason and (following her teacher, A. MacIntyre) on the embedding of the practical reason in historical narrative communities.

ture" of the human person could be changed as such, in the sense that one would take on a different nature and become something else. Rather, it is conceived as antithetical to the immutable divine nature, and this assumes a priori that the concept of the human person as such remains constant, underlying the historical epiphenomena of this nature in their illimitable variety; indeed, it is only this constant that makes possible the historical changes in the epiphenomena. One can also draw on the development of the modern concept of human dignity to show how the idea of the historicity of the human person and of his nature postulates a fundamental identity of human existence; for otherwise, all change in history would be transformation *into* another human existence, not the mutability of the human person *in* his human existence. Our concept of human dignity is concerned with the absolute kernel of human existence, and therefore presupposes a concept of the human person which is always and everywhere the same. Nevertheless, there is no one historical standpoint which would allow the formulation of an exhaustive catalogue of the essential conditions for the protection of human dignity; this is why each catalogue of human rights involves an anticipatory vision of a totality which can never be grasped to the full, yet is presupposed in each attempt at an approximation in history. There is an indissoluble dialectical relationship between the human person's "nature" and the forms in which this is realized in history. The consequence for the development of our ethos of human rights is that the concept of what is "naturally" correct can be realized only in the form of individual human rights, but all these rights, even taken as a whole, do not exhaust this concept.[104]

The human rights which are formulated in response to the experience of suffering injustice and in the face of the changing historical threats to human existence thus point beyond themselves to an idea of human dignity which they cannot expound completely; nevertheless, they necessarily presuppose this idea in the process of their elaboration within history. The dialectical unity between human dignity and its specific historical articulation in the form of particular human rights can help us understand the relationship between the "nature" of the human person and its changing historical realizations, and explain why the historical change in our moral ideas—as the overview in the first chapter has shown—concerns not only peripheral spheres, but also the very core of what human existence means,

---

104. On this, cf. S. König, *Zur Begründung der Menschenrechte: Hobbes-Locke-Kant*, Freiburg and Munich 1994, p. 60.

without, however, subjecting this core to merely arbitrary change. Accordingly, we must conclude by reflecting on the relationship between that which is always and everywhere identical in human "nature" and its changeable manifestations in the historical life of human beings. We shall do this in a context which many see as the sixty-four-thousand-dollar question in moral theology today, that is, the problem of intrinsically evil actions, those natural-law prohibitions which admit of no exceptions.

4. Prohibitions of the natural law, or intrinsically evil actions

In his early work *Die Einheit in der Kirche* ("Unity in the Church," published in 1825), the Tübingen theologian Johann Adam Möhler describes an inner law governing the development of doctrine in the church, which can help us understand the significance of theological controversies for the conceptual elaboration of the dogmatic truth of the faith. According to Möhler, the original wholeness and fullness of the living faith of the church is characterized by polarities and antitheses which are bound together in an unconscious unity, until they are called into question (either from outside the church or by theological reflection) in a manner that attempts to exclude one of these poles from the church. The antithesis, initially preserved as it were in the slumber of an unconscious unity with its opposite pole, thus becomes an open contradiction, which the church's consciousness of the faith attacks through the voice of the magisterium. This makes it necessary to stake out boundary lines; this in turn leads to a parting of the ways, which, however, is only an intermediary stage on the path to a higher unity, in which the element of truth which was maintained even in an irreconcilable contradiction is brought back into the body of the church's faith. In this higher unity, the original antitheses no longer lie alongside one another without any connection; now, they are received as reconciled polarities into a conscious unity, with their indispensable significance for each other acknowledged. If on the other hand it proves impossible to bring back the contradiction which was expelled from the church, the consequence is an impoverishment of the consciousness of the faith itself, since the excluded aspect puts at risk the wholeness of the faith and the fullness of its truth. Accordingly, no matter how necessary demarcations may be in the specific situation where contradictions must be confronted, dogmatic development cannot remain forever fixed in the attitude of opposition; rather, it must reconquer its own wholeness, if it is to possess, in a conscious unity which reconciles the opposites, the fullness of the deposit of faith which has been entrusted to it.[105]

Möhler draws on idealistic conceptions of history when he sets out the logic whereby theology penetrates the truth of the faith. His primary intention is to explain the history of the dogmatic statements taught by the church, but his observations can also help to make sense of moral-theological controversies within the church today and to grasp better why these are conducted so vigorously. Contemporary discussions of the moral-theological concept of *intrinsice malum* ("that which is intrinsically evil") offer a perfect example of the inner laws governing such controversies, as presented by Möhler. From the time of Augustine on, this concept was an unquestioned element of the tradition, which had never become problematic—and hence had never been the object of specific theological reflection. The questioning of this concept by an influential current within moral theology has led the ecclesiastical magisterium to portray the indispensability of this kind of argumentation in a way that suggests that the entire moral doctrine of the church depends on its acknowledgement. The thesis of the absolute validity of natural-law prohibitions (or of the intrinsic evil of the actions covered by these prohibitions) thus acquires a prominent symbolic meaning which was wholly unknown in the phase of its implicit acceptance, and the problems connected with intrinsically evil acts occupy the center of a methodological conflict with fundamental significance. Unfortunately, since this conflict has become entangled with the problem of artificial contraception and the controversial statements of the magisterium about sexual morality, it is often conducted in tones suggesting that the profession of faith itself is at stake.

In reality, the doctrine of *intrinsice malum* is appropriate neither as a shibboleth of orthodoxy within the church nor as a litmus test of an open, positive ethics. This is why its examination should be a sober matter, not weighed down by an argumentation aiming at all kinds of strategic goals in keeping with sideward glances at contemporary problems. This will allow us to see that the concept of intrinsically evil acts is not in the least a peculiarity of church doctrine, remote from the development of moral-philosophical thinking. Rather, it belongs to the common tradition shared by all non-utilitarian ethical systems from Aristotle, via Augustine and Thomas Aquinas, to Kant and modern proponents of a deontological jus-

---

105. Cf. J. A. Möhler, *Die Einheit der Kirche. Oder das Prinzip des Katholizismus*, Darmstadt 1957, pp. 152–57.

tification of morality. Along the trajectory of this tradition, it fulfills a necessary, but also a modest function, since—although its own defenders often overlook this point—it cannot count as a sufficient principle for justifying morality. This concept recalls what one may never do, but it does not draw up an exhaustive list of such actions, antecedently to each particular historical situation. Just as the idea of human dignity does not generate a complete catalogue of the human rights which are necessary for the protection of this dignity, so the concept of natural-law prohibitions, negative obligations to avoid some specific behavior, or intrinsically evil actions does not of itself indicate which concrete actions fall under this category.

Our overview of the historical changes in our moral ideas has shown that particular modes of behavior have been morally acknowledged and tolerated by the church in one historical epoch, whereas a later period saw them as infringements of human dignity, proscribing them by means of a categorical prohibition; on the other hand, particular modes of action which have long been viewed as morally reprehensible can also lose this classification, as in the case of the voluntary donation of organs, which was regarded by the church's magisterium for a long time as intrinsically evil, but is nowadays considered as ethically permissible under certain conditions. Thus even the assessment of specific actions as intrinsically evil and morally reprehensible under all circumstances is itself subject to the historicity of our moral knowledge. It does not in the least designate some irreducible kernel of moral insights exalted far above all historical change. If, however, the same variety of historical conditions applies to our recognition of intrinsically evil actions, which one may never perform, as to all our moral knowledge, what can it mean to employ such a category? We shall investigate this question in two stages, first asking what *malum ex genere* means within Thomas' theory of the *lex naturalis*, and then discussing the justification of this concept in contemporary moral philosophy.

4.1. The negative commandments of the natural law

Thomas agrees with Aristotle that human actions include not only those that are a priori ethically good and those that are ethically irrelevant, but also absolutely evil actions which remain reprehensible even when they are performed for a good purpose.[106] The classical examples of this group

---

106. Cf. *NE* II, 6 (1107a9–17), *Eudemain Ethics* II, 3 (1221b19–27); *In II Ethicorum*, lect. 6 (nr. 329); and *STh* II–II, q. 66, a. 7, obj. 2. When we bear in mind the explicitly teleological

of human acts mentioned by mediaeval authors are the killing of innocent persons, adultery, and theft, and above all falsehood: thanks to an inherently disordered condition, lying can never under any circumstances be ethically permissible. All these actions are disqualified a priori from an ethical perspective. They may indeed be performed from good motives—for example, by using other people's property to give alms, or by employing a falsehood to help someone whose life is endangered—but this does not remove the wickedness which attaches to them, or the disordered condition *(inordinatio)* linked to them.[107]

Thomas' inclusion of such kinds of behavior in the category of *malum ex genere* does not resolve all the problems connected with their ethical evaluation; from one point of view, this inclusion poses more questions than it answers, since the concept of intrinsically wicked actions presented mediaeval ethics with a further question, which it tended to discuss in the context of the question whether God can dispense from the prohibitions of the natural law. This may at first sight appear contradictory, but the Old Testament narratives about Abraham's intention to kill Isaac, about Abraham's lies when he said that Sarah was his sister, the theft of the Egyptian vessels, or Hosea's fornication made it necessary for the medieval theologians to justify exceptions from natural-law prohibitions which did not admit of any such exceptions. These transgressions of the natural law are related in a great variety of circumstances and linguistic genres, but they have one important feature in common: they obey an explicit command issued by God (Thomas read Hosea's adultery as an historical event, not as a symbolic prophetic action). Since God cannot contradict his own self in the individual acts of his will, it follows that these transgressions must at least initially be in accordance with the ethical order.

This assumption confronted Thomas and the scholastic theologians of his period with the question of how substantial deviations from the norms of the natural law could be compatible with the genuine concept of "natural law," especially with its formal character as something ordered by the

---

character of Aristotle's ethics, it is all the more remarkable that he should speak of intrinsically evil *(auta phaula)* actions.

107. Cf. *STh* I–II, q. 18, a. 2; q. 8, a. 8; q. 92, a. 2; *De malo*, q. 2, a. 4; and *Quodlibetum* 9, q. 7, a. 2, which states: *"quod actionum humanarum multiplex est differentia: quaedam enim sunt quae habent deformitatem inseparabiliter annexam, ut fornicatio, adulterium, et alia huiusmodi, quae nullo modo bene fieri possunt."* On the historical development of the dogmatic tractate on intrinsically evil actions, cf. S. Pinckaers, *Ce qu'on ne peut jamais faire. La question des actes intrinsèquement mauvais. Histoire et discussion*, Fribourg and Paris 1986, pp. 20–66.

reason. Thomas' explanation of this problem is particularly relevant to our modern debate about the *intrinsice malum* (a concept which he himself does not employ) because it also explains why it remains meaningful and necessary, despite the historical mutability of natural-law prohibitions, to speak of absolutely wicked actions.

Unlike his predecessors, Thomas is not content with the assertion that God gave Abraham or Hosea a special dispensation from the relevant prohibitions of the natural law, thereby giving an exceptional legitimation to murder and adultery. Thomas' question is more fundamental and acute: if these actions are truly carried out in obedience to God's will, can they still be called murder, adultery, or theft? In consequence of sin, God has ordained that all human beings, the just and the unjust, must die a natural death. If he commands that one particular human being be killed, the execution of this order entails no injustice. This means that it cannot be called "murder," any more than sexual congress with another woman can be called "adultery" or "fornication"—expressions which are meaningful only within the order of things laid down by God, where one woman is united to one particular man. Nor does taking possession of another person's property amount to theft, if this is done at God's command: God owns everything, and from his perspective, it is not the property of *another* that is taken, even if it seems so to us when we bear in mind what is ordained by the natural law.[108]

Such a solution poses problems about the relation between reason and will, knowledge and action in God, and Thomas reflected on these in the context of his doctrine of God. He attempts to avoid the alternative between a voluntarist, arbitrary God who commands one thing today and something else tomorrow and a God who is tied down by an antecedently posited rational ordering of things by making a distinction between the inner being of God and the expressions of the divine will *ad extra*. Considered in themselves, the will of God and the eternal law of his reason coincide in the divine being itself, and this means that the will of God is not *subject to* the eternal rational law, but is rather *identical to* this law. However, with regard to the creatures who are subject to the *lex aeterna*, the acts of his will are called "rational," since they wholly correspond to this law, which in God's wisdom is identical to his will.[109] Although later nominal-

108. Cf. *STh* I–II, q. 94, a. 5, ad 2; and *STh* II–II, q. 64, a. 6, ad 1. On this, cf. esp. L. Honnefelder, *Naturrecht und Geschichte*, pp. 14f.
109. Cf. *STh* I, q. 21, a. 1, ad 2; I–II, q. 93, a. 4, ad 1.

ist theologians no longer accepted this distinction as an explanation of the relationship between divine freedom and the rational ethical order, it is very helpful when we discuss the historical change of natural-law commandments. Here, in keeping with his insight into the *natura mutabilis* of the human person, Thomas has accepted in principle the possibility that historical change in the matters to which the commandments of the natural law refer can bring about a change in these commandments themselves. His attempts at an explanation of a divine charge—which is incomprehensible from a human standpoint—to "transgress" prohibitions of the natural law must assuredly be understood as boundary-statements; they do not in the least make the natural law subject to arbitrary change. Nevertheless, the point remains: the commands issued by God in the period of the Old Covenant are not a special dispensation from natural laws, nor did such commands place the natural law in abeyance for a time. Rather, there was a change in the nature of the matter to which the commandments of the law referred, so that Hosea's conduct was not merely permitted by way of an exception, but was in fact not adultery at all, given the specific circumstances. If one wishes to apply the distinction between immutable and mutable natural law to this situation and to the Ten Commandments themselves, one may say with Thomas that the commandments of the Decalogue are immutable only to the extent that they contain the concept of something that is "naturally just"; with regard to the specification of which concrete acts are to be considered murder, theft, or adultery, however, they are fundamentally mutable, either by divine authority or even (in certain circumstances) by human authority.[110]

If, however, the specific definition of what must count from an ethical perspective as murder, theft, or adultery can change, this presupposes a further distinction. When mediaeval theologians speak of the *spolia Aegyptorum* (the despoiling of the Egyptians at the exodus) or of Hosea's adultery, they assume without question that the conduct designated by these words resembles in some manner the conduct that they otherwise call "theft" and "adultery," even if it does not deserve the same ethical disapproval in these cases. This means that they make a distinction between

---

110. *STh* I–II, q. 100, a. 8, ad 3: *"Sic igitur praecepta ipsa decalogi, quantum ad rationem iustitiae quam continent, immutabilia sunt. Sed quantum ad aliquam determinationem per applicationem ad singulares actus, ut scilicet hoc vel illud sit homicidium, furtum vel adulterium, aut non, hoc quidem est mutabile: quandoque sola auctoritate divina, in his scilicet quae a solo Deo sunt instituta, sicut in matrimonio, et in aliis huiusmodi, quandoque etiam auctoritate humana, sicut in his quae sunt commissa hominum iurisdictioni."*

what we might call the *material* aspect of an action and its *formal* character which agrees or disagrees with the ethical ordering of things. Although Thomas is frequently obliged to use the same term, since language supplies him with only one single word, he nevertheless makes a very clear differentiation between instances in which we merely make a description of something, and instances in which we express ethical disapproval of the same matter. In other cases, however, he can employ two different concepts to make the intended distinction clear. For example, when the fifth commandment says "Thou shalt not kill," this apodictic formulation presupposes a priori the concept of that which is unjust and ethically reprehensible—a concept which, as such, is not necessarily linked to the expression "to kill."[111] Thomas elaborates this distinction most clearly in a Quodlibetum; for scholars of his period, this was the highest-ranking framework for an academic disputation. He replies as follows to the objection that killing in self-defense or as punishment for a crime is held to be justified:

To this, we must reply that the concept of 'murder' always denotes a sinful action, since it is inseparably linked to a state of disorder. 'Murder' *(homicidium)* means more than the killing of a human being *(occisio hominis),* just as composite concepts often mean more than their individual parts. Thus, 'murder' means the unjustified killing of a human being *(occisio hominis indebita).* Consequently, murder can never be permitted, whereas it is sometimes justified to kill a human being.[112]

Similarly, the concepts of "fornication" *(fornicatio)* and "theft" or "robbery" *(furtum, rapina)* already contain a negative ethical value-judgment, which however does not always apply to the material character of the acts in question, since these are called "sin" only when they contradict right reason or just order.[113] Hence, it can happen that one who obeys a divine directive, in agreement with the origin of all reason, performs an act which, considered by itself, would contradict that which the human rea-

---

111. *STh* I–II, q. 100, a. 8, ad 3: *"Occisio hominis prohibetur in decalogo secundum quod habet rationem indebiti: sic enim praeceptum continet ipsam rationem iniustitiae."* On this, cf. esp. J. F. Dedek, "Intrinsically Evil Acts: An Historical Study on the Mind of St Thomas," *The Thomist* 43 (1979) pp. 389–413, esp. 401ff.

112. *Quodlibetum* 8, q. 6, a. 4, ad 1. Cf. also 9, q. 7, a. 2: *"Sunt vero quaedam actiones quae absolute consideratae, deformitatem vel inordinationem quamdam important, quae tamen aliquibus circumstantiis advenientibus bonae efficiuntur; sicut occidere hominem, vel percutere, in se deformitatem quamdam importat, sed si addatur occidere malefactorem propter iustitiam, vel percutere delinquentem causa disciplinae, non erit peccatum, sed virtuosum."*

113. *STh* II–II, q. 154, a. 2, ad 2: *"Fornicatio dicitur esse peccatum, inquantum est contra rationem rectam."*

son generally considers to be correct.[114] In the case of adultery or fornication, Thomas reflects on this gulf between the material situation and the ethical evaluation of an action only in the case of the historically unique—and unrepeatable—case of the prophet Hosea. In the case of the prohibition of theft, however, he holds that a corresponding differentiation is always necessary. Theft is forbidden as a general rule, because taking other people's property is a contradiction of justice even if the intention is to help a third party; nevertheless, in extreme situations, it can be permissible to take other people's property to ensure one's own survival.

In keeping with the natural-law principles of his justification of the right to property, Thomas is certain that the poor have a claim on the superfluous goods of other people, and that the only reason why property owners are free to decide how to share out their superfluous goods is that otherwise a harmonious life in society would be impossible. Despite this generally necessary reservation, which restricts free disposal of property to its owner, situations of extreme need may permit one to take hold (publicly or secretly) of goods which he obviously needs to keep himself alive; such actions do not come under the category of "theft." In the case of *necessitas extrema*, the use of other people's property—Thomas speaks here with great precision of *uti re aliena*, in order to avoid the formally correct definition of "theft" as *acceptio rei alienae*—has therefore the character of self-defense or self-preservation. It is certain that it does not have the character of theft, even if such conduct is externally indistinguishable from those actions usually denoted by this word.[115] This makes it inappropriate to speak of a "justified exception" to the prohibition of theft; what is involved here is basically not an action that might in fact properly be called "theft" but (thanks to particular circumstances) does not fall under the general prohibition, but rather an action which in ethical terms is not in any sense theft: in material terms, it does indeed amount to the same thing, but such aspects alone are not decisive for its ethical evaluation, and must be disregarded when the totality of relevant aspects of the action—including the particular circumstances (here, the extreme distress of the one in need)—demand a different assessment.

How is this compatible with the affirmation that there exists a category of human actions with an inherent deformity which precludes their ever

---

114. Cf. ibid.

115. Cf. *STh* II–II, q. 66, a. 7, ad 3. Cf. also *Quodlibetum* 9, q. 7, a. 2 (quoted in n. 112 above).

198 The universal claim of natural law

being ethically good in any way *(nullo modo bene fieri possunt)?* If we take all of Thomas' statements on this question, such an affirmation is meaningful only if the insuperable *deformitas* of such actions is related, not to a material defect, but to their incompatibility with the order of reason or— where these actions concern not the person of the agent himself, but other persons—with the rule of justice. Every other interpretation breaks down at the very starting point of Thomas' analysis of behavior: for him, the moral quality of human acts is judged by the criterion specific to the human existence of the person, that is, by the rule of his reason. Naturally, this applies also to the *bonitas ex obiecto* or the *malitia ex obiecto,* because only an object which is in accord or disaccord with the order of reason can qualify human behavior from an ethical point of view and be a decisive factor in the evaluation of this behavior as good or bad.[116]

The principle that only the totality of all aspects of behavior, as recognized by the reason, decides the ethical evaluation of human acts, is not however identical with the idea that human conduct is always orientated to "pre-moral" goods external to itself, and that the ethical value of such goods is recognized only by the evaluative judgment of the reason. For Thomas, it is not the totality of all the *consequences* of an action and the evaluation of the goods which it realizes that is decisive for its ethical value, but the *total structure* of the action itself, which includes not only its object and the end of the agent, but also all the relevant circumstances.[117] If one follows Thomas in distinguishing the object (*what* a person does), the end (*the purpose* for which he does it), and the circumstances (*how* he does it), this does not mean that only the end (what later scholastic terminology calls the *finis operis*) imparts an inherent qualification to the action, while the end and the circumstances remain external to it; rather, these are the intentional origin and the concrete mode of the action, and are a part of the rationally-guided structure of the action which decides the ethical value of human conduct as a whole.[118] In the same way, the *electio,* which

116. *STh* I–II, q. 18, a. 8: *"Actus omnis habet speciem ab obiecto; et actus humanus, qui dicitur moralis, habet speciem ab obiecto relato ad principium actuum humanorum, quod est ratio."* Cf. also *STh* I–II, q. 1, a. 3, and *De malo,* q. 2, a. 4.

117. On this, cf. L. Honnefelder, *Natur als Handlungsprinzip,* p. 174, and the summaries by G. Stanke, *Die Lehre von den "Quellen der Moralität". Darstellung und Diskussion der neuscholastischen Aussagen und neuerer Ansätze,* Regensburg 1984, pp. 82–89; A. V. Maurer, *Homo agens. Handlungstheoretische Untersuchungen zum theologisch-ethischen Verständnis des Sittlichen,* Frankfurt et al. 1994, pp. 40–62.

118. *STh* I–II, q. 1, a. 3, ad 1: *"Finis non est omnino aliquid extrinsecum ab actu: quia comparatur ad actum ut principium vel terminus."* *STh* I–II, q. 18, a. 3, ad 1: *"Circumstantiae sunt*

determines the action in concrete terms (and comes closest to our idea of an evaluation of goods), is not a choice between various goods external to the will. It is a preferential choice among the appropriate means which are inherently related to the end of the action intended by the will.

We can see here a clear difference from modern theories which justify norms in teleological terms. This divergence is not only expressed in a different evaluation of individual actions as intrinsically evil;[119] it also indicates that the question is being posed in a fundamentally different perspective. Thomas is not content to ask about our knowledge of that which is ethically correct, although he naturally also discusses such *normative* questions in the narrower sense of the word; he also analyses the structure of human conduct, that is, he inquires in the framework of a comprehensive analysis of action into the relation between those factors which are decisive for the ethical evaluation of human acts. In this kind of *theoretical* perspective on conduct, it is not enough to consider human behavior under the aspect of its external consequences, or to compare the goods realized by such behavior in accord with particular rules about what one should prefer, for this kind of analysis does not do justice to the specific character of human praxis. Following Aristotle, Thomas distinguishes between two forms of human activity, only one of which—action in the sense of the Aristotelian *praxis*—can be the immediate object of a *moralis consideratio* in the sphere of practical science. Morally relevant questions do indeed arise in the other sphere of activity, viz. production in the sense of the Aristotelian *poiêsis*—questions about its goals ("What are we allowed to produce?") and means ("What criteria of appropriateness must we bear in mind here?")—but this common factor should not obscure the fundamental distinction between technical production and moral conduct.

While the first form of activity is always related to an external object which is produced or altered in keeping with technical rules in the process of production, action (the specific activity born of freedom) aims at the human existence of the person himself. This activity is done for its own sake; its only end is *eupraxia,* "good human praxis," which embraces both

---

extra actionem, inquantum non sunt de essentia actionis: sunt tamen in ipsa actione velut quaedam accidentia eius." In the *ad secundum* of this article, Thomas specifies that the circumstances of an action are to be considered as *per se accidentia* for its moral evaluation.

119. This is clearest in the evaluation of lying. For Thomas, falsehood is ethically impermissible, not only because of the harm done to one's neighbor and to human life in society, but also because of the inherent disorder which it causes in the liar himself. Cf. *STh* II–II, q. 110, a. 3, ad 4; on this, cf. J. F. Dedek, "Intrinsically Evil Acts," pp. 406ff.

the self-realization of the person of the agent and the communicative col-
laboration of all who share in the action. Activity in this higher manner,
which is possible only for human beings endowed with reason, is not primarily orientated to the realization of external goods, as is the case with
goal-orientated production in functional activity. Rather, it bears its own
meaning in itself. In scholastic terminology, we may say that specifically
moral activity is not yet in view when we consider action only as an *opera-
tio transiens* which brings about something in the sphere of things. Rather,
by analogy to the internal personal acts of the human person, his knowing,
thinking, and willing, it must be considered as an *actio immanens,* whose
first "result" is the practical perfection of the agent in the human existence
which he shares with others.[120] Accordingly, moral behavior does not mean
that one changes external conditions or situations; it is always the self-
expression of the agent before his own eyes and that of others in the world
he shares with them.

Using terminology common in ethics since the time of Schleiermacher,
we can also call this aspect of ethical praxis "representative" (as opposed to
"effective"), "expressive," or simply "meaningful" action.[121] These concepts
may be more familiar to us, but all they seek to do is to work out the specific course of the boundary-line between what Aristotle and Thomas call
the goal-orientated and the functional forms of human activity. Despite all
the conceptual differentiations, the variety of historical contexts, and the
difference in accentuation among the various thinkers, these approaches
agree on the decisive point: the issue in moral action is not some relationship between external goods or the sum of these, but whether the human
being himself succeeds or fails in his human existence and his quality as a
person. Only this position allows us to understand fully the basic principle
of Thomas' analysis of behavior, that is, that human actions can be evalu-

120. Cf. *In VI Ethicorum,* lect. 3 (nr. 1150–51) and lect. 4 (nr. 1167). On this, cf. esp. J. F.
Keenan, *Goodness and Rightness in Thomas Aquinas's Summa Theologiae,* Washington 1992,
pp. 81–85. Keenan points out that both sides in the modern controversy between teleological
and deontological ethics misunderstand the level on which Thomas analyses the "object" of
human action. This "object" is neither the moral order as a whole (which is damaged by individual acts) nor the total condition of the world (which is improved or worsened by the
external consequences of an action), but the inner orientation of the person to ethically correct behavior. This is why one does not do justice to the distinction made by Thomas if one
makes a sharp conceptual separation between ethical goodness and ethical correctness or
equates the former with the intention and the latter with the object of the action (an object
which in turn is understood as a pre-moral good).

121. On this, cf. F. Kaulbach, *Einführung in die Philosophie des Handelns,* Darmstadt 2nd
edn. 1982, pp. 135–47; A.V. Maurer, *Homo agens,* pp. 86–96.

ated ethically only in their totality, and not exclusively on the basis of their external consequences. And it is only in this context that one can correctly inquire about intrinsically evil actions, which recall what one is never permitted to do. Our question now is: do there exist modes of human conduct or individual human actions with an inherent structure opposed to the principle that allows the human being to succeed as such, so that these absolutely preclude his being accepted as a person?

4.2. Intrinsically evil actions, or the infringement of absolute rights

In the context of Thomas' analysis, it is not possible to dispense with the concept of *malum ex genere,* even if this does not yet possess the emphatic meaning often attributed to it by modern critics of a teleological ethics. It is not, however, possible on the basis of an exposition of Thomas alone to identify those actions which might deserve the predicate "intrinsically evil." Rather, if we take seriously the inherent historicity of moral thinking, we must reckon with the possibility that Thomas considers some human actions to be intrinsically evil, while we regard them as ethically permissible, whereas he in turn tolerates modes of conduct which seem to us absolutely reprehensible. For example, Thomas is willing to accept the torture of innocent persons as a part of ordinary legal process, whereas our modern legal sensitivity will not accept torture even in exceptional instances as a means of establishing truth in legal process.[122] This means that we must distinguish very clearly between the question *whether* it is possible in principle for actions to exist which must be qualified as morally reprehensible independently of their foreseeable consequences, and the historically changeable judgment about *which* particular actions come under this heading. Up to this point, we have followed the basic outlines of Thomas' theory of behavior in our description of intrinsically evil actions; in the second part of our investigation we shall debate with a number of positions in contemporary moral philosophy which concrete actions are considered by the insight of the practical reason today to belong to this category.

In order to indicate more clearly the meaning of the thesis that will be developed in what follows, let us here sketch briefly the answer that our investigation will disclose: a mode of conduct must always be considered as intrinsically evil and as incompatible with the personal dignity of another

---

122. Cf. *Expositio super Iob* X, 1, 5; on this, cf. F. Compagnoni, "Folter und Todesstrafe in der Überlieferung der römisch-katholischen Kirche," *Concilium* 14 (1978) pp. 657–66, esp. 659.

human being, when it attacks the irreducible minimum conditions for his human existence, which must be protected in order to give him the possibility of free ethical self-determination. To use a terminology more common among deontological ethicists and philosophers of law today, one may say that a mode of behavior is morally reprehensible in the strict sense if it offends the inalienable or "absolute" rights of another person, independently of the consequences this can have for the wellbeing of other persons who are also affected by this action.[123] The factual necessity of speaking of intrinsically evil actions, or of absolute rights of the human person infringed by such actions, will emerge from the following analyses of the intentional killing of innocent persons, of torture as a means of protection from terrorist threats, of rape as a crime against sexual self-determination, and (on a quite different level) of adultery as an offense against the essence of marital love. Our discussion will show why a purely teleological ethics does not provide an adequate framework for the ethical disapproval of these examples. This is why contemporary moral philosophy has developed modes of argumentation which employ other methods than the mere assessment of consequences and an evaluation of goods. Since this argumentation emphasizes human rights and duties in a manner which makes greater use of deontological concepts, it can be seen as a philosophical equivalent to the moral-theological concept of inherently evil modes of conduct.

a. The intentional killing of innocent persons   The example of the intentional killing of an innocent person is best suited to show what is meant by the infringement of the inalienable rights of an other person, or by an "intrinsically evil action." This prohibition, the kernel of the prohibition of killing, has always been upheld by the traditional understanding of morality, in keeping with the entire non-utilitarian tradition of European moral philosophy and the ethical convictions of the Christian churches. In the *Catechism* (1993) and the encyclical *Evangelium Vitae* (1995), the Catholic magisterium has emphasized in particularly strong terms its unconditional rejection of the killing of innocent persons. The linkage to the commandment of love adds a new note to the injunction not to kill: this takes up traditions of Reformed ethics and gives the prohibition a broader foundation.[124]

---

123. On this, cf. A. Gerwith, "Are There Any Absolute Rights?," in Idem, *Human Rights. Essays on Justification and Applications,* Chicago 1982, pp. 218–33, esp. 219.

124. Cf. *Lumen Gentium* 25; *Gaudium et Spes* 27; *Catechism of the Catholic Church* 2268 and 2320; and the encyclical *Evangelium Vitae* 57 and 75–77.

Nevertheless, even an unconditionally valid norm of the natural law such as the prohibition of killing requires the practical power of judgment, if it is to be correctly applied in each specific instance. The limitation to "innocent" persons does not in the least remove all the difficulties generated by the distinction between this absolutely valid norm and its verbal formulations. Apart from the classical exceptions to the prohibition of killing (self-defense, the death penalty, killing in a just war), there are other cases which—thanks to the concept of objective guilt presupposed here—cannot be appropriately grasped even by the limited norm which forbids the killing of *innocent* human beings. For example, violent persons who are mentally ill must usually be considered incapable of incurring guilt; nevertheless, we accept in our society that an insane man who is running amok may be killed by the police who have the task of protecting us, if he represents an acute danger to the life of uninvolved third parties and killing him is the only way to defuse the risk. Likewise, the legal rules governing warfare allow one to kill enemy soldiers, although the mere fact of their membership in the opposing army is not in the least sufficient to allow us to hold them "guilty." We can scarcely suppose that the authors of the encyclical *Evangelium Vitae* meant their unconditional formulation of the prohibition of killing an innocent person to be understood as categorically excluding these rules, which had previously enjoyed validity; rather, the context suggests that the encyclical intends to oppose a line of argument in contemporary debates in ethics of life, where new exceptions to the prohibition of killing are proposed, above all in the case of abortion and euthanasia. Here it is certainly apposite—indeed, in view of the arguments put forward, necessary—to recall the significance of the prohibition of killing. These examples show, however, how difficult it is to formulate this norm with such a degree of linguistic precision that it does not intentionally subsume cases that one would not in fact wish it to cover.

Accordingly, the unanimity with which otherwise very different ethical traditions maintain the absolute validity of this prohibition cannot disguise the fact that precisely its unconditional formulation provokes moral-philosophical objections which must be taken seriously. Some of these are pragmatic, as is indicated by the reference to situations of hopeless competition in which one life stands against another and a strict observance of the prohibition of killing would appear to contradict our spontaneous moral sensibilities. There are, however, also fundamental reservations vis-à-vis the claim that human life is an absolute value and *per definitionem* incommensurable with other values. In a finite world of contingent goods, only the ethical disposition of the human person is an absolute value, while his body and life, like all other "external" goods, belong to the sphere of pre-moral goods, where it is in principle permissible to weigh one against another. This means that it is impossible on the basis of a teleological ethics to maintain the absolute validity of the prohibition of killing an innocent person: for it is only when the goods at question in a particular case have been weighed that one can discern the ethically correct manner to deal with human life.[125]

A teleological ethics wishes to maintain the fundamental validity of the prohibition of killing, since its watering-down would lead to unforeseeable consequences, endangering its function of ensuring peace in society. Whereas, however, a deontological ethics is interested primarily in establishing moral principles, teleological ethics argues more on the basis of individual cases (e.g., the killing of a wounded comrade in war, or the shooting of a person trapped in a burning automobile after an accident) in which the unconditional observance of the prohibition of killing obviously runs contrary to the true interests of those whom it is meant to protect. Hence, teleological and utilitarian positions do not call into question the prohibition as such, but only its deontological justification in terms of the dignity of the human person and his "absolute" right to life, and the unconditional validity which is derived from this right. Proponents of these positions do however argue that there are strong reasons not to tamper in any way with the general acceptance of the prohibition of killing—either on the basis of the evaluation of the goods involved in individual situations of competition (the teleological perspective) or of the long-term consequences for life in society (the utilitarian perspective).[126] Before we now go on to plead in favor of a deontological justification of the prohibition of killing, it is important to explicitly acknowledge both this clarification and the necessary differentiation between a teleological evaluation of goods and a utilitarian maximizing of profit which goes beyond the boundaries of the individual.

Our first reply to the pragmatic objections to a deontological under-

---

125. On this, cf. B. Schüller, *Die Begründung sittlicher Urteile. Typen ethischer Argumentation in der Moraltheologie*, Düsseldorf 2nd edn. 1980, pp. 73–78; W. Wolbert, *Der Mensch als Mittel und Zweck. Die Idee der Menschenwürde in normativer Ethik und Metaethik*, Münster 1987, pp. 65–71.

126. On this, cf. D. Birnbacher, "Das Tötungsverbot aus der Sicht der klassischen Utilitarismus," in R. Hegselmann and R. Merkel (eds.), *Zur Debatte über Euthanasie. Beiträge und Stellungnahmen*, Frankfurt 1991, pp. 25–50, esp. 42.

standing of the prohibition of killing is that even an "absolutely" valid norm can envisage only those situations relevant in practical living, not extremely rare boundary-situations or sheerly fictitious constellations of circumstances, which can never be grasped beforehand by a normative consideration. The soldier who shoots a badly wounded comrade as they flee, in order that he may not fall into the hands of the enemy, or the policeman who turns his gun on a driver who cannot be extricated from his burning car, do not call into question the prohibition of killing, even if the external consequences of what they do allow us to describe their action as "killing." One may, however, raise the question whether this is not in fact to concede specific "exceptions" which allow us in hopeless boundary-situations to water down the absolute prohibition of killing—and while this may be understandable in human terms, would not the presuppositions of the deontological approach make it a serious self-contradiction in logical terms?

When faced with the objection that every attempt to reconcile absolute norms with the unacceptable consequences these can have in individual cases amounts to the task of squaring a circle, deontological ethicists seek to formulate the prohibition of killing with greater linguistic precision, so that it will be immune to criticism. Their intention is to make it impossible to employ intellectual sharpness to think up ever new dilemmas. With this in mind, the American philosopher Alan Gewirth proposes the following formulation of the prohibition of killing: "All innocent persons have an absolute right not to be made the intended victims of a homicidal project."[127] The "absoluteness" of the right not to be intentionally and foreseeably made a victim of murder is deduced here from the fact that every moral subject who is (actually or potentially) capable of action is an end in himself; within the framework of a deontological ethics, therefore, this absoluteness is based on the highest moral principle of the acknowledgment of the personal dignity of every other human being. The limitation to "intended" killings links the prohibition to a conscious intention to kill which follows a clear and considered plan; the intention is to exclude unforeseeable emergency situations such as those mentioned above. Gewirth gives another example of a situation of constraint which cannot be fully grasped in advance: when the brakes on his tram fail to function,

127. A. Gewirth, "Are There Any Absolute Rights?," p. 233. On this point, cf. the analysis of the argumentation Gewirth presents in support of his position by K. Steigleder, *Die Begründung des moralischen Sollens. Studien zur Möglichkeit einer normativen Ethik*, Tübingen 1992, p. 319.

the driver has only seconds in which to decide whether the inevitable crash will cost the life of one or several persons, and he does not "kill" when he instinctively throws the steering wheel to the side where only one single passenger is waiting. Nor does a doctor "kill" an incurable patient, who would long have been dead without his therapeutic interventions, when he decides to stop a treatment which has become hopeless.

When it is alleged that a teleological ethics must necessarily evaluate such actions as "killing," this is because this approach considers only the external consequences of our actions as relevant to an ethical judgment. If, however, one begins from the total structure of an action, where the agent's intention plays the decisive role, one will not evaluate the conduct of the tram-driver or doctor as "killings" in the ethical sense. The decisive cause of death in both cases is not the intentional behavior of human agents, but an event which occurs independently of all human action: the failure of the brakes, or the course of an incurable illness. The consequence for the debate about the absolute validity of the prohibition of killing is that neither the "tragic" boundary-cases nor the inevitable situations of conflict which are often adduced by teleological ethicists as contrary arguments are in fact admissible examples, since their qualification as "killings" demands an antecedent decision in favor of the teleological evaluation. In other words, its basis, logically speaking, begs the very question it wishes to resolve.

Naturally enough, this does not apply to an ethics which argues in purely consequentialist terms. If one makes a strict separation between ethical correctness and ethical goodness, drawing only on the external consequences for the normative judgment and rejecting any distinction between acting and merely allowing something to happen, one will be obliged to call the action of the tram-driver or doctor "ethically permitted killing." This ethics sees the differentiation between a death which is either passively or positively accepted as a consequence, and a death which one actively inflicts on another person, as a merely semantic sifting which dispenses certain boundary-cases from the prohibition of killing. A consistently teleological way of looking at things would have to argue that such distinctions are arbitrary definitions which merely obscure the fact that even a deontological justification of the prohibition of killing is de facto obliged to admit exceptions.

How are we to achieve clarity on this question? Taken by themselves, both approaches appear coherent and compelling; if, however, one takes each position in turn and considers the arguments put forward by the other approach, it is impossible to resist the impression that this debate is circular.

Is this controversy ultimately only a dispute about words, concerning mere-ly the linguistic question of whether specific forms of conduct which result inevitably in death—conduct held to be ethically permitted under certain circumstances—are or are not to be equated with active killing? Answers to this question are plausible only within the totality of each particular theory, so that clarity remains unattainable. Nevertheless, this is a remarkable result in the confrontation between the teleological and deontological justifica-tions of the prohibition of killing, since it at least means that this question cannot be resolved on the pragmatic level by referring to alleged or genuine "exceptions" to the prohibition—precisely because it remains a matter of debate whether these cases can in fact be called "killing."

On the level of fundamental principles, when it is asserted that an ab-solute right to life exists, derived from the inviolable dignity of the human person, it is objected that life *per se* is only a pre-moral value with no neces-sary relationship to the ethical self-realization of the person. Such an argu-ment fundamentally fails to recognize the anthropological significance of the unity of the human person as body and soul. The body and physical life are not "goods" external to the personal self-realization of the human being, with a purely instrumental relationship to his "genuine" self-realization— whether one might wish to call this sphere of human existence the "spirit," "soul," "reason," or "ethical self-determination." Rather, the body is the ab-solutely indispensable medium of expression in which the human person necessarily represents himself in all his acts, even in the loftiest activities of his spirit. This is why the human being must be considered as a unity of body and soul even when we are speaking of his capacity for ethical action, since he exists in his capacity for ethical self-determination only *in* his body and *through* his body.

Respect for human personal dignity may not be limited to his inner convictions and intellectual acts alone: it must also embrace the inviolabil-ity of his bodily existence. This principle is not contradicted by the fact that personal existence is based on the capacity for transcendental acts, nor by the Christian conviction that purely spiritual persons also exist; nor can we accept the objection that one must distinguish in the case of the human being, who is a finite person, between his human and his personal exis-tence, with the consequence that "the body cannot be an 'essential compo-nent' of the human being *qua* person."[128] Our personal existence and our

---

128. W. Wolbert, *Der Mensch als Mittel und Zweck,* p. 69. One is not surprised when this author appeals in support of his position to a "Platonic" philosopher like N. Hartmann. Such a thesis would have been unthinkable within the scholastic tradition of classical moral

ethical freedom are not lived out in a world of angels (where it is possible to conceive of ethical acts not linked to a body), but in a world where we, as finite beings, are subject to the laws governing our unity as body and soul. Since this anthropological unity of our human existence is a condition of life for every human person everywhere and at all times, we must respect ourselves as beings capable of ethical self-determination in our bodily dimension too—irrespective of all the divergent views about what ultimately makes life meaningful.

In this sense, the body is freedom's boundary. We can respect each other as subjects capable of moral action only when we respect each other in the expressive form of our bodily existence. Only so do we make it possible for each other to unfold a personal existence which is a goal in itself. Our unconditional respect for the bodily life of others is not only an expression of special esteem for some pre-moral value which would belong in principle to the external "goods" available to the human being in his ethical actions; rather, we respect in bodily life the representation of the freedom of another human being, the representation of his person, which is accessible to us—who are finite beings—only in the medium of its unity as body and soul. This means that the absolute validity of the prohibition of killing is not based on a highly exaggerated view of the value of life, allegedly a religious development specific to the Judaeo-Christian tradition, but on the anthropologically indisputable fact of the bodily dimension of our de facto existence, which is one of the absolute boundary-conditions which make human life possible.[129] It is sometimes objected here that this argument "proves" too much—and hence proves nothing at all, since it is inappropriate as an answer to questions concerning norms. We may indeed concede here that the argument about the unity of the human person is in fact employed by some Catholic moral theologians today in such a way that every intervention in bodily life and the physical laws which govern this must necessarily appear as a direct attack on the personal dignity of the human being;[130] such an extension of the principle commits the opposite

---

theology, which always maintained that the intellectual soul is the essential form of the body, so that there is only one single existent, which we call the human person, existing in the concrete unity of body and soul. This is why Thomas explicitly says that the soul can no longer be called a "person" when it is separated from the body, since it is no more capable on its own of fulfilling the requirements of personal existence than would be one single part of the body (cf. *STh* I, q. 29, a. 1, ad 5; and q. 75, a. 4, ad 2).

129. On this, cf. esp. F. Kaulbach, *Einführung in die Philosophie des Handelns*, Darmstadt 2nd edn. 1982, pp. 43–50.

130. Thus, moral theologians such as G. Grisez, W. May, or M. Rhonheimer wish to

error as regards the fundamental experience of the unity of our human existence in body and soul, by dissolving the person's relationship to his own self in his bodily existence into an immediate identity. A more precise phenomenological analysis (which need not be repeated here)[131] can show that the personal self-experience of the human being also includes the capacity to take up a distance vis-à-vis his own body; in German, one can make this distinction by saying that the *Leib* which we *are* is not identical with the *Körper* which we *have*. The complementary structure of human existence is formulated even more precisely by L. Honnefelder: "I *am* my *Leib*, which I also *possess* as *Körper*."[132] This intermediary position between "being" and "having" is the source of the person's liberty in his body *(Leib)*, a liberty which always includes a certain freedom of movement vis-à-vis one's own body *(Körper)*, and this finds expression in religious acts of fasting and voluntary renunciation, or in medical interventions in one's body. In Christian understanding, this freedom of movement can go as far as the total disposition of the person over his own body in the emergency situation of martyrdom.

This means that the reference to the unity of the person as body and soul does not disqualify every intervention in bodily life as ethically impermissible. Where this unity is proposed in a way that systematically obscures the freedom which the person enjoys vis-à-vis his own body, there are very good reasons for objecting to it. But the fact that too much evidential weight is sometimes attached to the inalienable unity of the person in his body does not mean that this is merely an anthropological formula devoid of content from an ethical perspective, which can be used to justify anything (and hence nothing at all). On the contrary, many moral precepts remain incomprehensible if we are unaware of the significance of the unity of the person as body and soul for the task of ethical self-determination. Here,

---

demonstrate that every act of "artificial contraception" which intentionally renders sexual intercourse incapable of procreation is an attack on the personal dignity of the marriage partners, since it brings about a "profound alienation between the personal self and his body," treating the body in a technical manner as a mere object and thus denying "that human bodiliness has the character of a subject" (M. Rhonheimer, *Sexualität und Verantwortung. Empfängnisverhütung als ethisches Problem*, Vienna 1995, p. 129). For a debate with this kind of argument, cf. D. Mieth, *Geburtenregelung. Ein Konflikt in der katholischen Kirche*, Mainz 1990, pp. 165ff.; H.-G. Gruber, *Christliche Ehe in moderner Gesellschaft. Entwicklung-Chancen-Perspektiven*, Freiburg 1993, pp. 201–12, 266.

131. On this, cf. E. Schockenhoff, *Ethik des Lebens*, pp. 95f.

132. L. Honnefelder, "Person und Gehirn—zur ethischen Beurteilung der Transplantation von Hirngewebe," in J. Fedrowitz et al. (eds.), *Neuroworlds. Gehirn-Geist-Kultur*, Frankfurt and New York 1994, pp. 380–88, at 383.

we must recall especially respect for the bodily inviolability of another person, esteem for the lives of sick and weak persons, and our obligation to exercise special care in dealing with the early stages of human life.

In all these cases, the following anthropological principle is decisively important: the dignity of the person unfolds only in his bodily existence, which shares in this dignity, because it is impossible for the human person to lead the rational existence to which he is destined otherwise than in the bodiliness of his practical life. This is why the prohibition of killing an innocent person marks an extreme boundary drawn by respect for the ethical dignity of every human being. In its strict version, this prohibition must be considered as based immediately in the highest moral principle, since the charge to exercise rational, ethical self-determination is adressed to a being who can fulfill this charge only in and through his bodily existence.

b. Torture and sacrifice of an innocent person for the sake of the common good The question is often posed in contemporary moral-philosophical debates about a deontological or consequential basis for morality whether one may sacrifice an innocent person for the good of the community, or even (in extreme situations) torture him in order to save the lives of a greater number of likewise innocent persons. This is a modern modification of Caiaphas' question of whether it is not better for one individual to die than for the whole people to perish (cf. Jn 11:50 and 18:14). In view of the fact that the individual has both rights and obligations in relation to the community, and that it is in principle possible to demand that he make sacrifices for the sake of the fellowship, Caiaphas' maxim can be translated as the following problem: are there absolute individual rights which may never be infringed, and must be respected even if this involves the risk that other innocent persons may die? Or are there extreme situations—such as the examples proposed in moral-philosophical analyses, which admittedly often seem highly artificial—where an individual may be sacrificed for the sake of the good of society or the prosperity of a majority of people? The moral theologian Bruno Schüller discusses this question in the light of an example:

The sheriff of a city in the southern United States, dealing with the case of a white woman who has been raped, is confronted with the alternative of declaring the guilt of a black suspect, whose innocence is in fact supported by irrefutable proof, or else conducting a long search for the true criminal. If the innocent black man is accused and condemned at once, this would spare the lives of many other innocent persons. If an action is assessed exclusively on the basis of its consequences, the condemnation of the black man must be viewed as the only ethically correct action; but everyone would condemn this as an unjust act crying out to heaven.[133]

It is not altogether clear, from this little story, how the two alternatives are connected: why should the condemnation of the innocent black man "spare the lives of many other innocent persons"? It may be that Schüller has in mind the lynching justice that one finds in many westerns, where the sheriff must sacrifice a symbolic victim to appease the wrath of the mob and prevent their violence from erupting in all directions. At any rate, the story clearly depicts the decisive question: must not a teleological ethics, which aims to resolve such situations of conflict by weighing up competing goods (in this case, the life of one innocent person and the lives of several innocent persons), view the death of the innocent black man as justified? Naturally, Schüller rejects this conclusion as a false insinuation employed by deontological ethicists to discredit the teleological approach. It is not, however, his response that is interesting here, so much as the reason he gives: he does not reject the execution of the innocent suspect because the innocent man has an absolute right to life which may not be sacrificed for the common good, but because his execution would not be an appropriate instrument to ensure the rule of law and long-term social peace. In the long run, such arbitrary acts by the judicial authority would not protect the common good; rather, they would undermine confidence in the meaning of the institution of "penal justice." Hence they would prove harmful to the good of society: "This is why the sheriff must accept that he is in fact forbidden to execute the one innocent person in order to save the lives of many innocent persons."[134]

There can be no doubt that Schüller abhors the execution of an innocent person just as decisively as deontological ethicists; the only difference is perhaps that the latter present the same view more emphatically. Yet is he arguing consistently on the basis of his own principles when he sees the personal dignity of the human person, who is an end in his own right, as the *ontological* reason why we ought to love him as our neighbor for his own sake,[135] but is unwilling to accept this personal dignity as a sufficient basis for a *normative* ethics which would protect an innocent suspect from

133. B. Schüller, *Die Begründung sittlicher Urteile*, p. 290. On the evaluation of this assessment within a teleological ethics, cf. also W. Wolbert, *Vom Nutzen der Gerechtigkeit. Zur Diskussion um Utilitarismus und teleologische Theorie*, Freiburg 1992, pp. 123f.

134. Schüller, *Die Begründung sittlicher Urtiele*, p. 291.

135. Cf. B. Schüller, "Das Geschick eines Wortpaares," in: Idem, *Der menschliche Mensch. Aufsätze zur Metaethik und zur Sprache der Moral*, Düsseldorf 1982, pp. 156–83, esp. 172, 183.

being executed? For (in Schüller's eyes) it is not the immanent value of the innocent black man that makes him worth protecting but only the consideration that the long-term harm to the common good that would result from the sacrifice of an innocent life outweighs the immediate usefulness of his death. If the only path to the conclusion that the sacrifice of an innocent person is morally unjustified entails taking the detour of an additional rule-utilitaristic argumentation, then it certainly appears that a human being has been made into a proper object for calculation—we would be obliged to respect the life of an innocent person only as long as there was no contradiction between this life and the (correctly understood) common good, and a judicial murder would undoubtedly be justifiable within the framework of such a theory, if the weighing of the goods involved led to a different conclusion about the appropriateness of bending the law as an instrument for maintaining public order. If we move from this example to the level of fundamental ethical argumentation, this means that a teleological ethics is not in principle obliged by the concept of "the personal dignity of the human person" to exclude the possibility that in situations of tragic conflict, an individual may be sacrificed to the good of society as a whole, or of a large number of persons.[136]

This is why the question proposed in the example of the sheriff can be given serious consideration only if one presupposes that, under given circumstances, the sacrifice of an innocent person might indeed be an appropriate means to ward off harm to a large number of people. The American philosopher Alan Gewirth constructs a particularly abhorrent example here, in order to set out the basic problem more clearly:

Suppose a clandestine group of political extremists have obtained an arsenal of nuclear weapons; to prove that they have the weapons and know how to use them, they have kidnapped a leading scientist, shown him the weapons, and then released him to make a public corroborative statement. The terrorists have now announced that they will use the weapons against a designated large distant city unless a certain prominent resident of the city, a young politically active lawyer named Abrams, tortures his mother to death, this torturing to be carried out publicly in a certain way at a specified place and time in that city. Since the gang members have already murdered several other prominent residents of the city, their threat is quite credible. Their declared motive is to advance their cause by showing how powerful they are and by unmasking the moralistic pretensions of their political opponents.[137]

136. On this ambivalence of teleological ethics, cf. also A. Anzenbacher, *Einführung in die Ethik*, p. 39; and esp. K. Steigleder, *Die Begründung des moralischen Sollens*, pp. 310f.
137. A. Gewirth, "Are There Any Absolute Rights?," p. 225.

The moral dilemma which the terrorists' attempt at blackmail intends to evoke in Abrams is comparable to the situation of the sheriff in Schüller's example, in that he is offered the possibility of rescuing the inhabitants of a large city from a probable death if he carries out an action which everyone—in normal circumstances—would abhor as an appaling crime. We need not reflect here on the point that the terrorists might not in fact carry out their threat if he refused, so that Abrams is faced only with a probable outcome of his choice (though in fact the probability is very high); the question which interests us here is whether a mode of conduct which we regard as "unspeakably evil" can lose this inherent quality, if it is done to the profit of a large number of people.[138] Gewirth denies this, defending the mother's right not to be tortured to death by her son as an "absolute" right which cannot under any conceivable circumstances be outweighed by the rights of other persons.[139] She possesses the right of bodily immunity not only vis-à-vis her son, but vis-à-vis every person. This means that the reason why Abrams is forbidden to torture his mother is not the particular fact that his victim would be his own mother (which of course makes the deed even more abhorrent); rather, her right not to be tortured to death corresponds to an absolutely binding obligation to abstain from a certain type of conduct. This obligation is incumbent upon everyone, and cannot be invalidated by any circumstances, nor by prevalent rights on the part of others. It follows that the prohibition of torturing an innocent person must be considered absolutely binding, since every infringement harms rights of other persons, which have a greater weight than any other considerations. To employ the vocabulary of classical natural-rights ethics: the torture of an innocent person must be counted among the list of intrinsically evil actions which remind us of what we are never permitted to do. Their inherent wickedness, which cannot be compensated for by any external consequences, consists precisely in the harm they do to the "absolute" rights of another person, attacking the inviolable protective sphere which deserves unconditional respect from everyone else, since it guarantees the possibility of that person's free self-determination.

The inquiry into the indispensable minimum conditions of our human

---

138. Ibid., p. 224. He understands this example as a reply to the strategy chosen by consequentialist ethicists who magnify beyond all scale the dreadful consequences that might ensue, if absolute rights are respected. It is not only the consequences that can be described in such a manner, however: one can also describe the circumstances of the action itself in such a way that the inherently repellent and abhorrent character becomes clear (p. 226).

139. Ibid., pp. 219–22.

existence also makes it clear that we consider torture morally abhorrent not only—as in the case of lawyer Abrams—because it is an especially cruel form of bodily harm and killing. Rather, every form of torture which robs a person of his capacity to exercise his own will in self-determination and seeks to destroy the core of his personality, must be seen as incompatible with the dignity of the person. Hence, the abhorrent quality of torture is not only the infliction of terrible pains, but also the fact that the victim cannot resist these pains, and that the threat or the actual infliction of torture turns him into an object without a will of his own.[140] This is why the moral disapproval of torture also applies to psychological terror, the mere threat of violence, the manipulation of personality by such means as drugs, or the withdrawal of sleep, which are calculated to break down systematically the resistance of a person, even if such methods may not involve the infliction of violence on his body, and cause no physical pains.

Does the recollection of what one is never allowed to do really suffice to free lawyer Abrams from his moral dilemma? If he refuses to go along with the terrorists' attempt at blackmail, is he not responsible for the death which they threaten to inflict on the millions who inhabit a great city? If he refrains from torturing his mother, how can he bear to see their death? According to a teleological ethics which evaluates his conduct exclusively on the basis of a consideration of its consequences, Abrams would indeed be obliged to consider himself responsible for all the foreseeable effects of what he does or refrains from doing. But such an immeasurable responsibility for the consequences could not resolve his moral dilemma; all it does is to leave him alone with a burden of responsibility grotesquely greater than any human being could ever bear. If the analysis of the situation into which Abrams is plunged by the terrorists' threats looks only at the consequences, it ends up by depriving him of the possibility of understanding himself as one who bears ethical responsibility, since this analysis possesses no criterion to identify those consequences which are *morally relevant*. If it argues consistently within its own categories, it is simply incapable of saying what responsibility Abrams might rationally be thought to bear in this situation.[141]

Does deontological ethics have a better starting point? It might begin by pointing to the traditional distinction between killing and allowing

---

140. Cf. W. Maihofer, *Rechtsstaat und menschliche Würde,* Frankfurt 1968, pp. 17–19, 33f.

141. On this point, we can apply to teleological considerations within Catholic moral theology the critique of utilitarianism proposed by J. L. Mackie, *Ethik. Die Erfindung des moralisch Richtigen und Falschen,* Stuttgart 2nd edn. 1983, pp. 157–78.

someone to die: it would remind Abrams that he is not actually killing the inhabitants of the city, but merely allowing their foreseeable death to occur, since he has no morally acceptable possibility of preventing it. Such an answer would indeed make Abrams' dilemma less acute, but according to Gewirth, it would not truly resolve it, since other persons' absolute rights not only entail the obligation to avoid particular actions, but also establish the positive duty not to allow them to be harmed. Even if one holds that the distinction between killing and allowing to die is indispensable in other cases, one must agree with Gewirth that Abrams will find little consolation in the thought that he has merely allowed the death of a great many persons to occur. This is why Gewirth proposes that one consider the dilemma provoked by the terrorists' threat not only from the perspective of its consequences, but also from another angle which can explain why Abrams bears no moral responsibility even if the blackmailers make good their threat.

This change of perspective leads us to ask *who* in fact bears responsibility for the death of countless persons, if the terrorists do decide to carry out their threatened plan. Even from this perspective, there is an external causal interconnection between Abrams' refusal to torture his mother and the nuclear attack on the city, but the "principle of intervening action" means that we are no longer obliged to interpret this as a closed chain of events for which Abrams alone would bear moral responsibility, since it was unleashed by his refusal.[142] This principle affirms that the moral responsibility for an action and its consequences remains with the agent who has provoked these through his own free decision and in awareness of all the relevant circumstances.

This may at first sight appear a trivial point, but reflection shows that it

---

142. A. Gewirth, "Are There Any Absolute Rights?," p. 229. Teleological concepts of ethics tend not to ask what the foreseeable consequences of other persons' actions mean for the moral evaluation of one's own conduct, even when such concepts attempt to make differentiations in the total sum of "consequences of action." For example, W. Wolbert distinguishes between *de facto* consequences (important for the subsequent evaluation) and *foreseeable* consequences (for the weighing which is necessary beforehand), between *foreseeable* consequences (for the discernment of that which is ethically correct) and *intended* consequences (for the judgment about what is ethically good), and finally between consequences which *will certainly occur* and those that are *hypothetical* (*Vom Nutzen der Gerechtigkeit*, pp. 49–60). But even if one agrees with this classification, it would still be necessary to include the foreseeable consequences of other persons' actions in the evaluation of the ethical correctness of one's own conduct. Since Wolbert provides no other appropriate criterion for such a differentiation, one would have to include these among the foreseeable consequences of one's own actions.

is decisively important. The moral dilemma which seems to afflict Abrams arises only if we accept that he is morally responsible for the totality of the consequences which are causally linked to his refusal to torture his own mother; and it is precisely this general premise, presupposed and taken for granted by teleological ethics, that the principle of intervening action calls into question. We can formulate this principle as follows: we are responsible only for the foreseeable consequences of our own actions, not for the consequences of other persons' actions which can be expected to occur, even when these are a foreseeable reaction to our own actions. While there is such a thing as shared moral guilt in other persons' actions, this is not caused by the mere fact that my own action occurs at an early point in the course of those events which ultimately add up to the total sum of "consequences of action" which would have to be included in a teleological evaluation. Rather, the concept of shared moral guilt in someone else's action presupposes that I freely approve of what the other person (who bears the responsibility) does, and that I integrate this into the context of my own actions by means of a forward-looking plan.

In an ethics of political resistance, one can ask whether it is ethically permissible to employ the foreseeable death of innocent civilian victims as a consciously intended instrument to stir the people to revolt against a foreign occupation. This question describes very precisely the strategic calculation of the Italian partisan leader Rosario Bentivegna during the Fascist occupation of his country, when he gave orders to attack German soldiers in the Via Rasella. He not only foresaw, but consciously provoked the vengeance taken by the SS, who (in keeping with the customs of international martial law) had threatened to shoot ten hostages for every solder killed; his intention was to mobilize his own people in support of the anti-Fascist resistance. According to the principle of intervening action, it would be ludicrous to charge him with moral responsibility for the death of the 335 hostages who were shot by the Nazis in the Ardeatine marshes twenty-four hours later. The moral responsibility for this abhorrent war-crime lies exclusively on the German side, first with Major Kappler, who personally decided to kill five hostages more than the pure logic of vengeance required, and then with his superiors in the German chain of command.

This, however, does not exonerate the Italian partisan leader from the obligation to scrutinize the ethical justification of his own strategy. In the logic of martial war, an attack on soldiers of the occupying forces may be morally justified; but can it be legitimate to employ the death of members of one's own people, who are held hostage by the enemy, as a means to destabilize the political situation? The barbaric shooting by the Nazis was not only accepted by the partisans as an inevitable subsidiary consequence of a military onslaught; it was in fact their intentional goal, integrated into the total strategy of the political resistance they were planning, because of its foreseeable effect on their own people.

This means that we must reply that it is reprehensible, even under the circumstances of a morally permissible resistance struggle, to sacrifice consciously the lives of innocent members of one's own people, whether uninvolved civilians or hostages held by the enemy. This kind of calculated instrumentalization cannot be justified by the political goals of the resistance, since it fails to respect the personal dignity of the victims. Unlike lawyer Abrams, who did not in the least wish the death of the inhabitants of a great city nor envisage this as a part of his own considered plan, the principle of intervening action does not absolve the Italian partisans from *all* share in responsibility for the hostages' death. In their case, we must ask, not whether they share guilt in the consequences of other persons' actions (which they foresaw and consciously provoked), but what the relation is between their share in moral guilt under the conditions of a political resistance struggle and the main guilt of those who actually carried out the shooting.

Let us return to the situation of lawyer Abrams, which we wished to clarify with the help of the principle of intervening action. Abrams is not guilty of the death of the inhabitants of the great city, since he possesses no ethically acceptable possibility of preventing it: the torture of an innocent person (and a fortiori of his own mother) is not an ethically legitimate means, even if it would save the lives of other innocent persons. The moral dilemma which appears to afflict Abrams so hopelessly is in fact based on a monstrous fiction, which can be constructed only on the basis of the unacceptable supposition that he is responsible for all the foreseeable consequences of his own actions and of the intervening actions, with no distinctions being drawn.

In reality, his alleged moral dilemma reveals only the limit of a teleological consideration of human behavior, when this is carried out with total consistency. The finitude of the human person means not only that we are mostly confronted in our behavior with contingent goods which can come into collision with other goods, but also that we are not responsible for all the foreseeable consequences of what we do. It asks too much of the human person to demand that he give up the unconditional certainty offered in many existential situations by deontologically formulated prohibitions in exchange for the burden of an unlimited weighing of goods; ultimately, this makes a nonsense of the idea of moral responsibility and abolishes the concept of moral action.[143] Full clarity may emerge only in extreme constellations of circumstances, but there are enough situations in daily life where the imperative is not to weigh things and reflect, but simply to avoid doing what one is never permitted to do. The recollection that it would be abhorrent and reprehensible to torture his own mother preserves Abrams from accepting the diabolical calculation of the blackmailers.

This critique of a purely consequence-orientated consideration of Abrams' situation thus leads to the conclusion that the strict refusal to torture an innocent person is the only morally justified mode of conduct; he is not morally responsible for the threatened destruction of a great city. The arguments presented against a teleological ethics in the discussion of his alleged moral dilemma are not, however, meant to give the impression that a consistent utilitarian would have had to counsel poor Abrams to accept the abhorrent crime and torture his own mother; most of the representatives of teleological ethics do in fact agree that the various kinds of torture—as punishment, as a way of ensuring proof or acquiring information—are no longer justified.[144] Where one is dealing with terrorist blackmail, there are indeed particular utilitaristic reasons for maintaining deontologically valid norms for conduct. Only the strict maxim that one may not abandon one's own moral convictions is capable in the long term of preventing blackmail; if nothing is done to refute the belief of the terrorists that a weighing of the goods involved might in some circumstances lead to acceptance of their demands, this will only increase their willingness to attempt blackmail again.

The goal of these reflections is not to call into question the seriousness of teleological ethicists' condemnation of torture. I do, however, doubt whether it is possible for a purely consequence-orientated ethics to provide a consistent justification for the conviction that such behavior is abhorrent, and whether one can maintain this justification without contradiction even in boundary-situations. My aim has also been to show that the task of a responsible weighing of goods and the concept of intrinsically evil

143. On this, cf. R. Spaemann, "Über die Unmöglichkeit einer universaltheologischen Ethik," *PhJ* 88 (1981), pp. 70–89, esp. 81ff.

144. On this, see the teleological justifications for the moral prohibition of torture in W. Wolbert, *Der Mensch als Mittel und Zweck,* pp. 108f.; W. Mommsen, *Christliche Ethik und Teleologie,* pp. 179f.

actions are not mutually exclusive, but rather require one another. Since the idea of intrinsically evil actions or of the absolute rights of others reminds us of what we are never permitted to do, it ultimately serves to keep open the free space within which we, as finite human beings, can bear moral responsibility for the consequences of our actions. Even in a teleological ethics, therefore, this deontological element is indispensable, just as a deontological ethics is compelled to exclude the unwished-for consequences of its own approach by additional teleological considerations.

c. Adultery and rape The examples discussed above may give the impression that intrinsically evil actions, through which we breach the inviolable personal area which protects another person, concern only extreme boundary-cases where the ethical verdict is clear a priori. The debate about whether torture, judical murder, the shooting of hostages, or the planned sacrifice of an individual to the interests of society are to be rejected because of their external consequences or because of their internal incompatibility with the ordering of reason can easily appear superfluous, since both modes of argumentation usually (though not in every particular instance) arrive at the same conclusions. Fortunately, the boundary-cases are extremely rare, and most of us are never called to put the reliability of our capacity to make ethical judgments to the test in this way. Nevertheless, this distinction helps us to understand our own moral judgments better in the daily situations of conflict that can occur in the personal world of every human being.

In this personal sphere, the concept of intrinsically evil actions, actions which one is never allowed to commit, has a further meaning connected with the general exonerating function of moral norms. The absolute prohibitions identify a core area where human persons share their lives with one another. This area never covers correct conduct, but only wrong behavior. By keeping us from doing what is wrong, the prohibitions preserve our ability to make ethical judgments so that we can employ this in situations where only a precise evaluation of all relevant circumstances will show us what is right. Hence, the ethical judgment that adultery is always and under all circumstances wrong behavior which contradicts the rational ordering of one's own sexuality, is not generated by an evaluation of external circumstances (which are often exceedingly complicated in complex situations between partners), but by internal insight into the ethical-personal character of marriage. The recognition that marital love makes claims on both partners in their personal selves and in their mutual relationship as subjects is also a recognition of the monogamous structure of marriage and of the obligation to marital fidelity. Fidelity to one's partner cannot be considered an external, pre-moral value, such that the prohibition of adultery would arise only from weighing other goods which lay outside the marriage itself; the very question of which other goods or special circumstances could make adultery ethically permissible is obviously inappropriate. Rather, the obligation to marital fidelity is a direct expression of the ethical-personal character of marriage, rooted in the fact that marriage, as a relationship between subjects, is itself an ethical institution in which human reason recognizes the expression of an ethos of human dignity in the field of human sexuality.[145]

Exclusivity and fidelity are necessary characteristics of marital love, but they are not external goods which could be in competition with other goods; accordingly, the recognition of the wrongness of adultery is not the result of weighing the relevant circumstances and the consequences that may be expected. Infidelity, cheating, and adultery are an obvious inherent contradiction of married love, and this is why they are always wrong. The only ethical evaluation which could be involved here would not be a weighing of external goods, but an inner conflict within the obligation to fidelity itself, that is, a conflict between equal personal values such as fidelity to oneself and fidelity to one's partner. It is a sign of human love's fallibility and capacity to error, and indeed ultimately a tragic indicator of the irreducible contingency of our existence, that two people can be led by their marriage partnership into a hopeless situation in which the only choice available is to leave the other in order to be faithful to one's own self.[146] The point of departure for such a choice is, however, fundamentally different from an evaluation of which competing goods pose a serious threat to the value of marital fidelity, and which goods this must outweigh if the prohibition of adultery is to be justified within the framework of a teleological ethics.

Even more clearly, rape must be recognized as reprehensible in all circumstances, since it is inherently an attack on the acknowledgment of the personal dignity of a human being. It contradicts not only the personal structure of love, but also the minimum conditions of human freedom which must be respected, if the possibility of ethical self-determination is to be maintained. No other action shows so unambiguously a lack of re-

---

145. Cf. P. Mikat, *Ethische Strukturen der Ehe in unserer Zeit,* Paderbrn 1987, p. 51; and esp. H.-G. Gruber, *Christliche Ehe in moderner Gesellschaft,* pp. 304f.

146. Cf. W. Weischedel, *Skeptische Ethik,* Frankfurt 1976, pp. 218f.

spect of another person's freedom and personal self-determination as the attempt to use violence, against her will and exploiting her bodily weakness, to make her the object of one's own sexual desire. The helplessness of the victim, the humiliating experience of being unable to protect herself, and the intentional exploitation of her fear in a sphere of special psychological vulnerability amount to a degradation of human dignity which is always and everywhere reprehensible and can never be justified by any other "usefulness." There can be no doubt that the ethical disapproval of such conduct is not generated only by an evaluation of its external consequences (e.g., the harm inflicted on the victim)[147] or by a consideration of special circumstances (e.g., where the victim was an employee of the rapist or where she was underage), but rather is the result of its inherent incompatibility with the dignity of the human being as a person, a dignity rooted in freedom and reason.

From the rapist's perspective, his crime expresses contempt for his victim, who is humiliated by this act of violence in a sphere central to her own self-esteem and the experience of her own identity. Since the sphere of sexual intimacy is as it were a forecourt to the sphere which protects the freedom and the personal self-determination of a human being, it can never be permissible to force someone against his or her will to engage in sexual activity. Since rape and the use of coercion in a sexual context are an attack on the sexual self-determination of the human person, they are intrinsically evil actions, and no further weighing of goods is needed for their ethical judgment. The inherent structure of these actions suffices to establish the ethical judgment that they are always wrong, because they are incompatible with respect for the personal dignity of another human being.

Once again, these reflections do not intend to sow doubt about the resolute disapproval of crimes of sexual violence by teleological ethics, still less to create the impression that—given a little imagination—one could even imagine situations where a teleological consideration would see rape as ethically permissible in order to attain some higher good. A consistent teleological evaluation has good arguments for seeing the prohibition of rape as absolutely binding; for if justified exceptions were allowed in particular instances, this would introduce a high degree of uncertainty into

---

147. On the consequences of sexual rape and the subsequent difficulties experienced by rape victims in rebuilding their identity, cf. H. Feldmann, *Vergewaltigung und ihre psychischen Folgen*, Stuttgart 1992; M. von Welser, *Am Ende wünscht du dir nur noch den Tod. Die Massenvergewaltigungen im Krieg auf dem Balkan*, Munich 1993; S. Kappeler et al. (eds.), *Vergewaltigung, Krieg, Nationalismus. Eine feministische Kritik*, Munich 1994.

human relationships, so that the social forces which bind human sexuality would increasingly give way to uncontrollable violence. From the perspective of a rule-utilitarianism, this danger may be enough to prompt the decided condemnation of rape. However, the decisive reason why we disapprove of rape and sexual violence is not a desire to prevent social ills, but the fact that every human being possesses an absolute right to remain protected from crimes against his or her own sexual self-determination, and an absolute right not to be forced against his or her will to engage in sexual activity.

As in the case of torture, the example of rape shows that we cannot do without the concept of intrinsically evil actions, for otherwise we lose the possibility of offering a consistent justification for our moral judgments in a core area of human conduct, where the mutual acknowledgment of the other as an ethical subject with personal dignity is at stake. Our reflections have, however, also made it clear that we must employ higher standards in using this type of argument than have been customary in Catholic moral theology up to now. If we apply the criterion of strict incompatibility with the personal dignity of human beings, not all actions which have been regarded in the past as intrinsically evil must in fact be considered as ethically impermissible under all circumstances.

A strict application of this criterion means that not every action which prevents the full realization of human dignity is intrinsically evil, but only conduct that is incompatible with the absolute minimum conditions for ethical freedom. In this restrictive sense, the category includes above all the infringement of fundamental human rights and behavior that directly contradicts those obligations which ethical freedom leads us to accept responsibly. This is why the killing of innocent persons, torture, and rape on the one hand, and the breaking of freely given promises, sexual infidelity, and adultery on the other can be considered paradigms of such intrinsically evil actions; on the other hand, a narrow criterion of intrinsically evil actions provides no help in making a comprehensive ethical evaluation of masturbation, homosexuality, and sterilization, or in distinguishing clearly between "natural" and "artificial" methods of contraception. Rather, an ethical judgment of these actions presupposes insight into the anthropological contexts in which they are meaningful, such as the significance of the dual gender of the human race, the unity of the various elements which give meaning to human sexuality, or the place of individual sexual acts within the totality of marital life. However, such an insight goes beyond the indispensable minimum conditions for human life, since it implies an answer to the question of how human life as a whole can succeed—and it is precisely such an answer that is lacking in the concept of intrinsically evil deeds that one may never perform.

When we look back at the dispute about theological and ethical methodology in the last two or three decades, this means that teleological ethics is correct to dismiss as circular and tautological the classical argument that certain actions were contrary to nature, and to reject the arguments used by traditional natural-rights ethics to justify the concept of the *intrinsice malum*. Teleological ethics is however wrong to infer from this that it can *never* be meaningful and necessary to employ this argument, and that the teleological weighing of goods is a sufficient criterion for the ethical evaluation of *all* situations of human conduct. Even in a deontological ethics, the weighing of goods retains an essential function when one must determine what is ethically right below this personal level; but where the moral rights of the human person and mutual respect for human beings as ethical subjects come into play, one cannot dispense with the recollection of what one is never permitted to do and the conscious justification of this by the concept of intrinsically evil actions. This means that the spontaneous convergence in classical moral theology of the two modes of argumentation which we today call teleological and deontological made good sense. The theoretical reason makes use of the complementarity of various explanatory models in order to achieve a scientific understanding of reality, and this is not to be dismissed as a logical inconsistency or a lack of systematic coherence in the sphere of the practical reason. The distinction between two normative levels of evaluation, emphasizing the distinction between the absolute protective sphere of the human person and other spheres of action, does better justice to the variety of existential situations in human life than an indiscriminate attribution of external consequences to our actions, in keeping with the status of ethics as a practical science. A purely consequential way of looking at things submits unnecessarily to the arrogant claim of a unilateral methodological ideal which was long ago abandoned by the theoretical reason in its own epistemological sphere.

❧ V. *The universal claim of biblical ethics*

THE PREVIOUS CHAPTERS have shown that the concept of nature embraces a variety of meanings. If we wish to speak of the universal validity of the natural law, this variety makes necessary a differentiation which the history of the philosophical and theological doctrines of natural law has tended to overlook. Since the appeal to human "nature" refers to those foundations of human existence which are always and everywhere the same and which the negative precepts of the natural law are intended to protect, the concept can be based at this level only on the initial presuppositions of human existence, which do not go beyond the absolute minimum conditions for the possibility of ethical self-determination, that is, for the freedom to live in a responsible manner. It follows that the universal claim of the natural law applies only to the minimum conditions contained in the ethical phenomenon itself. Such a reduced anthropology has nothing to say about the meaning of human existence as a whole and the totality of experience which is possible for human beings, and gives no indication of how one might realize one's fullest existential potential. Accordingly, the requirements of the natural law (which protect the sphere necessary to the development of the human person) never presuppose more than a critical employment of the idea of "human dignity": in other words, while they do not guarantee the realization of an existence worthy of the human person, they do ensure the external possibilities of such a life by excluding the most basic risks to human existence. Since the concept of human dignity functions only as an *exclusive* criterion limited to the irreducible initial conditions for human existence, the demands of the natural law on this level apply to every human being, irrespective of what ideas about the good life and what models of successful human existence may be valid within one's cultural self-understanding.

The critical demarcation drawn by the highest principles of the natural law and by the prohibitions anchored in these does not claim to offer any exhaustive definition of what an existence worthy of the human person might mean in positive terms. The common basis of the natural law, which establishes a culturally neutral lower boundary of human existence, is inherently open to more demanding anthropologies such as we find in mankind's philosophical traditions and in the religious ideas of the various peoples. On the level of these holistic conceptions, the "nature" of the human person denotes not merely the absolute minimum conditions for ethical self-possession, but that which brings the humanity of the human person to an integral fulfillment encompassing every sphere of his experience. In this reversed perspective, the idea of human dignity designates not primarily an inalienable *claim* which all must respect, but rather a *charge* to the human person to do justice to his own dignity in the various sectors of life. The answers given to the question of how human existence as a whole succeeds—or, to use the language of St. Thomas, how the human person attains his ultimate end and realizes the ultimate potential of his being— can be very various, depending on which *inclusive* understanding of human dignity is presupposed. On this level, in fact, ethical demands (especially those with a high ethical tendency) envisage different models of the human person, and this means that the universal claim which they propose must be conceived in a different way, one that does justice to the plurality of underlying anthropologies.

In today's world, the possibility of intercultural understanding in the field of ethics depends to a large extent on not suppressing the various anthropological presuppositions which might still lie concealed behind a superficial convergence of ethical ideas. The task for the church's moral proclamation is therefore to make a clearer distinction than has been customary in the past between the general initial conditions for human existence (which must be respected always and everywhere) and the consequences drawn from the meaningful answer offered by the Christian faith to the basic questions of human existence. The obligation to make an appropriate differentiation between the levels on which the church is speaking will certainly be seen by some people as a threat to the internal consistency of her moral teaching or a surreptitious attempt to weaken its universal claim. It is, however, also possible, in view of the intellectual challenge posed by the encounter with the world religions and the cultures of humankind, to see this as a positive chance to provide a better justification for the ethical claim of the Gospel, elaborating more clearly than in the classical doctrines of natural law how the truth of the Gospel protects the humanity of each human person. Indeed, we may find that this helps us to overcome the latent ambiguity which obscures the idea of a "Christian" natural law, as long as it is unclear whether this adresses an abstract essential nature of the human person, his nature as ruined by sin, or his nature as renewed in Christ. Bearing in mind the central theological objection to the church's classical doctrine of natural law, as set out in the first chapter of this book, this means that the distinction elaborated in philosophical discussion of the universal validity of human rights—between the absolute initial conditions for human existence and the richer substance of the anthropological ideas which have been developed against the background of various philosophical, metaphysical, or religious traditions— does not in the least endanger the inherent connection between these two elements. On the contrary, this distinction, which has become necessary today, indicates a path to resolve even the ultimate ambivalence which attaches to the idea of natural law in a theological context.

1. The background in anthropology and the theology of history

We must begin with the background in anthropology and the theology of history against which individual ethical directives in the biblical tradition are to be understood—especially the collections of precepts in the Decalogue and the Sermon on the Mount, which have had the greatest significance in the course of history. Some of these directives, exhortations, and paraenetic sapiential aphorisms are explicitly orientated to a high ethics. This is not to be explained as a quantitative surpassing or a substantial intensification of fundamental ethical commandments; rather, the claim they make must be interpreted against the background of the theological understanding of the human person and of his history which the biblical revelation generated in parallel to its traditional ethical materials. Without the anthropology and the conception of history specific to the Judaeo-Christian revelation, it is completely impossible to understand the meaning of ethical directives such as the demand for total fidelity in marriage, unlimited willingness to forgive, or renunciation of violence. Torn from their anthropological and salvation-historical context, they are bound to seem to be inhumanly excessive demands or rhetorical exaggerations; in either case, this means that they are not understood as seriously proposing ethical obligations. This charge, which is leveled (unjustly) against the universal prohibitions of the natural law, would therefore apply also to the ethical directives in Old Testament prophecy, in Jesus' Sermon on the Mount, or in the first Christian missionary proclamation. The high ethical directives of the Bible describe a path for human life, going beyond the minimum definition of the human person which underlies both the classical natural law and the modern ethos of human rights, and employing the terms "salvation" and "redemption" to portray the comprehensive success of human life.

1.1. Preliminary hermeneutical reflections

In order to understand these ethical affirmations, it is not, however, necessary to set out in systematic fashion all the aspects of the Bible's anthropology and understanding of history, still less to follow the history of the inspiration they have provided from the start to the philosophical anthropology of the twentieth century.[1] Nor need we set out the details of exegetical discussion in recent decades about the interpretation of the Old Testament texts which speak of the human person as created in God's image, or about the possibility of a theology which would embrace the whole Bible on the basis of a canonical exposition of both Testaments,[2] since the systematic understanding of the fundamental statements about biblical anthropology and the theology of history which moral theology necessarily presupposes cannot regard the literary-critical search for the earliest "stratum" or the original meaning of a text in the sense of tradition-history as anything more than a starting point. Where, however, biblical exegesis offers systematic theology a scientifically reliable access to the sources of theological knowledge, dogmatic and moral-theological reflection are obliged to make these exegetical insights the basis of their own work. Thus, a theological anthropology cannot simply pass by the results of exegetical investigation of the provenance of the idea of "image" in the Egyptian royal ideology, or the close connection in the Genesis narrative between this ideology and the gender polarity of the human person to whom God entrusts the creation.

Where, on the other hand, the biblical text disintegrates into ever new strata under the competition of literary-critical analyses and their attempts

---

1. On this, cf. B. Casper, *Das dialogische Denken. Eine Untersuchung der religions-philosophischen Bedeutung Franz Rosenzweigs, Ferdinand Ebners und Martin Bubers,* Freiburg 1967; Idem, "Der Zugang zu Religion im Denken von Emmanuel Levinas," *PhJ* 95 (1988) pp. 268–77; M. Theunissen, *Der Andere. Studien zur Sozialontologie der Gegenwart,* Berlin 2nd edn. 1977; W. Pannenberg, *Anthropologie in theologischer Perspektive,* Göttingen 1983, pp. 173–78; and, most recently, H. Schmidinger, *Der Mensch ist Person. Ein christliches Prinzip in theologischer und philosophischer Sicht,* Innsbruck and Vienna 1994.

2. Cf. H. Gese, "Erwägungen zur Einheit der biblischen Theologie, *ZTK* 67 (1970) pp. 417–36; and esp. B. S. Childs, *Biblical Theology of the Old and New Testament: Theological reflection on the Christian Bible,* London 1992.

at proposing a reconstruction, so that it is in fact dissolved by exegetical methodology, such results—which are more or less arbitrary—lose all relevance to further theological questions.[3] The only remaining alternative for systematic reflection is to recall the old hermeneutical principle that the total meaning of a biblical text includes both the history of its influence in later strata of the canon and the church's theological understanding of it.[4] But even so, the systematic interpretation of biblical texts and theological-ethical reflection on their relevance to human conduct must seek a methodologically sure access to the theological message of these texts; naturally, this entails due attention to all accessible results of investigation into biblical motifs and tradition-history. An example of the significance of such exegetical questions is the motif of the human person as God's image in the Old Testament. A theological anthropology based on this idea must pay heed to the fact that the relevant texts (Gn 1:26; 5:1–3; 9:6; Wis 2:23; Sir 17:3; Ps 8) had no immediate echo outside the creation-theological and sapiential traditions in Israel, and appear as an independent object of theological inquiry only in groups within hellenistic Judaism. Accordingly, if one wishes to make this idea the center of one's affirmations and use it to capture the richness of the perspectives of biblical anthropology, one will also have to take up other aspects of human existence suggested by the biblical writings.[5]

1.2. The image of God: the human person in his fundamental relationships

The theological interpretation of human existence on which the ethical directives of the Old and New Testaments are based does not limit itself to the minimum conditions which every human person must be thought to possess if ethical self-determination is to be a possibility; such conditions can be discerned by a transcendental reflection. Nor is it identical with the understanding of the person which has developed in philosophical reflec-

3. For an exegetical critique of this tendency, cf. F. Crüsemann, *Die Tora. Theologie und Sozialgeschichte des alttestamentlichen Gesetzes,* Munich 1992, pp. 42f.

4. On the hermeneutics of dogmatic and moral-theological exposition of scripture, cf. W. Kasper, "Das Verhältnis von Schrift und Tradition. Eine pneumatologische Perspektive" (1992), in: Idem, *Theologie und Kirche,* II, Mainz 1999, pp. 51–83; E. Schockenhoff, "Die Bedeutung von Schrift, Tradition und Lehramt für das Verständnis des christlichen Ethos," *Seminarium* 34 (1994), pp. 72–88.

5. I have written in greater detail about the substantial breadth of biblical ideas about "life" in my book *Ethik des Lebens. Ein theologischer Grundriß,* Mainz 1993, pp. 110–30.

tion as an exposition of the ontological self-understanding and the practical relationship to one's own self which the human person possesses thanks to his ability to assume responsibility for the conduct of his own life. Rather, the fundamental coordinates of the philosophical understanding of the person—especially selfhood, existence in relationship, and the unity of the human person as body and soul—are filled with new meaning by the light of revelation, so that the essential determination of the person achieves its fullest existential potential. Hence, biblical ethics presupposes a formally more demanding anthropology, one with a wider sweep which discloses the outlines of what successful human existence means.

If we look at the theological substance of the idea of "God's image," we find that it can be developed in four directions, indicating the biblical understanding of the four fundamental relationships in human existence. If we start with the emphatic affirmations in the priestly and Yahwist creation accounts about the human person as God's image, we are going beyond the significance that Gn 1:26 and similar texts possess de facto within the Old Testament itself; nevertheless, even a Jewish perspective justifies this, since the early rabbinic exposition of the doctrine of the human person as God's image connects this to central ethical questions. Naturally enough, the rabbis limit this to the exposition of the Jewish law, but they are more or less explicitly aware that the law has a universal human significance, embracing more than Israel alone. Indeed, many schools of rabbinic theology identify Israel with Adam, the human person, and this presupposes the profound insight that "the only true 'human being' is the one who follows the will of God which, according to the Old Testament, was revealed in a special manner on Sinai."[6]

a. The relationship to God (creatureliness)   As God's image, the human person lives constitutively *in relation to God.* This embraces every dimension of his existence, his transience and finitude, his creaturely needs and his mortality. He owes his creaturely existence neither to a decision taken by his own freedom nor to a gift bestowed by someone else, but only to the creative address by God's word. This means that he comes into existence as one called by God and is maintained in existence by the continuation of this creative adresss. The priestly creation narrative underlines this by means of a special divine decision, unlike the simple command whereby God creates the heavenly bodies and the earth, plants, and animals.

---

6. Cf. F. Mußner, *Traktat über die Juden,* Munich 1979, p. 101.

Through his creative word, God summons the human being to enter an immediate relationship to himself, which gives him the dignity of dialogue partner with God and makes him a human person. This means that it is not some particular characteristic (such as the intellect or the will bestowed on him rather than on the other creatures) that makes the human person God's image, but rather the relationship to God which sustains his life and allows him to transcend the empirical features of his humanity. When we speak of the human being as God's image and as person, we are not mentioning characteristics added onto his creaturely selfhood. Rather, we are speaking of his creaturely life as a whole, which can develop only in the fundamental relationship to his Creator and which surpasses the de facto reality of his empirical features. This is why one cannot locate the personhood of the human being in specific differentiating characteristics proper to his species. The intellectual elaboration of this fundamental biblical affirmation by theological anthropology has always understood this particular impossibility to mean that the human person cannot be conceived of as merely one section of the reality which is his milieu, or as one specific instance of a larger totality. Where anthropological reflection makes use of the verbal and intellectual concepts of Aristotelian-Thomistic ontology, it affirms this boundary by saying that the human person, unlike non-personal existents, is *quodammodo omnia,* that is, a totality in which the fullness of creaturely reality is present in a unique manner.[7]

b. The relationship to other human beings (shared humanity and the fact of two genders) The relationality of human existence, with its vertical foundation in God's creative adress, is prolonged on the horizontal axis by the dependence of the human person on *a human "thou."* This connection is conceived in such close terms in Gn 1:27 that it is simply impossible to affirm the human person as God's image independently of the concrete mutual relationship of man and woman: "So God created man in his own image, in the image of God he created him; male and female he created them."

Likewise, the central affirmation in the narrative in Gn 2:8–14 is that, while the animals are the human person's fellow creatures, they are not the real help and partner for which his life is designed. Only another human being, in the differentiation of the two genders, is the appropriate partner of a human being. It is only in the mutual help of woman and man that

7. On this, cf. Thomas Aquinas, *ScG* III, c. 122 (nr. 2860); *In III de Anima,* lect. 13 (nr. 790); *STh* I, q. 76, a. 5, ad 4.

the human being's humanity finds fulfillment. From the perspective of the relationship to God which sustains him in being, he is also destined to realize fundamental interpersonal relationships. Unlike a disastrous exegetical tradition which runs from the church fathers via the mediaeval theologians up to the present day, theological anthropology no longer interprets the idea of the mutual help of woman and man as referring to the way their sexual organs fit together for the purpose of procreating children; rather, they complement each other's shared humanity in a comprehensive manner which includes mutual understanding in dialogue.

When the Yahwist creation narrative relates the creation of the woman from the man's rib (cf. Gn 2:21), the primary intention is to affirm that the two genders belong together. A long-lived tradition has interpreted this as a reference to the patriarchal subordination of the woman under the man, but this too was a disastrous misunderstanding which distorts beyond recognition the biblical view of human sexuality. The archaic metaphor speaks rather of the dependence and mutual closeness of woman and man: "Then the Lord God said, 'It is not good that the man should be alone; I will make him a helper fit for him'" (Gn 2:18). According to both biblical creation narratives, human life can succeed only in a human fellowship based on the polar relationship of the two genders. The human person is summoned to enter a relationship with the animal world and to rule over the creation, but his existence cannot find fulfillment in these relationships with the created reality, which are subordinate to the relationship between human beings. As a being made for dialogue, the human person can exist only vis-à-vis a personal partner; this is how we attain fulfillment in our creaturely responsibility before God and in the relationship to others which is based on the gender polarity.[8]

It is surely rather remarkable that modern philosophical anthropology finds it so difficult to grasp adequately the meaning of human gender polarity and to relate this to the essential definition of human existence. What is the relationship between the personal existence of the human being (shared by woman and man alike) and the gender-specific expression of their human existence, where they differ? If the distinction between woman and man is an "essential" difference, then the classificatory logic of this philosophical term would mean that women and men were quite dif-

---

8. On the exegetical background, cf. C. Westermann, *Genesis, Kapitel 1–11*, Neukirchen 2nd edn. 1976 (*Biblische Kommentare/Altes Testament/1*), p. 309; H. W. Wolff, *Anthropologie des Alten Testaments*, Munich 1973, pp. 233–42; H. Schüngel-Straumann, *Die Frau am Anfang. Eva und die Folgen*, Freiburg 1989, pp. 103–11.

ferent beings, so that the concept "human species" would be merely a secondary summary of shared characteristics; hence, the attempt to understand the difference between the sexes in its existential significance for the
concrete mode of self-experience of the human person would risk abandoning the affirmation that human existence has an origin common to
both women and men. On the other hand, this shared human existence is
never an abstraction hovering somewhere "above" the differentiation of
gender. It exists only *in* the difference of women and men, as the concrete
experience of being a woman or a man. Otherwise, gender would be an accidental, arbitrary definition of the human person—and that would contradict both the fundamental biblical affirmation and the existential self-
experience of the human person.[9]

The philosophical and theological question about the meaning of human gender polarity may not limit itself to an analysis of the bodily and
psychological specificities of each gender, or the "existential themes" proper to each (to use Philipp Lersch's term); this was often the case in the philosophy of the twentieth century, with its anthropological orientation.[10]
Rather, a systematic understanding of the biblical affirmations about creation must examine the relationship between the essence of the two genders and the essence of the human person, and why personal existence
never occurs other than as female or male existence. One must conceive of
human gender polarity in such a way that this does not destroy the unity
of human essence, yet is more than merely a secondary, accidental definition. If an anthropological model is to succeed in explaining both what
distinguishes the sexes and what unites them, it must understand the genders as equally primary expressions of what it is to be a "human person,"
while at the same time making clear how this differentiation is rooted in
the being of the human person himself and is a component element in the
proper development of his being.

c. The relationship to oneself (totality) Another fundamental relationship of human existence concerns the relationship of the human person *to
his own self.* Biblical anthropology conceives of this not primarily as a con-

9. On this, cf. R. Schulte, "Sein und Verwirklichung der menschlichen Geschlechtlichkeit. Ein theologischer Versuch," in: N. A. Luyten (ed.), *Wesen und Sinn der Geschlechtlichkeit,* Freiburg and Munich 1985, pp. 301–72, esp. 317–88; H. M. Baumgartner, "Gleichheit und Verschiedenheit von Mann und Frau in philosophischer Perspektive," in: Ibid.
pp. 271–300, esp. 272–76.

10. On this, cf. J. Burri, *'Als Mann und Frau schuf er sie'. Differenz der Geschlechter aus
moral- und praktisch-theologischer Sicht,* Zurich 1977, esp. pp. 34–40.

scious relationship of the intellect to itself, but as a total unity of human life, embracing body and soul. We see this in the language chosen in Gn 2:7 with a succinctness that is difficult to translate: "Then the Lord God formed man of dust from the ground and breathed into his nostrils the breath of life; and the man became a living being." Behind the translation "living being" is a Hebrew construction which indicates that we human beings do not possess our *nephesh*—an expression which means much more than our word "soul"—but rather are a *nephesh* and live as a *nephesh*. Whereas Greek thought makes a sharp distinction between body and spirit as antithetical poles of human existence, the fundamental anthropological terms used in biblical language *(nephesh, ruach,* and *basar)* do not designate strata laid on top of each other in the human being in such a way that they construct his essence. Rather, when the human being is called "soul," "spirit," or "flesh," the intention is to speak of the entire person, from the variety of perspectives in which he experiences himself in the concrete unity of his existence.

If we wish to make more precise definitions of these terms with their overlapping meanings, we may say that *nephesh* denotes the bodily or intellectual concerns of the human person, *ruach* his vitality and passionate quality, and *basar* his weakness and transitoriness.[11] These concepts range over a wide field of meanings, but they have one basic characteristic in common: the fundamental words "soul," "spirit," and "flesh" are initially related to specific organs and vital biological functions, employing a variety of perspectives to indicate the possibilities open to the human person. They look at the totality of his existence, in his need and his frailty, the yearning of his intellect and the demands made by his body, in his social relatedness and his individual selfhood. In all these dimensions, human life is determined by its sustaining relationship to the creative, life-giving power of God. Even when the Bible speaks of two poles of human existence, the antithesis between "flesh" on the one hand and "soul" and "spirit" on the other does not denote any anthropological contradiction in the human person himself, but antithetical ways of relating to his Creator.

d. The relationship to the creation (responsibility)   In addition to the human person's creaturely dependence on God, his dialogic existence in the

---

11. On this, cf. W. H. Schmidt, "Anthropologische Begriffe im Alten Testament," *EvTh* 24 (1964), pp. 375–88, esp. 387; J. Schabert, *Fleisch, Geist und Seele im Pentateuch* (Stuttgarter Bibel Studien 19), Stuttgart 1966; and esp. H. W. Wolff, *Anthropologie des Alten Testaments,* pp. 21–123.

polarity of two genders, and his life in the holistic unity of body and soul, the biblical creation narratives emphasize above all the *special status of the human being* with regard to the creation that surrounds him. Although he is created on the same day as the land-animals, he is given lordship over them. The commission to represent God vis-à-vis the creation is based exclusively on the divine blessing which is invoked on the first human couple immediately after their creation: "God blessed them, and God said to them, 'Be fruitful and multiply, and fill the earth and subdue it; and have dominion over the fish of the sea and over the birds of the earth and over every living thing that moves upon the earth'" (Gn 1:28). This commission to rule over creation is given to the human being along with the Creator's blessing for his own life: it follows that it is not a *carte blanche* for the exploitation of nature. Rather, this human lordship over creation is meant to be the channel that brings the divine blessing to creation too. The unique dignity which his immediate relationship to God gives the human person is thus displayed in the special commission which he receives for the other beings within creation.

If it is true to say that the idea of the human person as God's image is derived from the Egyptian royal ideology by a democratization of the idea of the ruler as God's representative, this means that we encounter a very early stratum of the biblical anthropology here. We may agree with Lothar Ruppert's formulation of the earliest meaning of this idea: "In the human person, God himself encounters his creatures 'as in an image.' The human person points by the very fact of his existence to the Creator whom he represents before the creation as in an image."[12] When later theological reflection speaks emphatically of the special status and role of the human person as the "crowning" of creation, it certainly takes up one basic trait of the biblical texts; in Genesis itself, however, the prominence of the human person is linked to the bestowal of a commission which he cannot delegate to the other creatures. His task is to serve his Creator in the representative function of establishing God's peaceful sovereignty over creation.

In keeping with the two poles of the basic structure of the biblical affirmations—that God continuously maintains the world in existence by his creative word, and that he entrusts it to the hands of human beings—this means that the divine summons to live as "God's image" always entails human responsibility for creation. In the biblical understanding, the human

---

12. L. Ruppert, Genesis. *Ein kritischer und theologischer Kommentar, 1. Teilband: Gen 1,11–11,26,* Würzburg 1992, p. 92. On this, cf. also E. Otto, *Theologische Ethik des Alten Testaments,* Stuttgart et al. 1994, p. 94.

person is not called into being only so that he may live from the gifts of the creation and lead his natural existence in self-sufficiency; rather, he lives in accordance with God's image, in which he was created, only when he is open to God and to a human partner, and does not refuse his commission vis-à-vis creation. In other words, when the Bible speaks of the human person, it does not envisage partial functions, external roles, or individual aspects, but always the entire human being who is meant to respond to his Creator in all the dimensions of his life, in body and in soul.

1.3. The image of the human person: Jesus Christ as the symbol of true human existence

In a systematic perspective, with the task of reflection on the theological unity of both testaments, new light is cast on the fact (mentioned above) that, apart from the priestly writings, the idea of the human person as God's image long remained a marginal motif in Old Testament anthropology. Although the awareness that *all* human beings are created in God's image is indeed one of the most prominent affirmations in the Old Testament, to which the New Testament occasionally appeals in justification of ethical demands (cf. 1 Cor 11:7; Jas 3:9), these few isolated statements are not central to the various strata of Old Testament tradition. In the New Testament, however, the idea that the human person is created in God's image becomes much more important, so that it takes on a dominant status vis-à-vis all other anthropological themes. In the new covenant, the idea that the human person corresponds to God is not only an end towards which he is *en route* or a commission that he must fulfill; rather, this has become historical reality in one specific human being, in the life and death of Jesus of Nazareth and in his resurrection from the dead. Since then, it is present in history as the ultimate possibility available to every human person.[13] In Jesus Christ, there has entered the history of Israel a human being who was completely one with God and who brought the meaning of God's relationship in history with human beings to fulfillment "once and for all" (Heb 7:27; 8:12) by means of his life and death.[14] In Jesus Christ, however, we see not only a human being who lives completely

---

13. These presuppositions of Christian ethics in the theology of history have been studied especially by K. Demmer, *Deuten und handeln. Grundlagen und Grundfragen der Fundamentalmoral,* Freiburg 1985, pp. 120–27. Cf. also Idem, *Moraltheologische Methodenlehre,* Freiburg 1989, pp. 66–70.

14. On this, cf. G. von Rad, *Theologie des Alten Testaments,* II: *Die Theologie der prophetischen Überlieferung,* Munich 1965, p. 435.

236 The universal claim of biblical ethics

in accordance with the image of God; in him, it is God himself who appears in the image of this particular human being in order to be with every human being in the fullness of his love and grace. A human being who lives totally on the basis of his partnership with God, and a God who has drawn close in the image of this human being—this is the basic formula of the biblical anthropology which emerges in New Testament christological reflection.

For the New Testament, Jesus Christ is the true and only "image of the invisible God" (Col 1:15; cf. Rom 8:29; 1 Cor 15:45–49; 2 Cor 3:18). In baptism, we are renewed by being configured to him through God's grace, and we are called to share in his glory by means of a life in keeping with our baptism. In Jesus Christ, the true face of the human person emerges, without the disfigurements and obscurities which attach to every image that the human person makes of his own self or that others make of him. God himself shows us his image and likeness in order that we may know the dignity to which we are called. This means that the highest end and the supreme fulfillment of our life have drawn close to us in Jesus Christ; since he is the prototype of true human existence, he shows us what a life in freedom and love, justice and solidarity means for all human persons. This certainly does not remove the abiding difference between the symbolic, archetypical fullness of Christ and the fragmentary, incipient anticipation of perfected human existence in our ethical conduct.[15] The theologians of the early church employed a terminological specification, suggested by the verbal doublet of the biblical creation narratives, when they attempted to explain the abiding difference which means that Christ, as the *only* image of God, always lies ahead of us human beings, who are created *in view* of this image: Jesus Christ is in an exclusive sense *the* image in which the invisible God has appeared among human beings, who are created, not *as* the image, but *according to* the image of God, which they are to portray in their lives. This allows us to understand the ethical conduct of the human person as an historical path between two fixed poles. On the one hand, the idea of the perfect human being, who makes the correct response to God in every dimension of his existence, has already become reality in Jesus Christ, so that the historical possibility lies open to every human person. On the other hand, the one who is renewed in baptism and receives the grace of Christ is an imperfect and finite being: hence, he must be *in via*

15. On this, cf. E. Schockenhoff, *Zum Fest der Freiheit. Theologie des christlichen Handelns bei Origenes*, Mainz 1990, pp. 333f.

throughout his life, in order to correspond ever better to the end for which he was created.[16]

2. The universal significance of the Ten Commandments

If asked to name a biblical text which gives a concise summary of the ethical precepts of the Old and New Testaments, most people, whether Christian or not, would think spontaneously of the Decalogue. The Ten Commandments have been regarded by Christian preachers since Augustine and Martin Luther as a paradigmatic synthesis of the moral precepts of the Old Testament, and they serve in catechetical instruction even today as a kind of compendium of elementary basic rules for ethical conduct. They enjoy a high measure of plausibility thanks to their inherent reasonableness and their accord with what people experience in daily life. This interpretation, which sees the Decalogue as a document belonging to the whole of humanity, has a long history. The classical natural-law doctrines of early Christian and mediaeval theology understood it as a brief résumé of all the moral commandments of the Old Testament, which they then compared to the special ethical directives and counsels of the New. The earliest declarations of human rights in the modern period appealed to the Decalogue. The same is true of popular instruction in the Enlightenment, where the Ten Commandments were seen as a counterpart to the categorical imperative of a formal rational ethic, since they were adapted to the intellectual capacities of the simple people. From the nineteenth century onwards, the "ten words" of Israel have been regarded in the ecumenical dialogue of the world religions as the magna carta of an ethos applicable to the whole of humanity. Together with similar formulations in the sacred texts of other world religions (which are often summarized in chains of five precepts), the Decalogue contains the "five great commandments of humane living," which stipulate the maxims of a universal idea of humane existence.[17]

No other text in the Judaeo-Christian tradition has had a comparable

16. On this, cf. esp. E. Jüngel, "Der Gott entsprechende Mensch. Bemerkungen zur Gottebenbildlichkeit des Menschen als Grundfigur theologischer Anthropologie," in: H.-G. Gadamer and P. Vogler (eds.), *Philosophische Anthropologie*, I, Munich 1975, pp. 342–72; I. U. Dalferth and E. Jüngel, "Person und Gottebenbildlichkeit," *CGG* XXIV, cols. 66–86.

17. Cf. H. Küng, *Projekt Weltethos*, Munich and Zurich 1990, p. 82; Idem, *Das Judentum. Die religiöse Situation der Zeit*, Munich 1991.

influence outside the traditions of Jewish and Christian faith; within Judaism and the ecumenical sphere of the Christian church, the only texts that might stand comparison are the Lord's Prayer and the Sermon on the Mount. Why does the Decalogue have this unique significance? To begin with, it is one of the major texts shared by Jews and Christians; at the same time, it offers "a link to universal human morality and makes it possible for the Christian proclamation to speak of the world."[18] If our systematic reflection on the universal claim made by the Ten Commandments wishes to serve both the dialogue with Judaism and the worldwide encounter between the great religions of humankind, we must try to maintain this dual horizon in our investigation of the relevant issues. The moral-philosophical tools developed by classical natural-law ethics—especially the distinction between the ceremonial laws and the moral precepts in the two tablets of the Decalogue and the equation of the latter with the natural law—certainly aimed in the right direction and made a number of correct affirmations. However, one cannot simply repeat these in today's context, since they do not do justice to the gradated justification of the natural law, nor to the special historical-theological background to the Decalogue and to Israel's experience of God.[19]

2.1. To whom does the Decalogue belong?

A vigorous controversy among exegetes in recent years has debated whether this kind of universal claim can be justified within the Old Testament itself, or whether it was only the reception of the Decalogue in the early church and its later influence that allowed such a claim to be made.[20] The reason for this controversy is that the unique position enjoyed by the Decalogue for many centuries in the church's moral instruction does not actually accord with its status within the Old Testament: the brief summaries of the biblical faith which it offers are texts such as "Hear, O Israel" (Dt 6:4) or the various credal formulae which recall Yahweh's mighty deeds of liberation and the experience of the exodus. Nor do the Ten Commandments of Mount Sinai stand alone: there are other similar texts, such as the "cultic decalogue" in Ex 34, the list of curses at Dt 27:15ff., or the collec-

18. H.-G. Fritzsche, "Decalog IV. Ethisch," *TRE* VIII, cols. 418–28, at 418.
19. On this, cf. G. Müller, "Der Dekalog im Neuen Testament. Vor-Erwägungen zu einer unerledigten Aufgabe," *ThZ* 38 (1982), pp. 79–97, esp. 94f.
20. On the different reception of the decalogue before and after Augustine, cf. G. W. Locher, "Der Geltungsgrad der zehn Gebote," *ZEE* 13 (1969), pp. 129–45, esp. 136.

tions of precepts in the holiness code of Leviticus (cf. esp. Lv 19:11–18); and this form-historical comparison scarcely suggests that the Ten Commandments played some significant role of their own.

The negative impression is strengthened when we look at the tradition-history of the Decalogue within the Old Testament. A negative interpretation can appeal above all to two fundamental data of tradition-history. First of all, the pre-literary stratum of tradition, on the basis of which Gerhard von Rad reconstructed the so-called "historical creed" of Israel, does not refer either to the Sinai tradition or to the handing-over of the law; this early historical tradition in Israel does not mention the Sinai tradition, but goes directly from oppression in Egypt, via liberation from servitude, to the occupation of the land. Secondly—and even more remarkably—this historical picture (even in the phase after the exile) has nothing to say about the Decalogue and the Torah.

Within the Old Testament, there is only *one* strand of tradition-history which accords the commandments of the Decalogue an ever greater significance vis-à-vis the other lists of commandments and prohibitions, viz. the Deuteronomist theology. Only in this tradition does the Decalogue acquire a central significance, with "the claim to be a universal and perennially valid basic law."[21] Nevertheless, it is striking that the post-Deuteronomist theology scarcely ever refers to the Decalogue. This means that—as we see in the historical Psalms 105 and 136 and in texts such as Joshua 24:2–13 or Deuteronomy 6 and 26—the making of the covenant at Sinai and the revelation of the Ten Commandments played no role in Israel's traditional view of its history until well into the post-exilic period.[22]

This state of affairs, which is not disputed even by those exegetes who see the Decalogue as a substantially correct statement of Yahweh's will vis-à-vis his people, has led Frank Crüsemann to propose that it is misleading to attribute some special role to the Ten Commandments. In addition to the tradition-historical data which we have mentioned, he bases his case in particular on the fact that, apart from the direct address by God which distinguishes the Decalogue from the transmission of the law by Moses and Aaron, there are no recognizable exegetical indications of any special role. Despite its impressive linguistic formulation, he sees the Decalogue at best

---

21. F.-L. Hossfeld, *Der Dekalog*, Freiburg 1982, p. 283.

22. This has been set out with especial clarity by F. Crüsemann, *Die Tora*, pp. 44f. Cf. also the conclusion by L. Perlitt, "Dekalog I. Altes Testament," *TRE* VIII, cols. 408–13, at 412: "There is no trace of the decalogue in the post-Deuteronomist literature of the Old Testament." For a critique of this viewpoint, cf. n. 26 below.

as "the tremendous prelude" to the Torah, "but not in any sense a summary of what follows."[23] This means that the ending of God's direct address and the introduction of Moses' mediatorship in Dt 5:28f. are *not* intended to give prominence to the Decalogue as a special summary of the divine will. On the contrary, these stylistic devices are meant to ensure the fundamental equality in rank of all the laws in the Old Testament legal tradition. "According to the canonical text of the Old Testament, the Decalogue is not God's will in any other sense than all the rest of the Torah. It is not a summary of the Torah—not even of the supratemporal principles of the Torah."[24]

Crüsemann does not accept the obvious objection, viz. that this juxtaposition and mingling of legal texts which are often hard to reconcile (and indeed frequently contradict one another) leads to an inescapable contradiction within the Torah. Indeed, he holds that this objection can be turned into an argument in favor of his basic thesis, since he sees the juxtaposition as evidence of an ancient Persian legal principle which underlies the Jewish Torah too. Since all written law in Israel is regarded as promulgated in the name of God—unlike royal legislation in the ancient Orient—it must retain its validity forever, even when this means the juxtaposition of contradictory elements. Whereas (as we shall see below) many other exegetes discern an increasing tendency to systematization behind Israel's work on the Decalogue, Crüsemann proposes that Israel's canonical legal tradition follows what we might call a principle of toleration: "God's will is not a more or less closed system, nor a principle which integrates many truths into one unity. It includes things which are mutually exclusive."[25]

This thesis, that a unified and exemplary synthesis of God's will would fundamentally contradict the essence of the Torah, is a radicalization of Crüsemann's earlier affirmation that the substantial limitation and the restricted social-historical background of the Decalogue mean de facto that it could never possess universal significance.[26] This conclusion is based on

23. F. Crüsemann, *Die Tora*, p. 412; cf. p. 59.

24. Ibid., p. 413.

25. Ibid., p. 407.

26. Cf. F. Crüsemann, *Bewahrung der Freiheit. Das Thema des Dekalogs in sozialgeschichtlicher Perspektive,* Munich 1983, pp. 8–11, 36. For a critique of this position, cf. J. Schreiner, *Die Zehn Gebote im Leben des Gottesvolkes,* Munich 1988, p. 29; N. Lohfink, "Kennt das Alte Testament einen Unterschied von 'Gebot' und 'Gesetz'? Zur bibeltheologischen Einstufung des Dekalogs," *JBTh* 4 (1989), pp. 63–89, esp. 78, 84.

the fact that central topics of Old Testament ethics, especially the attitude toward weak and disadvantaged members of society which is typical of Israel's law of privileges, are not found in the Decalogue; this in turn is read as an indicator that the Ten Commandments were originally adressed, in seventh-century Israel, only to free men who possessed land. It is obvious that such a thesis, if exegetically correct, would have considerable consequences for systematic theology. The entire history of Christian reception of the Decalogue up to the present day has emphasized the universal intention of the Ten Commandments; but this would be an error, the result of overlooking the simple fact that the Decalogue is only one part of the Torah, formulated not for humanity as whole nor for the church, but only for Israel.

2.2. Exegetical notes on the understanding of the Decalogue

A thesis which completely reduces the significance of the Decalogue, relegating it to history and fragmenting its contents, can, however, easily turn out to be a boomerang from a systematic point of view. Its outcome is the material irrelevance of a text shared by Jews and Christians, a text on which Israel reflected for a long period and which did not lose all its importance within and outside Israel's sacred texts once its "great hour" in one particular phase of Deuteronomist literary history had passed.[27] From the Christian perspective, such a thesis would cast doubt on the legitimacy of the Christian reception of the Ten Commandments; and this would scarcely further the task of reminding the Christian church of its salvation-historical roots in Israel's vocation to be God's chosen people. Before we answer Crüsemann's thesis by demonstrating the abiding significance of the Decalogue within Christian ethics and its indispensable importance in Jewish-Christian dialogue, we must first note other approaches and tendencies in exegetical study of the Ten Commandments in recent decades. An overview of the results of the various investigations shows that the Decalogue itself, even from an exegetical perspective, provides a broader measure of support than might at first sight appear likely for the later sys-

---

27. The phrase in quotation marks is Norbert Lohfink's. The fact that the decalogue as a whole is no longer quoted in the post-Deuteronomist literature is not proof of its unimportance. Instead of literal quotations, we also find a freer way of dealing with it in this literature, where the decalogue is reduced to its "innermost essence" in the sabbath commandment, or is assumed into larger textual units (N. Lohfink, "Kennt das Alte Testament," p. 85). Outside literature, the decalogue was at any rate recited regularly in synagogue worship!

tematic reflection which follows Augustine, Thomas, and Martin Luther. The radically destructive thesis either completely ignores the following observations about the biblical text or unacceptably reduces their significance; however, it is here that we find evidence of the exegetical basis for the later reception of the Decalogue.

First, we are not compelled to interpret the theophany and the direct divine address employed when God gives Moses the Decalogue as an indiscriminate leveling-down of all the individual precepts in the Torah. Like the "toleration hypothesis," this interpretation is based on an importation of non-exegetical considerations; a completely different interpretation is also possible, as in the diametrically opposite view of N. Lohfink, who argues that the comparison between the commandments of the Decalogue, given in the direct divine adress, and the the other "statutes and ordinances" (cf. Dt 5:31; 6:20) of the Deuteronomist legal text gives the Decalogue a particularly prominent position within the Torah as a whole. The Decalogue presents the unchangeable and perennially valid *basic principles* of the Torah, as opposed to the time-conditioned and historically revisable *unfolding* of these principles in the rest of Yahweh's law. Hence, when the individual laws of Deuteronomy are developed in the exilic and post-exilic periods, they are given a structure which corresponds more and more clearly to the sequence of precepts in the Decalogue.[28] Eckart Otto interprets in a similar manner the phrase "statutes and ordinances" (Dt 12:1), which functions as a heading in the context of 12:1–4, arguing that it is a caesura, employed to indicate that the Deuteronomist editors see the Decalogue as valid always and everywhere, whereas the constitution sketched in Dt 12–26 applies only to life in cultivated land (from a post-exilic perspective, this means that it applies to the establishing of the new Israel).[29] If this exposition is correct, then the biblical text is at least open to the classical understanding in the Christian tradition, which regarded the transmission of the commandments by means of a direct divine address to each human person as a theological justification of the separation of the *praecepta decalogi* from the other precepts of the *lex vetus.*[30]

Secondly, the thesis that there are no distinctions among the precepts of the Torah overlooks the process of differentiation between *law* and *ethos* which takes place in the various strata of Old Testament tradition, and is

28. Cf. Ibid., pp. 80, 86.
29. Cf. E. Otto, *Theologische Ethik des Alten Testaments,* p. 218.
30. Cf. Thomas Aquinas, *STh* I–II, q. 100, a. 3.

reflected with especial clarity in the Ten Commandments. The transition from law to ethos is indicated already in the collections of trial-law in the Book of the Covenant, for example, in the prohibitions of twisting law, intended to protect the poor (cf. Ex 23:3, 6); unlike the prohibitions of perjury from the pre-exilic period, these no longer threaten a prosecution in court, but rather appeal to the interior attitude of the human person. The detachment of ethos from law in the Decalogue can be seen above all in the fact that it lacks any descriptions of crimes or stipulations about penalties. The same differentiation can be seen in the concluding prohibitions of "lust," which "round off the Decalogue as a whole with the appeal to respect the sphere of one's neighbor's life, thus accentuating its character as the summary of an ethic."[31]

Thirdly, considerations of *form-history* support the supposition that a conscious universalizing intention stands behind the Decalogue. A comparison with the Egyptian Book of the Dead or the long lists of prohibitions in the Surpu series shows that the prohibitions in these texts, which resemble those in the Decalogue, are juxtaposed to completely insignificant individual precepts, whereas the typical features of the Decalogue are a "concise compilation of central prohibitions"[32] and the "fundamental, wide-reaching universality of its demands."[33] The tenfold formulation in both versions of the Decalogue in the Old Testament can likewise be interpreted against this background. It is true that this appears only at a late stage in form-historical terms, since the prohibitions were originally formulated as individual precepts or in pairs or triads; however, as Hermann Gunkel suggested many years ago, the intention of the tenfold formulation was to make it easier to learn the commandments by heart, using one's ten fingers. The only explanation for such a praxis is the intention to give special prominence to this particular traditional material. Further, if it is correct to see the Decalogue as composed of five pairs of commandments which progress systematically from God to one's fellow human beings and have their point of departure in our way of thinking in dual concepts (upper and lower, right and left, male and female, day and night), this idea of a "symmetrical completeness" would be an especially eloquent expression of the universality which the ethical directives of the Decalogue were intend-

---

31. E. Otto, *Theologische Ethik,* p. 213. Cf. also pp. 84–88.

32. J.-J. Stamm, *Der Dekalog im Lichte der neueren Forschung,* Berne and Stuttgart 2nd edn. 1962, p. 304.

33. J. Schreiner, *Die Zehn Gebote im Leben des Gottesvolkes,* pp. 50f.

ed to possess. This would also help to explain the old tradition that the tablets of the Ten Commandments were written on both sides; the tendency to systematization which can be seen in the Decalogue itself would support the idea of "two tablets" of the Decalogue, with the first four commandments on the first tablet and the rest on the second.[34]

Fourthly, the brevity and concision typical of the Decalogue entail a *limitation on its contents* which sheds further light on its position in the transion from law to ethos. The principal difference between the "ten words" and the cultic precepts and legal ordinances in the rest of the Torah tradition is the lack of any reference to legal consequences and penalties. The primary scope of these rules for conduct and directives for living which Yahweh imparts is the internal disposition of the human person: this is the legal sphere that is to be protected by sanctions. Nevertheless, the Ten Commandments do not contain any summary list of *all* the requirements of the covenant God. They are limited to certain "fundamental negations" which preserve the sphere of life opened up by God and specify the boundary-zones which recall Yahweh's sovereign rights over the entire life of the human person.[35] Precisely by refusing to issue maximum demands and by being content with warding off elementary risks to human life in society, "the Decalogue in all its Ten Commandments watches over the human existence of human beings."[36] With the exceptions of the commandments concerning the Sabbath and one's parents, all its demands are formulated negatively; they do not exhort one to do something, but to avoid conduct that is incompatible with fellowship with God. Instead of describing the ethos in all its specific requirements, they localize it by indicating where its boundaries lie. The commandments of the Decalogue affirm what is possible within the community of Israel, and what utterly shatters and destroys the relationship to God.[37] The substantial incompleteness and open-ended formal character of the Decalogue can be grasped appropriately only by a systematic interpretation which pays heed to the specific, intermediate position of such a minimal ethic in the transi-

34. On this, cf. H. Gese, "Der Dekalog als Ganzheit betrachtet," in: Idem, *Vom Sinai zum Zion. Alttestamentliche Beiträge zur biblischen Theologie,* Munich 1974, pp. 63–80, esp. 79f.

35. G. von Rad, *Theologie des Alten Testaments,* I: *Die Theologie der geschichtlichen Überlieferung,* Munich 1969, p. 208.

36. Ibid., p. 209.

37. Cf. W. H. Schmidt, *Die Zehn Gebote im Rahmen alttestamentlicher Ethik,* Darmstadt 1993, p. 22.

tion from a legal sphere to a comprehensive ethos which embraces the totality of human life in every sphere of conduct.

Fifthly, since they protect the existing fellowship with God and are in conformity with the salvation wrought by Yahweh, the immediate validity of the precepts of the Decalogue concerns the people of Israel.[38] Unlike the prohibition of killing at Gn 9:6, the Ten Commandments are not yet adressed to humankind as a whole. Indeed, when we consider the first two commandments, the milieu in which Israel lived would have made a loosening of this restriction unthinkable. Nevertheless, a *universalizing tendency* is incipiently present in the Ten Commandments, aiming from the outset to widen the sphere of their validity both *inwards* and *outwards.* An element common to all human persons and obligating them all was discovered in the Torah and in the Decalogue when these were linked to the theology of the priestly document, with its central affirmation that every human person is created in the image of God. On this point, the Decalogue also agrees with the holiness code in Lv 18:2–5, the provisions for protection in society made by the law of privileges, and the "legal spirituality" of the Psalms which draws on sapiential (and hence universal) motifs.

While all these requirements mark a boundary vis-à-vis the norms of the other peoples, since they are legitimated in theological terms by the will of Yahweh, it is also true that "life is promised to everyone who follows Yahweh's commandments, and this means in principle that the same promise is made to all the peoples."[39] No consistent exploitation was made of the possibilities for universalizing the ethos provided by the creation-theological and sapiential traditions of Israel; nevertheless, this tendency is at work in many strata of the transmission of commandments within the Old Testament. Accordingly, the fact that the primary validity of the Torah concerns Israel need not contradict the affirmation that it serves the function—especially in the summary made by the Decalogue—of limiting the lordship which one human being may exercise over another and of protecting human beings from their own selves. It is indeed true that it is legitimated in theological terms by the will of God and is rooted in Israel's

38. Here we must agree with F. Crüsemann, *Die Tora,* p. 71. It is impossible to put Crüsemann's point too strongly: "In terms of substance, everything depends on the connection between exodus and demand. Liberation and commandment belong inseparably together, even in the temporal dimension" (p. 56). This last phrase, "even in the temporal dimension," should not however be understood to mean a limitation to the original historical situation in which Israel first experienced the link between God's salvation and God's commandment.

39. Cf. E. Otto, *Theologische Ethik des Alten Testaments,* p. 258; cf. also p. 267.

experience of the exodus; nevertheless, if it is read backwards (so to speak) from the creation-theology in the priestly document, the Decalogue also "presents" humankind as a whole with "a fundamental condition and a fundamental demand applicable to all human persons, an ethical minimum which is a necessary condition for life itself."[40] These exegetical data mean that a systematic understanding of the Decalogue must avoid false alternatives in the interpretation of the basis of the Ten Commandments (natural law *or* divine will) and of the sphere within which they are intended to be valid (Israel *or* humankind).

2.3. Theological-ethical interpretation of the Decalogue

The suppression of awareness of the salvation-historical origin of the church in the vocation of Israel entailed a profound contradiction in the theological understanding of the Decalogue by Christian thinkers from the very beginning. The Decalogue is acknowledged today as a document which concerns all of humankind, and this is due only to the influence it has enjoyed within Christianity; at the same time, the neutralization of the salvation-historical dimension meant the loss of the original meaning of the Ten Commandments, which is tied to the liberation of Israel. The universal significance of the Decalogue was purchased at a high theological price. This situation will change only when we as Christians learn to understand the "ten words" in a way that overcomes the disastrous theological schism between Israel and the church and the consequent separation of the universal significance of the Decalogue from its historical origin.

a. The significance of the introduction The dichotomous attitude vis-à-vis the Old Testament law finds expression as early as the New Testament, in the remarkable fact that the introduction to the Decalogue—"I am the Lord your God, who brought you out of the land of Egypt, out of the house of bondage" (Dt 5:6; Ex 20:2)—is never once quoted, although it plays a formally and substantially indispensable role in Jewish self-understanding.[41] All the New Testament writers, including Paul, agree that the traditional commandments of the Torah are (at least substantially) a valid expression of God's will and provide a generally reliable orientation for the ethical demands made by Jesus.[42] Nevertheless, the detachment of

---

40. W. H. Schmidt, *Die Zehn Gebote im Rahmen alttestamentlicher Ethik*, p. 13.

41. Cf. G. Müller, *Der Dekalog im Neuen Testament*, p. 85.

42. On this, cf. W. Schrage, *Ethik des Neuen Testaments*, Göttingen 2nd edn. 1989 (*Das Neue Testament deutsch* IV), p. 61.

these precepts from the fundamental profession of Israel's faith in Yahweh's mighty deeds of liberation deprives them of the decisive introductory note which makes the Torah what it is in Jewish eyes, that is, the pattern of liberation, the path of salvation which shows the way to life.

The law cannot *only* be a path of salvation, since the dialectic of promise and threat, which intensifies in Israel with the passing of time, belongs to the Torah from the very beginning.[43] The fundamental theological structure of the Old Testament ethos must, however, be taken seriously from a Christian perspective too, since without this basic theological affirmation it is impossible to understand the meaning of the Decalogue. The critique of the law in the New Testament, expressed in the obvious distance taken by Jesus vis-à-vis the Sabbath observance and the ritual commandments of contemporary Judaism, and radicalized in the Pauline antithesis between law and Gospel, exposes in a particularly acute manner the dialectic of the law and thus contains a necessary element of theological criticism of the law, pointing to the immanent dangers and possibilities of abuse which appear in paradigmatic form in the Jewish "legal spirituality" of Jesus' time. Nevertheless, even in its most radical form, New Testament critique of the law presupposes that it was not the antithesis of grace from the very beginning. The New Testament also sees it as the original form taken by God's salvific intervention in favor of his people. Hence, the law is an initial expression of his abiding closeness to human beings, which of course can be displayed in the new covenant even *without* the law—and, as the death of Jesus shows, ultimately even *against* the law. The New Testament perspective does not require us to abandon the theological characterization of the law as the pattern of God's liberation, but the exact meaning of this term must be grasped more clearly. In the new covenant, the law can no longer have a soteriological role, since it has been fulfilled once and for all in God's unconditional intervention in favor of humankind (something the law already portrayed in the old covenant) and in the perfect obedience of Jesus Christ (something completely new in salvation history, both recapitulating and transcending the history of disobedience). Salvation is granted without any prior conditions; but since salvation entails the task of preserving through appropriate behavior the gift one has received, the law defines the consequences of salvation.

The original theological character of the law can be seen with special clarity in the introductory formula to the "ten words" in the biblical tradi-

---

43. On this, cf. W. Zimmerli, *Das Gesetz und die Propheten,* Göttingen 1963, pp. 46ff.

tion. In the preamble to the Decalogue, Yahweh appears, not simply with the authority of a divine legislator (as the Christian reception of the Decalogue has uncritically assumed), but as the savior of his people. Yahweh has freed Israel from slavery in Egypt, led the people through the wilderness, and given them the land he had promised; this last point is particularly important for the Deuteronomist theology. Accordingly, a life according to the commandments of its God could be understood in Israel only as the response to a gift already received, as the expression of a blessing bestowed by God and made visible in the occupation of the promised land. This is why the following principle applies, not only to the New Testament ethos, but already to the Old Testament ethos and to its ethical commandments: "God gives before he demands. He makes demands as the one who has previously demonstrated that he is the God of liberation."[44]

When exegetes speak of the mutual relationship of gifts and tasks, or the response of the acting person to the salvation he has received, or God's act which "makes [human] action possible" (in Helmut Merklein's phrase),[45] they are describing a fundamental quality found throughout the biblical ethos: ethical conduct involves God's grace and God's demand. The combination of law and covenant, Torah and salvation, commandment and salvation, is the fundamental theological structure of *every* biblical ethics, a common note which is retained even in the passage from the Old Testament to the New. Emphases and accentuations may change within this fundamental structure: as God's sovereign rule draws near, ethics acquires a more strongly eschatological motivation. But these are only modifications, which do not call the starting point into question. This is why it is not the Beatitudes in the Sermon on the Mount that first establish the theological horizon of promise and commitment against which human ethical conduct is to be interpreted from a biblical perspective; this horizon is already portrayed in the divine address which introduces the Decalogue. One of the most important tasks in today's dialogue between Jewish and Christian

44. H. J. Boecker, *Recht und Gesetz im Alten Testament und im Alten Orient,* Neukirchen-Vluyn 2nd edn. 1984, pp. 184f.; cf. also C. Westermann, "Bedeutung und Funktion des Imperativs in den Geschichtsbüchern des Alten Testaments," in: R. Mosis and R. Ruppert (eds.), *Der Weg zum Menschen. Zur philosophischen und theologischen Anthropologie* (Festschrift for A. Deissler), Freiburg 1989, pp. 13–27. On the basis of a careful grammatical investigation, Westermann rejects the antithesis between the indicative (for God's action) and the imperative (for his commandments and laws) and shows that the imperative too is employed in Hebrew as a "linguistic form for God's salvific action" (p. 26).

45. Cf. H. Merklein, *Die Gottesherrschaft als Handlungsprinzip. Untersuchungen zur Ethik Jesu,* Würzburg 3rd edn. 1984, p. 139.

ethics is the rediscovery of this theological dowry from the Old Testament and its fruitful integration into the Christian understanding of the Decalogue.

b. The Decalogue as elaboration of the commandment to love The divine self-presentation which introduces the Decalogue is absolutely essential to the theological self-understanding of Judaism. When this is omitted, the empty space is filled in the reception of the Decalogue in the New Testament and the early church by a functional equivalent: the individual precepts are understood as an exemplary exposition of the commandment to love. The consistency and radicality of this new summary of the Decalogue are not commonly found in the Old Testament. This entails not only a substantial shift in significance, but also an unmistakable relativization,[46] as we see in the fact that the Decalogue as a whole is never quoted anywhere in the New Testament, and only extremely seldom in early Christian literature before Augustine.[47] The preaching of Jesus contains at most occasional echoes of individual commandments from the Decalogue (cf. Mt 5:21; 5:27; 5:33; 15:19; 19:18); the reference is particularly clear in the pericope about the rich young man (Mk 10:11–22), where Jesus quotes several precepts word for word: "Do not kill, Do not commit adultery, Do not steal, Do not bear false witness, Do not defraud, Honor your father and mother" (10:19). This is the most detailed quotation from the Decalogue in the New Testament, changing the order of the commandments and citing them in a very free form. The decisive point in Jesus' answer is that these precepts, which he assumes his hearers know, are both confirmed and relativized. They are still a valid account of the divine will, but they are no longer sufficient, now that the kingdom of God is dawning. They are superseded by Jesus' demand that the young man also abandon his possessions and his inherited wealth in order to be free for discipleship. A similarly critical evaluation of the commandments, or at least a measure of reservation with regard to them, lies behind the antitheses in the Sermon on the Mount, where the individual precepts from the Decalogue function only as starting points which must be left behind, since they are superseded by the new commandments given by Jesus.

Besides this eschatological relativization of the Decalogue, however, we also find in the New Testament a tendency to confirm it; this is especially prominent in the Letter to the Romans. In the Letter to the Galatians,

---

46. On this, cf. G. von Rad, *Theologie des Alten Testaments,* II, p. 434.
47. On this, cf. H. Hübner, "Dekalog III. Neues Testament," *TRE* VIII, cols. 415–18.

Paul's radically antinomistic attitude leads him to understand Jesus' one commandment to love as replacing the plurality of commandments in the Torah (cf. 5:14); in Romans, however, he anticipates the later Christian understanding of the Decalogue by acknowledging it as a substantial elaboration of the new commandment to love. The individual commandments are subsumed in love, which thus becomes the true motivation for conduct. In this function, the commandment to love replaces the salvation-historical introductory formula in the version of the Decalogue in Deuteronomy. In this new context, however, the individual precepts retain the important task of delineating the substance of those spheres of life where love must become active. Indeed, they remain indispensable in Paul's eyes, since they specify what is meant by the one commandment to love: "He who loves his neighbor has fulfilled the law. The commandments, 'You shall not commit adultery, You shall not kill, You shall not steal, You shall not covet,' and any other commandment, are summed up in this sentence, 'You shall love your neighbor as yourself'" (Rom 13:8–9).[48] Two contradictory tendencies thus dominate the theological understanding of the Decalogue within Christianity: while the Ten Commandments are relativized by Jesus' proclamation of the kingdom of God, they are also confirmed anew in the ethical paraenesis of Paul (who is not unfamiliar with natural-law arguments)[49] as substantial elaborations of the commandment to love. Where one trajectory indicates the influence of the Sermon on the Mount within Christianity, the other gives the Decalogue an autonomous rank as a fundamental ethical formula applicable to the whole of humanity.

A new weight attaches in this second trajectory to the question of the systematic internal structure of the Decalogue and the problem of its substantial incompleteness. The "challenging insufficiency" and the "transformative dynamics" found in the Decalogue itself[50] are brought only to a temporary conclusion in the synthesis of its Ten Commandments in the one commandment of Jesus, since this conclusion in turn points beyond itself. The requirement to love is not limited to the observance of the commandments, although these play an indispensable role as the substantial

48. This has been clearly set out in recent years by W. Schrage, *Ethik des Neuen Testaments,* p. 223; and E. Lohse, *Theologische Ethik des Neuen Testaments,* Stuttgart et al. 1988, pp. 103f., arguing against the situation-ethical interpretation of Paul by Bultmann's school.

49. Cf. the balanced presentation by U. Wilckens, *Der Brief an die Römer* (Rom 1–5) (*Evangelisch-katholischer Kommentar zum NT* VI,1), Zurich et al. 2nd edn. 1987, p. 135.

50. J. Schreiner, *Die Zehn Gebote im Leben des Gottesvolkes,* p. 125.

elaboration and concretization of love. If we ask in detail what love means, we find that it demands more than the observance of the boundaries drawn by the Decalogue; many areas of life in which love is meant to be active are mentioned only implicitly (or indeed not at all) in the Decalogue. Examples are conduct vis-à-vis the weak and the poor or one's attitude to one's own self. Systematic reflection on the position of the Decalogue in Christian ethics has always been aware that it is not a complete list of all ethical commandments, precisely because it does not mention some essential spheres of action and tasks of love. In his *Summa Theologiae*, Thomas Aquinas devotes an article to the question *utrum praecepta decalogi convenienter enumerentur* (I-II 100, 5), where his "objections" are basically a list of the various areas about which the Decalogue says *nothing*. He gives a double reply to the question why it nevertheless can count as a summary of the commandment to love, specifying further the position of the Ten Commandments within the moral law from the formal and material perspectives.

c. The Decalogue as fundamental ordering of justice Thomas interprets the fact that the narrative framework in the Bible depicts the Ten Commandments as directly revealed by God as a first indication that they contain only what everyone can discern "without too much effort" *(modica consideratione)* from the common principles of the *lex naturalis.* This means that the Ten Commandments are a kind of rule of thumb of our everyday understanding. No expert ethical knowledge or special moral virtuosity is required in order to discern them, because reason or faith makes them universally obvious. The *prima et communia principia* of the natural law do not belong to the Decalogue, nor do the further consequences drawn from these common first principles by legal experts and wise persons. Nevertheless, they are included in the Decalogue—the first principles as its necessary presuppositions, the consequences as appropriate inferences.[51]

---

51. Cf. *STh* I–II, q. 100, a. 3: *"Illa ergo praecepta ad decalogum pertinent, quorum notitiam homo habet per seipsum a Deo. Huiusmodi vero sunt illa quae statim ex principibus communibus primis cognosci possunt modica consideratione: et iterum illa quae statim ex fide divinitus infusa innotescunt. Inter praecepta ergo decalogi non computantur duo genera praeceptorum: illa scilicet quae sunt prima et communia, quorum non oportet aliam editionem esse nisi quod sunt scripta in ratione naturali quasi per se nota, sicut quod nulli debet homo malefacere, et alia huiusmodi, et iterum illa quae per diligentem inquisitionem sapientium inveniuntur rationi convenire, haec enim proveniunt a Deo ad populum mediante disciplina sapientium."* Cf. *STh* I–II, q. 100, a. 5; and II–II, q. 122, a. 1.

What is one to make of this interpretation, which so neatly adapts the basic formula of biblical ethics to Thomas' own theological conception and inserts it into a systematic structure of ethics? We may tend today to see the direct linking of a process of systematic reflection to a biblical narrative—in this case, to the stylistic device of a direct divine address—as showing little respect for the literary meaning of the text; this, however, is in fact how Thomas takes the biblical text seriously, acknowledging its claims to truth on the level of substantial theological affirmations. If we bear in mind today's exegetical discussion, sketched above, we can scarcely deny that his formal assignment of the Ten Commandments to a position between the absolute first principles of the practical reason and the complete exposition of the commandments in the experiential wisdom of ethical "experts" does in fact do justice to the intermediary position of the Decalogue in the transition from law to ethos.[52]

Thomas even finds a convincing reason for the *substantial* incompleteness of the Decalogue, explaining what this means in the Bible itself and also satisfying systematic theology's need to discern some kind of meaningful structure in the traditional sequence of the Ten Commandments. For Thomas, the Decalogue is not simply identical with the moral precepts of the natural law; rather, it is limited to the basic demands of justice entailed by human beings' relationship to God and to one another. This insight leads to the first structural principle, whereby the Ten Commandments are assigned to the two tablets of the Decalogue in keeping with these two basic human relationships. Since Augustine's way of reckoning the commandments on the second tablet displays an especially clear logical order—a distinction between *concupiscentia carnis* and *concupiscentia oculorum* is possible only if one separates the prohibitions of lust—Thomas follows it in preference to the traditional biblical division.[53]

If the Decalogue is understood as a universally obvious fundamental ordering of justice both vis-à-vis God and in the intimate interpersonal sphere, this allows us to perceive an internal structure in the Ten Com-

---

52. This is also the assessment of O. H. Pesch, *Das Gesetz,* Heidelberg et al. 1977 (Kommentar zur deutschen Thomas-Ausgabe 13), pp. 634f.: "The question which forms the title of the present article reflects the academic methodology emplyed in pre-critical exegesis, a methodology which expresses the systematic theologian's respect for the Bible as document of faith . . . Using his own tools, Thomas has in fact grasped the biblical meaning of the decalogue, which contains the basic requirements entailed by the human person's relationship to God and to his fellows. Every believer can grasp the evidential character of these requirements; no special level of education is necessary."

53. *STh* I–II, q. 100, a. 4–6; II–II, q. 122, a. 1.

mandments, despite the gaps in their contents. This means that, formally speaking, they are a structured whole. Nevertheless, the initial impression is that the concentration of the Ten Commandments on the fundamental requirements of justice merely creates a new confusion, since this summary function makes the Decalogue a competitor to the New Testament commandment to love—which in turn functions as a summary of the commandments in the Decalogue. This impression of a superfluous doublet disappears, however, when we look at the structural principle and the consistent intellectual form in Thomas' theology: in his architectonic structure, love and justice are not rival principles, but have the same mutual relationship as do grace and freedom or revelation and reason. Just as revelation does not extinguish the light of the natural reason, and grace does not destroy human freedom, so love works *in* and *through* justice. The actions of justice are, so to speak, the concrete form in which love accomplishes its own work.

There is no competition between justice and love, as if love would begin only where justice ceased, or justice meant that love would have to be extinguished in order to make possible the establishment of a neutrally objective social order. Rather, justice and love are related to each other like two concentric circles which enclose all the individual commandments of the Decalogue in both a narrower context and a broader horizon. In Thomas' language, which is accustomed to draw clear distinctions, this means that love is the goal of all the Ten Commandments, but their immediate concern is with the actions of justice in which love must be displayed, if it is not to destroy the ordering of penultimate matters *en route* to its goal.[54] This idea becomes very concrete in the context of the exposition of the Decalogue, for it is obvious that one cannot love one's neighbor and at the same time cheat on him by means of adultery, rob him of his property, or throw doubt on his honor, still less plan to murder him. The manner in which Thomas defines the relationship between the principles of love and justice, leading him to interpret the Decalogue as the magna carta of justice under love's demand, is therefore a fundamental systematic insight which is applicable under other theological presuppositions too. In other words, its essential point can be detached from the historical form of Thomas' theology.[55]

54. *STh* II–II, q. 122, a. 1, ad 4: *"Praecepta decalogi pertinent ad caritatem sicut ad finem: secundum illud I ad Tim. 1:5:* finis praecepti caritas est. *Sed ad iustitiam pertinent, inquantum immediate sunt de actibus iustitiae."*

55. To take one example: Paul Tillich, the Protestant theologian and philosopher of

The other correspondences and gradations which Thomas elaborates in order to uncover a logic behind the individual commandments in the Decalogue owe their genesis to the contemporary tendency to systematization; as Otto Hermann Pesch once joked, Thomas' period could not imagine the human author of sacred scripture and God himself "otherwise than as a professor of systematic theology who had been trained in Aristotelian logic."[56] But even if we would wish to query details of the connections which Thomas makes, they can aid a theological understanding of the Decalogue, since they show that it was not by pure chance that the individual commandments landed in the place they occupy in the Decalogue, and that they do not simply stand alongside one another without any interconnections. Thomas discerns a meaningful and gradated ordering especially in the commandments on the second tablet, which follow the hierarchy of the goods protected by the precepts or the diminishing gravity of the sinful assaults on these goods. *Secundum ordinem gravitatis peccatorum,* the killing of an innocent person is more serious than adultery, which affects his immediate private sphere; but adultery in turn, which attacks a high personal good, is more serious than theft, which attacks the external goods of life. This gradation is continued in the distinction between sinful deeds (killing, adultery, theft), sins of the mouth (lies, false testimony), and sins of the heart (prohibition of lust); here, the decisive factors are the external tangibility and the growing closeness to performance of the sinful deed.[57]

Thomas discerns a meaningful reason even behind the deviation from the other commandments of the Decalogue in the formulation of the precepts concerning the Sabbath and one's parents. While the primary prohibitions in the moral law establish a negative obligation (i.e., to abstain from specific conduct) which applies to all human persons whatsoever, irrespective of how distant or close our relationship to them may be, there are also persons to whom we are linked by a *relatio specialis* which entails a special obligation of gratitude to them. On the basis of this distinction, the two commandments in the Decalogue which are formulated in positive terms point to our two most important relationships, to God who gave us life and to our parents who were the first to accompany our life

---

culture, is led by a phenomenological description and an ontological analysis to posit a structurally comparable relationship between these concepts: "Liebe, Macht, Gerechtigkeit" (1954), in: Idem, *Gesammelte Werke* XI, Stuttgart 2nd edn. 1976, pp. 143–225, esp. 189–99,

56. O. H. Pesch, *Das Gesetz,* p. 637.

57. Cf. *STh* I–II, q. 100, a. 6; and II–II, q. 122, a. 6, ad 2.

with their loving care. The positive formulation of these two commandments reminds us that we cannot really repay the good things that we have
received from God and our parents by means of our love and gratitude.
But this means that we may not be content with a negative lower boundary that tells us what we may not do: rather, we must do all in our power
to fulfill both commandments.[58] We are obliged to respect the life and
property, the marriage and family, the honor and personal good reputation
of all persons; but since we can never make a full response to the super-
abundance of good things we have received from God and our parents, we
owe them a particular measure of love which surpasses the observance of
negative boundaries.

Let us repeat that even if the particular cross-references, correspondences, and subtly articulated antitheses which Thomas pursues even in the
case of stylistic deviations in individual formulations are the product of a
contemporary style of thinking, this criticism does not apply to his basic
underlying conception, which grasps the biblical meaning of the Decalogue with astonishing precision. The Ten Commandments protect "the
great goods in life which the human person has received from God,"[59] viz.
his life, his marriage, his freedom, his good reputation, his property. This
is the indispensable basis for human life, and it must be preserved from attack by others in order that a fundamental ordering of life in society be not
destroyed. The impressive strength of the formulations in the Decalogue
lies in the fact that the commandments do not go beyond acknowledgment of the indispensable basis of our neighbor's life. They have a power
which no one can evade.

3. The universal significance of the Sermon on the Mount

If one seeks a New Testament counterpart to the Decalogue, the obvious candidate is the great discourse composed by Matthew in his Gospel.
Christian theologians soon saw this as a summary of the *lex nova* of the
Christian faith; when they described the novelty of the Christian ethos
and the characteristics which distinguished it from the surrounding pagan
milieu, they did so largely by quoting the words of the Sermon on the
Mount. To be more precise, the earliest Christian exegetes combined *logia*

58. Cf. *STh* I–II, q. 100, a. 7; and II–II, q. 122, a. 6, ad 1.
59. J. Schreiner, *Die Zehn Gebote des Gottesvolkes,* p. 101.

from the two versions of the discourse in Matthew and Luke, which we call the "Sermon on the Mount" and the "Sermon on the Plain." The first name has left a profound impression upon Christian memory ever since Augustine entitled his exposition of Jesus' first great discourse, which Matthew locates on a mountain, *De Sermone Domini in monte,* and all the Christian churches and denominations employ this term today, not only with reference to the requirements transmitted specifically in Mt 5–7, but as a *synecdoche* for Jesus' ethical teaching as a whole. No other New Testament text has disturbed and disquieted the church throughout its history in a manner comparable to the Sermon on the Mount, whose demands continually confront the church with its own failures and at the same time preserve it from complete assimilation to the society in which it lives. The Sermon on the Mount is an abiding protest against a worldly church, and the soil from which reforms within the church and new social movements on the margins of the established church draw the spiritual force which nourishes them. The various forms of ecclesial ethos and social structures which have come into being in the two thousand years of Christian history have their origins in the varied (and often contradictory) responses that have been given to the provocation of the Sermon on the Mount.

3.1. Whom does the Sermon on the Mount address?

The various interpretations generated by the theological understanding of the Sermon on the Mount in the course of history differ above all in the answers they give to two fundamental questions, viz. the *persons adressed* by the Sermon, and its *function.* The question of the actual intention of Jesus' instruction can be decided only on the basis of a holistic theological-ethical understanding of the Sermon, but the question of its addressees is a connecting thread which will allow us to follow the exegetical and theological alternatives taken by the interpreters. Whom does the Sermon on the Mount adress? All peoples, so that it is to be understood against the background of a universal human ethos, and its demands must in principle be followed in every period and by every person? The democratic state under the rule of law, which is to anticipate future international guarantees of peace by renouncing now the use of violence against other states and by testing on the world-scale the strategy offered by the Sermon on the Mount for the resolution of conflicts? The church, which is to become a light for the peoples by a common existential praxis shaped by the teaching of Jesus, in order to fulfill its task of bearing witness to the Gospel? A group of elite Christians within the church, who are called to a special form of discipleship and orientate their life on the counsels imparted in the Gospel *(consilia evangelica)?* Or individual Christians, who are subject to the demands of the Sermon in their private life, especially in marriage and family—but who must bow to the pragmatic principles of civil government, if they occupy public office or bear political responsibility for the security of their people?

Each of these answers represents one interpretative model of the Sermon on the Mount, and each model in turn presupposes one particular understanding of Christian existence as a whole, developed at various times and places in church history. The liberal thesis about the essence of Christianity (whose supratemporal significance coalesces with the humane achievements of European cultural history), the literal observance of commandments (typical of a charismatic sect on the borders of the established churches), the two-storied ethics of the mediaeval church with its division into clergy and laity, and the two-realms doctrine of Protestantism are thus all explanatory models of the Sermon on the Mount, each of which has been dominant at one particular epoch of church history or in one particular confessional sphere of Christendom.[60]

The new characteristic of the debates about the Sermon on the Mount in recent years is that the traditional types of exposition are no longer restricted to one particular confession. The various disciplines—New Testament exegesis, theological ethics, and moral philosophy—discuss comparable questions which point in the same direction, and one can discern a structural correspondence between the dominant exegetical tendency in recent years, which understands the ethos of the Sermon as the specific group ethos of the earliest community, and one tendency in moral philosophy, which emphasizes the relevance of small, manageable groups for the genesis of convictions about moral values and the learning of moral conduct. Within biblical research, one can note other structurally analogous perspectives which have far-reaching consequences for our understanding of the Decalogue and of the moral teachings in Jesus' ethics.

60. Cf. the overviews presented by W.-D. Wendland, *Ethik des Neuen Testaments,* Göttingen 2nd edn. 1975 (NTD-Ergänzungsband 4), pp. 16–22; P. Stuhlmacher, "Jesu vollkommenes Gesetz der Freiheit. Zum Verständnis der Bergpredigt," *ZThK* 79 (1982), pp. 283–322, esp. 294–308; U. Luz, *Das Evangelium nach Matthäus (Mt 1–7),* Zurich et al. 3rd edn. 1992 *(EKK I/1),* pp. 191–97. Individual monographs worthy of special note are: K. Beyschlag, "Zur Geschichte der Bergpredigt in der Alten Kirche," *ZThK* 74 (1977), pp. 291–322; U. Berner, *Die Bergpredigt. Rezeption und Auslegung im 20. Jahrhundert,* Göttingen 2nd edn. 1983 *(Göttinger theologische Arbeiten (GTA)* 12).

For the exposition of the Sermon on the Mount, this means that the ethical teachings of Jesus, especially the commands to love one's enemies and
renounce the use of violence, are not seen as isolated individual demands
which are then compared with prominent statements in Old Testament
Jewish ethics or hellenistic-Roman ethics. Instead, scholars concentrate on
the social-historical background, the *Sitz-im-Leben* in the early church, and
the group to which these teachings are adressed. However, even if the exegetical methodology and the guiding questions are different, these various
approaches agree on one decisive point: Jesus' ethical demands are not
adressed to *all* human persons without distinction, but speak primarily to
the community of disciples in one very specific historical-political situation
in the Palestine of his period. Just as the social-historical interpretation of
the precepts in the Decalogue sees them as conceived for one sociological
sector of the Jewish people in one restricted phase of its history, viz. for full
citizens in the seventh century who possessed large tracts of land, so too Jesus' commands in the Sermon on the Mount referred originally to "a specific social event."[61] This means that they are not to be understood as universally binding ethical regulations; they describe only "an attitude demanded
of Christians in situations of resistance."[62] This attitude distinguishes the
disciples of Jesus from the world around them. Accordingly, his commandments are to be understood only as urging attitudes which are consciously
different from prevalent modes of conduct. Scholars may indeed interpret
these attitudes in a variety of ways—e.g., the renunciation of violence is
seen as directed against the Zealots and political-national messianic movements,[63] as an expression of the defenselessness of persecuted wandering
charismatics,[64] or as "solidarity with the poor" at a period when the existing
political-religious and social-economic conflicts in Palestine were escalating
further[65]—but all these attempts at a social-historical reconstruction agree

61. L. Schottroff, "Gewaltverzicht und Feindesliebe in der urchristlichen Jesustradition,
Mt 5,38–48, Lk 6,27–36," in: G. Strecker (ed.), *Jesus Christus in Historie und Theologie,*
Tübingen 1975, pp. 197–201.
62. Ibid., p. 201.
63. This is the view taken by M. Hengel, *War Jesus Revolutionär?,* Stuttgart 1970, p. 22,
and P. Hoffmann, *Studien zur Theologie der Logienquelle,* Münster 1972, p. 76.
64. See esp. G. Theißen, "Gewaltverzicht und Feindesliebe (Mt 5,38–48/Lk 6,27–38),
und deren sozialgeschichtlicher Hintergrund," in: Idem, *Studien zur Soziologie des Urchristentums,* Tübingen 1979, pp. 160–97, esp. 185–87.
65. P. Hoffmann, "Tradition und Situation. Zur 'Verbindlichkeit' des Gebots der Feindesliebe in der synoptischen Überlieferung und in der gegenwärtigen Friedensdiskussion,"
in: K. Kertelge (ed.), *Ethik im Neuen Testament,* Freiburg 1984, pp. 50–118, at 79.

that the ethical directives of Jesus are adressed neither to isolated individual ethical subjects nor to "humankind" as a whole. Rather, their audience is a community of Jesus' disciples who live in a very specific political-social situation and acquire a new group identity precisely by behaving in a way that goes beyond what mere solidarity within the group would lead one to expect.

Gerhard Lohfink has developed a more strongly community-related understanding of the Sermon on the Mount. Although he neglects its social-historical background, he agrees with recent exegetical approaches in rejecting a universalistic, abstract interpretation of its demands. His own approach adheres to the exposition of the Sermon by the "community theology" of the 1930's, but he takes new paths of his own in the exegetical arguments he proposes to support his case.[66] Beginning from the narrative framework, which he identifies as the whole summary of the words and works of Jesus at Mt 4:23–5:2, he postulates a situation in the history of Jesus which can be exactly reconstructed and a corresponding *Sitz-im-Leben* of Jesus' disciples. The Sermon is not adressed to individuals, but to the Israel of the final ages; Lohfink assumes a time when Jesus still counted on a basic openness on the part of Israel as a whole vis-à-vis his new exposition of the will of God. After Israel rejects this teaching, it is adressed to the community of disciples in the narrower sense; after Jesus is rejected by the religious leaders of his people, this community represents the Israel which is willing to repent. As such, the group of disciples is summoned to lead a life guided by the alternative commandments of Jesus and thus to form the contrasting society that is sketched in the examples of the Sermon on the Mount.[67] In support of individual points in his thesis, Lohfink appeals to the conscious rejection of the disciples by the crowds of the people, to the significance of the group of the Twelve as representing all Israel, to the careful selection of place names from among the cities in the Decapolis, and to the function of the Sinai typology which shows that the Sermon on the Mount is an eschatological exposition of the Torah.

---

66. According to U. Berner, *Die Bergpredigt*, pp. 44–47, this group includes the expositions by O. Riethmüller, H. Asmussen, and D. Bonhoeffer. They saw the Sermon on the Mount as "community regulations for the city on the hill" (in Riethmüller's phrase) which Christ creates as his own new people, no longer limited to one nation but transcending all ethnic barriers.

67. Cf. G. Lohfink, "Wem gilt die Bergpredigt? Eine redaktionskritische Untersuchung von Mt 4,23–5,2 und 7,28f," *ThQ* 163 (1983), pp. 264–84. Cf. also Idem, *Wie hat Jesus Gemeinde gewollt?*, Freiburg 1982, pp. 63–70b.

The primary function of the great programmatic discourse which Matthew elaborates in the Sermon on the Mount is therefore the calling of the disciples and the formation of the community. It is not intended as a free-floating ethical instruction, but in a very specific sense as "*didache* for the formation of disciples."[68] The close relationship assumed here between discipleship and the teaching of Jesus depends, however, on the decisive point that the disciples are portrayed not as individual hearers, but as representatives of the new people of God, called to be the salt of the earth and the light of the world (cf. Mt 5:13–16) and to bear witness to the Gospel before the world. According to Lohfink, the main presupposition of this commission is that this "people of God which is to be gathered together" (and which later became the church) forms a "separate living space" as a community where people live and deal with one another in a way other than that which is normal in the world. This entails clear boundaries vis-à-vis the world.[69] This limitation of the validity of the Sermon on the Mount is indeed meant only as something temporary, since Jesus' teachings certainly envisage the whole of humankind, in an indirect manner; nevertheless, the further influence of the Sermon, which is to be transmitted by the church, is not conceived in terms of the images of salt and yeast, which see individual Christians as working in their society as the ferment of a new way of life. Rather, Lohfink gives unambiguous prominence to the alternative image of the city of God built on a hill to give light to the peoples. This means that while the rest of humankind is envisaged by the Sermon on the Mount, this is only "via the church, which is to make all the peoples into communities of disciples."[70] According to this model, the communities of disciples are not thought of only as an exemplary fellowship of proclamation and witness, with an alternative lifestyle meant to attract outsiders to the Sermon on the Mount. Rather, the Sermon and discipleship are so closely interconnected that the goal of the Sermon on the Mount is not primarily the proclamation of God's sovereignty and the transformation of humankind as a whole, but the formation of new communities of disciples in which Jesus' contrasting model will live on. Only within such communities of faith, which bear the imprint of the Gospel, is it possible to fulfill the ethical directives of the Sermon on the Mount. Outside this sphere, it is completely (or at least virtually) impossible to practice them.

68. G. Lohfink, "Wem gilt die Bergpredigt?," p. 279.
69. Cf. Ibid., p. 283.
70. Cf. Ibid., p. 284.

3.2. Exegetical observations on the understanding of the
Sermon on the Mount

The theory that the Sermon on the Mount has a limited validity sees its strong point precisely where other interpretative models allegedly confront a dilemma: it claims to be able to indicate a specific context within which the ethical requirements of Jesus can be fulfilled. For the individual as an isolated subject, or for humanity as a collective unit, this will always remain an insuperable demand. But in the social milieu of the community of disciples, this becomes possible thanks to God's mighty deeds, which this community continues to experience. Hence, the question of the ecclesial *Sitz-im-Leben* of the Sermon on the Mount aims to restrict the message of Jesus to the church, since this is considered the only way to ensure that his ethical directives can in fact be put into practice.

Apart from the fact that the reference to the disciples' ethical conduct as something made possible by God's mighty deeds is hardly convincing, this kind of solution in principle remains caught in the dilemma we have already seen: either the degree of obligation of the Sermon must be reduced, or else its claim to validity must be lessened. This is where the central question must be posed to the "community model" solution; from a theological-ethical perspective, this is weightier than the historical objections which can be made to some of the individual arguments, and which indeed call into question the exegetical foundations of this whole attempt at reconstruction (e.g., the limitation of Jesus' ministry to the Israel which was willing to repent, the function of the Twelve which is assumed by the community of disciples after Israel rejects Jesus, the hypothesis of a "discontinuity" in Jesus' public ministry, and the meaning of the pilgrimage motif).[71] Besides this, a number of individual traits in the narrative and motif-critical and redaction-historical particularities in the biblical account offer exegetic arguments against eliminating the claim to universal validity in Jesus' ethical demands. These aspects are overlooked by the "community model." I offer a summary of them here, drawing on the voluminous exegetical literature on the Sermon on the Mount, in order to show the biblical basis of the following theological-ethical interpretation.

First, the fact that this Sermon, like the law of Sinai in the past, is proclaimed on a mountain need not mean only the superseding of the law of

71. On this, cf. P. Hoffmann, "Tradition und Situation," p. 105; A. Vögtle, "Ein 'unablässiger Stachel'," in: H. Merklein (ed.), *Neues Testament und Ethik* (Festschrift for R. Schnackenburg), Freiburg 1989, pp. 53–70, esp. 64–67.

Moses, or the establishing of a binding social order for the new people of God; in addition to the reference back to the events of Sinai, the introduction to the Sermon on the Mount also points ahead to the conclusion of Matthew's Gospel. It is not only the pre-Easter figure of the historical Jesus who stands behind the Sermon on the Mount: here, we also hear the authority of the risen and exalted Christ who sends his disciples to the peoples, to teach them everything that he has commanded them (cf. Mt 28:18–20).[72] The historicization in Matthew's portrait of Jesus has always paradigmatic significance for the idea that the disciples are to be drawn from all the nations and for the evangelist's idea of the lordship of the Son of Man over all the peoples of the world, which he elaborates as a contrast to the Pharisaic and national-Zealot messianic ideals of his own day. Accordingly, we must not forget that when Matthew looks back to the proclamation of the historical Jesus, he is reflecting on its universal significance for the debate between his own community and other messianic ideas. "The directives once given by Jesus now take on a universal dimension as obligatory commandments for the group of disciples drawn from all peoples, until the end of this age of the world."[73]

Secondly, the contrast which Matthew consciously constructs between the disciples and the crowds means that the Sermon on the Mount adresses two "concentric circles of hearers, so to speak,"[74] and this at any rate excludes a "disciple ethics" in the narrower sense, viz. an ethics for perfect Christians or a two-storied ethics within the church. Although the Sermon is adressed directly to the disciples, the "crowds" are also envisaged, representing the fellowship of disciples who are to be gathered from among the nations to whom the Gospel of God's kingdom will be proclaimed. The metaphors of "salt of the earth" and "light of the world" which follow the Beatitudes (cf. Mt 5:13–16) give the Sermon the quality of a "recruiting adress"[75] with a horizon that transcends the disciples who stand around Jesus. The disciples are the first to hear the Sermon, and their witness is to work like a ferment among the peoples so that everyone may be confronted with the claim of unrestricted justice and love which has become visible in Jesus Christ. Apart from the commission to the disciples to preach to all the peoples, it is above all the parable of the judgment of the whole world

---

72. On this, cf. A. Vögtle, "Ein 'unablässiger Stachel'," p. 64; E. Lohse, *Theologische Ethik des Neuen Testaments,* p. 45.
73. P. Hoffmann, "Tradition und Situation," p. 90.
74. U. Luz, *Das Evangelium nach Matthäus,* p. 197.
75. Ibid.

(Mt 25:31–46) which expresses Matthew's conception of the widening horizon of the proclamation: here, the "church" and the "disciples" are no longer mentioned as specific units, and membership in the community has no longer any significance for God's eschatological judgment.[76]

Thirdly, the universal horizon of the Beatitudes and antitheses of Matthew's Sermon on the Mount can be discerned in a number of verbal particularities. Where Luke presents the Beatitudes as macarisms adressed directly to the disciples ("Blessed are you . . ."), Matthew formulates them in the third person, thereby broadening their address. This more general form goes beyond the promise of a reward to the group of disciples and discloses fundamental traits of an understanding of the human person which appears when God reveals his unconditional love. Likewise, the Golden Rule which introduces the conclusion to the Sermon on the Mount (Mt 7:12) is formulated without any limitation to praxis within the group of disciples. The comparison in the clause "whatever you wish that others would do to you" makes this a universal rule for conduct, summarizing the ethical requirements which govern the disciples' dealings with every human person.[77]

Fourthly, the "separate living space" with clear boundaries *ad intra* and *ad extra* which, according to the "community model," determines the sociological context of Jesus' ethos, is a questionable concept. It imports into the Sermon on the Mount the Johannine concept of "brotherly love" (which has undoubtedly a stronger relation to the community), instead of interpreting the Sermon from its highpoint in the commandment to love one's enemies—although this is suggested by the ever higher demands which the Sermon makes of its hearers. The restriction to the group of disciples also fails to note that the wider circle of hearers of the Sermon do not share the wandering existence of the disciples, but remain where they have lived hitherto. These persons are meant to realize the ethical directives of the Sermon on the Mount, not under some special conditions, but in the concrete existential situations in which Jesus' message reaches them. Accordingly, the interpretative parameter of Jesus' ethical teachings is not only the group of disciples (within its present or future boundaries), but all the "public social sphere of people's lives in Palestine: this is the world which God adresses as lord."[78]

76. On this, cf. P. Hoffmann, "Tradition und Situation," p. 93.

77. On this, cf. E. Lohse, *Theologische Ethik des Neuen Testaments*, p. 48.

78. P. Hoffmann, "Tradition und Situation," p. 105; cf. also A. Vögtle, "Ein 'unablässiger Stachel'," pp. 65f.

Fifthly and lastly, the command to love one's enemies also implies a criticism of the attitude which would water down the requirement of love so that it applied only to one's neighbor, whether in the community of disciples or in one's social milieu. Exegetical discussion about the original meaning of the term "enemy" has helped to shed light on the concrete social-historical background against which Jesus' requirement is transmitted by the source "Q," the Matthaean redactor, or the author of the two-volume Lucan work. Knowledge of this context is not in the least irrelevant to our understanding of this commandment, since there is a great difference between demanding love of enemies as the individual's attitude vis-à-vis a personal foe, as the generous attitude of a ruler vis-à-vis his subjects, as the refusal to seek revenge when one is defeated, or as non-violent resistance in a situation of persecution.[79] However, the various contexts in the history of transmission must not be allowed to detach the interpretation of the commandment to love one's enemies from Jesus' original intention, which aimed at overcoming every barrier to love of neighbor. Insight into the social, religious, or political-national context in which Jesus' demand was transmitted by New Testament tradition identifies the specific situations and real existential conditions in which this demand was heard at each point of its transmission; but such insights do not contradict the universal validity intended in Jesus' words.

The fundamental significance of the command to love one's enemies, which in principle embraces every concrete situation, is emphasized in Matthew's Sermon on the Mount both by its absolute, unconditional formulation and by its justification in terms of sapiential and creation theology. The precept, "Love your enemies and pray for those who persecute you, so that you may be sons of your Father who is in heaven; for he makes his sun rise on the evil and on the good, and sends rain on the just and the unjust" (Mt 5:44–45), contains no specifying limitation on its validity, nor any concrete definition of the circumstances to which it is meant to apply. Rather, it is issued in general terms, without any presuppositions; and precisely this "simple" formulation gives it a radicality vis-à-vis any special parallel texts in Jewish literature.[80] Matthew's text "consciously refrains from explaining who is meant by 'enemy,' doubtless because this—like the Jewish discussion of the question, 'Who is my neighbor?' (cf. Lk 10:29–

79. On this, cf. L. Schottroff, "Gewaltverzicht und Feindesliebe in der urchristlichen Jesustradition," pp. 202ff.

80. On this, cf. G. Strecker, *Die Bergpredigt. Ein exegetischer Kommentar,* Göttingen 1984, pp. 92–95, 184.

37)—would merely establish a new casuistry, once again laying down legal rules for the radical loving service of one's fellow human being, and thereby stripping the demand of its radicality."[81]

The only motivation that the Sermon on the Mount offers for the demand to love one's enemies lacks any description of the specific relationship which we might have to our enemy. An ethics of gradated reciprocity, where even "evil" persons greet and do good to one another, is undermined by the simple reference to the goodness of the heavenly Creator, whose love makes no distinction between persons. God's behavior in his creation allows his perfection to be understood as a model which enables human beings to overcome boundaries, barriers, and prejudices in their conduct towards each other. "In contrast to the world established by human beings, a world full of differences, contradictions, and hostilities, we see an image of what the world could be as God's creation."[82]

3.3. Theological-ethical interpretation of the Sermon on the Mount

In view of the contemporary state of exegetical, hermeneutical, and theological discussion, the starting point for theological-ethical understanding of the Sermon can be described as a tension between two poles. On the one hand, we must try to get behind the dogmatic, confessional, or political-ideological influences which dominated the various types of exposition in the past; on the other hand, we must preserve the elements of theological insight contained in these past expositions (even if they have been presented in a unilateral exaggeration which ignores other aspects), where these are in agreement with the original intentions of the biblical text. The attempt at a substantial critique of the various theological-ethical expositions on the basis of the intentions of the Sermon (to the extent that these can be uncovered by exegesis) cannot begin from some neutral standpoint far removed from the controversies of the past. Every such attempt is the continuation of one particular expository trajectory, and it is important that one remain hermeneutically conscious of one's own presuppositions. The appropriation of this tradition which brings it into the present day finds its necessary counterpart in a (self-)critical debate with the objections proposed by other traditions.

81. H. Merklein, *Die Gottesherrschaft als Handlungsprinzip*, p. 235.
82. P. Hoffmann, "Tradition und Situation," p. 107.

a. The Sermon on the Mount as synthesis of a perfect Christian life The understanding of the Sermon on the Mount in Catholic theology, with fundamental outlines bearing the imprint of Augustine and Thomas, is in fact more differentiated than may seem from the perspective of the Reformation polemic against the distinction between *praecepta* and *consilia* and the two-storied ethics which the mediaeval church allegedly built on this distinction.[83] Thomas' exposition of the Sermon has been the most influential attempt at systematization in Catholic theology, and his distinction between commandments and counsels supplied the theological justification for religious life which was dominant in the church for many centuries until it was corrected by the Second Vatican Council. This important distinction, which is supported in principle by good biblical reasons (although it cannot be derived exegetically from one text alone, viz. Mt 19:21), does not however play any key role in his exposition of the Sermon on the Mount. Rather, Thomas agrees with Augustine in affirming explicitly: "All the perfection of our lives is summarized in this discourse of the Lord."[84] The theological location of the Sermon in the ground plan of Thomas' thinking is a further confirmation that its goal is to lead all Christians to perfection. Thomas reads the Sermon on the Mount as a systematic theologian, and finds in the Beatitudes the goal of that highest existential possibility towards which all human beings are necessarily *en route*, even if they follow different paths in keeping with their various ideas of happiness.[85] The Sermon contains the commandments which lead to this common goal of human existence—in his exposition, Thomas always speaks of *praecepta,* never of *consilia*—and the instruments which help us to observe these commandments on the way that leads to the highest end.

In this way, the exposition of the Sermon on the Mount is as it were a prism which allows Thomas to make a synthesis of the great outlines of his theological-ethical thinking. He agrees with the dominant tendency in early Christian exposition by maintaining that the commandments in the Sermon are universally valid for all Christians and that they can be ob-

---

83. A balanced presentation of the Catholic expository tradition can be found today in Protestant scholars such as U. Berner, *Die Bergpredigt,* pp. 69–71, and U. Luz, *Das Evangelium nach Matthäus,* pp. 193f.

84. Thomas Aquinas, *Lectura super Matthaeum* V, 2 (nr. 403): *"in isto sermone Domini tota perfectio vitae nostrae continetur."*

85. Ibid., (nr. 404): *"Sciendum tamen quod in istis verbis includitur omnis plena beatitudo: omnes enim homines appetunt beatitudinem, sed differunt in indicando de beatitudine; et ideo quidam istud, quidam illud appetunt."*

served in this life.[86] At the same time, however, he emphasizes that the Sermon contains a definitive answer to the fundamental question of every human existence, taking up the human yearning for happiness and bringing this to a definitive fulfillment which lies beyond all partial sensuous experiences. This is the theme of the virtuoso link which Thomas makes, on the basis of his anthropological analysis of the *desiderium naturale,* between the individual biblical topics of faith, hope, and love, the gifts of the Holy Spirit, and the Beatitudes, presenting these as three configurations with the same fundamental meaning. Once again, we need not investigate in detail here the ramifications of the hidden correspondences which Thomas discerns between the traditional biblical materials; sometimes the linkage does violence to the texts themselves.[87] Our only interest, when we attempt to take up his approach and make use of it today, is in the basic outlines of a theological interpretation of the Sermon on the Mount which combines the universal validity and practicability of its commandments with the goal of a definitive overcoming of the basic existential contradictions in the human person and a definitive fulfillment of his natural yearning for meaning.

Such an interpretation maintains its systematic potential even today, since it is able to take up the individual results of modern exegesis and integrate these into a theological-ethical explanatory model. If one inquires into the hermeneutical meaning of the affirmations in the Sermon on the Mount, one must distinguish three textual levels in the biblical transmission process. The succession of these levels allows us to see the decisive theme for the practical life of the hearers of the Sermon. The structure of the Sermon as a whole has a variety of meanings: *first,* we encounter the historically given original text in Jesus' proclamation, *secondly,* we encounter the Gospel text to which Matthew has given a literary shape, and finally we encounter a *third* text, which is the primary goal of the first two textual forms, viz. the text "that is to be formed in theological thought and in one's own existence."[88] This means that the only way to define the theological-ethical intention of the Sermon is to ask in all three textual strata about the intention of Jesus' words and about Matthew's literary strategy when he

86. On this, cf. esp. K. Beyschlag, "Zur Geschichte der Bergpredigt in der alten Kirche," pp. 313ff.

87. Cf. Thomas Aquinas, *STh* I–II, qq. 68–69; and *Lectura super Matthaeum* V, 2–9 (nr. 404–43).

88. H.-D. Betz, "Die hermeneutischen Prinzipien in der Bergpredigt," in: E. Jüngel et al., *Verifikationen* (Festschrift for G. Ebeling), Tübingen 1982, pp. 27–41, at 31.

combines Jesus' original logia about killing, adultery, and swearing with the other antitheses (which are the work of the evangelist himself), thus creating an open list.[89] Matthew employs the repetition of a formally unusual and substantially provocative introduction here as a stylistic means to attain a precise goal: he intends to "direct the reader" away from his literary text and to point the readers or hearers to the "text" that must be written in their own lives.[90] The verbal crescendo in the list of antitheses generates a movement that leads to something new and impels the readers in a direction where they can recognize the claim Jesus is making.

b. The antitheses as illustrations of the greater righteousness In the parable of the Good Samaritan (cf. Lk 10:25–37), Jesus does not offer any general definition of one's "neighbor," but leads his hearers to behave as a neighbor in concrete situations. Similarly, the individual antitheses have their starting point in conflicts that arise in every sphere of daily life in human society, and sketch the contrasting picture of a situation in which the "greater" righteousness becomes reality, in response to the claim made by love. Hence, they all display a parallel correspondence between the old conduct, which must be altered, and the new situation which is to take shape in the behavior of the hearers. If we draw a sketch of these correspondences, we find on the one side a list of conflictual situations which are provoked by the contradictory desires in the human person and the insistence *ad extra* on the claims of law: conflicts and lawsuits with one's neighbor (Mt 5:21), sexual passion without a goal in the human person himself (Mt 5:27), conflicts in one's marriage (Mt 5:31), the misuse of language to deceive and cheat (Mt 5:33), the violent resolution of conflicts, in keeping with the law of revenge (Mt 5:38), and finally, as the true root of all injustice, enmity among human persons (Mt 5:43).[91] Corresponding to these, we find on the other side the individual paths of reconciliation which give exemplary outlines to the goal of a perfect Christian life (cf. Mt 5:48). Thus there is formed the image of a reconciled world, which begins with the healing of the human person in his own heart and allows the image of a comprehensively successful life to emerge in ever wider concentric circles. The first step in the private sphere is the re-establishing of the original mutuality

89. On the exegetical distinction between the "primary" and "secondary" antitheses, cf. P. Hoffmann and V. Eid, *Jesus von Nazareth und eine christliche Moral,* Freiburg 1975, pp. 73–79; H. Merklein, *Die Gottesherrschaft als Handlungsprinzip,* pp. 253–60.

90. On this, cf. W. Egger, "Handlungsorientierte Auslegung der Antithesen Mt 5,21–28," in: K. Kertelge (ed.), *Ethik im Neuen Testament,* pp. 119–44, esp. 131.

91. Cf. ibid., p. 124.

between woman and man (cf. Mt 5:32) and the assurance that one can rely on the veracity of human speech in the presence of the transcendent God (Mt 5:37). The reconciliation intended by the Sermon on the Mount is not limited to the narrower circle of marriage and family, but goes beyond this, breaking through the deadly cycle of violence in every human relationship (Mt 5:39) and indicating the path to a universal brotherhood among human beings (Mt 5:44–45). Accordingly, the Sermon on the Mount is the pure and undistorted expression of the will of God, which lays claim to all of reality. It does not teach an interim ethics for a brief period at the end of time, nor a partial ethics which would apply only to one limited sector of life. Since the law and the prophets are fulfilled in the Sermon (Mt 5:17; 7:12), it contains the perfect will of God, which always was so, and is valid everywhere.

In face of this claim, the antitheses in their harsh form will inevitably be felt as a provocation and an impossible demand. The spontaneous reaction on the part of the hearers is a defensive attitude. One who is angry with another has not yet done any violence to him, far less killed him; to look at the wife of another man and take pleasure in her is not necessarily the prelude to committing adultery with her. Giving one's unjust accuser the whole of one's cloak, or turning the other cheek to one who strikes does not lead to any constructive resolution of a conflict. Matthew certainly envisages spontaneous associations of ideas such as these: he intends to provoke his readers and break through their encrusted thinking, so that they will be alert to the claim Jesus is making. His hyperbolic language intends to disorientate people in the practical understanding they bring to everyday life, so that they can be opened up to the will of God in their thinking and action.[92] Naturally, one can become accustomed to this verbal provocation, so that this instrument no longer functions as intended. This is above all the case when the Sermon is heard only on the second level, and the hearer does not allow himself to be called into question by what he hears.

If, however, one is willing to set out on the path intended by Matthew, one discovers suddenly that on the first two levels of the text of the Sermon, where we hear his message as it is mediated by the exaggerated language of the evangelist, Jesus is doing much more than merely proposing

---

92. P. Ricoeur has studied this intentional effect in the case of the biblical parables, in which modern exegetes recognize the verbal form chosen by Jesus himself: "Stellung und Funktion der Metapher in der biblischen Sprache," in: Idem and E. Jüngel, *Metapher. Zur Hermeneutik religiöser Sprache*, Munich 1974, pp. 45–70, esp. 67f.

paradoxical individual requirements or surpassing Old Testament commandments. His concern is to heal the wickedness of the hearer's heart and to establish the basic personal rights of the hearer's neighbor. The anger in my heart or the lustful glance of my eyes can indeed make it difficult to acknowledge the claim which is made on me by the personal existence of another human being. But we do not begin to act against the value and dignity of another only when we harm those fundamental goods of his life which are protected in the external sphere of law; we do so at a much earlier point, for example when we harbor evil thoughts or anger against him. And if our neighbor is truly to be respected, more is needed than a simple recourse to legal standpoints when conflicts arise; respect for the personal dignity of the other also includes respect for his marriage, and this in turn entails more than the observance of legal regulations and abstaining from flagrant adultery. My eye too can harm the existential milieu of another person when my lustful glance penetrates the sphere that must be protected. Following the same logic, Jesus refuses both the husband and the wife (cf. Mk 10:12) the option to limit married love by appealing to the Old Testament law of divorce, for the legally-guaranteed freedom one claimed for oneself would set a boundary to married love. Thus, the individual antitheses indicate the contours of a way of life in which the "greater" righteousness of God intends to overcome all the legal regulations which are marked by a compromise with evil. The hearers are forbidden to appeal to the legal state of affairs in order to limit the love they must show their neighbor. God's praxis, which knows no limitations, becomes their model; instead of the limitations of the old law, their internal attitude is to become the new law. "The law is no longer a boundary, but the appeal to a conduct without any boundaries."[93]

c. Jesus' radical commands as a challenge to undivided love   Although Jesus decrees a new way of life in view of the dawning of God's kingdom, giving renewed access to the original meaning of the Torah as the will of God, the phrase "intensification of the Torah," which has become common among exegetes, is fuzzy and open to great misunderstandings. It suggests that Jesus introduces an intensification which transcends the commandments of the Old Testament law, but this fails to note that, although Jesus does indeed take the law of Moses as the point of reference for the

93. W. Egger, "Handlungsorientierte Auslegung," p. 123; cf. also H. Merklein, *Die Gottesherrschaft als Handlungsprinzip,* p. 253.

"intensified" formulations of his own precepts, he employs the antithetical introduction to his ethical directives to make a contrast between his own legitimation as the authoritative interpreter of God's will and the legitimation of Moses and his law. Since his intention is to use his own authority to set out God's will and to enforce it to the full now that God's kingdom is coming, the antitheses in the Sermon on the Mount are not "radicalized commandments from the Torah," but "commandments of Jesus which surpass the Torah in radicality."[94] But in what sense must we understand the ethical teachings of Jesus as more radical, further-reaching, or harder to keep? While the Pharisees divided the commandments into easy and difficult precepts and insisted on their fulfillment, Jesus asserts that despite the higher claims he makes, it is "easy" to keep his commandments (cf. Mt 11:30). In terms of the *quantitative* effort demanded, they are not difficult, for unlike the 624 individual precepts of the Torah, they ultimately consist "only" in acknowledging one another with an undivided heart, thereby fulfilling the whole law in the one commandment to love (cf. Mt 5:17). In another sense, of course, Jesus' commandments in the Sermon on the Mount are very difficult, even harder than the crushing quantity of individual precepts in the Old Testament, and this is why it is not entirely wrong to say that Jesus "intensified" the law. If we look at the commandments in the light of the *inner, qualitative* resistance which must be overcome before they can be observed, then we see that his commandments do in fact require a greater effort and strength.[95]

Unlike the Decalogue, a fundamental ordering of justice which regulates only the external mutual relationships of human persons, Jesus' demands concern the perverted needs in the human person which oppose a life in common in a new, reconciled order of life where all are in agreement. Jesus does not only want to limit evil once it has already broken out. Rather, he wants to tear its roots out of human hearts (cf. Mk 7:15), which are the origin of everything that human beings wish and do—and hence of human existence in the deepest sense. This is why the antitheses to the

94. H. Merklein, *Die Gottesherrschaft*, p. 256. On the concept of "intensification of the Torah," which goes back to the Protestant exegete H. Braun, see the critical observations by W. Schrage, *Ethik des Neuen Testaments*, pp. 64f.

95. On this, cf. H.-D. Betz, "Die hermeneutischen Prinzipien in der Bergpredigt," pp. 37f., and G. Strecker, *Die Bergpredigt*, pp. 181f. On the rabbinic understanding of the unity and inviolability of the Torah, cf. R. Dillmann, *Das Eigentliche der Ethik Jesu. Ein exegetischer Beitrag zur moraltheologischen Diskussion um das Proprium einer christlichen Ethik*, Mainz 1984, pp. 99f.

commandments of the old law which he propounds concern the antago-
nism between human instincts and passions on the one hand and the end
[goal] of an undivided capacity to love on the other. In Thomistic terms,
Jesus is concerned with the *inordinationes circa seipsum* which keep people
prisoners in a desperate desire for possession, hindering them from realizing their true potential for life.

The mirror-image of the genuine, authentic fulfillment of the beatitudes and the antitheses of the Sermon on the Mount speaks of the perverse inclinations of the human hearts and the "evil impulse" which must
be overcome within us, if our external relationships too are to be free from
violence and willing to seek reconciliation.[96] It is precisely here that the
newness of Jesus' ethical teaching and the specific difference between the
Sermon on the Mount and the requirements of the Old Testament law are
to be found: Jesus uncovers the original meaning of the Ten Commandments afresh by demanding their "radical" fulfillment out of a spirit of undivided love. Even the teaching about the renunciation of revenge and violence and about love of one's enemies, which goes beyond the basic
structure of the Ten Commandments, appears "easy" to fulfill once the
false desire, the perverted wish for self-assertion, and the fearful concentration on one's own person have been overcome. This allows us to call these
highest peaks of Jesus' ethics "more radical commandments"—not because
they demand something harder of the human person, but because their
fulfillment goes further than the external limitation of conflicts which the
law could achieve. They are not intended to place impossible demands on
the human person, nor to confront him with his hopeless condition and
his incapacity to do good (as supposed by one dogmatic interpretative tradition, which has continued even into our own days to read Paul's understanding of justification into the Sermon on the Mount). The only reason
why Jesus' commandments are to be called radical is that they demand a
total and undivided gift of self along the path of love. In this sense, the
Beatitudes go so far as to affirm that the fulfillment of these commandments offers the human person an incomparable, unique path to his true
happiness. With every step he takes in love, forgetting himself and breaking through the vicious circle of self-preservation, he anticipates the experience of undivided wholeness which God gives him independently of all
his moral endeavors.

96. On this, cf. H.-R. Reuter, "Die Bergpredigt als Orientierung unseres Menschseins
heute," *ZEE* 23 (1979), pp. 84–104, esp. 95–98; and A. Vögtle, "Ein 'unablässiger Stachel',"
p. 67.

d. Is it possible to live personally in accordance with the Sermon on the Mount? The Sermon on the Mount is aware that the human person has not yet attained the end [goal] of a perfect Christian life: in the Bible, only the triune God, who in himself is love, is called absolutely perfect and good (cf. Mt 19:17). However, the triune God already gives the human person here on earth a share in his own perfection by showing him the vision of a happines that makes a total and undivided claim on him. But this is bestowed, not as a mere gift for passive recipients, but as instructions for human conduct: this happiness comes about "by doing." When the Sermon on the Mount summons the hearers to take certain steps along the path of love, the intention is certainly that these actions should truly be performed. Although the antitheses are not legal regulations in the technical juridical sense, they are seriously meant as requirements which must be fulfilled by those who are receptive to the kingdom of God and who acknowledge his lordship. In Matthew's view, these requirements can actually be met. It is true that some precepts, such as the requirement to turn the other cheek, have a deeper meaning which goes beyond the literal sense of the words, so that a mere literal observance is not enough to fulfill them truly; but this does not entitle us to hold that the Sermon as a whole is "not intended literally," still less that it is fundamentally impossible to put it into practice.

This is confirmed by the fact that some of the antitheses, especially the logion about adultery, are formulated in an obligatory manner similar to that of laws, so that they can be characterized as "potential" eschatological divine law.[97] A refusal to put these precepts into practice in concrete action would be a complete misunderstanding of the fundamental theological-ethical affirmation of the Sermon on the Mount. Although its requirements are presented in the form of verbal hyperbole, these are no mere paradoxes, but are meaningful exaggerations which confront the hearers with the claim made by the kingdom of God—the kingdom which must take shape in their conduct here and now. One may object to the term "conditions for admission" to the kingdom of God (analogous to the commandments of the Decalogue in the old covenant, whose observance opened the way into the promised land), since it threatens to reverse the priority of God's unconditional turning in love to the human person, replacing this with a prior achievement on the part of human beings. Nevertheless, we can still agree with the lapidary observation of the exegete Hans

97. On this, cf. U. Luz, *Das Evangelium nach Matthäus*, pp. 272f.

Windisch, when we consider the theological-ethical intention of the Sermon on the Mount: "It is certainly expected that everyone who hears and reads these requirements, which are set out so clearly and urgently, will also put them into practice. Praxis is the natural and normal thing here."[98]

Nevertheless, the ethical directives of the Sermon cannot be fulfilled in the manner of the Ten Commandments, which (especially in their prohibitive form) designate a lower boundary drawn by the basic requirements of justice. The demands made in the Sermon are obligatory points of orientation for a life which accepts the claim made by the kingdom of God, and hence they are genuine commandments. However, they show the human person an open boundary which he will never completely attain, far less leave behind him; all he can do is to take one step after another in the right direction. The ethical directives of Jesus, presented in the examples and focal points collected by Matthew in his series of antitheses, are genuinely meant to be fulfilled, but not as if they provided a blueprint for each individual step. Rather, we are meant to employ our freedom to discover afresh, in each new existential context, what these directives demand of us.

The Sermon on the Mount describes paths towards the end [goal] of a perfect Christian life. Here, the human person receives his greatest potential for life and responds to God's categorical assurance of salvation. But these paths of the "greater" righteousness of the kingdom of God are not simply sketched in the Sermon in the form of a completely articulated program. One can speak of these paths only by comparing and contrasting them to the conduct that can usually be expected of human beings, and this is why the element of contrast plays a decisive role in the antitheses. The ethical demands made by Jesus, with a strangeness that is at first sight shocking, intend to address the imagination of the hearers and stimulate them to take the step from the text of the Sermon on the Mount, which they have only heard or read (i.e., the second level) into their own lives, transposing into the focal points of their own existence the series of logia about renunciation of recourse to lawsuits and revenge, the prohibition of oath-taking, and the commandments about non-violence and the love of enemies. This means that the ethical directives of the Sermon on the Mount can be called "ethical models" or "ethical perspectives,"[99] provided

---

98. H. Windisch, *Der Sinn der Bergpredigt. Ein Beitrag zum Problem der richtigen Exegese,* Leipzig 1929, p. 69; on the description of the Matthaean antitheses as an entry-ticket to the kingdom of God or as "a new legislation for the eschatological kingdom of God," cf. pp. 10f., 131.

99. On this, cf. esp. P. Hoffmann and V. Eid, *Jesus von Nazareth und eine christliche*

that one does not forget that the unlimited service of one's neighbor in love which Jesus requires must lead, in the new situations into which his perspective is to be translated, to more than merely an analogous attitude or a purified consciousness.[100] Rather, this must lead to a praxis which is just as concrete as that described in the examples of the original antitheses.

When moral theologians speak of "commandments that must be fulfilled" and "commandments indicating an end [*telos*]," they are displacing the difference between the Ten Commandments and the ethical directives of Jesus, rather than identifying it precisely. The precepts of the Sermon on the Mount are also meant to be kept, even if in a non-legal manner which puts an end to assumptions about the power of evil in human life. The concept of "commandments indicating an end [*telos*]" contrasts the conduct required when one accepts the claim made by the kingdom of God to the observance in concrete praxis which is typical of the commandments in the Old Testament law; but this contrast defers the praxis envisaged by the Sermon into some far horizon outside the specific situations which lay an obligation on the human person here and now. This gives the Sermon as a whole an element of utopian inaccessibility which soon leads to a resigned compromise with the wretched state of the world and with one's own imperfection. For Jesus, however, the kingdom of God and its "greater" righteousness are not a distant ideal which can be approached by human persons only asymptotically in an infinite—but ultimately futile—approximation. The kingdom of God is not a moral "ideal," and one cannot rest content with the idea that an imperfect realization is all that is ever possible in one's life. On the contrary: Jesus proclaims the kingdom of God as a reality in which God's new world has already dawned and everyone is definitively assured of the perfection of his own human existence.[101]

Moral, pp. 23f. The concept of "ethical perspective" is intended to make it clear that the ethical directives of the New Testament always include the interpretative response of the individual communities to the challenge issued by Jesus' proclamation. "The perspectives hold fast to the concrete element in Jesus' proclamation, but they make it possible to transpose this into action and to develop it further, by taking up the meaning of the demand which Jesus makes in each case and handing it on in such a way that they motivate to action" (ibid.). On the concept of "ethical model," cf. also R. Dillmann, *Das Eigentliche der Ethik Jesu*, pp. 39–42.

100. F. Böckle speaks of "elements which purify the ethical consciousness in view of the *basileia*," but he goes on to explain this ambiguous expression by affirming that Jesus' ethical directives contain both more than a law (since they are more comprehensive than a legal definition) and less than a law (because they lack the character of legal coercion): *Fundamentalmoral*, Munich 1977, p. 213.

101. On this, cf. K. Demmer, *Entscheidung und Verhängnis*, Paderborn 1976, p. 109;

The basic commandment of the Sermon on the Mount obligates every human being to take hold of this perfection in concrete praxis. Matthew describes the observance of this commandment as the path of greater righteousness, and the individual requirements serve as examples of how this is
to be done.

This is why the Sermon is not an exhaustively detailed program which
reviews in advance every conceivable situation in Christian existence; nor is
it limited to an appeal to adopt a new interior attitude. It not only demands
that one act *on the basis of* love: it also provides specific indications of *what*
love does, and *what* kind of conduct vis-à-vis one's neighbor is compatible
with love. These counsels are not mere points for orientation which the individual is free to accept or reject—but nor are they legal regulations which
would obligate all individuals equally. Rather, they instruct us how to discover in free obedience what is required of us here and now. The Sermon
on the Mount sees Christian existence as a path and a process: not a path
that can be taken in any old way, but a path "aiming at perfection, with a
direction and a radicality clearly marked off by the individual commandments which shine with a light they draw from their end."[102] Different
Christians may make varying progress along this path, and they may not all
come equally far in the course of their lives, but this does not dilute the validity of the common end, viz. the perfection of a Christian life. In all the
variety of the paths they take and the stages they have reached, all the individuals are making towards the same end, provided that they fulfill the
commandment to love and the exemplary demands of Jesus in accordance
with their specific situation and the possibilities that they have.

  *e. Is it possible to act politically in accordance with the Sermon on the
Mount?* The path of Christian existence has many strata, many ramifications, and many faces. It leads individual Christians towards the common
end, namely the *tota perfectio vitae nostrae,* in keeping with the multiplicity
of their existential circumstances and the varying degree of their moral capacity. If we bear in mind that people differ, and evaluate this plurality

---

H.-G. Fritzsche, "Dekalog IV. Ethisch, *TRE* VIII, col. 421: "What is involved is not simply a
new 'concept of God,' but new concepts of history, the world, and the human person as a
whole; no doubt these are ultimately implied in the concept of God. One must become
aware of the *caesura,* the turning point in history introduced by Jesus Christ, and one must
become convinced that from now on, it is objectively possible to fulfill the commandments,
because the work of Christ has overcome the curse of tragic hopelessness, what Augustine
calls *non posse non peccare."*

  102. U. Luz, *Das Evangelium nach Matthäus,* p. 189; cf. also p. 313.

positively, we can see the abiding justification for the Catholic differentiation between various paths and stages within the one end, namely Christian perfection,[103] while the classical Protestant distinction between two realms or a double "governance" whereby God exercises his lordship over the world *(regimen Dei spirituale—regimen Dei corporale)* proves its worth in another field.[104] When we consider that the Christian is both a public and a private person, we can combine these two: the differentiation *among* the various existential forms of Christian living is complemented by a gradation *within* the sphere of personal responsibility in which the individual Christian is called to put Jesus' ethical directives into practice. This approach contains a substantial element of truth, which is not to be disqualified by the memory of the fatal separation (already implied in Luther) which led in the theory of "two kingdoms" in twentieth-century German Lutheran theology to a complete surrender of civil and political life into the hands of the alleged autonomy of divinely-willed state structures.

There is no doubt that the Lutheran polarity between civil profession and political office on the one hand and private life in one's family and marriage on the other was over-simplified. If, however, one refuses to specify gradated areas of responsibility and involvement, this too can unintentionally promote a new neutralization of the Sermon on the Mount. For if this text is read as a political program or a societal utopia, supplying immediate solutions for the decisions which are to be taken in the conflicts of day-to-day politics, this merely makes it easier for the individual to dispense himself from the demands which the Sermon propounds with regard to his specific praxis. Here, the Protestant interpretation of the Sermon is correct to insist that the reshaping of the world under the claim made by God's greater righteousness begins with each individual, whose selfhood is irreducibly his own. According to the logic of the Sermon on the Mount, this reshaping must begin by overcoming the inner conflicts in human hearts, their perverse needs, their struggle to acquire possessions and to assert themselves, and the belief that they must force their own standpoints on others; for thereby, one will overcome the erroneous attitudes which are the root of the structural violence found in external relationships between human beings.

103. On this, cf. Thomas Aquinas, *STh* II–II, q. 184, a. 1 and 3.
104. On this, cf. Martin Luther, "Wochenpredigten über Mt 5–7" (1530–32), in: *D. Martin Luthers Werke: Kritische Gesamtausgabe*, 32, Weimar 1883ff., pp. 299ff.; on this, cf. H.-G. Geyer, "Luthers Auslegung der Bergpredigt," in: Idem et al. (eds.), *"Wenn nicht jetzt, wann dann?"* (Festschrift for H. J. Kraus), Neukirchen-Vluyn 1983, pp. 283–93, esp. 289f.

If a social-critical reading of the Sermon on the Mount takes it as an unmediated political program with concrete directives for the praxis of citizens in the state, or between one state and another, it makes an illegitimate detour around the logic appropriate to the spheres of society, politics, and economics, leaping over the level on which conflicts must be dealt with—but it is on this level that the contrasting images of the Sermon are intended to operate. It is indeed true that these images speak of the claim made by the kingdom of God on every sphere of life, and of the human person's undivided obedience; they speak of a world without violence, of overcoming hatred, and of universal reconciliation among human beings. But they do not suppress the reality of violence or the awareness of the destructive power of evil in human history. The history of the path which God has taken with his Son is inseparably linked to the revelation of non-violence as the definitive power, the final judgment over all violence; the same applies to the other ethical requirements made in the Sermon on the Mount. It is only the life-story of Jesus of Nazareth, who accepted death vicariously and was raised by God, that discloses the full consequences of the conflict addressed by the provocative directives in the Sermon. From its perspective, non-violence and love of enemies must be seen as distinguishing signs of the kingdom of God and as a protest against the violence which reigns in the structures of the world. But these directives do not dispense us from forming an appropriate judgment about when non-violence is to be chosen for the sake of legitimate ends, or from assessing its suitability as a strategic political instrument for the attainment of such ends.

The exhortations in the Sermon to renounce revenge and violence, and to love one's enemies, warn against restricting love too narrowly to the private interpersonal sphere, where its force of gravity (so to speak) will naturally urge us to practice solidarity. In particular, the command to love one's enemies—which is not simply meant as the zenith of a "natural" human love—is intended to remind us how far love must be ready to go, and what provocative expressions love can take, if we follow Jesus' will.[105] The exaggerated formulations of his message bring out with especial clarity the particular character of his ethical instructions, but not even these intend to specify in advance the route to be taken in every conceivable political situation, or to define the path that will de facto lead to peace among human beings and justice among the nations. Nor do they intend to anticipate the individual's discovery of the specific task in which he can express his

---

105. On this, cf. U. Luz, *Das Evangelium nach Matthäus,* pp. 317f.

obedience and his love. The Sermon on the Mount does not counsel a withdrawal from the political world (e.g., in the form of a refusal to participate in political life), nor does it permit us to despise the role played by accurate perception and knowledge in the evaluation of political strategies. But it does warn against neutralizing the path of non-violence and the initial steps on the road to reconciliation, which it encourages us to take: these must not be reduced to a political utopia or to an anthropological wishful thinking which remains blind to the causes of violence in human society.

4. Natural law and biblical ethics

Our interpretation of the two most influential literary compilations in biblical ethics has demonstrated their universal intention. Both texts, the Decalogue and the Sermon on the Mount, speak in their own way of fundamental risks and perverted needs which pose a threat to the human existence of every person; although initially addressed to Israel and the community of disciples, they also envisage all humankind—the whole world. Such a claim must, however, stand the test of argument and be capable of rational justification, not only within the special relationship of the chosen people to God or under the conditions governing discipleship in the community, but also in the context of universal human experiences and hopes. But does not this contradict everything that we have said about the theological character of biblical ethics as a covenant ethos dependent on God's salvific action in history and on the unconditional antecedent love which he has shown humankind? One may also ask, from the neutral platform of general human reason, how a universal claim which embraces the human existence of every person can be made from *one* particular standpoint, such as the tradition of Jewish-Christian salvation history. Only a satisfactory answer to these two questions will allow us to attribute universal significance to the high biblical ethos in a manner that is theologically and philosophically legitimate.

Such an answer presupposes that the "universal" meaning which is intended (and which we must still define more precisely) is distinct from the indisputable minimum conditions for human existence which have been shown by a transcendental reduction to be the absolutely essential kernel of the natural law. The Ten Commandments already go beyond the initial minimum of presuppositions, claims to protection and personal rights which are indispensable for an existence worthy of the human person, in which one assumes responsibility for one's own ethical conduct; this is still more true of the Sermon on the Mount. For example, the modest presuppositions of a neutral, partial anthropology cannot convincingly demonstrate the validity of the prohibition of adultery and divorce which is established in the Decalogue and freed in the second and third antitheses of the Matthaean text from subsequent limitations; but both these prohibitions make sense against the background of an anthropology which recognizes a positive value, essential to the success of human living, in the mutual partnership of woman and man and the unconditional reliability of their life in common. Similarly, the precept of absolute respect for the minimal conditions which make human existence possible does not suffice on its own to justify the requirements to love one's enemies and seek reconciliation. Like all the other high ethical directives of the Bible, these presuppose a demanding understanding of the human person and of his personal dignity. But how then is it possible to attribute to the high ethical demands of the Bible a universal significance which is valid under other basic anthropological and cultural presuppositions too?

As far as the internal aspect of the Jewish-Christian tradition is concerned, the biblical consciousness of faith responds by affirming that neither Israel nor the church have ever considered the biblical ethos and its demands as their *exclusive* possession, as something to be protected or hidden from the other peoples. It is indeed true that the Old Testament ethos contains not only traditional materials common to all humanity and justified in sapiential terms, but also particular ethical norms intended to keep Israel separate from the peoples, such as the regulations of the holiness code, the laws about societal protection which were based in salvation history (e.g., the jubilee year, when the land was not to be worked and debts were to be remitted), or the regulations governing care for the poor and the manumission of slaves. Since this ethos is based in Israel's election, the historical experience of liberation, or God's blessing when he gave his people the chosen land, it finds a natural limitation at the boundaries of the people; at the same time, however, the theological legitimation of such norms of conduct is accompanied by a tendency to internalization and universalization which seeks to submit every sphere of daily life to the sovereignty of God.[106] Initially, this tendency is limited to life in Israel, but the idea of God's love and the revelation of his righteousness inspire a uni-

---

106. On this, cf. E. Otto, *Theologische Ethik des Alten Testaments,* pp. 98, 215f.

versalization of the ethos beyond the national boundaries: for example, the concept of "neighbor" is extended beyond the group of full Jewish citizens, so that the foreigner in Israel is entitled to the protection given by the law about care of the poor (cf. Lv 19:34). Although this inspiration had no lasting effect in many areas of the tradition, it nevertheless helped reduce the separation between morality *ad intra* and morality *ad extra,* and served to promote an ethical universalism.

The motif of God's love pointed ethical reflection in Israel toward a trajectory which was ultimately more powerful than any concerns about preserving boundaries, and created the awareness that, in God's plan for history, the special path taken by Israel had a significance for the other peoples too. Although an ethical particularism frequently recurred in the legal, ethical, and societal ideas of Israel (a phenomenon widespread in the history of all religions), Israel never exclusively or even predominantly conceived of its relationship to the peoples in terms of such a model. Rather, it lived its election in the ethical sphere as a *mission entrusted to it on behalf of the peoples.* This found theological interpretation in the category of *vicarious representation,* which played a central role in Israel's consciousness of its election.[107] In the Bible, Adam is thought of as the representative of all humanity; after Adam falls, God elects the people of Israel as the representative of all the peoples (cf. Gn 12:3). Even after Israel proves unfaithful to its mission vis-à-vis the peoples, the consciousness of being chosen for "the many" in a universal function with no boundaries remained alive and found new expression in the idea of the sacred remnant (cf. Is 1:9; 10:21), in the tradition about the Servant of Yahweh, and in the motif of the pilgrimage of the peoples to Mount Zion. In particular, the cultic traditions of Israel bear a universal significance for the Gentile world; here, it celebrates God's presence in the midst of a world full of hatred and violence, and this cult is a privilege entrusted to Israel on behalf of all the peoples. Just as the irruption of violence into the history between God and human beings changed the life of all human beings for the worse, so the response which God gives by the setting-up of the sanctuary, by the dwelling of his glory in Israel, and by the expiatory cult performed at Sinai, brings benefits to humanity as a whole. "The world, i.e. in the last analysis all peoples, can survive only because God has established the expiatory cult in Israel. That which humankind as a whole still lacks, that

---

107. On this, cf. A. Deissler, "Stellvertretung als Prinzip der Heilsgeschichte," *LS* 30 (1979), pp. 339–45; K. H. Menke, *Stellvertretung. Schlüsselbegriff christlichen Lebens und theologische Grundkategorie,* Freiburg 1991, pp. 29–51.

which they need because of the reality of violence, is realized in Israel."[108]

In this way, the motif of Israel's representative function vis-à-vis the peoples serves to remove all boundaries from the idea of salvation history, which initially provided theological legitimation for special ethical norms. The priestly document interpreted the history of God's dealings with his people—beginning with the promise to Abraham and culminating in the establishing of the sanctuary on Sinai and the pilgrimage of the peoples to Mount Zion—as a wide-reaching undertaking set in motion by God in order that humanity may survive and his threatened creation may not perish. This universal theological conception of history allows us to understand the central affirmation of the priestly creation narrative, that the human person is created in God's image. This affirmation does not mention any special religious role for Israel; rather, it claims to apply to the humanity of *every* person, and explicitly refrains from limiting the bestowal of divine dignity to the biblical person alone. Belief that the human person is God's image entails the profession of faith that "every human being in every religion, and in every sphere where the religions are no longer acknowledged, is created according to the image of God."[109] The universal breadth of Israel's basic anthropological and salvation-historical conception necessarily leads to the conclusion that its traditional ethical materials too, such as the Decalogue, the exhortations in the wisdom literature, and a fortiori the ethos of the prophets, intend to lay an obligation upon the whole of humanity.

In this perspective, not even the Torah, which was handed over to Israel as an abiding memorial of Yahweh's salvific deeds, can ultimately be seen as the exclusive possession of Israel. Just as God created the world for every person, so his commandments protect the human life of every person. Rabbinic theology saw this claim symbolized in the fact that the Torah was not imparted in the land of Israel, but in the wilderness, a land with no ruler, that is, in the no man's land that belongs to all peoples in common. According to this theological argument, the Torah was imparted in the wilderness, in fire and water—i.e., in public and as a common possession available to all human beings, just like the elements of the creation—in order that the peoples would have no excuse to reject the Torah: "Just as the elements of creation are freely available to all who dwell in the world, so too is the Torah freely available to all who dwell in the world."[110]

After what we have written above, it is scarcely necessary to state here

108. E. Otto, *Theologische Ethik des Alten Testaments,* p. 230.
109. C. Westermann, *Genesis, Kapitel 1–11,* p. 218.
110. Mekhilta on Ex 20:2, quoted from F. Mußner, *Traktat über die Juden,* p. 156.

that the ethical universalism generated in the Old Testament world marks the intellectual world of the New Testament too. The instructions in the Sermon on the Mount, the parables of Jesus, and even the hyperbolic logia about non-violence and love of enemies refer not only to the circle of the first hearers, but also to the whole world. The community of disciples is to practice these teachings in a representative manner: first for all Israel, in view of its conversion, and then for the peoples of the entire populated world, that is, for all human beings, who are meant to acknowledge the sovereignty of God. Even if Jesus' high ethical directives are initially valid for the community of disciples, their aim is not the propagation of a special, religious group-ethos; here, they take the same line as Israel's Torah. As our exposition has demonstrated, their primary concern is not the intensification of individual commandments, but the fundamental right of the other *qua* person. This is why they envisage, not only the community of disciples, but humankind as a whole. The life and praxis of Christians, who are the new people of God, are to bear witness before humankind and on behalf of all persons to what the world could be as God's creation, if they were willing to accept the demands made by his kingdom.

From a theological perspective, the salvation-historical model in the Bible, which interprets the universal demands of the Decalogue and the Sermon on the Mount as an ethical truth which must be attested vicariously for all the peoples, succeeds in making a plausible connection between the particular provenance of the biblical ethos and its universal significance. This, however, resolves only one aspect of the problem, that concerning the self-understanding of Israel and of the church. It does not establish a platform for dialogue with the other world religions which likewise confront the human person with demanding interpretations of his existence. If the high ethical demands of the Jewish-Christian tradition are to demonstrate their significance for the ethical consciousness of humanity in this context too, more is required than the theological legitimation supplied by biblical salvation history: they must also find an answering echo in the ethical reason of the human person. In theological terms, this rational self-explication of the biblical ethos is a process which entails the recognition that the eschatological dynamic of God's love, revealed in Jesus Christ, is the dowry which Jewish-Christian salvation history brings to the development of the ethical consciousness in humankind up to the present day, and likewise the discovery that its future potential is by no means exhausted.

According to such a model, however, the intercultural and interreligious dialogue of the world community cannot be content with the search for a lowest common denominator among the various human traditions, since this would force the individual world religions to regress to a level of ethical consciousness lower than that which their own traditions had already reached.[111] Rather, this encounter must take the form of an open contest about the *humanum,* where the various world religions, political utopias, and secular humanisms challenge each other. This would give the Christian churches the opportunity to bear witness to the inherent rationality of the high ethical teachings contained in the biblical history of revelation, without thereby claiming an exclusive monopoly on the interpretation of absolutely all ethical demands—since such a claim would deny any autonomous access to ethical truth on the part of non-Christians. The truth which is discovered and lived (doubtless in a fragmentary and imperfect manner) within the faith community of the church does not seek to replace the paths of ethical experience in the other world religions; it wishes to lead these to grasp the highest possibilities which they possess and to set them free to realize their own inherent fullness. This is why Christian truth need not disqualify those aspects of successful human existence which have been further developed or better preserved in other cultural spheres than in the Western civilization which bears the imprint of the Gospel message. On the contrary, the model of a common contest and of a vicarious existence on behalf of others suggests that we should be able to learn from the ethical traditions of the other peoples. Their testimony reminds the church that she is the eschatological community of salvation to which God has entrusted the revelation of his love, and that she is always *in via* towards full knowledge of the truth.

If the endeavors of the world religions and human cultures to attain ethical agreement are to go beyond a superficial consensus diplomacy, they must take the form of a contest about a deeper and more appropriate knowledge of ethical truth itself. An interreligious dialogue which was guided only by accepted procedures for reaching agreements, but which did not recognize any substantial criterion of truth, could be carried on honestly only if the participants had already abandoned their own convictions about the truth, or had (so to speak) bracketed these off for themselves before beginning the conversation—something that would contradict the idea of religious tolerance. In an intercultural dialogue conducted

---

111. On the structural dilemma to which a transposition of the model of parliamentary consensus to the dialogue among the world religions leads, cf. E. Schockenhoff, "Brauchen wir ein neues Weltethos? Universale Ethik in einer geschichtlichen Welt," *ThPh* 70 (1995), pp. 224–44, esp. 239f.

in sincere mutual respect and in the spirit of genuine tolerance, the awareness of one's own contingency and finitude is linked with the hope that one may encounter a new aspect of the truth in the mirror held up by the other positions, so that both sides may make progress in their knowledge of the truth, each along its own path.

This is why the Jewish-Christian contribution to an ethical dialogue which embraces all humankind may not restrict itself to the minimal standards of some declaration about the "world ethos"; the obligatory character of such statements falls short of the treaties which already guarantee human rights in international law, and they provide less orientation than the traditions proper to the various religions. Rather, the Jewish-Christian contribution will present the highest demands of biblical ethics in the contest about the *humanum,* backed by arguments which show why it is precisely the high ethical instructions about non-violence or love of enemies that offer the right answer to the deep-seated dangers and fears which beset humankind on its path into the future. The demands that one refrain from revenge, that one should be unreservedly willing to seek reconciliation, and that one should love one's enemies, undoubtedly go against the grain of practical everyday human understanding, and those who live in a world with a common-sense ethos based on pure reciprocity will find these teachings implausible. The hyperbolic demands made by Jesus do not simply lie at the upper end of some universal understanding of humanity which contains a full picture of the possibilities of our "natural" human existence. There exists a rationality of love which transcends these more obvious possibilities, and it takes time for this rationality of love to discover its own individual potential for action; a fortiori, a lengthy process is needed before the historical-political and legal-institutional structures entailed by an ethos of universal love of neighbor can be discerned and put into practice.

In our own European cultural sphere, many centuries of historical experience were required before the idea of non-violence in human relationships led to institutionally regulated forms for the resolution of conflicts between states and to a stable societal peace under the rule of law. When we consider the conflicts between national interests on the global scale, we see that human beings are only beginning to recognize that there is no long-term alternative to a strategy of "intelligent love of one's enemies,"[112] even if the peace that has been achieved is continually threatened by out-

112. On this, cf. C. F. von Weizsäcker, "Intelligente Feindesliebe," *Reformatio* 29 (1980), pp. 413–18.

breaks of violence and hatred. In the intimate personal sphere, the requirement that we love our enemies finds an echo in the reason of every human person as soon as he begins to grasp that the double end of this precept— that we overcome the impulse to vengeance in our own heart and cease to regard an opponent as an "enemy"—is the only viable path to the definitive overcoming of interpersonal enmity.[113]

In the same way, the requirement of forgiveness, originally proposed by Jesus in a religious context (i.e., the revelation of God's unconditional love for every human person), can be seen to be reasonable in human terms. Indeed, the Jewish philosopher Hanna Arendt has called the ability to forgive an "action equal in rank to the original praxis" which needed forgiveness: in other words, it gives us an outstanding opportunity to act in a truly human way. In forgiveness granted without cost—corresponding to the logic of God's love, which he bestows unconditionally—the philosopher discerns the supreme instance of creaturely freedom. Although forgiveness is a response to another person's unjust conduct, it is an unforeseeable and autonomous reaction which can free both the one who forgives and the one who is forgiven from the consequences of this injustice.[114] Like the exhortations to renounce violence and to love one's enemies, the demand for unlimited forgiveness belongs to the outstanding statements of the high biblical ethos. These contain a fullness of meaning epistemologically inaccessible to the ethical reason on its own, a meaning which points beyond the original context in which these precepts were formulated.

113. On this, cf. P. Lapide, *Die Bergpredigt. Utopie oder Programm,* Mainz 1982, pp. 99–108.

114. On this, cf. H. Arendt, *Vita activa oder vom tätigen Leben,* Munich and Zurich 3rd edn. 1981, pp. 234–37.

✣ VI. *The meaning of the distinction between law and morality*

WE SHALL NOW review the discussion and argumentation in this book and summarize the most important fruits of our reflections on the potential usefulness of the concepts of "natural law" and "human dignity" in a systematic ethics. We have defined a basic core of natural-law thinking which is impervious to the classical objections by critics of the natural law. Although this critique was often very acute, indeed apparently devastating, it nevertheless did not succeed in eliminating the real questions in fundamental ethics and legal philosophy which are designated in our philosophical and theological tradition by the two concepts of "natural law" and "human dignity." On the contrary, these questions have continued to be posed, in a different terminology, by thinkers who consciously saw themselves as champions of the natural law under changed intellectual conditions. In philosophy and jurisprudence, "natural law" was now called historical law, the right to existence, or a personal and rational law; in this way, even when the term "natural law" was avoided because it suggested misleading associations, the matter itself remained on the agenda.[1]

The two most important new approaches in contemporary Catholic moral theology, autonomous morality and teleological ethics, cannot disguise their provenance in natural law. They share the goal of taking up anew, in the context of the modern consciousness of freedom and scientific-technological rationality, intellectual motifs which once belonged to natural-law thinking. I have endeavored to emphasize this continuity in the discussions in this book, even if I do not wish to deny my critical distance vis-à-vis the unilateral claim to justification and the reductionist problems posed by a teleological ethical conception.

The aim of my analyses is not, however, limited to a debate among the-

---

1. On this, cf. E. Wolf, *Das Problem der Naturrechtslehre. Versuch einer Orientierung,* Karlsruhe 1955, pp. 101–5; H. D. Schelauske, *Naturrechtsdiskussion in Deutschland,* Cologne 1968; K. Kühl, "Naturrecht V. Neuere Diskussion," *HWPh* VI, cols. 609–23.

ologians. I have not sought to give an account of earlier debates within Catholic moral theology,[2] nor to draw up a balance-sheet of the guilt incurred by the fearful attacks by the church's magisterium or by the lack of loyalty by moral theologians in the past and the present. My intention has been to engage in a dialogue with historical thinking and with the most important moral-philosophical tendencies of the twentieth century, in order to demonstrate the truth of a claim which has never been the object of dispute between moral theology and the magisterium, that is, that our moral judgments are capable of expressing the truth in a universally valid manner. The bitter controversy about whether unconditionally-formulated norms (especially the negative prohibitions of the natural law) possess a validity which allows no exceptions, or whether the practical judgmental capacity or *epikeia* is always required in order to apply these norms to concrete instances, should not blind us to the fact that such a question can be posed *only* on the basis of a cognitive conception of morality that elaborates individual norms backed up by substantial argumentation, and that claims unconditional validity for these norms. This presupposition is the common foundation of all the tendencies in Catholic moral theology. Paradoxically, this is often overlooked precisely by those critics within the church who claim that only their own moral theory is valid.

1. The difference in degree between natural law and human dignity

This foundation, which remains valid, was anchored in the past in the idea of natural law, but it is, of course, another question whether one should continue to employ the concept of "natural law" here. The continuity of natural-law thinking in European and non-European intellectual history, as well as the fact that these terms are used with much less hesitation outside the German linguistic sphere, certainly suggest that we should do so. It is possible to avoid undesirable linguistic associations—the naturalistic fallacy in argumentation or concealed circular arguments—if one understands the concept of that which is always and everywhere constant in our human existence, in the way set out in this book. All the basic concepts employed in the language of moral reflection are open to misunder-

2. On this, cf. esp. W. Nethöfel, *Moraltheologie nach dem Konzil. Personen, Programme, Positionen,* Göttingen 1987; E. Gillen, *Wie Christen ethisch handeln und denken. Zur Debatte um die Autonomie der Sittlichkeit im Kontext katholischer Theologie,* Würzburg 1989.

standings; this risk is not greater with "natural law" and "human dignity" than with the modern key-word "autonomy" or the concept of a teleological evaluation of consequences, which is borrowed from a technical, scientific model of rationality. In terms of substance, "natural law" recalls more strongly than other concepts the nature of the human person as a unity of body and soul and his creaturely milieu, which are the indispensable preconditions underlying the ethical self-realization of the person and his commission to lead an existence in accordance with reason. The idea of natural law entails that human life can never succeed if it disregards the natural parameters laid down in advance, and that these parameters must be employed in a rational manner by the human person who bears responsibility for his own praxis. Precisely the mutual convergence of these two guiding concepts, "natural law" and "human dignity," which accords with their close connection in Thomas' theory of the *lex naturalis,* is able to capture the tension between already-established parameters and the task which is given, between nature and person, between creaturely limitation and the open potential of ethical freedom—and every ethical theory must reflect on these questions.

The dialectical relationship beween these two poles determines the conditions under which a natural-law ethics can arrive at norms based on a substantial argumentation. This ethics must have recourse to the fundamental elements of an anthropological theory of goods. When we bear in mind the history of scientific development, we see that such a theory can be proposed today only on an experiential basis, related to history and in close contact with the empirical human sciences. If a natural-law ethics gives a critical account of the mutual correspondences that link anthropology and ethics and uncovers the anthropological presuppositions of these connections, it will be able to establish substantial norms in the light of its own universal moral principles without succumbing to a naturalistic fallacy or insisting on the opposite standpoint, viz. an ahistorical formalism. The history of philosophical and theological doctrines of the natural law teaches us in no uncertain terms how precarious the equilibrium between nature and person remains. Many examples show how this dialectical relationship is dissolved in favor of one side or the other; we find only a few models which succeed in maintaining the correct balance. One of these is Thomas' theory of the *lex naturalis* with its complementary inclusive relationship between the practical reason and natural endeavor; the present outline of a theological-ethical doctrine of natural law is situated on the trajectory from Thomas' thinking.

An ethical theory which takes its starting point in the fundamental capacity of the practical reason to discern the truth, and which claims universal validity for its affirmations, must remain aware of its own strengths and limitations. Its strength is that its results can be proposed without distinction to all individuals, peoples, and cultures, since they do not go beyond the initial conditions for human existence, and guarantee only the absolute protective sphere within which a life worthy of the human person can develop.[3] However, this universal applicability of its conclusions also reveals the limits of an ethical conception which argues in terms of the natural law. To speak of the natural rights of every human person is to presuppose only a modest anthropology which has nothing definitive to say about the comprehensive ends in life which allow our human existence as a whole to succeed and which help us to realize our fullest potential. Thus, natural-law affirmations remain in a "preliminary sphere" which points beyond itself to that "fullness of the basis of life" to which the biblical revelation bears witness.[4] This is why the natural law is the indispensable basis of an international human-rights politics, although it does not supplant the constructions of meaning offered by the world religions and the high ethical traditions of humanity. It would be a fatal misunderstanding, if one were to extend the validity of the natural law to embrace an integral ethos which comprehended every sphere of life and showed the path to an authentic realization of human existence. The result would not be a strengthening of the foundations of natural-law argumentation, but rather their demolition.

However, the anthropology of human rights points beyond itself to an idea of human dignity which it cannot completely formulate or comprehensively interpret. The insights of natural law are not simply unrelated to the anthropological constructions of meaning that offer us an image of

3. On the difficulties involved in the political realization of the idea of human rights, cf. L. Kühnhardt, *Die Universalität der Menschenrechte. Studie zur ideengeschichtlichen Bestimmung eines politischen Schlüsselbegriffs*, Munich 1987, pp. 294–303; T. Hoppe, "Menschenrechte als Basis eines Weltethos?," in: M. Heimbach-Steins (ed.), *Brennpunkt Sozialethik. Theorien, Aufgaben, Methoden* (Festschrift for F. Furger), Freiburg et al. 1995, pp. 319–33. One may question—at least in the case of Confucianism—whether the political ethics of Far Eastern political philosophies are acquainted only with objective obligations of the ruler vis-à-vis the common good, not with obligations vis-à-vis the individual subjects of his kingdom (cf. ibid., p. 325). On this, cf. T. A. Metzger, *Escape from Predicament: Neo-Confucianism and China's Evolving Political Culture*, New York 1977; W. T. de Bary, "Neo-Confuzionism and Human Rights," in: L. S. Ronner (ed.), *Human Rights and the World's Religions*, Indiana 1988, pp. 183–98, esp. 188f.; H. Roetz, *Die chinesische Ethik der Achsenzeit*, Frankfurt 1992, pp. 195–228.

4. K. Demmer, "Naturrecht und Offenbarung," in: M. Heimbach-Steins (ed.), *Brennpunkt Sozialethik*, pp. 29–44, at 30.

successful human existence; rather, these insights are inherently open to more substantial anthropologies. When (as in the Jewish-Christian tradition) such holistic interpretations of life and the high ethical directives which acquire plausibility against the background of these interpretations, intend a universal validity, this lies on a different level than the universal validity which is postulated of natural-law principles or the general acknowledgement of human rights. This second level, which has often found an echo in moral-theological tradition in the idea of a christological natural law, has been described in the present book, with the help of a category drawn from the biblical understanding of faith, as "vicarious representation." In other words, the commandments of the "perfect" righteousness which expound God's unabbreviated will in Jesus' Sermon on the Mount and show what the human person can be in the eyes of his Creator, are meant to be lived by God's people, as the representative of all peoples, in the hope that this testimony will create a resonance in the ethical reason of humankind. The encounter with revelation not only confirms the ethical reason in the level of insight which it has already reached; it also opens a new perspective for subsequent ethical reflection, and this can lead to a deeper penetration of moral truth.[5]

Although the insights of the natural law must be accessible to the practical reason, they are not merely neutral "forecourts" to the high ethos which has been elaborated in response to the demand made by revelation. Rather, they stand a priori in the sphere which is determined by the historical fact of revelation. Even a secular or humanist ethics remains affected by the questions generated by the intellectual encounter with this fact. This means that, on the first level of natural-law insight, the recourse to the natural initial conditions for human existence must be seen in theological terms as a methodological abstraction which prescinds from the concrete historical situation of the natural law. This intellectual abstraction is, however, essential, if we are to discern the constant element in our human existence which is present always and everywhere, as well as the logical reason for the validity (independent of revelation) of the practical truth.

The limitation of the natural law to the original demand that human existence be respected—a claim which covers every human being, simply because he or she belongs to the species—has also consequences for the exercise of the church's magisterium, whose genuine competence primarily concerns the preservation, exposition, and transmission of the truth of the faith and of the presuppositions necessary to protect this truth (cf. *Lumen*

5. Cf. Ibid., p. 41.

gentium 25). At the same time, however, the Catholic church has become the advocate of human-rights demands in the world arena to a greater degree than any other religious group. She justifies this commission by arguing that she lives among the peoples as the sacrament of unity, sent to all human beings with the comprehensive salvific mission of proclaiming the word of God. The truth of the Gospel also includes the natural rights of the human person and those requirements of the ethical law which everyone can recognize in the light of the natural reason. This is the key affirmation in the encyclical *Veritatis splendor:* "Inasmuch as the natural law expresses the dignity of the human person and lays the foundation for his rights and duties, it is universal in its precepts and its authority extends to all mankind" (par. 51).[6] The reflections in this book are meant as a contribution to the correct understanding of this statement.

The debate with ethical relativism and with the basic positions of historical thinking has confirmed the universal validity of natural-law requirements and the universal claim made by human rights. Since it is possible from every standpoint to recognize the dignity of the human person (at least as far as the initial conditions for his ethical self-determination are concerned), the rights and obligations inferred from this dignity can be demanded of all persons. When the church demands that every state in the world, regardless of the religious and cultural traditions to which it might appeal, must respect the rights of the human person, this refers to the core of preconditions for existence and existential possibilities which are inseparable from human existence as such. This is why the group of indispensable human rights is limited to the sphere that must be considered the absolute presupposition for a life in freedom and human dignity, where the person bears responsibility for his own existence. In principle, this applies to all the rights to participation in society and the so-called third-generation human rights just as much as to the original rights of the individual to self-defense, since the former category too protects the natural living sphere within which each person must exercise ethical self-determination in structuring his own existence.[7]

6. On the understanding of human rights in the church, against the background of Catholic social doctrine, cf. J. Punt, *Die Idee der Menschenrechte. Ihre geschichtliche Entwicklung und ihre Rezeption durch die moderne katholische Sozialverkündigung,* Paderborn et al. 1987, pp. 175–221; G. Putz, *Christentum und Menschenrechte,* Innsbruck and Vienna 1991, pp. 121–233; K. Hilpert, *Die Menschenrechte. Geschichte—Theologie—Aktualität,* Düsseldorf 1991, pp. 138–73; F. Hafner, *Kirchen im Kontext der Grund- und Menschenrechte,* Freiburg 1992, pp. 128–48.

7. On the position of the third-generation rights in the tension between law and

It follows that human rights and the idea of the natural law formulate no more than a minimal claim, in the sense described above, which applies to every human being by virtue of his humanity, whether or not he is aware of these rights and is in a position to demand that the political order in his native land respect them. Where the church speaks out against torture and rape, discrimination and persecution, the death penalty, abortion and enforced sterilization, or defends fundamental rights of the family against state interventions, she is demanding respect for the natural rights which every human person *per se* possesses. She is not asking the state to accord some special protection to her own moral views, but only to observe those principles of righteousness which the practical reason recognizes with certainty and which no one can dispute without entangling himself in contradictions. This means that the church's action when she demands the universal observance of human rights is perfectly compatible with the distinction between law and morality and with respect for the cultural identity of the various peoples, states, and nations.

2. The differentiation between law and morality

Natural-law thinking has often been accused of reluctance to accept the necessary separation between law and morality and of a failure to see the relevance to legal theory of the tension between that which ought to be and that which is. This accusation of an impermissible confusion between law and morality refers to the double nature proper to the natural law, the conceptual polyvalency which we have seen earlier in this book. The concept of that which is "naturally" right can, however, function as a bridge between both positions: this is the thesis which we shall now elaborate in debate with other positions in legal philosophy. This is because the idea of natural rights of the human person, the basis both of the classical natural law and (in another manner) of Kant's rational law, makes it possible to justify laws by employing a supra-positive criterion of normative principles of justice to evaluate existing law without needing to postulate a complete congruence between the basis in moral values and the positive legal ordering.

---

morality, cf. D. Witschen, "Menschenrechte der dritten Generation und internationales Ethos," *ZkTh* 117 (1995), pp. 129–51.

2.1. The dilemma of legal positivism

The objection that natural-law thinking tends to water down the differentiation between law and morality is, of course, not completely wrong; it is quite correct to observe that an ethical or legal-philosophical theory based on natural law cannot accept a strict separation between these two spheres. This, however, is not because the natural law is in principle unable to cope with the complexity of modern societies; rather, there are good objective reasons at work here. We may note that it is also possible to give a wrong account of the distinction between law and morality if one neglects their common foundations and the intersection in their contents which binds them together, irrespective of all the differentiation which is necessary in modern societies. Such a separation was urged in the twentieth century above all by legal positivism, the classical antagonist of the natural law, and by a theory of systems which saw law and morality as two mutually independent spheres, each with its own sociological norms. At the root of these dissociative models lies the idea of legal positivism, which affirms that the obligatory character of law (unlike the claim to validity proposed by ethical norms) is not deduced from its agreement with moral principles and natural rights, but from a pure act of positive promulgation: according to functional theories of law, the laws which are in force are based on the will of the legislator and on the readiness of the community under law to submit to this will. Accordingly, promulgation in keeping with the proper norms and the societal reality are the only presuppositions of the concept of law, formally speaking; in material terms, any contents whatever can be "law."

The basis of legal validity here is no longer the acknowledgment of a supra-positive criterion of human dignity or natural law, but only the constitution of the specific state-community. A law is legitimated within the system by the principle of conformity to the constitution, which in turn (in order that this appeal may not lead to an infinite regression) must be anchored in the acknowledgment of a so-called "fundamental norm." This, however, is no longer conceived as an objective claim antecedent to every civil legal order—like the claims made by the idea of human dignity or of the human person's inalienable rights. Rather, the "fundamental norm" functions as a merely imaginary concept in theoretical reflection and is completely devoid of contents. It serves to explain the necessary presupposition which allows one to claim that the legal prescriptions which then are formulated have a normative, binding character. Hence, the "fun-

damental norm" means only that every citizen is to behave in keeping with
the prescriptions of the constitution.[8] Its transcendental-logical status is
the explicit contradiction of the attempt to base existing law on the criterion of that which is "naturally" just. This, however, does not mean that legal positivism, as a system of *legal* philosophy, can dispense altogether with
any particular *moral* philosophical theory. It usually accepts the basic suppositions of ethical relativism and refuses to admit moral elements into the
concept of law, since it fears that ultimately every judge could pass sentence in accordance with his own arbitrary private morality, if one were to
accept the presuppositions of a non-positivistic justification of law which
acknowledged normative criteria for the discernment of "correct" law.[9]

In the eyes of its proponents, the greatest advantage of a positivistic justification of law is that, whereas all natural-law intellectual models maintain the tension between ideal and reality, between moral claim and societal reality, the positivistic line dissolves this tension by giving basic
precedence to *legal security.* A natural or rational law supports the legal-
philosophical principle that legal norms are distinguished from moral prescriptions primarily by the *vis coactiva,* the "authority to coerce." The positivistic justification of law sees this as a constitutive difference.[10] Despite
all the imperfection and fragmentariness of the law, its enforceability gives
it a strength of its own, which no other ordering can replace. Only an ordering which can be enforced, and thus possesses "the power to shape reality," deserves the name of law.[11] Legal positivism fears that if there existed
criteria of a higher, "correct law" based in the natural law, against which
one could test existing law, then this would lead in situations of conflict to
uncertainty about whether the written law or the higher law should apply.
This is why priority is given in principle to legal certainty rather than to
the realization of substantial justice; in cases of extreme injustice, however,
some proponents of this priority would reverse their choice.[12]

8. Cf. H. Kelsen, *Reine Rechtslehre,* Vienna 2nd edn. 1960, pp. 197–204. On the legal-
philosophical debate about this position, cf. R. Alexy, *Begriff und Geltung des Rechts,*
Freiburg and Munich 2nd edn. 1994, pp. 154–97.

9. Cf. G. Radbruch, *Rechtsphilosophie,* Stuttgart 3rd edn. 1973, p. 175; N. Hoerster, "Zur
Verteidigung des Rechtspositivismus," *NJW* 39 (1986), pp. 2480–82.

10. Cf. Thomas Aquinas, *STh* I–II, q. 96, aa. 2–3, ad 5; I. Kant, *Die Metaphysik der Sitten,* A35 (Werkausgabe, ed. W. Weischedel, VIII, p. 338).

11. H. Welzel, *Naturrecht und materiale Gerechtigkeit,* Göttingen 1951, p. 163. Cf. also
Idem, "Naturrecht und Rechtspositivismus," in: W. Maihofer (ed.), *Naturrecht oder Rechtspositivismus?,* Darmstadt 1962, pp. 322–38, esp. 333.

12. This is the meaning of Radbruch's celebrated formula. In the wake of his experiences
under the Nazi terror regime, the most famous representative of German legal positivism

Positivistic-functional thinking emphasizes another characteristic of the law too: legal sanctions are not naturally immanent consequences of a crime or transgression, but are determined by the legislator, who decides what is appropriate and what kind of law is politically feasible. They are not simply the natural consequences of an action, but are reactions prescribed by the community under law. One can expect these reactions, as long as it is de facto possible to enforce the legal consequences that are threatened. When this is no longer the case, the argument about the power of law to shape reality can give way to the opposite consideration, so that the law legitimately bows to a changed societal reality. In order to maintain a just social ordering, it may be necessary to suspend the enforceability of legal demands for a time, or even to cancel them permanently. This argument reverses the original negative position taken vis-à-vis the natural law; in such conflicts, theories of law based on the natural law often maintain the normative validity of the law with greater decisiveness, though such reflections say nothing *per se* about the possibilities of enforcing a law in the reality of a specific society.

The strengths of legal positivism make it seem irrefutable, but its weaknesses are just as obvious—above all, its inability to give a satisfactory answer to the questions which erupt whenever the gulf between the legal order and the moral order grows too wide. Its own approach does not allow legal positivism even to pose such questions, since they can only undermine the claim of existing law. Critics of the classical positivistic theory of law have confronted it above all with problems like the right to political resistance, the binding character of obviously immoral legal prescriptions, or the possibility for judges to develop jurisprudence in their sentencing. In today's societal debates, the dilemma of legal positivism can be seen most clearly when long-term shifts in the moral consciousness of society turn groups that demand the continued observance of a basic consensus about the legal order into a minority, or when general legal awareness fails to keep pace with the development of ecological consciousness or with the sensitivity to ethical issues about peace on the part of groups of citizens. The acknowledgment of the principle of legality may indeed be essential, if a democratic legal culture is to be preserved; but the appeal to this prin-

---

was no longer willing to maintain the absolute validity of the principle of legal certainty, and he wrote: "One should resolve the conflict between justice and legal certainty by giving the priority to the positive law which is guaranteed by promulgation and power, unless the contradiction between the positive law and justice becomes so intolerable that the law, as an 'incorrect law', must yield to justice" (Idem, *Rechtsphilosophie,* p. 345).

ciple is no longer sufficient on its own to suppress questions about the legitimacy of the legal order as a whole. Such situations of conflict display the dilemma of legal positivism with acute clarity. On the one hand, the law cannot protect itself against the eruption of such questions about its legitimacy by the mere decision to maintain its formal validity; but on the other hand, since a positivistic-functionalist understanding allows it only to lay down the rules that are valid within its own ordering, it can contribute nothing to ensure the foundations of societal consensus and the ethical basis which provides the legitimation for the entire system of rules.

This consideration points to a further dilemma of the positivistic approach: legal positivism can accept diametrically opposite political structures, depending on whether it is united to a strong or a weak understanding of the state. In a totalitarian state, it risks being misused by a dictatorial elite to legitimate its rule, since it facilitates the identification of the executive and the judicial powers, depriving the political opposition a priori of any legal basis. Where the legal-philosophical theory of positivism is linked to the conception of a libertarian state, as in most Western democracies, it succumbs to pressure to provide legitimation in the opposite direction. Since it cannot survive in the long term if it disregards the ethical convictions of the majority of citizens, it is confronted by the expectation that it will create the legal expression for each change in societal attitudes. In many cases this may seem unproblematic, or indeed the expression of a more humane relationship between the citizens and their state, something that contributes to the preservation of legal peace; an example is the liberalization of sexual penal laws. In other cases, however, especially when basic elementary rights such as that to life and bodily integrity are affected, a retreat on the part of the legal order can make a consensus on the part of the community under law even more difficult. And if the heedless infringement of basic rights became a widely accepted societal phenomenon, or the numerical majority claimed the right to disregard the rights of others without suffering any consequences from their own actions, legal positivism would ultimately be obliged to accept this, since it has no possibility of effectively expressing the disapproval of the legal order vis-à-vis such a development. Even to speak of an "ethical minimum" underlying the law is foreign to this theory, since it can no longer understand the basic norm of obedience to the state constitution in the sense of a supra-positive claim on the part of justice.

2.2. The objective justification of the value of the law

At this point, natural-law thinking resembles the legal-ethical foundations which underlie democratic states. Democracy's precedence over all other forms of political governance is not based only on the majority principle or the basic principle of conformity to the constitution, but also on the acknowledgment of those human rights which exist antecedently to action by the state and the mutual dealings of individuals. Accordingly, when the constitution obliges a democratic legal state to observe neutrality in terms of its worldview, this must not be practiced as an equidistance vis-à-vis all the moral convictions which are de facto followed in society. Since it is the guarantor of the free democratic legal order, the state cannot simply understand itself as value-neutral.[13] If the variety of opinions held in society means that a state under the rule of law no longer protects any sphere of the law whatever from challenge by changing majorities, it imperils the basis of its own legitimation—and without this basis, it cannot continue to exist in the long term. If we consider the political-ethical foundations of the legitimacy of the modern state, we can indeed assert that systems of norms (whether hypothetical or actually existing) which fail to fulfill basic criteria of justice no longer correspond to the concept of legal order.[14] The political-ethical advantage of a state under the rule of law vis-à-vis all other forms of state is hence bound de facto to the "values" which it embodies and protects. The encyclical *Evangelium vitae* (par. 70–71) gives the following examples: the dignity of the human person, the inalienable rights of the person, solidarity among individuals, and the common good. When the various groups in society pursue their own interests, they must orientate their activities to these values.

Many legal scholars in Germany after the Second World War were attracted to the idea that the law had an objective basis in values, since this seemed to offer the possibility of overcoming legal positivism without needing to have recourse to the idea of a law "deriving from nature." They too, however, objected strongly to the thesis that law must be understood as an ordering of values that finds its substantial basis in the moral and so-

---

13. On the distinction between neutrality in terms of worldview and neutrality in terms of values in the democratic legal state, cf. G. Brunner, *Grundwerte als Fundament der pluralistischen Gesellschaft. Eine Untersuchung der Positionen von Kirchen, Parteien und Gewerkschaften in der Bundesrepublik Deutschland,* Freiburg 1989, pp. 176–85; and M. Gante, *218 in der Diskussion. Meinungs- und Willensbildung 1945–1976,* Düsseldorf 1991, pp. 202–22.

14. On this, cf. O. Höffe, *Politische Gerechtigkeit,* Frankfurt 1978, pp. 159, 170.

cial values that it realizes, since this idea entails all the difficulties involved in a philosophical definition of the concept of "value," which are scarcely smaller than the problems of basing law in the natural law. Viewed from the standpoint of today's discussion, the expectation that an ethics of substantial values would provide a surer foundation for legal validity must seem wholly illusory.

In the context of legal philosophy, the practical impossibility of achieving an intersubjectively binding consensus about the significance, the decisive character, and the hierarchy of the individual values presents an even greater difficulty than the unclarified theoretical questions about what legal validity is and how it may be recognized. The distinction between the fundamental quality of a value and its dignity can be employed to show why one of the primary tasks of the legal order in a state is to enforce the prohibition of killing and to give life the greatest possible protection.[15] This, however, does not amount to a complete preferential system which would allow us to determine the relationships between the values of that which is useful (basic economic and material needs), that which is true (science and education), that which is beautiful (art, leisure and play), and that which is holy (religion) in the legal system as a whole. The idea of a gradated hierarchy of values can help us in the ethical order to pursue our ends in life in accordance with the rank that each of these values possesses, but this does not solve the problem of the relationship within a general legal order between the ends of freedom and equality, education and health —or, to take a more concrete example, between the duty of the public media to provide information and the right of the individual person to protection of his privacy. Hence, the attempt to justify law in terms of objective values does not genuinely free us from the dilemma of legal positivism, since it too must appeal to the subjective views about value which de facto exist in society; it does not possess any legally binding criterion with which it might undertake a normative evaluation of these views. If one seeks to provide a philosophical basis for law, it is a serious disadvantage that the phenomenological ethics of value—unlike the natural law— was initially elaborated as a purely ethical theory to provide orientation for our ethical conduct.[16]

15. On this, cf. E. Schockenhoff, *Ethik des Lebens. Ein theologischer Grundriß*, Mainz 1993, pp. 194f.
16. On the debate with the legal theory drawn from a philosophy of value, cf. G. Luf, "Zur Problematik des Wertbegriffs in der Rechtsphilosophie," in: H. Miehsler et al. (eds.), *Jus Humanitatis* (Festschrift for A. Verdross), Berlin 1980, pp. 127–46, esp. 141f.; and above

The view that the legal order is as an order of values—evaluating the democratic state under the rule of law exclusively on the basis of the moral values which it realizes or fails to realize—overlooks another aspect which is decisive for the self-understanding of modern states, that is, that even when the political-ethical legitimation of a free state under the rule of law is understood on the basis of a supra-positive basis and measure of law, this legitimation cannot be sought *only* in the external realization of normative ideas about justice. On the contrary, legal ethics also attributes high significance to the *internal* principles of legality, for example, the universal validity of positive laws, the obligation to act publicly, or the prohibition of enacting laws with retrospective validity; usually, this significance can be grasped *e contrario,* in the mirror held up by the experience of injustice suffered at the hands of an arbitrary coercive government. This means that a legal order does not lose its legality simply because some of its legal regulations contradict moral commandments or no longer adequately fulfill the requirements of such commandments. This is the case only when the contradiction or lack of agreement with the moral order affects central areas of life in society and crosses a threshold which calls into question the moral legitimation of the entire legal system.[17]

Pope John Paul II clearly believes that the Western democracies are exposed to such a danger, as we see from the passages in his encyclical *Evangelium vitae* mentioned above. He argues that these democracies must act more effectively against surreptitious tendencies to disregard basic human rights, especially the elementary claim of the human person to life and physical integrity from the beginning of earthly existence to its close. His own biography gave John Paul II a special sensitivity to the appalling experiences of the twentieth century, and (unlike most of his superficial critics) he has not forgotten these. This means that one can scarcely question the seriousness of his inexorable diagnosis of our age. At the same time, however, even if one shares the Pope's concern, one may regret the gloomy tone which runs through his analysis and the one-sidedness of his argumentation. It is, after all, one fruit of the experiences of injustice in the twentieth century that Christians have a positive attitude to the secular state under the rule of law, since this guarantees freedom, even if not every manifestation of societal reality lives up to the claim which the state itself makes.

all, E.-W. Böckenförde, "Zur Kritik der Wertbegründung des Rechts," in: Idem, *Recht, Staat, Freiheit. Studien zur Rechtsphilosophie, Staatstheorie und Verfassungsgeschichte,* Frankfurt 1991, pp. 67–91.

17. Cf. R. Alexy, *Begriff und Geltung des Rechts,* p. 84.

The encyclical goes on at great length about the moral foundations of the democratic state under the rule of law; the reader who grew up in such a state would have been happy to see a positive word about the genuine value of an independent legal order and a free democratic legal culture. This would have been a good complement to the papal doctrinal statements about political ethics to which the encyclical itself refers (cf. par. 70).

2.3. *The natural rights of the human person as basis of the legal order*

Neither the radical thesis of a separation, on which legal positivism is based, nor the thesis of a close link, proposed by the program of an objective justification of the legal order in terms of values, leads to an appropriate understanding of the differentiation between law and morality. The concept of natural rights of the human person and the idea of that which is "naturally" right seem to offer an alternative which deserves serious consideration. At the very least, one must examine in such situations whether natural law—so often proclaimed dead—has in fact proved useless, or whether it can make a contribution to the philosophical justification of law which no competing theory can offer. When all the players have made their bids, the cards are mixed anew and the play can start again, with an open outcome. Naturally, the weaknesses of legal positivism, which have come to light in periods of harsh conflicts about societal values, and the impossibility of deriving the validity of the law from a presupposed order of values are not sufficient in themselves to restore the natural law to its old place; this card too must demonstrate its own strength. The failure of other attempts to supply a philosophical justification of the law does not automatically tell us what the idea of that which is "naturally" right can contribute here. When the problem is posed in different terms, this idea must prove its own potential by indicating how we can grasp the essence and the character of the law in its specific relationship to morality.

If a definition of the essence of law is to explain what its distinction from the moral order means, it cannot simply take an intermediate position between legal positivism and a theory of objective values. Since natural-law thinking anchors the validity of the legal order in the highest principles of the practical reason, thereby tracing the concept of law back to the origin which it shares with the moral order, it is closer to the justification in terms of values than to a purely functional explanation. This allows us to see the natural-law interpretation of the validity of law as a form of the linkage thesis, centered on the conception of natural rights rather than on the category of value. It is impossible to ascertain the substantial contents of this concept independently of the specific historical, cultural, and societal conditions which make rational knowledge possible; but we can say that it embraces the totality of rights which every human being *qua* person possesses. The legal order is constituted by the intersubjective acknowledgment of these rights. It is not possible to explain the concept of natural rights by presenting an exhaustive compilation or a definitive list of such rights; the logical status of this concept is comparable to a regulative rational idea which must be defined specifically in each historical context. The natural rights which every person *per se* possesses are not in the least identical with the ensemble of all the civil rights one enjoys as a member of a civil society governed by laws; but the acknowledgment and historical validity of these rights, like the development of the legal order as a whole, are specified and elaborated upon in an historical process which goes hand in hand with the historicity of human knowledge as a whole.

This convergence of natural and civil rights can be understood as analogous to the two stages which, as we have shown, determine both the concept of natural law and the idea of human dignity from a theological-ethical perspective. The concept of "natural rights of the human person" is employed by natural-law thinking to reconstruct, in keeping with the available insights of historical-social reason, the minimal conditions which must be fulfilled if the human being is to be considered as a moral subject who bears ethical responsibility for his behavior. Besides this, every legal system contains a further group of rights which every human being de facto possesses but which are not essential components of the concept of his moral responsibility. These civil rights can display a much greater variety from one society to another, since they are accorded to the person, not because each person in fact possesses them, but because they are laid down in the legal order. They are not based on something that is naturally right, but on positive law, and they correspond to the legal articulations implied by the societal function of the legal system in each state.[18]

The chief advantage which this approach to justifying law has over the theory of values is that the concrete discernment of natural rights in the light of the highest principles of justice avoids the unresolved problems posed by the thesis of an intersubjectively obligatory order of values. Compared to legal positivism, the strength of this approach is its development

18. On this, cf. esp. L. L. Weinreb, "Natural Law and Human Rights," in: R. P. George (ed.), *Natural Law Theory. Contemporary Essays,* Oxford 1992, pp. 278–305, esp. 291–97.

of the reflexive justification of law on the basis of the idea that all the members of a community under law accept one another's inalienable rights. The idea of a recourse to "natural" rights which demand mutual recognition corresponds to the transcendental-logical status of a "basic norm," which is intended to avoid an infinite regression to ever higher levels of justification. Basically, however, all this does is to make it impossible to deduce the sphere of positive law from some higher level of validity which would also have a legal nature. When the legal order is constructed on other foundations, which are antecedent to law and morality—in keeping with the idea of mutual acknowledgment on the part of free rational beings—there is no danger of regression into an endless series of justifications. Another advantage is that the sphere of law need not be understood only as a coercive system external to the human person: this approach can also see it as an historical manifestation of the practical reason, similar to that found in the moral convictions and values adopted by individuals.

Philosophically speaking, a decisive weakness of the functional theories of law is their inability to see law as based in the personal nature of the human being and hence as an expression of interpersonal solidarity within a community governed by law. The objection which has often been made to the idea of natural law, that is, that law belongs only to the sphere external to the person, or else to the sphere of external life in society, is incorrect, just as it is wrong to assert that law is based only on a social-psychological mechanism, namely the mutual fear which people would experience if there were no law. One can indeed distinguish law from the sphere of morality, but there is also common ground: the elementary ends in life and basic social goods, which ethics and law each in its own way are meant to realize and protect, are laid down in advance.[19] Since it is possible for the practical reason to recognize these fundamental ends in life and fundamental goods antecedent to the law, and since the reason is able to discover these in keeping with the specific historical-cultural parameters involved in each case, the substantial legitimation of the law is not based only on its social effectiveness or on some kind of promulgation. Rather, since the legal order is orientated to the free personal nature of the human being and his elementary ends in life, the reason is able to discern the foundations of its legitimation. This makes possible a critical examination and an historical development of existing law.

Since the discovery of that which is naturally right is inseparable from

19. On this, cf. A. Kaufmann, *Recht und Sittlichkeit,* Tübingen 1964, p. 26.

the state of knowledge possessed by the practical reason, this can occur only via the path of *historical* testing and convincing argumentation. This insight is centrally important for historical natural-law thinking. The acknowledgment that the practical reason has the public character of a process, and that its knowledge is historically and socially conditioned, distinguishes this position from the deductive natural-law doctrines of the past, which have lost their validity even for those who think in terms of the natural law: even the most decisive defenders of scholastic natural law today explicitly recognize the necessity of developing the natural-law justification of the law in this direction. For example, the Catholic social ethicist Arthur Friedolin Utz defines the basic idea of a non-positivistic legal theory in such a way that it is completely impossible to confuse natural law with a complex of norms comparable to positive law, but with a higher validity:

> The natural law is not a catalogue of legal norms which have been given exhaustive formulation once and for all. It consists in the practical reason, which is of such a character that it recognizes principles in order to realize the ends of existence within each specific society, with all its economic and societal conditions. Natural law grows along with the culture and the concrete societal situation, especially with the consciousness of law on the part of the members of society, but it is not identical with these societal factors. At the same time, it offers the possibility of engaging in a critical debate with existing economic conditions and with the general state of society.[20]

The definition offered by Ernst-Wolfgang Böckenförde, a legal philosopher who is open to natural-law thinking, likewise emphasizes that the natural law cannot be understood as a catalogue of pre-existing legal norms deduced from some constant, essential nature of the human person—a catalogue which would lay down *e supra* what positive legal precepts may or may not state. Rather, he understands the natural law as "a mode of thinking on the part of the practical reason which tends to control existing legitimations of legal praxis by means of the criterion of the fundamental ends in human life and the extent to which these are realized, and which accordingly tends to promote criticism, development or even the legitimation of existing law."[21]

20. A. F. Utz, "Naturrecht als Sammelbegriff nicht-positivistischer Rechtstheorien," *ARSP* (Supplement I: *Zeitgenössische Rechtskonzeptionen,* Teil 4) 70 (1979), p. 13.

21. E.-W. Böckenförde, "Die Begründung des Rechts auf Werte oder auf das von Natur Rechte," in: R. Brinkmann (ed.), *Natur in den Geisteswissenschaften,* I, Tübingen 1988, pp. 181–202, at 200; Idem, "Staatliches Recht und sittliche Ordnung," in: H. Fechtrup et al. (eds.), *Aufklärung durch Tradition* (Festschrift for J. Pieper), Münster 1994, pp. 87–107, esp. 92ff.

If the validity of the legal order remains tied in this way to the criterion of that which is naturally right—a criterion which in turn is orientated substantially to the personal rational nature of the human being and his elementary ends in life—one must naturally ask what meaning such a natural-law justification of law attributes to the coercive character of the law and to internal procedures for positing and developing positive law. The concept of that which is naturally right is capable of demonstrating that a one-sided concentration on the coercive character of the law is the product of a misunderstanding of the difference between law and morality, a differentiation which is constitutive of the concept of "law" itself. Although the enforceability of its demands is the specific difference between law and an ethos or a shared morality which is based on internal sanctions, the legal order as a whole is not based on the threats uttered by the legislator, but on mutual acknowledgment on the part of free rational beings, who thus respect each other's personal dignity and give birth to the law as the sphere of their common freedom.[22] If the law is to fulfill this task, it must be based on more than fear and coercion alone; rather, its validity is based on an "interplay of acknowledgment and coercion."[23] In other words, the mere presence of coercion does not denote the presence of law; but where the law exists, coercion may and must be exercised.[24] For example, without this element of mutual acknowledgment, it would be completely impossible for the concept of law to embrace treaties in international law or the binding solidarity which married partners show one another in their life together. Accordingly, even though the concept of law cannot dispense with the requirement that it be possible to enforce sanctions, the coercive character of the law does not suffice to explain the entire spectrum of manifestations of the law.

When the law is justified in terms of the natural law, this does not mean that the procedures laid down in the legal order to posit and enforce legal prescriptions lose their significance; for it is precisely when the criterion of that which is naturally right is no longer available in the form of a comprehensive complex of norms, but must be discerned afresh under the condi-

22. J. G. Fichte was the first to deduce such a transcendental philosophical justification of law from the idea of the intersubjective constitution of human freedom. The entire legal theory of this philosopher is based on the distinction between law and morality. Cf. Idem, *Grundlage des Naturrechts* 4 (1796), in: J. G. Fichte (ed.), *Fichtes Werke*, III, Berlin 1971, pp. 41–47. On this, cf. H. J. Verweyen, *Recht und Sittlichkeit in J. G. Fichtes Gesellschaftslehre*, Freiburg and Munich 1975, pp. 84–94.

23. G. Otte, "Recht und Moral," *CGG* XXII, cols. 6–36, at 13.

24. Cf. A. Kaufmann, *Recht und Sittlichkeit*, p. 34.

tions of rational agreement, that it becomes decisively important to observe the framework established by positive law, which gives the possibility of debating about what is naturally right. The existence of a positive legal order is a necessary presupposition if that which is naturally right is to be discerned under conditions which remain compatible with the claim it makes. This means that the natural law itself requires the existence of positive law. Even for a non-positivistic theory of law, the essential presuppositions of a peaceful civil order include the guarantee of legal certainty, the maintenance of formal legal procedures, the effective enforcement of the state monopoly on coercive force, and the creation of a final judicial body from which no further appeal is possible. Without these, it is impossible for the law to fulfill its task of ensuring the mutual acknowledgment of free rational beings in their inalienable rights.

Our concern here is with the philosophical foundations of the validity of law. This means that we need not discuss the procedures and necessary legal processes involved in the discernment of that which is naturally right; this belongs to the juridical interpretation of the constitution and the interpretation of laws, a sphere which should be kept as free as possible from the influence of competing theories about the justification of law. However, our attempt at a natural-law justification of the law has still to indicate how it defines the differentiation between law and the moral realm. Accordingly, after this lengthy expedition into the area of legal philosophy, we return to our original moral-theological question. This was the starting point for our reflections on the relationship between natural law and human dignity: since the church's moral teaching declares that the legislation of the secular state must take account of ecclesial affirmations, where these presuppose the natural rights of the human person, the relationship between the moral and legal orders has always been a topic in theological ethics and the various kinds of natural-law argumentation which this has employed.

Let us therefore conclude by recalling once again the real meaning of the distinction between law and morality from the perspective of a theological-ethical theory which is aware that the law too is based on the idea of that which is naturally right. The legal order is founded on the acknowledgment of the human person's inalienable rights and of the duty to interpersonal solidarity within a community under the rule of law. It protects the absolute minimum sphere which a human person needs if he is to develop in his ethical self-determination. It follows that, since the goal of the law is to *make possible* an existence worthy of the human person, it leaves it up to the free responsibility of the individual to *realize* such an existence. All that the legal order can do is to protect the external presuppositions of an existence worthy of the human person, who is to exercise self-determination and take responsibility for his own life—and this applies both to the basic rights guaranteed in individual states and to the human rights recognized in the international community. To determine how individuals employ this freedom, in accordance with their personal goals in life, and whether they do full justice to their own human dignity, is no longer the task of law, but of morality. This is where the individual's conscience must provide orientation, since the responsibility of each person for the success of his own life cannot be delegated to anyone else. On this level of personal ethical responsibility, the church addresses her faithful by means of the proclamation of the Gospel. On the same level, she speaks to all those of "good will" when she seeks to achieve the enforcement of human rights by appealing to those ethical principles which can be recognized by the natural reason. This means that the church's moral teaching cannot desire too close a link between law and morality; this would risk an unthinking equation of legal and moral norms, leading many people (including a great number of Christians) to orientate their conscience, not to ethical truth, but to the minimum standards of their society as these are expressed in its laws.

Bibliography

Alexy, R. *Begriff und Geltung des Rechts.* Freiburg and Munich, 2nd edn., 1994.

Antes, P. "'Ethik' im Islam." In C. H. Ratschow (ed.), *Ethik der Religionen. Ein Handbuch.* Stuttgart 1980.

Antes, P. et al. (eds.). *Der Islam. Religion-Ethik-Politik.* Stuttgart 1991.

Anzenbacher, A. *Einführung in die Ethik.* Düsseldorf 1992.

Apel, K. O. *Diskurs und Verantwortung. Das Problem des Übergangs zur postkonventionellen Moral.* Frankfurt 1988.

Arendt, H. *Vita activa oder vom tätigen Leben.* Munich and Zurich, 3rd edn., 1981.

Arntz, J. T. C. "Die Entwicklung des naturrechtlichen Denkens innerhalb des Thomismus." In F. Böckle (ed.), *Das Naturrecht im Disput,* 87–120. Düsseldorf 1966.

Aubert, J. M. "Pour une herméneutique du droit naturel." *Rech. de Sc. Rel.* 59 (1971): 449–92.

Auer, A. "Die Erfahrung der Geschichtlichkeit und die Krise der Moral." *ThQ* 149 (1969): 4–22.

Bary, W. T. de. "Neo-Confuzionism and Human Rights." In L. S. Ronner (ed.), *Human Rights and the World's Religions,* 183–98. Indiana 1988.

Bauer, G. *Geschichtlichkeit. Wege und Irrwege eines Begriffs.* Berlin 1963.

Baumgartner, H. M. "Gleichheit und Verschiedenheit von Mann und Frau in philosophischer Perspektive." In N. A. Luyten (ed.), *Wesen und Sinn der Geschlechtlichkeit,* 271–300. Freiburg and Munich 1985.

Becker, G. *Neuzeitliche Subjektivität und Religiosität. Die religionsphilosophische Bedeutung von Heraufkunft und Wesen der Neuzeit im Denken von Ernst Troeltsch.* Regensburg 1982.

Belmans, T. G. *Les sens objectifs de l'agir humain: Pour relire la morale conjugale de Saint Thomas.* 1980.

Berner, U. *Die Bergpredigt. Rezeption und Auslegung im 20. Jahrhundert (GTA* 12). Göttingen, 2nd edn., 1983.

Betz, H.-D. "Die hermeneutischen Prinzipien in der Bergpredigt." In E. Jüngel et al., *Verifikationen* (Festschrift for G. Ebeling), 27–41. Tübingen 1982.

Beyschlag, K. "Zur Geschichte der Bergpredigt in der Alten Kirche." *ZThK* 74 (1977): 291–322.

Bianco, F. "Dilthey und das Problem des Relativismus." In E. W. Orth (ed.), *Dilthey und die Philosophie der Gegenwart,* 211–29. Freiburg and Munich 1985.

Birnbacher, D. "Das Tötungsverbot aus der Sicht der klassischen Utilitarismus."

In R. Hegselmann and R. Merkel (eds.), *Zur Debatte über Euthanasie. Beiträge und Stellungnahmen*, 25–50. Frankfurt 1991.

Bloch, E. *Naturrecht und menschliche Würde* (Gesamtausgabe, II). Frankfurt, second edn., 1991.

Böckenförde, E.-W. "Die Begründung des Rechts auf Werte oder auf das von Natur Rechte." In R. Brinkmann (ed.), *Natur in den Geisteswissenschaften*, I, 181–202. Tübingen 1988.

Böckenförde, E.-W. "Kirchliches Naturrecht und politisches Handeln." In F. Böckle and E.-W. Böckenförde (eds.), *Naturrecht in der Kritik*. Mainz 1973.

Böckenförde, E.-W. "Staatliches Recht und sittliche Ordnung." In H. Fechtrup et al. (eds.), *Aufklärung durch Tradition* (Festschrift for J. Pieper), 87–107. Münster 1994.

Böckenförde, E.-W. "Zur Kritik der Wertbegründung des Rechts." In E.-W. Böckenförde, *Recht, Staat, Freiheit. Studien zur Rechtsphilosophie, Staatstheorie und Verfassungsgeschichte*, 67–91. Frankfurt 1991.

Böckle, F. *Fundamentalmoral*. Munich 1977.

Boecker, H. J. *Recht und Gesetz im Alten Testament und im Alten Orient*. Neukirchen-Vluyn, 2nd edn., 1984.

Bollnow, O. F. *Dilthey. Eine Einführung in seine Philosophie*. Stuttgart, 2nd edn., 1955.

Bormann, F.-J. Review of *Aquinas's Theory of Natural Law: An Analytic Reconstruction*, by A. J. Lisska. *Theologie und Philosophie* 74 (1999): 425f.

Bormann, F.-J. *Natur als Horizont sittlicher Praxis*. Stuttgart 1999.

Breuer, S. *Sozialgeschichte des Naturrechts* (Beiträge zur sozialwissenschaftlichen Forschung 42). Opladen 1983.

Brunner, G. *Grundwerte als Fundament der pluralistischen Gesellschaft. Eine Untersuchung der Positionen von Kirchen, Parteien und Gewerkschaften in der Bundesrepublik Deutschland*. Freiburg 1989.

Bubmann, P. "Naturrecht und christliche Ethik." *ZEE* 37 (1993): 267–80.

Burkhard, F.-P. *Ethische Existenz bei Karl Jaspers* (Epistemata: Reihe Philosophie 13). Würzburg 1982.

Burri, J. *'Als Mann und Frau schuf er sie'. Differenz der Geschlechter aus moral- und praktisch-theologischer Sicht*. Zurich 1977.

Casper, B. *Das dialogische Denken. Eine Untersuchung der religionsphilosophischen Bedeutung Franz Rosenzweigs, Ferdinand Ebners und Martin Bubers*. Freiburg 1967.

Casper, B. "Der Zugang zu Religion im Denken von Emmanuel Levinas." *PhJ* 95 (1988): 268–77.

Cathrein, V. *Die Einheit des sittlichen Bewußtseins der Menschheit. Eine ethnographische Untersuchung*, I. Freiburg 1914.

Childs, B. S. *Biblical Theology of the Old and New Testament: Theological reflection on the Christian Bible*. London 1992.

Compagnoni, F. "Folter und Todesstrafe in der Überlieferung der römisch-katholischen Kirche." *Concilium* 14 (1978): 657–66.

Crüsemann, F. *Bewahrung der Freiheit. Das Thema des Dekalogs in sozialgeschichtlicher Perspektive.* Munich 1983.

Crüsemann, F. *Die Tora. Theologie und Sozialgeschichte des alttestamentlichen Gesetzes.* Munich 1992.

Dalferth, I. U., and E. Jüngel, "Person und Gottebenbildlichkeit." *CGG* XXIV, cols. 66–86.

Deckers, D. *Gerechtigkeit und Recht. Eine historisch-kritische Untersuchung der Gerechtigkeitslehre des Francisco de Vitoria (1483–1546).* Freiburg i.Ue. 1991.

Dedek, J. F. "Intrinsically Evil Acts: An Historical Study on the Mind of St Thomas." *The Thomist* 43 (1979): 389–413.

Deissler, A. "Stellvertretung als Prinzip der Heilsgeschichte." *LS* 30 (1979): 339–45.

Demmer, K. *Deuten und handeln: Grundlagen und Grundfragen der Fundamentalmoral.* Freiburg 1985.

Demmer, K. *Entscheidung und Verhängnis.* Paderborn 1976.

Demmer, K. "Geschichtlichkeit," In H. Rotter and G. Virt (eds.), *Neues Lexikon der christlichen Moral.* Innsbruck 1990.

Demmer, K. *Ius Caritatis. Zur christologischen Grundlegung der augustinischen Naturrechtslehre.* Rome 1961.

Demmer, K. *Moraltheologische Methodenlehre.* Freiburg 1989.

Demmer, K. "Natur und Person. Brennpunkte gegenwärtiger moraltheologischer Auseinandersetzung." In B. Fraling (ed.), *Natur im ethischen Argument.* Freiburg 1990.

Demmer, K. *Sein und Gebot: Die Bedeutsamkeit des transzendentalphilosophischen Denkansatzes in der Scholastik der Gegenwart für den formalen Aufriss der Fundamentalmoral.* Munich et al. 1971.

Dihle, A. *Die Goldene Regel. Eine Einführung in die Geschichte der antiken und frühchristlichen Vulgärethik.* Göttingen 1962.

Dillmann, R. *Das Eigentliche der Ethik Jesu. Ein exegetischer Beitrag zur moraltheologischen Diskussion um das Proprium einer christlichen Ethik.* Mainz 1984.

Dilthey, W. *Der Aufbau der geschichtlichen Welt in den Geisteswissenschaften.* In *Gesammelte Schriften,* VII, Stuttgart and Göttingen, 8th edn., 1992.

Dilthey, W. *Einleitung in die Geisteswissenschaften. Versuch einer Grundlegung für das Studium der Gesellschaft und der Geschichte.* In *Gesammelte Schriften,* I, Stuttgart and Göttingen, 8th edn., 1990.

Drescher, H. G. *Ernst Troeltsch: Leben und Werk.* Göttingen 1991.

Droesser, G. *Freiheitspraxis im Prozeß. Zur geschichtsanthropologischen Grundlegung einer Theologie des Ethischen.* Frankfurt 1992.

Dupré, W. "Kultur und Ethos. Zum Problem der Sittlichkeit in Primitivkulturen." In C. H. Ratschow (ed.), *Ethik der Religionen.* Stuttgart 1980.

Egger, W. "Handlungsorientierte Auslegung der Antithesen Mt 5,21–28." In K. Kertelge (ed.), *Ethik im Neuen Testament,* 119–44. Freiburg 1984.

Feldmann, H. *Vergewaltigung und ihre psychischen Folgen.* Stuttgart 1992.

Fichte, J. G. *Grundlage des Naturrechts 4* (1796). In J. G. Fichte (ed.), *Fichtes Werke,* III, 41–47. Berlin 1971.

Finance, J. de. "Sur la notion de la loi universelle." In J. de Finance, *Personne et valeur,* 151–76. Rome 1992.

Finnis, J. *Fundamentals of Ethics.* Oxford 1983.

Finnis, J. *Natural Law and Natural Rights.* Oxford 1980.

Flückiger, F. *Geschichte des Naturrechts,* I: *Altertum und Frühmittelalter.* Zurich 1954.

Fritz, K. von. "Teleologie bei Aristoteles." In G. A. Seeck (ed.), *Die Naturphilosophie des Aristoteles.* Darmstadt 1975.

Fritzsche, H.-G. "Decalog IV. Ethisch." *TRE* VIII: cols. 418–28.

Fromm, E. *Die Anatomie der menschlichen Destruktivität.* Hamburg 1974.

Fromm, E. *Psychoanalyse und Ethik. Bausteine zu einer humanistischen Charakterologie* (*Gesammelte Werke* II). Stuttgart 1980.

Gadamer, H.-G. *Wahrheit und Methode. Grundzüge einer philosophischen Hermeneutik* (*Gesammelte Werke* I). Tübingen, 6th edn., 1990.

Gante, M. *218 in der Diskussion. Meinungs- und Willensbildung 1945–1976.* Düsseldorf 1991.

Gayhart, B. A. *The Ethics of Ernst Troeltsch: A Commitment to Relevancy* (Toronto Studies in Theology 53). Lewiston 1990.

Gerwith, A. "Are There Any Absolute Rights?" In A. Gerwith, *Human Rights. Essays on Justification and Applications.* Chicago 1982.

Gese, H. "Der Dekalog als Ganzheit betrachtet." In H. Gese, *Vom Sinai zum Zion. Alttestamentliche Beiträge zur biblischen Theologie,* 63–80. Munich 1974.

Gese, H. "Erwägungen zur Einheit der biblischen Theologie." *ZTK* 67 (1970): 417–36.

Geyer, H.-G. "Luthers Auslegung der Bergpredigt." In H.-G. Geyer et al. (eds.), *Wenn nicht jetzt, wann dann?* (Festschrift for H. J. Kraus), 283–93. Neukirchen-Vluyn 1983.

Gillen, E. *Wie Christen ethisch handeln und denken. Zur Debatte um die Autonomie der Sittlichkeit im Kontext katholischer Theologie.* Würzburg 1989.

Ginsberg, M. "Basic Needs and Moral Ideals." In M. Ginsberg, *On the Diversity of Morals,* 130–48. London, 2nd edn., 1962.

Ginsberg, M. "On the Diversity of Morals" (1953). In M. Ginsberg, *On the Diversity of Morals.* London, 2nd edn., 1962.

Grisez, G. "The First Principle of Practical Reason." In A. Kenny (ed.), *Aquinas: A Collection of Critical Essays.* London 1969.

Grisez, G. "A New Formulation of a Natural-Law Argument against Contraception." *The Thomist* 30 (1966): 343–61.

Grisez, G. et al. "Every Marital Act ought to be Open to New Life: Toward a Clearer Understanding." *The Thomist* 52 (1988).

Gruber, H.-G. "Autonome Moral oder Moral der Autonomie." *SdZ* 118 (1993): 691–99.

Gruber, H.-G. *Christliche Ehe in moderner Gesellschaft. Entwicklung-Chancen-Perspektiven.* Freiburg 1993.

Habermas, J. *Zur Rekonstruktion des historischen Materialismus.* Frankfurt 1976.

Hadot, P. *Exercices spirituels et philosophie antique.* Paris 1981.

Hafner, F. *Kirchen im Kontext der Grund- und Menschenrechte.* Freiburg 1992.

Hall, P. M. *Narrative and the Natural Law. An Interpretation of Thomistic Ethics.* Notre Dame and London 1994.

Hare, R. M. *Die Sprache der Moral.* Frankfurt 1972. [English translation: *The Language of Morals,* 1952].

Harman, G. "Moral Relativism Defended." *PhRv* 84 (1975).

Hegel, G. W. F. *Grundlinien der Philosophie des Rechts, 100 (Theorie Werkausgabe, VII).* Frankfurt a.M. 1970.

Heidegger, M. *Sein und Zeit.* Tübingen, 9th edn., 1976.

Hengel, M. *War Jesus Revolutionär?* Stuttgart 1970.

Herfurth, T. *Diltheys Schriften zur Ethik. Der Aufbau der moralischen Welt als Resultat einer Kritik der introspektiven Vernunft* (Epistemata 119). Würzburg 1992.

Herskovits, M. J. "Statement on Human Rights." *American Anthropologist* new series 49 (1947): 539–43.

Hilpert, K. *Die Menschenrechte. Geschichte—Theologie—Aktualität.* Düsseldorf 1991.

Hirschi, H. *Moralbegründung und christlicher Sinnhorizont.* Freiburg 1992.

Hoerster, N. "Zur Verteidigung des Rechtspositivismus." *NJW* 39 (1986): 2480–82.

Höffe, O. "Ein transzendentaler Tausch. Zur Anthropologie der Menschenrechte." *PhJ* (1992): 1–28.

Höffe, O. *Politische Gerechtigkeit.* Frankfurt 1978.

Hoffmann, P. *Studien zur Theologie der Logienquelle.* Münster 1972.

Hoffmann, P. "Tradition und Situation. Zur 'Verbindlichkeit' des Gebots der Feindesliebe in der synoptischen Überlieferung und in der gegenwärtigen Friedensdiskussion." In K. Kertelge (ed.), *Ethik im Neuen Testament,* 50–118. Freiburg 1984.

Hoffmann, P. and V. Eid. *Jesus von Nazareth und eine christliche Moral.* Freiburg 1975.

Honnefelder, L. "Die ethische Rationalität des mittelalterlichen Naturrechts: Max Webers und Ernst Troeltsch Deutung des mittelalterlichen Naturrechts und die Bedeutung der Lehre vom natürlichen Gesetz bei Thomas von Aquin." In W. Schluchter (ed.), *Max Webers Sicht des okzidentalen Christentums: Interpretation und Kritik.* Frankfurt 1988.

Honnefelder, L. "Natur als Handlungsprinzip. Die Relevanz der Natur für die Ethik." In L. Honnefelder (ed.), *Natur als Gegenstand der Wissenschaften,* 151–83. Freiburg 1992.

Honnefelder, L. "Naturrecht und Geschichte. Historisch-systematische Überlegungen zum mittelalterlichen Naturrecht." In M. Heimbach-Steins (ed.), *Naturrecht im ethischen Diskurs,* 1–27. Münster 1990.

Honnefelder, L. "Person und Gehirn—zur ethischen Beurteilung der Transplantation von Hirngewebe." In J. Fedrowitz et al. (eds.), *Neuroworlds. Gehirn-Geist-Kultur,* 380–88. Frankfurt and New York 1994.

Hoppe, T. "Menschenrechte als Basis eines Weltethos?" In M. Heimbach-Steins (ed.), *Brennpunkt Sozialethik. Theorien, Aufgaben, Methoden* (Festschrift for F. Furger), 319–33. Freiburg et al. 1995.

Hossfeld, F.-L. *Der Dekalog.* Freiburg 1982.

Höver, G. *Erfahrhung und Vernunft. Untersuchungen zum Problem sittlich relevanter Einsichten unter besonderer Berücksichtigung der Naturrechtsethik von Johannes Messner.* Düsseldorf 1981.

Höver, G. *Sittlich handeln im Medium der Zeit: Ansätze zur handlungsorientierten Neuorientierung der Moraltheologie.* Würzburg 1988.

Hübner, H. "Dekalog III. Neues Testament." *TRE* VIII: cols. 415–18.

Hünermann, P. *Der Durchbruch geschichtlichen Denkens im 19. Jahrhundert: Johann Gustav Droysen, Wilhelm Dilthey, Graf Paul Yorck von Wartenburg: Ihr Weg und ihre Weisung für die Theologie.* Freiburg 1967.

Husserl, E. "Philosophie als strenge Wissenschaft." *Logos* 1 (1910–1911): 323–41.

Ilting, K.-H. "Naturrecht." *GGB*, IV: cols. 245–313.

Ilting, K.-H. "Naturrecht II." *GGB*, IV: cols. 270–73.

Ineichen, H. "Wilhelm Dilthey." In O. Höffe (ed.), *Klassiker der Philosophie,* II, 187–202. Munich 1981.

Isensee, J. "Die katholische Kritik an den Menschenrechten. Der liberale Freiheitsentwurf in der Sicht der Päpste des 19. Jahrhunderts." In E.-W. Böckenförde and R. Spaemann (eds.), *Menschenrechte und Menschenwürde.* Stuttgart 1987.

Jaspers, K. *Philosophie* II: *Existenzerhellung.* Berlin et al., 4th edn., 1979.

Jaspers, K. *Vom Ursprung und Ziel der Geschichte.* Munich, 3rd edn., 1952.

Jüngel, E. "Der Gott entsprechende Mensch. Bemerkungen zur Gottebenbildlichkeit des Menschen als Grundfigur theologischer Anthropologie." In H.-G. Gadamer and P. Vogler (eds.), *Philosophische Anthropologie,* I, 342–72. Munich 1975.

Kappeler, S. et al. (eds.). *Vergewaltigung, Krieg, Nationalismus. Eine feministische Kritik.* Munich 1994.

Kasper, W. "Das Verhältnis von Schrift und Tradition. Eine pneumatologische Perspektive" (1992). In W. Kasper, *Theologie und Kirche,* II, 51–83. Mainz 1999.

Kasper, W. *Wahrheit und Freiheit. Die "Erklärung über die Religionsfreiheit" des II. Vatikanischen Konzils* (Sitzungsberichte der Heidelberger Akademie der Wissenschaften). Heidelberg 1988.

Kaufmann, A. *Recht und Sittlichkeit.* Tübingen 1964.

Kaufmann, F.-X. "Wissenssoziologische Überlegungen zu Renaissance und Niedergang des katholischen Naturrechtsdenkens im 19. und 20. Jahrhundert." In F. Böckle and E.-W. Böckenförde (eds.), *Naturrecht in der Kritik,* 126–64. Mainz 1973.

Kaulbach, F. *Einführung in die Philosophie des Handelns.* Darmstadt, 2nd edn., 1982.

Keenan, J. F. *Goodness and Rightness in Thomas Aquinas's Summa Theologiae.* Washington 1992.

Kelsen, H. *Reine Rechtslehre.* Vienna, 2nd edn., 1960.

Kissling, C. *Gemeinwohl und Gerechtigkeit. Ein Vergleich von traditioneller Natur-rechtsethik und kritischer Gesellschaftstheorie.* Freiburg 1993.

Kluxen, W. *Philosophische Ethik bei Thomas von Aquin.* Hamburg, 3rd edn., 1998.

Knoll, A. M. *Katholische Kirche und scholastisches Naturrecht: Zur Frage der Frei-heit.* Vienna et al. 1962.

Kohlberg, L. *Moral Stages: A Current Formulation and a Response to Critics.* Basle et al. 1983.

König, S. *Zur Begründung der Menschenrechte: Hobbes-Locke-Kant.* Freiburg and Munich, 1994.

Korff, W. "Der Rückgriff auf die Natur. Eine Rekonstruktion der thomanischen Lehre vom natürlichen Gesetz." *PhJ* 94 (1987): 285–96.

Korff, W. *Norm und Sittlichkeit. Untersuchungen zur Logik der normativen Ver-nunft.* Mainz 1973.

Kosellek, R. "Geschichte, Historie." In *GGB* II: cols. 593–717.

Kosellek, R. "Geschichte, Historie. V. Die Herausbildung des modernen Geschichtsbegriffs." *GGB* II: cols. 647–91.

Kühl, K. "Naturrecht V. Neuere Diskussion." *HWPh* VI: cols. 609–23.

Kühnhardt, L. *Die Universalität der Menschenrechte. Studie zur ideengeschichtlichen Bestimmung eines politischen Schlüsselbegriffs.* Munich 1987.

Küng, H. *Das Judentum. Die religiöse Situation der Zeit.* Munich 1991.

Küng, H. *Projekt Weltethos.* Munich and Zurich 1990.

Kutschera, F. von. *Grundlagen der Ethik.* Berlin and New York 1982.

Lapide, P. *Die Bergpredigt. Utopie oder Programm.* Mainz 1982.

Leher, S. *Begründung ethischer Normen bei Viktor Cathrein und Wahrheitstheorien der Sprachphilosophie.* Innsbruck and Vienna 1992.

Lehu, L. *La raison, règle de la moralité d'après Saint Thomas d'Aquin.* Paris 1930.

Léonard, A. *Le Fondement de la Morale: Essai d'éthique philosophique générale.* Paris 1991.

Lieber, H. J. "Geschichte und Gesellschaft im Denken Diltheys." *Kölner Zeit-schrift für Soziologie und Sozialpsychologie* 17 (1965): 703–42.

Linares, F. "Jaspers' Geschichtsdenken." In F. Linares, *Beiträge zur Staats- und Geschichtsphilosophie.* Hildesheim et al. 1988.

Lisska, A. J. *Aquinas's Theory of Natural Law: An Analytic Reconstruction.* Oxford 1997.

Locher, G. W. "Der Geltungsgrad der zehn Gebote." *ZEE* 13 (1969): 129–45.

Lohfink, N. "Kennt das Alte Testament einen Unterschied von 'Gebot' und 'Gesetz'? Zur bibeltheologischen Einstufung des Dekalogs." *JBTh* 4 (1989): 63–89.

Lohfink, G. "Wem gilt die Bergpredigt? Eine redaktionskritische Untersuchung von Mt 4,23–5,2 und 7,28f." *ThQ* 163 (1983): 264–84.

Lohfink, G. *Wie hat Jesus Gemeinde gewollt?* Freiburg 1982.

Lohse, E. *Theologische Ethik des Neuen Testaments.* Stuttgart et al. 1988.

Luf, G. "Zur Problematik des Wertbegriffs in der Rechtsphilosophie." In H.

Miehsler et al. (eds.), *Jus Humanitatis* (Festschrift for A. Verdross), 127–46. Berlin 1980.

Luhmann, N. *Das Recht der Gesellschaft.* Frankfurt 1993.

Luther, M. "Wochenpredigten über Mt 5–7" (1530–32). In *D. Martin Luters Werke: Kritische Gesamtausgabe*, 32. Weimar 1883ff.

Luz, U. *Das Evangelium nach Matthäus (Mt 1–7) (EKK I/1).* Zurich et al., 3rd edn., 1992.

Mackie, J. L. *Ethik. Die Erfindung des moralisch Richtigen und Falschen.* Stuttgart, 2nd edn., 1983.

Maihofer, W. *Rechtsstaat und menschliche Würde.* Frankfurt 1968.

Manser, G. M. *Angewandtes Naturrecht.* Freiburg i.Ue. 1947.

Maurer, A. V. *Homo agens. Handlungstheoretische Untersuchungen zum theologischethischen Verständnis des Sittlichen.* Frankfurt et al. 1994.

Menke, K. H. *Stellvertretung. Schlüsselbegriff christlichen Lebens und theologische Grundkategorie.* Freiburg 1991.

Merklein, H. *Die Gottesherrschaft als Handlungsprinzip. Untersuchungen zur Ethik Jesu.* Würzburg, 3rd edn., 1984.

Merks, K.-W. "Naturrecht als Personrecht? Überlegungen zu einer Relektüre der Naturrechtslehre des Thomas von Aquin." In M. Heimbach-Steins (ed.), *Naturrecht im ethischen Diskurs*, 28–46. Münster 1990.

Merks, K.-W. *Theologische Grundlegung der sittlichen Autonomie: Strukturmomente eines "autonomen" Normbegründungsverständnisses im Lex-Traktat der Summa theologiae des Thomas von Aquin.* Düsseldorf 1978.

Metz, J. B. *Christliche Anthropozentrik. Über die Denkform des Thomas von Aquin.* Munich 1962.

Metzger, T. A. *Escape from Predicament: Neo-Confucianism and China's Evolving Political Culture.* New York 1977.

Mieth, D. "Das 'christliche Menschenbild'—eine unzeitgemäße Betrachtung? Zu den Wandlungen einer theologisch-ethischen Formel." *ThQ* 163 (1983): 1–15.

Mieth, D. *Geburtenregelung. Ein Konflikt in der katholischen Kirche.* Mainz 1990.

Mikat, P. *Ethische Strukturen der Ehe in unserer Zeit: Zur Normierungsfrage im Kontext des abendländischen Eheverständnisses.* Paderborn et al. 1987.

Möhler, J. A. *Die Einheit der Kirche. Oder das Prinzip des Katholizismus.* Darmstadt 1957.

Mommsen, W. *Christliche Ethik und Teleologie.* Altenberge 1993.

Moore, E. G. *Principia Ethica* (1903). Cambridge edn. 1971.

Morel, J. "Soziologische Wertrelativierung. Thematisierung eines Anliegens." In W. von der Ohe (ed.), *Kulturanthropologie. Beiträge zum Neubeginn einer Disziplin* (Festschrift for E. K. Francis). Berlin 1987.

Müller, G. "Der Dekalog im Neuen Testament. Vor-Erwägungen zu einer unerledigten Aufgabe." *ThZ* 38 (1982): 79–97.

Müller, M. *Erfahrung und Geschichte.* Freiburg and Munich 1971.

Mußner, F. *Traktat über die Juden.* Munich 1979.

Nethöfel, W. *Moraltheologie nach dem Konzil. Personen, Programme, Positionen.* Göttingen 1987.

Nothelle-Wildfeuer, U. '*Duplex ordo cognitionis*'. *Zur systematischen Grundlegung einer katholischen Soziallehre im Anspruch von Philosophie und Theologie* (Abhandlungen zur Sozialethik, 31). Paderborn 1991.

Oening-Hanhoff, L. "Mensch und Recht nach Thomas von Aquin." *PhJ* 82 (1975): 10–30.

Otte, G. "Recht und Moral," *CGG* XXII: cols. 6–36.

Otto, E. *Theologische Ethik des Alten Testaments.* Stuttgart et al. 1994.

Pannenberg, W. *Anthropologie in theologischer Perspektive.* Göttingen 1983.

Pannenberg, W. "Die Begründung der Ethik bei Ernst Troeltsch." In W. Pannenberg, *Ethik und Ekklesiologie: Gesammelte Aufsätze,* 70–96. Göttingen 1977.

Patzig, G. *Ethik ohne Metaphysik.* Göttingen 1983.

Perlitt, L. "Dekalog I. Altes Testament," *TRE* VIII: cols. 408–13.

Pesch, O. H. *Das Gesetz* (*Kommentar zur deutschen Thomas-Ausgabe* 13). Heidelberg et al. 1977.

Pieper, A. *Ethik und Moral. Eine Einführung in die praktische Philosophie.* Munich 1985.

Pinckaers, S. *Ce qu'on ne peut jamais faire. La question des actes intrinsèquement mauvais. Histoire et discussion.* Fribourg and Paris 1986.

Pinto de Oliveira, C.-J. "Die theologische Originalität von Johannes Paul II." In O. Höffe et al. (eds.), *Johannes Paul II. und die Menschenrechte,* 60–91. Freiburg i.Ue. 1981.

Punt, J. *Die Idee der Menschenrechte. Ihre geschichtliche Entwicklung und ihre Rezeption durch die moderne katholische Sozialverkündigung.* Paderborn et al. 1987.

Putz, G. *Christentum und Menschenrechte.* Innsbruck and Vienna 1991.

Rad, G. von. *Theologie des Alten Testaments,* II: *Die Theologie der prophetischen Überlieferung.* Munich 1965.

Rad, G. von. *Theologie des Alten Testaments,* I: *Die Theologie der geschichtlichen Überlieferung.* Munich 1969.

Radbruch, G. *Rechtsphilosophie.* Stuttgart, 3rd edn., 1973.

Ratzinger, J. "Naturrecht, Evangelium und Ideologie in der katholischen Soziallehre." In K. von Bismarck and W. Dirks (eds.), *Christlicher Glaube und Ideologie,* 24–30. Stuttgart 1964.

Reiner, H. "Zu Flückigers 'Geschichte des Naturrechts I.'" *Archiv für Rechts- und Sozialphilosophie* 41 (1955): 528–61.

Reuter, H.-R. "Die Bergpredigt als Orientierung unseres Menschseins heute." *ZEE* 23 (1979): 84–104.

Rhonheimer, M. *Natur als Grundlage der Moral: Eine Auseinandersetzung mit autonomer und teleologischer Ethik.* Innsbruck and Vienna 1987 [Eng. tr.: *Natural Law and Practical Reason: A Thomist View of Moral Autonomy,* New York 2000].

Rhonheimer, M. *Praktische Vernunft und Vernünftigkeit der Praxis: Handlungstheorie bei Thomas von Aquin in ihrer Entstehung aus dem Problemkontext der aristotelischen Ethik.* Berlin 1994.

Rhonheimer, M. *Sexualität und Verantwortung. Empfängnisverhütung als ethisches Problem.* Vienna 1995.

Ricken, F. *Allgemeine Ethik.* Stuttgart et al., 2nd edn., 1989.

Ricken, F. "Naturrecht I." *TRE* 24: 132–53.

Rickert, H. *Die Philosophie des Lebens. Darstellung und Kritik der philosophischen Modeströmungen unserer Zeit.* Tübingen, 2nd edn., 1922.

Ricoeur, P. "Stellung und Funktion der Metapher in der biblischen Sprache." In P. Ricoeur and E. Jüngel, *Metapher. Zur Hermeneutik religiöser Sprache,* 45–70. Munich 1974.

Rippe, K. P. *Ethischer Relativismus. Seine Grenzen, seine Geltung.* Paderborn et al. 1993.

Roetz, H. *Die chinesische Ethik der Achsenzeit.* Frankfurt 1992.

Rombach, H. *Strukturontologie: Der menschliche Mensch.* Freiburg and Munich 1987.

Rotter, H. (ed.). *Heilgeschichte und ethische Normen.* Freiburg 1984.

Ruppert, L. Genesis. *Ein kritischer und theologischer Kommentar, 1. Teilband: Gen 1,11–11,26.* Würzburg 1992.

Schabert, J. *Fleisch, Geist und Seele im Pentateuch* (Stuttgarter Bibel Studien 19). Stuttgart 1966.

Schallenberg, P. *Naturrecht und Sozialtheologie. Die Entwicklung des theonomen Naturrechts der späten Neuscholastik im deutschen Sprachraum (1900–1960).* Münster 1993.

Schelauske, H. D. *Naturrechtsdiskussion in Deutschland.* Cologne 1968.

Scheler, M. *Der Formalismus in der Ethik und die materiale Wertethik* (*Gesammelte Werke* [*GW*] II). Berne and Munich, 6th edn., 1980.

Scheler, M. *Wesen und Formen der Sympathie* (*GW* VII). Berne 1974.

Scherer, G. *Welt—Natur oder Schöpfung?* Darmstadt 1990.

Schmidinger, H. *Der Mensch ist Person. Ein christliches Prinzip in theologischer und philosophischer Sicht.* Innsbruck and Vienna 1994.

Schmidt, W. H. "Anthropologische Begriffe im Alten Testament." *EvTh* 24 (1964): 375–88.

Schmidt, W. H. *Die Zehn Gebote im Rahmen alttestamentlicher Ethik.* Darmstadt 1993.

Schockenhoff, E. "Brauchen wir ein neues Weltethos? Universale Ethik in einer geschichtlichen Welt." *ThPh* 70 (1995): 224–44.

Schockenhoff, E. "Die Bedeutung von Schrift, Tradition und Lehramt für das Verständnis des christlichen Ethos." *Seminarium* 34 (1994): 72–88.

Schockenhoff, E. *Ethik des Lebens. Ein theologischer Grundriß.* Mainz 1993.

Schockenhoff, E. "Personsein und Menschenwürde bei Thomas von Aquin und Martin Luther." *ThPh* 65 (1990): 481–512.

Schockenhoff, E. *Zum Fest der Freiheit. Theologie des christlichen Handelns bei Origenes.* Mainz 1990.

Schottroff, L. "Gewaltverzicht und Feindesliebe in der urchristlichen Jesustradition, Mt 5,38–48, Lk 6,27–36." In G. Strecker (ed.), *Jesus Christus in Historie und Theologie*, 197–201. Tübingen 1975.

Schrage, W. *Ethik des Neuen Testaments* (*Das Neue Testament deutsch* IV). Göttingen, 2nd edn., 1989.

Schreiner, J. *Die Zehn Gebote im Leben des Gottesvolkes*. Munich 1988.

Schröer, C. *Praktische Vernunft bei Thomas von Aquin*. Stuttgart et al. 1995.

Schüller, B. "Das Geschick eines Wortpaares." In B. Schüller, *Der menschliche Mensch. Aufsätze zur Metaethik und zur Sprache der Moral*, 156–83. Düsseldorf 1982.

Schüller, B. "Die Bedeutung des natürlichen Sittengesetzes für den Christen." In G. Teichtweiher and W. Dreier (eds.), *Herausforderung und Kritik der Moraltheologie*, 105–30. Würzburg 1971.

Schüller, B. *Die Begründung sittlicher Urteile. Typen ethischer Argumentation in der Moraltheologie*. Düsseldorf, 2nd edn., 1980.

Schüller, B. "Zur theologischen Diskussion über die lex naturalis." *ThPh* 4 (1966): 481–503.

Schulte, R. "Sein und Verwirklichung der menschlichen Geschlechtlichkeit. Ein theologischer Versuch." In N. A. Luyten (ed.), *Wesen und Sinn der Geschlechtlichkeit*, 301–72. Freiburg and Munich 1985.

Schulz, W. *Grundprobleme der Ethik*. Pfullingen 1989.

Schulz, W. *Philosophie in der veränderten Welt*. Pfullingen 1972.

Schüngel-Straumann, H. *Die Frau am Anfang. Eva und die Folgen*. Freiburg 1989.

Schuster, J. *Ethos und kirchliches Lehramt. Zur Kompetenz des Lehramtes in Fragen der natürlichen Sittlichkeit*. Frankfurt 1984.

Semmelroth, O. "Kommentar zur Pastoralkonstitution 'Gaudium et Spes.'" In *LThK*, supplementary vol. III: col. 366.

Singer, M. G. *Generalization in Ethics*. London 1963.

Spaemann, R. "Über die Unmöglichkeit einer universaltheologischen Ethik." *PhJ* 88 (1981): 70–89.

Specht, R. "Naturrecht. Mittelalter und frühe Neuzeit," *HWPh* VI: 571–82.

Stace, W. T. *The Concept of Morals*. London, 2nd edn., 1932.

Stamm, J.-J. *Der Dekalog im Lichte der neueren Forschung*. Berne and Stuttgart, 2nd edn., 1962.

Stanke, G. *Die Lehre von den "Quellen der Moralität". Darstellung und Diskussion der neuscholastischen Aussagen und neuerer Ansätze*. Regensburg 1984.

Steigleder, K. *Die Begründung des moralischen Sollens. Studien zur Möglichkeit einer normativen Ethik*. Tübingen 1992.

Strauss, L. *Natural Right and History*. Chicago and London 1953.

Strecker, G. *Die Bergpredigt. Ein exegetischer Kommentar*. Göttingen 1984.

Stuhlmacher, P. "Jesu vollkommenes Gesetz der Freiheit. Zum Verständnis der Bergpredigt." *ZThK* 79 (1982): 283–322.

Tanner, K. *Der lange Schatten des Naturrechts: Eine fundamental-ethische Untersuchung*. Stuttgart et al. 1993.

Theiler, W. *Zur Geschichte der teleologischen Naturbetrachtung bis auf Aristoteles.* Berlin, 2nd edn., 1965.

Theißen, G. "Gewaltverzicht und Feindesliebe (Mt 5,38–48/Lk 6,27–38), und deren sozialgeschichtlicher Hintergrund." In G. Theißen, *Studien zur Soziologie des Urchristentums,* 160–97. Tübingen 1979.

Theunissen, M. *Der Andere. Studien zur Sozialontologie der Gegenwart.* Berlin, 2nd edn., 1977.

Tillich, P. "Liebe, Macht, Gerechtigkeit" (1954). In P. Tillich, *Gesammelte Werke* XI, 143–225. Stuttgart, 2nd edn., 1976.

Troeltsch, E. *Die Absolutheit des Christentums und die Religionsgeschichte.* Tübingen, 3rd edn., 1929.

Troeltsch, E. *Die Soziallehren der christlichen Kirchen und Gruppen* (Gesammelte Schriften, I). Tübingen 1919.

Troeltsch, E. *Der Historismus und seine Probleme* (Gesammelte Schriften, III). Tübingen 1922.

Troeltsch, E. *Der Historismus und seine Überwindung.* Berlin 1924.

Troeltsch, E. *Grundprobleme der Ethik (GS* II: *Zur religiösen Lage, Religionsphilosophie und Ethik).* Tübingen, 2nd edn., 1922 (reprint Aalen 1962).

Troeltsch, E. "Naturrecht, christliches." *RGG,* V, cols. 697–704. Tübingen, 1st edn., 1913.

Topitsch, E. "Restauration des Naturrechts?" In E. Topitsch, *Sozialphilosophie zwischen Ideologie und Wissenschaft.* Berlin 1961.

Utz, A. F. "Die Ethik des Thomas von Aquin." In W. Ockenfels (ed.), *Ethik des Gemeinwohls: Gesammelte Aufsätze 1983–1997.* Paderborn et al. 1998.

Utz, A. F. "Naturrecht als Sammelbegriff nicht-positivistischer Rechtstheorien." *ARSP* (Supplement I: *Zeitgenössische Rechtskonzeptionen,* Teil 4) 70 (1979): 13.

Verweyen, H. J. *Recht und Sittlichkeit in J. G. Fichtes Gesellschaftslehre.* Freiburg and Munich, 1975.

Vögtle, A. "Ein 'unablässiger Stachel.'" In H. Merklein (ed.), *Neues Testament und Ethik* (Festschrift for R. Schnackenburg), 53–70. Freiburg 1989.

Wagner, F. "Naturrecht II," *TRE* 24: cols. 153–85.

Weber, H. *Allgemeine Moraltheologie: Ruf und Antwort.* Graz et al. 1991.

Weber, M. *Wirtschaft und Gesellschaft. Grundriss der verstehenden Soziologie.* Tübingen, 5th edn., 1972.

Weinreb, L. L. "Natural Law and Human Rights." In R. P. George (ed.), *Natural Law Theory. Contemporary Essays,* 278–305. Oxford 1992.

Weischedel, W. *Skeptische Ethik.* Frankfurt 1976.

Weizsäcker, C. F. von. "Intelligente Feindesliebe." *Reformatio* 29 (1980): 413–18.

Welser, M. von. *Am Ende wünscht du dir nur noch den Tod. Die Massenvergewaltigungen im Krieg auf dem Balkan.* Munich 1993.

Welte, B. *Geschichte und Offenbarung,* edited posthumously by B. Casper and J. Feige. Frankfurt 1993.

Welzel, H. *Naturrecht und materiale Gerechtigkeit. Problemgeschichtliche Untersuchungen als Prolegomena zu einer Rechtsphilosophie.* Göttingen, 4th edn., 1960.

Welzel, H. "Naturrecht und Rechtspositivismus." In W. Maihofer (ed.), *Naturrecht oder Rechtspositivismus?* 322–38. Darmstadt 1962.

Wendland, W.-D. *Ethik des Neuen Testaments* (NTD-Ergänzungsband 4). Göttingen, 2nd edn., 1975.

Westermann, C. "Bedeutung und Funktion des Imperativs in den Geschichtsbüchern des Alten Testaments." In R. Mosis and R. Ruppert (eds.), *Der Weg zum Menschen. Zur philosophischen und theologischen Anthropologie* (Festschrift for A. Deissler), 13–27. Freiburg 1989.

Westermann, C. *Genesis, Kapitel 1–11* (BK/AT/1). Neukirchen, 2nd edn., 1976.

Westermarck, E. *The Origin and Development of the Moral Ideas.* London 1908.

Wieland, G. "'Secundum naturam vivere'. Über den Wandel des Verhältnisses von Natur und Sittlichkeit." In B. Fraling (ed.), *Natur im ethischen Argument,* 13–31. Freiburg and Vienna 1990.

Wilckens, U. *Der Brief an die Römer (Rom 1–5) (Evangelischer-katholischer Komentar zum NT* VI,1). Zurich et al., 2nd edn., 1987.

Williams, B. *Morality: An Introduction to Ethics.* New York 1972.

Windisch, H. *Der Sinn der Bergpredigt. Ein Beitrag zum Problem der richtigen Exegese.* Leipzig 1929.

Wirz, S. *Vom Mangel zum Überfluß: Die bedürfnisethische Frage in der Industriegesellschaft.* Münster 1993.

Witschen, D. "Menschenrechte der dritten Generation und internationales Ethos." *ZkTh* 117 (1995): 129–51.

Wolbert, W. *Der Mensch als Mittel und Zweck. Die Idee der Menschenwürde in normativer Ethik und Rechtsethik.* Münster 1987.

Wolbert, W. *Vom Nutzen der Gerechtigkeit. Zur Diskussion um Utilitarismus und teleologische Theorie.* Freiburg 1992

Wolf, E. *Das Problem der Naturrechtslehre. Versuch einer Orientierung.* Karlsruhe 1955.

Wolff, H. W. *Anthropologie des Alten Testaments.* Munich 1973.

Zelinska, U. *Normativität der Natur—Natur der Normativität. Eine interdisziplinäre Studie zur Frage der Genese und Funktion von Normen.* Freiburg 1994.

Zimmerli, W. *Das Gesetz und die Propheten.* Göttingen 1963.

Index of topics

Prohibitions *(continued)*
207, 208, 210, 213, 218, 219, 220, 221,
224, 226, 239, 243, 245, 252, 254, 274,
280, 288, 299, 300
Promiscuity, 19
Promises, 76, 77, 78, 81, 222, 245, 247, 248,
263, 282
Property, 48, 73, 81, 122, 135, 169, 173, 193,
194, 197, 253, 255; private, 13, 96
Prostitution, 39
Prudence, 140, 142, 143, 144, 152, 156, 166
Purpose, 13, 14, 16, 17, 93, 94, 97, 100, 102,
102, 122, 178, 192, 198, 231

Rape, 81, 202, 210, 219–22, 293
Rational principle, 72, 162, 163
Recapitulation theory, 22, 23, 247
Reconciliation, 22, 27, 85, 97, 190, 191, 205
Redemption, 22, 23, 27, 29, 113, 227
Relativism, cultural, 46, 54, 61, 63, 67, 71;
ethical, ix, x, 4, 44, 45, 46, 47, 50, 52, 53,
54, 55, 59, 60, 61, 62, 63, 64, 65, 66, 67,
68, 70, 71, 72, 73, 75, 80, 82, 83, 108, 111,
131, 179, 292, 295; fundamental, 71; historical, 35, 36, 102
Religion, freedom of, 37, 38
Resistance struggle, 216, 217, 258, 264, 296
Responsibility, 3, 39, 43, 72, 76, 125, 126,
164, 174, 184, 185, 214, 215, 216, 217, 218,
219, 222, 224, 229, 231, 233, 234, 257,
277, 280, 289, 292, 302, 307
Rights, basic, 297, 307
Rights, human, 4, 6, 22, 37, 39, 127, 128,
132, 186, 189, 192, 202, 222, 226, 227,
290, 291, 292, 293, 298, 300, 307; decla-
ration(s) of, 45, 66, 67, 105, 237, 285,
307
Ritual commandments, 247
Rule, commission to, 231, 234
Rule-utilitarianism, 212, 222

Salvation history, 2, 23, 26, 27, 30, 31, 47,
154, 226, 246, 247, 279, 280, 282, 283
Scholasticism, late, 28, 30, 188
Self-defense, 75, 196, 197, 203
Self-determination, 202, 207, 208, 209, 210,
213, 214, 224, 228, 292, 306; sexual,
220–22

Selfhood, 95, 109, 111, 114, 229, 230, 233, 277
Sermon on Mount, x, 25, 61, 63, 226, 238,
248, 249, 250, 255–79, 280, 283, 291
Sexual taboo, 43, 81
Sexuality, 19, 20, 38, 49, 145, 165, 166, 182,
219, 220, 222, 231
Sin, 18, 21, 22, 30, 133, 194, 196, 225, 254
Skepticism, 48, 82, 84, 90, 95, 128; moral,
62
Slavery, 18, 19, 39, 40, 42, 63, 74, 77, 248,
280
Social Darwinism, 17
Social teaching, 26, 30
Social theory (critical), 84
Sociobiology, 58, 178
State under rule of law, 211, 256, 285, 298,
300, 301, 306
Sterilization, 222; compulsory, 293
Stoa, 6, 7, 13, 15, 18, 134
Structural context, 88, 115
Suicide, 38, 39
Suttee, 74
Syllogismus operativus, 153
Synderesis, 148, 153
Systems theory, 9, 11, 294

Theft, 51, 65, 73, 75, 81, 108, 172, 173, 193,
194, 195, 196, 197, 249, 250, 254
Tolerance, 37, 40, 65, 68, 70, 71, 201, 284,
285
Torah, 239, 240, 241, 242, 244, 245, 246,
247, 248, 250, 259, 270, 271, 282, 283;
intensification of, 270, 271, 283
Torture, 38, 39, 40, 42, 63, 68, 69, 201, 202,
210, 212, 213, 214, 215, 216, 217, 218, 219,
222, 293
Treatment, interruption of, 206
Truth, capacity for, 167

Universalism, 281, 283
Universals, moral, 53, 80, 83
Usury, prohibition, 37, 42, 173

Value(s), 5, 10, 15, 16, 18, 19, 20, 34, 35, 37,
39, 44, 45, 46, 47, 52, 53, 54, 58, 59, 60,
61, 62, 63, 67, 73, 74, 78, 80, 82, 86, 92,
93, 94, 95, 97, 99, 100, 101, 102, 103,
104, 105, 106, 107, 108, 111, 116, 121, 122,

Index of persons

Natural Law & Human Dignity: Universal Ethics in an Historical World was designed and composed in Adobe Garamond by Kachergis Book Design, Pittsboro, North Carolina; and printed on 60-pound Glatfelter Natural and bound by Edwards Brothers, Inc., Lillington, North Carolina.